OMAR KHAYYĀM

POET, REBEL, ASTRONOMER

HAZHIR TEIMOURIAN

SUTTON PUBLISHING

First published in the United Kingdom in 2007 by
Sutton Publishing, an imprint of NPI Media Group Limited
Cirencester Road · Chalford · Stroud · Gloucestershire · GL6 8PE

British Library Cataloguing in Publication Data
A catalogue record for this book is available from the British Library.

Hardback ISBN 978-0-7509-4715-2

Typeset in Goudy.
Typesetting and origination by
NPI Media Group Limited.
Printed and bound in England.

Contents

Acknowledgements

Never of teachers did I go deprived;
Then more theorems I myself contrived.
Seventy-two years, day and night, I thought:
Only to conclude that I knew naught!

A friend who encouraged the venture from the start and spent time reading and criticising the new translation was the late John Kilbracken. John's mastery of English was legendary, to the extent that the editors of the *Oxford Concise Dictionary* once thanked him for his corrections of their work. As a reminder of his help, and in memory of his lifelong friendship, I treasure his pocket edition of FitzGerald which he had bought on 23 July 1943, around the time of my third birthday, when he was on shore leave from an aircraft carrier escorting supply convoys to Russia. He had jotted down some of his own earliest poems inside its covers and subsequently kept it as a token of his youth as the youngest squadron commander in the Fleet Air Arm of the Royal Navy. Yet he gave it to me during one of my visits to Killegar, his home in County Leitrim, Ireland, where we buried him in August 2006. Over the years, particularly after 1989 when we shared a house in Wapping after our marriages had ended, he became the elder brother I would not otherwise have had in England, my beloved country of adoption. Through him, Ireland also won my heart.

When John moved to Ireland permanently, following the expulsion of most hereditary peers from the House of Lords in 1999, his place in my life was somewhat filled by a younger brother, Christopher Lee, the historian and playwright. To him, too, I am grateful for his love, wisdom and uplifting optimism. I have incorporated in the new translation his catch phrase of 'We're still here', because it happened also to be Khayyām's, in a slightly different version. He subsequently became firm friends both with my superb literary agent, Sonia Land of Sheil Land Associates, and Jaqueline Mitchell, my wonderful editor at Sutton Publishing. On the latter subject, my thanks are due also to Jane Entrican, Assistant Publisher of Biography at Sutton, who took over responsibility for the book after Jaqueline had left the company.

Another friend, Suzanne Hodgart, a former deputy pictures editor of *The Sunday Times Magazine*, who found and chose the photographs, cannot possibly know how grateful I am to her, as I am also to friends Jon Swan in Massachusetts and Jim McCue and David Morphet in London for their critiques of the new translation. As with 'JK', they all said politely that they would have pursued a different route! They are brought up in English poetics and rightly protective of FitzGerald. But their suggestions were nevertheless of great value to me. Dr Fuad Megally helped me over some of the more ambiguous passages in three poems in Arabic that remain of Khayyām, and Elliot Levine shared with me his thoughts on Khayyām's mathematics.

But the greatest gratitude is owed to my wife Christabel King who has been a helper, as well as partner. Since we got together in 1992, her love and enthusiasm have been the key to a new serenity in my life and she has been an inspiration to Shlair and Russell, the delights of my eyes from my previous marriage to Georgina Walker. Christabel did not even once become jittery around the dinner table in Limehouse as I stood up yet again to tell friends stories from the book she had heard many times previously. May Khayyām continue to inspire them all.

Apart from the original medieval sources, I have benefited most from the works of Rahīm Rezāzādeh Malek, who is, without doubt, the world's most prolific researcher on Khayyām. He has collected together, and annotated in one volume in Iran, all the known writings of the great man. He has also written a short volume on the life and poetry of Khayyām, enumerating exactly where and when and by whom each stanza first came to light. Even though I found myself in disagreement with some of his interpretations, without his devotion to wiping the ancient dust off Khayyām's much-abused face, this work would have been much harder to contemplate.

Also instructive were a number of books published in recent times by other Iranians at home and abroad. They do not qualify as 'biography' in the modern Western sense of the word. They are brief and often polemical. But in all of them I found important points, or at least stimulation. Among them, my thanks are due to Ali-Rezā Zekā vati Gharagozlou in Tehran, a philosopher whose hard work in tracing the history of every quatrain attributed to Khayyām before the middle of the fifteenth century was of enormous help to me. As I could not travel to Iran myself, friends searched the libraries there for any new scholarship on Khayyām on my part. Ali Tavakkoli deserves a special mention.

I benefited also from a volume on Avicenna, Khayyām's great hero, by Sādiq Gowharīn of Nishapur, beside a history of that city by Freydoon Grayeli, the man who, in 1962, actually lifted Khayyām's remains from his old grave to move them to his new mausoleum. Professor D.S. Richards of Oxford deserves my deep gratitude for his extensive annotations and corrections of Ibn al-Athīr's *Annals of the Saljuq Turks*, as do historians Joseph H. Lynch on the history of the Western church in medieval times, Michael Angold on Byzantium, and W.B. Bartlett on the Assassins.

I am indebted also to Professor G.S.P. Freeman-Granville, formerly of the State University of New York. His invaluable book on the Islamic and Christian calendars enabled me to convert Islamic lunar dates into modern solar ones without pain. Otherwise, this work would almost certainly be riddled with dozens of inaccuracies.

As for libraries, special thanks are due to the librarians of my club, the Athenaeum, in Pall Mall, as well as the staff of the London Library in nearby St James's Square, the largest subscription lending library in the world. The former, Sarah Dodgson and Kay Walter, made available to me all their treasures on FitzGerald, and the latter gave me the key to their Edward Heron-Allen collection on Khayyām and FitzGerald. I also used the magnificent British Library, the home of many manuscripts of Persian literature and a FitzGerald print that boasts the most expensive binding of any book in history.

I have striven to the best of my ability over a decade to make this report the most accurate account ever told of Khayyām's life. It is, certainly, the most thorough. A number of previously unnoticed facts of significance came to light in the course of my research. No doubt, however, there are shortcomings. In places I have had to speculate more than I would have liked. I hope they are minor, but they may not be. I hope that readers will write in with suggestions to improve both the story and the new translation of the poems for possible future editions.

Hazhir Teimourian
Limehouse, London, 2007
www.KhayyamByTeimourian.com

Prologue

'In the whole of the world, I could not think of another like him'

One Friday morning in the spring of 1135, a visitor to the city of Nishāpur in north-east Iran made his way slowly among the orchards to the south of the city's walls. He had employed a guide to take him to his destination and the two men exchanged few words. The stranger, in scholars' robes of long coat and high conical hat, was preoccupied. He wanted to visit the cemetery of Heira, the burial ground of Nishāpur's powerful and noble citizens.

Eventually the two men reached the graveyard and the guide led his employer inside towards a corner, where a neighbouring orchard marked the end of the enclosure. Two large trees of apricot and pear spread their branches over the wall. One of them had shed so much blossom over the ground that the grave could not be seen.

The guide pointed to a spot under the flower petals. The visitor bowed his head and began to cry quietly. He later wrote in his diary: 'In the whole of the world, I could not think of another like him.'

The visitor was Nizāmi Arūzi Samarqandi (Nizāmi 'the Prosodist' of Samarkand) who would gain fame later as the writer of a book on science and literature. The man lying under the earth was his former employer, Dr Omar Khayyāmi, the great astronomer, physician, philosopher and secret poet. Four years after Khayyāmi's death, Nizāmi had come to Nishāpur to pay his respects and to carry out some research. Later he recalled that, as he stood in front of the grave, the memory of a particularly happy day came to his mind. Some twenty-three years earlier, when he had been the great man's secretary, he had accompanied him to lunch at the home of a friend in the city of Balkh and there, as the wine flowed and the fine china tinkled, 'my lord Omar said he had chosen a spot for his grave where every spring shed blossoms over him twice'. Nizāmi had been puzzled. But now he saw he ought not to have been. Pear and apricot trees blossomed at different times of spring. The old man continued to entertain his friends beyond the grave.

*   *   *

'I shall never know or meet his like upon earth'

On the afternoon of Tuesday, 19 June 1883, when the meadows and parklands of Suffolk in East Anglia basked in the glory of an English summer, a small group of elderly men removed a coffin from a horse-drawn carriage and slowly carried it on their shoulders to a little parish church hidden behind trees. This was the hamlet of Boulge and the dead man, known to local children as 'Dotty' for his unkempt appearance, was one of England's most accomplished sons. Edward FitzGerald, poet and patron of the arts, shy recluse and toast of learned academies, the man who had translated the Rubāiyāt of Omar Khayyām into English verse, had died at the age of seventy-four, finally at peace with England.

There was no grand memorial service to honour him at Westminster Abbey. Too many years spent in rejection of London society had made certain of that. But Alfred, Lord Tennyson, who would probably have not climbed the heights without years of secret funding by the dead man, wrote a long poem in his memory. Another friend, Frederick Spalding, expressed the pain of his loss more privately in his diary. He wrote: 'I shall never know or meet his like upon earth . . .'

*   *   *

'A heavy-weight champion wrestler, with big bones and a very large head'

On 18 May 1962, which was, by coincidence, Khayyām's 914th birthday, his tomb in the ruins of old Nishāpur was opened for the first

time since his burial on 5 December 1131 to remove his remains to a
new mausoleum that the shah of Iran had built for him. As his fame
had spread throughout the world in recent times, due to the success of
Edward FitzGerald translating him into English, his grave was
attracting an increasing number of foreign visitors and Iran wanted to
be seen honouring him. The problem was that, after Khayyām's death,
the mausoleum of a later Muslim saint had grown to incorporate his.
The poet could not be honoured without dishonouring the saint. So a
new monument was erected for him about 100m away.

The man chosen to descend into the tomb to lift the remains was a
young man aged twenty. Many years later, after he had written a
history of Nishāpur, Dr Freydoon Gerāyeli recalled his experience. He
said: 'The tomb looked like a cistern, an underground water store, and
it was very deep, at least 2m deep. . . . They had not poured earth over
the body, as is the Muslim custom. They had just laid it on the floor of
the chamber and then built an arch over it. . . . The skeleton was
completely undamaged. . . . I kissed the skull as I picked it up and they
photographed everything. I had imagined Khayyām to be the
intellectual type, a small man with a thin body. Not so. We found a
heavy-weight champion wrestler, with big bones and a very large
head. The circumference of his skull was 61 or 62cm. . . . The tomb
had very strong brick walls.'

But why was Khayyām buried in a Zoroastrian-style burial chamber?

*   *   *

'Omar and Edward would have understood'

On 2 August 1996, yet another foreign visitor asked local farmers in
Suffolk for direction to Boulge churchyard and, yes, he sought the
grave of Edward FitzGerald. When he found it, he sat on the dry earth
of the churchyard beside the tombstone and fell silent for a long time
in harmony with the deserted countryside. The only sounds were the
cooing of oriental collar doves in the trees and the gentle rustle of
leaves in the breeze. A familiar wild rose spread its branches over the
stone. A plaque said its seed had been brought over from the graveside
of Khayyām in Nishāpur, grown at Kew Gardens in London and

planted there, in Boulge, by the Omar Khayyām Club of Great
Britain.

The visitor eventually moved over to the modest church and
pushed the door open. Inside, he found a memorial book placed beside
the alter. Pilgrims from all over the world, particularly the US and
Canada, had written movingly of their sentiments for both FitzGerald
and Khayyām.

Khayyām's fellow countryman similarly signed his name. In the
column for nationality, he wrote 'Stateless'. Then he added: 'Omar
and Edward would have understood!' He thought of telling their story,
one day.

CHAPTER ONE

The Fire Temples of Nishāpur

What a handsome face, what beautiful hair!
My height a cypress, my skin so fair.
And yet my Maker, what purpose did He
Assign to my life when He painted me?[1]

It is Wednesday, 10 May 1066, and a numbing fear grips the whole of
mankind, though perhaps nowhere so deeply as here in the dukedom
of Normandy, on the western edge of the world. Night has just fallen
and everywhere knots of people have gathered to peer into the sky to
gaze at a new visitor from the heavens. What terrible omen does this
wondrous long-tailed star, that has streamed across the sky for the past
three nights, bring for the young men now being recruited by Duke
William to invade England across the water? Some say it is the Angel
of Death riding a herd of white flying horses, come from Hell to pay us
a closer visit before a new plague. Old men kneel and pray. Women
weep. Will not a bishop, sage or bard try to persuade the Duke to
change his mind? If not they, what about one of his mistresses?

England's king, Edward the Confessor, died in January and William
regards himself as his cousin's appointed successor. On the other hand,
Harold Godwineson, the Earl of Wessex, has already been proclaimed
king in England. He is one of the bravest generals that the Anglo-
Saxons have ever produced. A terrible blood-letting beckons.

One man who knows 'William the Bastard' too well to hope for a
compromise is a nobleman by the name of Otho Geraldino. He is a
Norman like everyone else, but owes his fancy Italian name to an
ancestor among the dukes of Tuscany. As one of William's most
trusted commanders, he has already discussed the matter at court and

heard the duke say that the new star was exactly the divine signal he had waited for. It heralded victory for the rightful king and doom for the usurper.

But William would say so, would he not? He too, like his old friend and enemy, Harold across the sea, is battle-hardened and a gambler. He has known no peace since he became ruler at the age of seven, thirty-one years ago. Besides, he has been planning this day for years; he has sunk too much gold into the building of all those ships and the forging of this great army and would lose too much face to change his mind now. He has even won the pope's support for his venture. The banner of St Peter is on its way from Rome to accompany him.

As Geraldino gazes upon the comet[2] in fear and awe, he hopes that William's bravura will prove justified once more, and that he himself will also survive the battle. He sees everywhere the new star imposing itself upon everyone's mind. What he certainly does not know – and could never imagine – is that some 3,000 miles to the east, in a great city he has never heard of, at this very moment, there gazes upon the same star a precocious, eighteen-year-old youth, with a 'handsome face, beautiful hair, my height a cypress, my skin so fair', whose name will, one day, be forever linked to his, Geraldino's.*

* * *

It is eighteen years earlier, Wednesday[3] 18 May 1048, and dawn breaks over the valley of Nishāpur to reveal a countryside of fruit-laden orchards and swaying wheat fields. In the middle of the valley nestles its precious possession and source of fame, the great city itself.

The mood in Nishāpur's arcaded bazaars, each devoted to the craft of a particular tradesman – hat makers, booksellers, fur merchants, perfume blenders, even cooks – is sullen and expectant. As the hooves of the occasional horse strike the paving stones and break the calm of the early morning, a few shopkeepers sprinkle water in front of their stores to reduce the dust of the long, hot day ahead. Others are having breakfast. Some have ordered porridge – made with crushed wheat shoots and garnished with cinnamon in sizzling, molten butter – to be

---

*   Geraldino is the first known ancestor of the FitzGeralds of England and Ireland.

delivered to their shops. Some have settled for the more humble lentil soup or baked beetroot.

In this city, on this day, Ebrāhīm Khayyāmi, a herbal physician who heads one of the city's upper-middle-class families, will announce the birth of his first son.[†] There will be celebrations in the extended family. The infant's mother will be showered with presents and there will be prayers that the baby might survive to a grand old age.[4]

Little Omar will, indeed, survive to become the patriarch of his clan. But he will become much, much more. His fame will transcend empires for centuries after his death and, in his own time, he will be honoured with exotic and pompous titles: *Abulfath Ghiāthaddin Hojjatol Haqq Malik al Hokamā Hakīm Omar bin Ebrāhīm al Khayyāmi*, 'The Father of Fath,[‡] the Saviour of the Faith, the Proof of the Truth, Philosopher Laureate, Doctor Omar, the Son of Ebrāhīm Tentmakers'.

He is expected to settle for the comfortable profession of his father, and he will, indeed, spend a few years as an apprentice in the family surgery. But he will go on to become one of the most important mathematicians of all ages, a confidant of kings, an emperor's personal doctor, and a renowned astronomer.

He will also, suddenly and dramatically, fall from grace. Few will want to know him. He will be pursued by enraged mobs and stalked by trained assassins. He will go into hiding for many a year and be forced to choose bitter, isolated exile. He will write rebellious, inquisitive, reflective poems.

Omar was born in the capital city of Persia's – or Iran's[5] – vast eastern region of Khorāsān. Every day, large caravans arrived in Nishāpur from all directions, including the Silk Road to the east, carrying the best cloths of China and the most sought-after spices of India. Caravans also exported from Nishāpur its fine woollen fabrics and other products, to the east as well as to the west, to such dreamt-of places as Isfahan, Baghdad, Constantinople.

On the day of Omar's birth, however, the throbbing bustle of life in the city's bazaars was only part of the recent story of the people of

---

[†] See later in this chapter for an explanation of why we think we know Khayyām's date of birth precisely.

[‡] Fath was the name of his eldest son. The 't' and 'h' are pronounced separately.

Nishāpur. Their city breathed resentment and sorrow. Everywhere sullen faces spoke of the hard times that had befallen 'the Bride of Cities', 'the Pride of the East'. This was a community under alien rule and in conflict with itself.

Only ten years earlier, in 1038, the city's elders had decided that it was no longer possible to resist the marauding Saljuq Turkish nomads from Asia who had menaced them for a generation. The Saljuqs had strangled the trade that had made Nishāpur prosperous and nearly destroyed the agriculture that fed it. The elders had agreed to negotiate and had, in addition, yielded to paying a huge treasure in gold and silver to the invaders' chief warlord, Toghril, in return for a promise to respect the citizenry's private possessions. Still, many had been slain and much property seized by the invaders.

A near-contemporary writer and traveller, Rabbi Benjamin of Tudela in Spain, has left us his own, terrified vision of these first Turks to come out of north-eastern Asia. He wrote: 'They worship the wind and live in the desert. They eat no bread and drink no wine, but endure a diet of raw meat and, being without noses, breathe only through two small holes in their faces.' How strange in mentality and alien in race they must have appeared to the common people of Nishāpur.

More appalling yet had been the rescue attempt organised by the rightful king, the drunkard Sultan Mass'ud of the Ghaznavid dynasty based in the city of Ghazni, far in the east in today's central Afghanistan. Belatedly, the sultan had turned his attention from looting and massacring the Hindu regions of western India for the glory of Allah (and a future Pakistan!) to repossess Nishāpur, the most glamorous city in his empire. But the venture had coincided with the worst drought in memory, and this he had compounded by stationing in the city his large, hungry army. The livestock had died, when not eaten, and the wretched poor had resorted to cannibalism. The sultan had then committed the worst possible mistake. He had chased the Saljuqs into the central Asian deserts, only to have his army reduced there to a scattering of thirsty, hungry, cursing former soldiers fleeing in all directions. The combination of the drought and the Turks' mobility had first killed off his horses and elephants. Then his troops had become a posse of dazed, near-mutinous infantry. A final flight towards India had seen the sultan slain by his own slaves.[6]

Now, eight years later, most farmers had returned from the hills and Toghril's younger brothers – for the chief himself was already far into western Iran on new conquests – had begun to nurture the caravan traffic once more. It was good to see the underground canals emerging in town with cool, clear water from the hills. It was reassuring to hear, every morning, the cries of the officials who divided the streams on their way to the various districts. Green shrubs lined the streets once more.

But beyond these tentative signs of recovery, the city's former joyous spirit had deserted it, seemingly for ever. Toghril had reaffirmed his conversion to Islam to win recognition from the caliph in Baghdad, the spiritual head of Sunni Islam. He wanted to be acknowledged as the new Shāhanshāh, King of Kings, successor to the emperors of old Iran, and he wanted to be declared the new Lord of all Muslims – 'King of the East and West'. To this effect, he had imposed Islamic Shari'a law on the whole of Transoxania and Khorāsān. Worse still, he had drawn his enforcers of the law from among fierce bands of Arab immigrants who had previously been despised in Nishāpur and elsewhere in Iran.

So, gone were the days of glory – still lingering in the mind of the elderly – when a poet such as Daqiqi could sing with pride at royal audiences:

> Four blessings above all has Daqiqi chosen
> In this battleground of beauty and repellence:
> The ruby of lips, the cry of the harp,
> The taste of old wine and the creed of Zarathustra.[7]

Now the public expression of any such attachment to the joys of life, let alone preference for the ancestral religion, could result instantly in the confiscation of a man's home and the sale of his children into slavery.

A new visitor did not have to read the broken hearts of the vanquished Persians in their grim faces alone. As he walked the streets, he saw how they had to dismount and stand aside with bowed heads to make way for any Turkish soldier or Arab cleric who passed by.

One contemporary poet, Assadi Tūsi,[8] wrote a poem called 'My House'. It grieves for the people of Khorāsān from homesick exile:

> The house is ruined,
> The garden wilted,
> The pillars are down,
> The light has died.

Another, Manūchehri Dāmghāni, writing earlier as Turkish numbers gathered force to the north in central Asia, spoke of autumn and 'the cold wind that blows from Khārazmia'.[9]

As for those who still clung to the region's older religions, Zoroastrianism, Christianity and Judaism, they had to praise Islam in public and, even then, they were tolerated only if they worshipped in secret and paid the heavy *jizyah* tax that Islam decrees against certain religions it may tolerate. The houses of these lesser believers could not be taller than their Muslim neighbours' and Jews had to wear patches of yellow cloth on their chests and backs to warn Muslims not to touch them. Buddhists were classed as idol worshippers and put to the sword unless they converted or submitted to slavery.

Nor was that all. The city's various Muslim sects themselves regularly clashed in riots and burned down one another's houses, mosques, schools, libraries and hospitals, on the perception of any slights. The riots were so frequent that they had acquired a name of their own: *shahr jang*, city war.

Between the bouts of communal madness, the downtrodden multitude and their champions clung to the use of the Persian language and resorted to humour as a weapon to help them to resist the efforts of the authorities to replace their ancient tongue with Arabic.

One joke that has survived from those times reveals how deeply the resentment of the vanquished people ran: 'A magpie sits on the edge of a roof and feasts on a dog's defecation. As he does so, he recites, in heavily glottal Arabic, the saying "Breakfast nails the body together". A man passes underneath in the lane and is disgusted. He shouts: "Surprise, surprise! You eat shit and vomit Arabic." '[10]

*   *   *

Nishāpur bears the name of Shāhpūr I, the second emperor of the Sasanian dynasty that fell to the invading Arabs in the seventh century.[11] But an important garrison town and trading centre had occupied the site for centuries under the previous Parthians and possibly even the Achaemenids, the Great Kings of classical Persia. The town had been favoured for its strategic position by Shāhpūr's father, Artaxerxes 'the Kurd' Pāpakān, who had overthrown the last of the Parthians in 224 CE. When Artaxerxes appointed his son Shāhpūr as the governor of the region, the latter strengthened the town's fortifications and drained the marshes around it to convert them into productive arable land. It is thought to have been at this time that the city's older name, Abar[12] Shahr, was formally abandoned, even though many writers continued to use it long into Islamic times.

Nishāpur was further expanded by Shāhpūr II, 'the Great', whose formal reign began even before he was born in 310 CE. On the death of his father, the imperial crown was hung above the head of the pregnant queen as she sat on the throne to deputise for her unborn child. Later still, the emperor Yazdgard II (443–457) chose Nishāpur as his favoured residence. It was then that it acquired a large Christian population and became the seat of the Nestorian bishops of Iran. The emperor remained in Nishāpur until he died 'as the result of a kick by a water horse', for which we may read an embarrassing tussle in the ruling family itself.[13]

In 487, the most renowned of the Sasanians, Anūshak Rabān (known commonly today as Anūshīrvān the Just) was born in Nishāpur to a native noblewoman and went on to follow his father in choosing his queen from the city.

Those were the good times of the storytellers in the herbal tea houses of Nishāpur, an age, now passing into legend, when Zoroastrian emperors celebrated the beauty of their queens on their coins and young women chose only heroes for husbands.

Popular immersion in that world of pre-Islamic Iran, always conveyed in theatrical, outlandish Persian, had been – and remained – another crucial factor in frustrating the attempts of the Muslim clergy to make the language of the mosque the language of the home in Nishāpur. Countless romantic, historical and scientific books in the old language, Middle Persian or Pahlavi, still circulated and fetched high prices as investments.

The bulk of such literature is now lost. A few dozen volumes have survived and some – such as the so-called *Arabian Nights*[14] – were translated or plagiarised into Arabic. They remind us of the vast amounts of money that the Sasanians spent on new writers before they went down. We may speculate endlessly on what glories Iran might have achieved if its intellectual development had not been interrupted by Islam. It had already reached an advanced stage by 529 CE when most of Constantinople's Aristotelian philosophers fled Christian persecution to make Sasanian Iran their home.

* * *

It has just passed 2 a.m. on 4 July 1054, and it is a pleasantly cool, clear night in China's imperial capital city, Beijing. The wooden beds of the citizenry can be seen everywhere; on flat roofs, balconies, verandas, in courtyards and among the flowerbeds, to relieve the stifling heat. Some older people have difficulty falling asleep. For a few, it is their profession to stay awake. These include the emperor's astrologers who watch the skies for any new events that might affect the life of the emperor or the fate of his divine state. Some are already tired, having recorded the movements of the planets against the background of the constellations since dusk, as well as tutored their pupils' aspiring eyes.

Suddenly, one teacher falls silent in mid-speech as he describes the constellation of Taurus. He does not respond to questions and begins to rub his eyes. He thinks he sees a bright new star to the south east of the lower horn of the Bull. But surely, that cannot be. Only half an hour ago, there was no such thing, and nor is it a 'broom star'. It has no tail. On the other hand, if it is really there, what could it mean? Something calamitous, obviously. Should he wake the Astrologer Royal, Yang Wei-te? Perhaps the emperor would like to see?

We do not know the precise chain of events that followed immediately, but we can make a fair guess. The Astrologer Royal was awakened; he was as much at a loss as were his underlings; prayers were said and heads were shaken; all began to tremble as the sun broke above the eastern horizon and the new star did not disappear along with all the other heavenly bodies.

The new star remained visible all day, that day, and for twenty-three more days. At night, it shone so brightly that some young people made a point of reading by it.

The Beijing account, as told in *The Essentials of Sung History* by Chang Te-hsiang, says that the event put the astrologers in a dilemma. It was not a broom star or comet and its remaining visible by day had no precedent. But who would dare tell the emperor? Eventually, someone said he saw a yellow glow at one corner of the new star, and was not yellow the imperial colour of the Sung dynasty? So, on 27 August, when the new star no longer shone by day, the Astrologer Royal sought audience before the emperor to give his imperial majesty a most uplifting piece of news:

> Prostrating myself before your Imperial Majesty, I hereby report that a guest star has appeared. Above the star in question, there is a faint glow, yellow in colour. If one carefully examines the prognostications concerning your Royal House, the interpretation is as follows: the fact that the guest star does not trespass against *Pi*, the lunar mansion in Taurus, and because its brightness is full, means that there is a person of great wisdom and virtue at the helm of this land. I beg that this be handed over to the Bureau of Historiography.[15]

Nine and a half centuries later, we know that the heavenly phenomenon of 4 July 1054 was not the birth of a new star, but the death of one. It was a supernova, a massive sun exploding after exhausting nearly all of its hydrogen fuel and imploding upon itself to make a neutron star, a tiny, immensely dense body. In the process, the enormous gravitational forces that resulted from the death of the old giant caused new nuclear reactions and a new spectacular explosion. It gave up more energy than whole galaxies at a time. The region then became a giant, but near-invisible, mass of dust or nebula with a pulsating source of radio waves at its centre.

There are four other independent surviving records of the supernova of 1054, what we now call the Crab Nebula. Three of them were written elsewhere in China, the other in Japan. There are also some rock carvings by the natives of central and northern America dating from the eleventh century that appear to be depictions of the supernova with the crescent of a new moon nearby. But the absence of any account of the event in the surviving histories of the Middle East and Europe takes some explanation. Astronomers are unanimous in believing that the explosion would have been noticed by virtually the whole of mankind, and its visibility in daylight regarded as ominous. Certainly, weather conditions would have not been unfavourable everywhere for the 21½ months that the new 'star' remained visible at night.

The puzzle may not be difficult to solve. In the Middle East, thousands of historical documents vanished in the Turkic, Mongolian and Tartar invasions of the subsequent centuries (see next segment in this chapter about the historian Abul Fadl Beihaqi) and Europe was in the grip of a censorious church that believed creation had already been completed. New stars were not supposed to come into being, while comets were regarded as only an atmospheric phenomenon.

Whatever the reasons for the absence of historical records on the birth of the Crab Nebula in the Middle East, there can also be no doubt that the people of Khayyām's Nishāpur were as shaken by it on that special 4 July as were the astrologers of China and Japan. Perhaps even more so. With memories of recent wars and famines still weighing on their minds, Nishāpurians would have been forgiven if they were especially frightened. Did it mean that the governor would rebel against the new king, for example, and plunge them into another war? Was it the sign of another draught coming? Or even more Turks from over the horizon?

The fear of more 'kith and kin' from Central Asia bursting onto the plains of Khorāsān was now the greatest fear of the ruling Saljuq Turks themselves, as they began to grow urban, soft and fat. What no one guessed was that, before too long, even rival royal wives would rebel to start new civil wars.

How did the general excitement surrounding the celestial newcomer affect young Omar, who had only recently celebrated his sixth birthday? We may speculate that he saw how it preoccupied his family. The little boy later displayed an early and unusual enthusiasm for astronomy and mathematics. Was it because the explosion in the sky made a local hero of a relative or teacher who dabbled in astronomy and astrology? We shall see shortly that two of his future mathematics teachers were published astronomers.

* * *

While the new star still shone in the sky in daylight that July of 1054 and terrified populations everywhere, a wholly unexpected act by a foreign diplomat in Constantinople outraged the ancient city that had already seen so much. The man had arrived from Rome with the specific mission of trying 'to heal the wounds that pushed asunder the two wings of Christendom'. Yet his tactics gave notice of a new internecine war among the Christians, precisely at a time when they were being pressed on two sides by barbarians and heathens. Was it not proof of the astrologers' worst fears about the unwelcome visitor from the Heavens?

The diplomat was no less a magnate than Cardinal-Bishop Humbert of Silva Candida, the pope's right-hand man and theological guide. He had arrived with a letter from his master that hoped the two sides would overcome their differences in the interest of Christian unity. He had been received in ceremony and given free access to the emperor, Constantine Monomachos, who had ordered the burning of a pamphlet that denounced Roman teachings. Yet the cardinal had resorted to harsh words wherever he had gone and demanded immediate compliance with doctrine as formulated by the See of Peter.

Some of his demands were small-minded, some comical and some bizarre. He wanted the easterners to stop leavening the bread of the sacrament, he objected to the sacramental wine, 'the blood of Christ', being diluted with water, and he disagreed with Constantinople on 'the procession' of the Holy Spirit. Over the course of several centuries and starting in far-flung Spain, the Romans had drifted towards the initially heretical belief that the Holy Spirit had emanated both from the Father and the Son, whereas the easterners still believed that it had arisen from the Father *through* the Son. The fact that the dogma was so abstruse that even many priests did not understand it, let alone the laity, was deemed immaterial.

On their side, the Byzantines, or 'the Greeks' as the Romans called them to dismiss them for the mere provincials that they had been in old Rome, posed obstinacies of their own. They excommunicated any priests who shaved their chins and trimmed their hair. They allowed the secular clergy – those who did not live in monasteries – to marry – as opposed to the concubinage – or con *cubare*, 'lying together' – that Rome tolerated.

But really, at the deeper level, the confrontation had its roots in the ancient rivalry between civilised, ancient Greeks and the upstart Romans. Rome, now as ever, wanted to boost its prestige, particularly as it was locked in a political battle for supremacy with the Holy Roman Empire based in Germany. To justify its position, Rome resorted to the claim that the pope occupied the chair of St Peter and was thus the automatic head of Christ's church on earth.

The Byzantines replied that there was not the slightest historical evidence for the claim. But their established church was in a weak position when it came to doctrinal disputation. It did not have the mental equipment to reject the popes' alleged connection with Peter, nor even challenge the authenticity of the so-called Donation of Constantine. This document was a notorious forgery from the end of the eighth century by Pope Leo III that claimed that the leadership of Christianity had forever been conferred on the bishops of Rome by the emperor Constantine. The Byzantine patriarchate pointed out, instead, the moral corruption that afflicted the papacy, even though the present pope, Leo IX, was doing his best to curb some of the outrageous practices of his clergy. Had not, for example, the previous pope bought his job, that is, the papacy, from his godson? And had not the godson inherited it from his father when popes were supposed to be celibate?

And yet the present Byzantine patriarch, Michael Cerularius, was a mere political appointee and, furthermore, he had committed many un-brotherly acts. He had taken advantage of his weak and indolent sovereign, Constantine IX, to close all Roman Catholic churches in the eastern empire for their refusal to preach according to Greek Orthodox usage, and he had challenged the authority of Rome in the west itself. He had ordered one of his underlings to send a letter to the 'most reverend pope and all the other Frankish bishops' to criticise Roman practice. If Constantine had been stronger, he would have almost certainly prevented the letter from being sent, for his army was at that very moment allied to the pope's forces in southern Italy in their combined effort to stem the rising power of the Normans there. In fact, the pope, Leo IX, had been languishing in a Norman prison at the time and deserved greater respect. The patriarch's outrage had forced the head of the present Roman delegation, Cardinal Humbert, to react similarly badly. He had published a pamphlet called *The Crimes of the Greeks.*

Still, now the pope was released from captivity and the cardinal had come to Constantinople with the official task of letting bygones be bygones. He had come to show the goodwill of the Holy Father in the greater interest of both wings of the church of Christ while their prospects became more desperate by the day. In southern Italy, the papal and Byzantine estates were falling to the Normans regularly and, in the east, heathen barbarians, the Turks, were laying waste to Christian Armenia and Georgia.

However, Humbert had found that he was knocking his head on a stone wall, albeit one covered with velvet. Even his many appeals addressed to the emperor in person to order an attempt at doctrinal convergence had not made the slightest difference. What was he to do now?

He resolved on a most dramatic gesture, one that even risked his life. On the morning of 16 July 1054, as the Orthodox clergy in their silken robes and long beards administered to a great throng of the faithful in the ancient cathedral of Constantine the Great, the Santa Sophia, he and his companions suddenly raised a banner and marched to the altar with loud and defiant voices. There they lay upon the altar a lengthy proclamation in the name of the pope that excommunicated Patriarch Michael and all who followed him. In fluent Greek, Humbert denounced the whole Byzantine church as heretical. The long, abusive tract, in Latin, ended thus:

Wherefore we, abhorring the violence and insults done unto the Holy and First Apostolic See, and seeing that the Catholic faith is many ways violated, do by the injunctions of the Holy and Indivisible Trinity, and the Apostolic Throne (whose messengers we are), and of all the Orthodox Fathers of the Seven Councils, hereby subscribe that anathema which our Lord the most reverend pope hath passed unto the said Michael and all his followers (if they be not penitent) in these terms: Michael the pseudo-patriarch, the neophyte, who donned the monastic garb merely out of human fear and is now notorious as the author of many dreadful crimes, and with him Leo, so-called Bishop of Ochrida, and Nicephorus, chancellor of the said Michael, who in sight of all trampled on the sacrifice of the Latins with his feet, and all who follow them in the heresies aforesaid and the crimes aforesaid, shall be anathema marantha, as with Simoniacs, Valesians, Arians, Donatists, Nicolaites, Severians and Manichaeans, and as with those who teach the animation of leavened bread and all other heretics, nay, as with the Devil himself and his angels, unless they do turn aside. Amen, Amen, Amen.[16]

The cardinal and his entourage then marched out of the stunned cathedral, faces flushed and steps determined. Some of the Orthodox clergy ran behind them to plead with them to take back their proclamation. In their haste, they dropped the tract and picked it up again and the congregation laughed. Eventually they found the Romans outside the cathedral ceremoniously shaking the dust from their shoes to cleanse them of the filth of the blasphemers before mounting their horses for Rome.

In the event, the cardinal was persuaded by Emperor Constantine to remain a little longer in the city in the hope of persuading the patriarch to compromise. But the weak emperor failed. Cerularius reasoned that some of the pope's beliefs were clearly heretical. 'If the head of the fish is rotten, how could the rest of it be healthy', he said.

According to one account, the pope had died three months earlier on 15 April and Cardinal Humbert, as one of the seven cardinal-bishops of the church of Rome, must have been informed by express messenger. If true, he did not divulge the news to his hosts. It would have undermined the validity of his proclamation. Nor is it clear if, even before leaving Rome, he had obtained the approval of the pope for excommunicating the Byzantine patriarch if the patriarch refused to submit.

In analysing Humbert's act, it would make sense to assume that he had an eye on the papacy himself. He was aged fifty-four now and at the height of his powers. He had a reputation in Rome for being a decisive and visionary reformer. Surely, his turn to be pope was around the corner. In the event, this was not to be. After writing three books that laid the theoretical foundation for the supremacy of popes over kings and emperors – and by extension making possible the Crusades – he died seven years later at the age of sixty-one, when his turn really did seem to have arrived. His legacy, however, would prove more enduring than that of many a pope. His insult, perhaps designed to harvest maximum publicity to enhance his career, made virtually final the schism between the two great wings of Christianity. It would take until 4 May 2001 before a pope would be allowed into the presence of the patriarch of the Greek Orthodox church to apologise for past wrongs symbolised by Humbert's sacrilege at the altar of Santa Sophia on that 16 July 1054.[17]

* * *

At some unspecified date between January 1055 and August 1056 in Constantinople, a young army commander was brought before Empress Theodora, who had overthrown her brother-in-law Constantine to rule as sole *Autocrat* and last emperor of the Macedonian imperial house. The young man bore a famous name, Romanus Diogenes, and his charge of rebellion did not surprise many. His father, Constantine Diogenes, a leading army general as *dux* of Thessalonica in northern Greece, had 'committed suicide' in 1031 as he was being interrogated for rebellion. He had previously been blinded.

What was not expected was that the hard-hearted empress, now in her seventies and with a gruesome record of blindings of her own, should be reduced to tears by the sight of the youth. Perhaps it had something to do with the unproven accusation twenty-six years earlier that she had conspired with the young rebel's father to overthrow her sister, Empress Zoë and her husband, Constantine Monomachos. Had she and the soldier's father been lovers, as some rumours claimed? Was she actually his mother, as even wilder rumours said? We are fortunate in having a vivid account of the encounter. Michael Attaleiates, a contemporary historian and courtier, described the interrogation:

> The man did not only surpass others in his good qualities, but he was also good to look at in all respects. His broad chest and back gave him a fine

appearance, and his very breath seemed noble, if not actually divine. He seemed more handsome than others and this was enhanced by his bright eyes. His complexion was not exactly white, nor very dark, but as though mixed by artifice with nature and somewhat ruddy. In all these, his gentleness could be observed and he gave evidence, as the comedian (Aristophanes) says, of a form worthy of worship.[18]

Fortune rode high for the solider this time. He was forgiven and sent back to his lands in the Anatolian east with his titles restored. But Constantinople would have mixed sentiments about him one day, though not history. Had he later achieved what he wanted above all, the shape of the Middle East and, perhaps, the whole world, would have been different now.

*   *   *

It is the late afternoon of Saturday, 24 January 1058 and ceremonial Baghdad is dressed up for the most important event of many years. Toghril, the paramount chief of the Saljuqs, is in town for the second time and he will, today, be invested by the caliph as the new 'Shāhanshāh'. As such, he will be recognised for what he is, the undisputed temporal ruler of all the eastern lands of Islam, including here, Baghdad, the seat of the caliphate. But the event will have symbolic importance, too. It will be a recognition that the recent Persian Shia domination of the largely Sunni caliphate is truly over. It has been replaced by the rule of the Turks who, as new converts to Sunni Islam, are imposing its precepts everywhere ruthlessly, as well as putting a heavy hand on the caliph's shoulder himself. Allah's deputy on earth will enjoy the new era probably even less.

The last time Toghril arrived in the city, the caliph did not receive him at all. For the whole thirteen months of his unwelcome stay, all communication between the two sides was carried out by their viziers. The caliph, as every good Sunni knows, has been bestowed with such divine beauty that many a mortal would be stricken dead if they were to lay eyes on him. Toghril may well be the most powerful man in the world and the caliph's protector, but he knows his place. He is just a humble mortal and has no wish to raise the wrath of God.

It would seem as if the whole population of the great city has gathered around the royal palace, though this is not true. Many Shias have stayed away as they mourn the end of Persian rule. Certainly during the last stay of Toghril's Turks in the city, they bore the brunt of the atrocities. The Turcomans were billeted in their homes and 'indulged in every crime possible' to the extent that the caliph threatened to leave the city in protest.

Anyhow, for the moment, such memories of the recent past are being left at home, the jubilant crowds betraying no hint that the frequent bloodshed between Sunnis and Shias make Baghdad essentially a dysfunctional city.

Bands of musicians play their joyous tunes and dancers and tightrope walkers thrill with their arts. There is hardly a vacant place in the surrounding streets. Infantry and cavalry struggle to keep the thoroughfares open. Large numbers of the gentry and the heads of the main mercantile houses are inside the palace to be fêted throughout tonight, after the breaking of the Ramadan fast at sunset.

In the innermost hall of the palace, the huge coronation chamber, the most important personages of the new order, including Saljuq princes and their Persian viziers, have been waiting for some time for the ceremony to begin. Incense burners are moved around the hall to kill off the body odour – mixed with the stench of garlic on their breaths and goat cheese stuffed into their pockets – of so many rough Turks from the steppe whom the Persians have not managed yet to civilise. At the top end of the hall is erected an enclosure for the Holy Presence. The finest tapestry in the region hangs around the throne to shade the caliph from unworthy eyes. Among all those gathered here, only one outsider will be able to see the Successor to the Prophet, al-Qa'im Bi Amrallah, Steadfast by the Command of God, the Abbāsid caliph, this day. Toghril Beg, the paramount chief of the Saljuq clan, will be that chosen man.

At last the proceedings start with a band of trumpeters blaring a pompous tune, and the master of ceremonies ushers the Saljuq chief, on foot and unarmed, into the enclosure. Having waited for so long to be allowed into the presence, the mighty warlord, without whose protection the caliph would be murdered inside a week, falls upon his knees and kisses the ground at the foot of the throne. The lower ends of the hangings are high enough for everyone in the hall to see the Turk humiliating himself. The Commander of the Faithful, wearing the black cloak of the Abbāssids and holding the mace of Muhammad in his right hand, smiles upon the Turk and, with his eyes, guides him to a smaller throne next to his.

Then, after a recitation from the Kor'an, the caliph solemnly, but indirectly, addresses Toghril through the chief of the palace staff, 'the Chief of Chiefs':

> Say to him: The Commander of the Faithful is grateful to you for your efforts, praises your deeds and is delighted to have your society. He has placed you in control of all the lands that God gave to *his* control. He has entrusted to you the care of His servants. Fear God in this commission and recognise His graciousness to you therein. Strive to spread justice and restrain evil and benefit the people.[19]

The palace chief then proclaims a decree from the caliph ordering all Muslims to regard Toghril as their overall, temporal lord. Seven robes of honour and seven young girls are presented to him, to symbolise the seven regions of the caliphate, and a golden brocade, scented with musk, is draped over his head. This is surmounted by twin crowns to symbolise the kingship of Arabia and Persia and, to complete the pageant, Toghril is girded with two swords to signify his now being 'the ruler of the east and west'.

A great feast is held long into the evening for the good and the great. Among those present are Toghril's Grand Vizier or chancellor, the wily Abu Nassr Mansūr Kondori. He is suspected by many of wrapping Toghril round his little Khorāsānian finger. Certainly without his strategic genius and diplomatic skill, Toghril would not have forged such an empire so rapidly. Among Kondori's recent decisions is the choice of the city of Isfahan in central Iran as the new capital. Toghril's nephew, prince Alp-Arslān is also here, and so is Alp-Arslān's young vizier, again from Khorāsān, Hasan Tūsi.

As they gaze upon the scene and go through the motions of paying one another their sincerest compliments in the most noble spirit of camaraderie, few among the gathered throng try seriously to gaze into the future. An exception, perhaps, is the young man, Tūsi, who has himself come a long way from being a refugee and the son of a tax collector. Toghril is in his seventies now and childless. What will happen when – or if – his nephew Alp-Arslān succeeds him? It would be natural if the prince kept Kondori in place in the office of the Grand Vizier. The whole of the army seems to be under Kondori's thumb. But Kondori eyes Tūsi with suspicion. He is right to do so. The younger man scrutinises every little movement of the older man's eyebrows to learn the secrets of his success. However, it does not occur even to him that he, young Tūsi, will one day order the severed head of the great man to be delivered to his door for proof of his execution.

Even less does it occur to the rising star that in the ages to come, he will not be remembered primarily for the awesome power that he will wield. It will rather be for the part he will play in the life of a seven-year-old boy now going through the motions of early schooling in Nishāpur, in the same school where he, Tūsi himself, was educated.

*   *   *

Even invaders look kindly on doctors, and this gave Ebrāhīm Khayyāmi the chance to become one of the beneficiaries of the new peace.

By the late 1050s, the Saljuq ruling class was already on its way towards becoming absorbed into Iranian life. One of Toghril's frequent statements was: 'We are not as sophisticated as you Persians', and he was ambitious and a fast learner. He had surrounded himself with Iranian advisors and administrators. His armies were inundated by volunteers wanting to fight for Islam and the plunder that accompanied the jihad, especially in the demoralised and neglected Christian lands of eastern Byzantium. Inside Toghril's new Muslim domains, trade and industry were making a profit again.

Perhaps the most important clue we have to the extent of Ebrāhīm Khayyāmi's prosperity is his recording and preservation of the precise date of birth of his son. He ordered a horoscope to be drawn up to describe the exact position of the planets and stars at the moment of the baby's birth. The practice was mainly the preserve of princes, landowners and the richest merchants. Such was the harsh daily struggle of most families that they had neither the money nor the inclination to record their family histories.§

Yet another indication of Ebrāhīm's wealth was to employ some of the most renowned teachers of Khorāsān to give his young son personal tuition in the various specialities. Furthermore, Ebrāhīm was of a liberal frame of mind, wealth and liberalism often being close companions, for at least one of the tutors he employed was the mathematician Bahmanyār, a proud Zoroastrian. In an age when devout Muslims would not shake hands with Zoroastrians, Jews and Christians for fear of being contaminated by impurity, the decision must imply the broad horizons that Ebrāhīm inhabited.[20]

Some commentators have suggested that Omar's father was a tent maker, a *Khayyām*. No historical source makes any such claim, and all refer to Ebrāhīm as Khayyāmi, not Khayyām. This suggests the collective name of a family or clan whose founder may have been a man of that trade. Family names or surnames were common among professionals and the nobility. The assertion does not preclude Omar's family remaining in possession of a merchant's business that produced or sold tents. The confusion has arisen from his later adoption of the pen name *Khayyām* in the quatrains, but more about that later.

Ebrāhīm's profession as a doctor comes down to us in only one source, but it is a solid one and contemporary. It is, again, Khayyām's mini-biographer, Ibn Funduq,[21] who knew him. He writes: 'He had a great hand in medicine, which was due to his ancestors, and he spent his life studying it.' It makes sense. In a culture where young men automatically followed in the footsteps of their fathers, it explains why young Omar pursued science and medicine, rather than some other profession. Nevertheless, some Greek philosophy that did not

§   Khayyām's horoscope is preserved in Abul-Hasan Beihaqi's *Tatimmah Sewwān al-Hikmah*, or *Supplement to Bibliotheca Philosophica*. The man is also known as Ibn Funduq. As a child, he visited Khayyām together with his father and impressed visitors by recalling the occasion for the rest of his life. The Indian researcher Govinda Tirtha referred the horoscope to the Institute of Theoretical Astronomy of the Academy of Sciences of the former Soviet Union. The astronomers calculated that the particular position of the stars and planets as recorded in the horoscope could have only occurred on 18 May 1048. *The Nectar of Grace: Omar Khayyam's Life and Works*. Allahabad, 1941.

clash with Isalmic doctrine, Islamic law, Arabic language, Persian
poetry and music would have been among the subjects with which the
aspiring doctor had to be familiar.[22]

* * *

It is mid-morning on a spring day in 1058 and an elderly man of urbane
appearance climbs to the roof of his house in the village of Hāreth
Ābād, near the city of Beihaq in western Khorāsān. He has looked
forward to this day for weeks. An old friend and colleague is coming
to stay with him for a few weeks and he is eager to have early
confirmation of the arrival, as soon as the distant specks of several
horsemen, the visitor and his servants, appear on the horizon.

Examining him, you might think he was a typical local noblemen, a
dehghān, a landowner of old Persian stock. His peers cling to their pre-
Islamic family titles, and their wealth enables them to send their heirs to
the great cities, such as Nishāpur, for their education. He wears a
traditional Iranian robe over his tunic and trousers, with a shawl around
his waist, and he moves with a dignity instilled in him in a distant youth.
But this particular man has been much more than a country landowner.
He has been private secretary to no less than five sovereigns, two of
them emperors. He advised his imperial masters at crucial moments of
their reigns, his gossip was sought by chancellors and princes, he ran the
imperial postal service, and he became rich – 'very rich' some said –
although later he lost all. Or, perhaps not quite all. The wealth that he
had inherited in his native Khorāsān escaped the clutches of his enemies
at the Ghaznavid court. Khorāsān is now in the possession of the Turks,
and so this, his father's estate in the village of his birth, remains his.

His full name is Khājeh Abul Fadl Muhammad Ben Hussein e
Beihaqi e Dabīr, the Lord Secretary Muhammad, Father of Fadl, Son
of Hussein, of Beihaq. One day, he will be hailed as an important
historian of these accursed times. For the moment, he is a broken man
and lives in the past. He misses his former life constantly, especially
that invigorating nearness of power, that intoxicating thrill of urgent
news, that privileged peerage of purposeful men.

From early childhood, his lordship has been a restless soul. Even
now, at the age of sixty-three, he wakes maddeningly early for his

servants, rides a couple of hours before breakfast and writes late into the night.

While in office, he kept a secret diary for twenty years and, what is more, he smuggled home copies of many a confidential letter and treaty. Did he always dream of leaving a history behind? He will not deny that he was something of an exhibitionist – 'ah, well, that's youth for you?', he says – and he will not object to being called a gossip, let alone a storyteller. Now, in his last years in 'this rubbish dump of redundancy', as he calls his estate, writing history saves his sanity. The company of the local landowners who talk only of racehorses, hunting dogs and male heirs he shuns. But they, too, find him irritating. He has picked up too many decadent, courtly habits. For example, even though he writes in Persian, not Arabic, he brings into the language far too many words from that foreign tongue, and he cares too much for his former masters. Were the Ghaznavid Turks not as uncouth as the latest barbarians, the Saljuq Turks?

His lordship screws his eyes once again on the winding road that stretches far away to the distant hills. But it is no use. His vision blurs.

He wants his old friend, the Lord Secretary Abu Sa'd Abdul-Qaffār Fākher bin Sharīf here, not only to reminisce about the good old days, but also for any corrections to books he has completed. He hopes, too, that his old friend will write some of his own recollections into the history, particularly about when young Prince Mass'ud had the walls and ceiling of a great hall painted with erotic images and his father's spies told on him. That early example of debauchery surely portended the tragedy that would later befall the empire?[23]

*   *   *

One aspect of the city of Omar's birth that had not been damaged in either the famine or the war in 1040 was its physical appearance. A stranger visiting Nishāpur for the first time would have first been impressed by the ancient great gates that had been built into the city wall, between tall towers that could subject the ill-intentioned to a barrage of arrows. The gates were made of hard wood covered with thick iron plates to resist fire. Once inside, the visitor found grand squares, multi-storied institutions with immaculate tiled façades, dancing fountains and peaceful parks.

Some detailed descriptions of Nishāpur have survived to enable us to speculate about the plan of the city. Chief among the accounts are *The History of Nishāpur* by Hākim of Nishāpur, a judge who lived only a generation or so before Khayyām.[24]

From such sources it becomes clear quickly that Nishāpur had retained its essential Sasanian plan of a large city in three distinct parts. The Kohan Dezh, or Old Castle, was the seat of the government, where the emperor, his chief ministers and his standing army lived. Its walls were the strongest, built to resist a long siege even after the other parts of the city had fallen, and it had only two gates in order not to present an enemy with too many weak points. The numerous watchtowers were constantly manned. The vital treasury, prison and emergency grain stores were also in Old Castle.

Another part, also with walls of its own, was the Shahristān, or 'City'. In pre-Islamic times, beside the remaining official institutions, such as fire temples, synagogues and churches, it housed the bazaars and caravanserais. It was Nishāpur's commercial district.

The third area consisted of the suburbs, known in Khayyām's time by an Arabic name, the Rabad or outskirts. It had began as the equivalent of the modern industrial estate or 'business park', with workshops for making cloths, shoes, carriages, arms, ceramics, and the like. In more recent times, some of the functions of the Shahristān and the Rabad had merged. While the lower classes remained in the Rabad, some rich families had moved into new mansions there to take advantage of the greater availability of land.

Nishāpur's largest mosque, the Friday Mosque, was in the Rabad, and so were some new bazaars, including one that pushed special-isation to extremes: the Pistachio Breakers' Bazaar. As such expensive assets could not be transferred in emergencies to the Shahristān, the Rabad had also acquired thick walls and watch towers to protect it. The names of some of its gates have come down to us and are evocative: Burnt Gate, War Gate, the Head of Shīrīn Gate.[25]

Here is a passage from Hākim's *History* which refers to the district of Heira, where Khayyām lived:

Nishāpur's districts were 47 in number. And a medium district – neither large, nor small – was, for example, the District of the Weavers. It had 300 lanes. . . . The district of Heira was the most desirable, the district of notables and nobility. Its bazaar was very large, the largest of all. One end of it was at the head of Heira and the other near the Park of Sultan Hussein of Karmīr. That is nearly one farsang, all of it covered.[26]

Omar owned a grand house in Heira, of which more later, and he would be buried in its cemetery in a plot of land that he would buy there long before his death.

Hākim's description of the bazaar of Heira might seem an exaggeration – a covered bazaar that was over three miles long would have been rare, if not unique, unless we have received an erroneous measure of 'farsang' from those times. In any case, the bazaar was a place to visit, or, more advisedly, to explore over a whole day. Apart from its numerous enchanting shop fronts, it had many 'guest houses' and caravanserais with restaurants and professional entertainers to tempt the passer-by.

For the caravan owner or merchant who wanted to stay in the city for weeks at a time, self-contained apartments could be hired on upper floors, while shops, offices and stables occupied the ground level. For recuperation, native and visitor alike sat for hours on cushioned benches around the cool, covered mews and chatted over cakes and herbal infusions, or they played backgammon or chess while waiters hurried about and musicians and singers performed in the background. The larger eating houses had ponds with fountains and goldfish.

At dusk every night, the roads and passages that linked Heira to other districts in the city were closed by the police and a curfew imposed from late evening to dawn. Torch-carrying patrols would ask strangers for the night's password.

The bathhouses of Heira served as places of gossip and networking, as well as of bathing. They had hot pools, colonnaded steam chambers, cool fountains and resting rooms. They were served by a retinue of masseurs and towel bearers. Bathing usually took half a day, especially for women, and so the staff served light lunches and dinners. Young Omar would have been taken to a women's bath by his mother for his first five or six years, until other women complained that he stared at them!

*   *   *

The former Lord Secretary Abu Sa'd Abdu-Qaffār eventually did arrive at Beihaqi's home in western Khorāsān and was genuinely enthusiastic about the five volumes that his friend had written so far. 'People are already forgetting what happened. Fantasy rules their heads, now', he told Beihaqi.

Beihaqi lived on in his 'rubbish dump of redundancy' for another eighteen years until September 1077, when he died at the age of eighty-three. He wrote thirty volumes of memoirs and history on the rise and fall of the Ghaznavids and each volume was immediately copied numerous times for the hungry book market. Sadly, though, only six volumes have survived. Perhaps one of the lost ones contained an account of the birth of the Crab Nebula of 4 July 1054, for there was little that the keen eye of Beihaqi missed and, almost certainly, the historian's multitude of readers included young Omar. Beihaqi would have known the Khayyāmi family and might have mentioned them somewhere. He had studied in Nishāpur and later journeyed there every year if the safety of the roads permitted.

What makes Beihaqi special is his conscience as a writer, and it is touching how frequently he feels he has to apologise for divulging the privileged information he had about his masters. In one place, apparently feeling low, he writes: 'There is no way out for me but to record these events, for it will increase awakening and the future needs help if it is to take a better course. . . . I shall not write a single word that is exaggerated or biased so that the readers of these lines might say "Shame on you, old man". . . . This chapter ends here and I hope that the wise, even though I have spoken at length, will approve, for there is no writing that is not worth reading a second time. After this age, the people of other ages will refer to it and know [better].'

Of his own turbulent story, Beihaqi gives us only a hint: 'As long as the king [Sultan Mass'ud] lived, my superior honoured me. But then he changed, and I, too, made my mistakes. Then Life chose to reveal its rougher edges to me. I was caged [imprisoned]. I fell and rose and experienced hard and soft, a full twenty years. It is over, now'.

He does not quite say what those mistakes were, but implies that, by 1049 when he was made chief of the postal service, he had accumulated more wealth than was prudent for a man constantly in the eye of other courtiers. His enemies 'poisoned the mind of His Majesty' and the king appointed a Turkish slave called Nūyān to investigate him. The result was that all his property was confiscated. In 1051, when another Turkish official by the name of Toghril the Infidel seized the throne for two months, Beihaqi was imprisoned again. On being released, he decided no longer to stay in Ghazni, but to return to his village of birth, a thousand miles to the north-west.

It is intriguing that the formal reason for his dismissal was 'not repaying in full the dowry of his wife after he had divorced her'. While this could surely not have been the whole reason, it might indicate that his wife wielded some influence at court.

* * *

Soon after being exiled from the women's baths, a second milestone on the road to manhood awaited the sons of middle-class families. This was to be sent to school to start their formal education in Persian, Arabic, 'Indian accounts' or arithmetic, history, logic, rhetoric and Islamic law. The names of several prestigious schools of the time, that would have been eager to win the favour of the Khayyāmis, have come down to us. They had been founded in a variety of ways. Most were attached to mosques and catered for members of the sect that had built them. Others had been erected by philanthropists or even noblemen for their teachers as a mark of gratitude. One such was the Beihaqiya, founded and run by a relative of the historian. It had accommodation for hundreds of boarders and was so prosperous that it could give dozens of scholarships each year.

It is quite likely, however, that by the time young Omar celebrated his seventh birthday in May 1055, he had already had several years of tuition at home. We know from the autobiography of the great Avicenna that this was the case with him. His father employed the most revered teachers in Bukhara to give him tuition at home and one of them was even persuaded to live with the family. As a result, Avicenna tells us, he mastered logic so rapidly that, when he reached the age of fourteen, the tables had been turned. He had to explain Aristotle and Porphyry to his renowned tutor Nāteli. By the age of sixteen, expert physicians worked under him and, a year later, no less a personage than the king gave him precedence over his other doctors. Here he describe his earliest schooling:

> . . . my father employed for me a teacher of the Koran and a teacher of literature. By the time I was ten, I had learned the Koran and much of the literature, and it was in those early years that I showed some unexpected signs that surprised my teachers . . . then my father sent me to a man who sold greens and knew Indian accounts, so that he could teach it to me.[27]

Avicenna's recollections of 'the man who sold greens' went back to about 985, but cultures and lifestyles changed slowly in those times. Although the fall of Khorāsān into Saljuq hands meant that philosophy – that is, mathematics and the sciences – was now regarded with disdain and had to be learned surreptitiously, even now, in only the second decade of their conquest, the new rulers were beginning to relax and Nishāpur looked forward to normality once more.

The names of two of Khayyām's teachers have come down to us, and they were no ordinary men. As we shall see shortly, they were pioneers in geometry and astronomy whose writings have survived to our time.

On his way to the homes of his tutors, young Omar would regularly have passed through bustling streets and bazaars not dissimilar to those in the Old City of Jerusalem today. Here is a description of Nishāpur's awesome grand mosque by Hākim earlier in the century:

> The city's largest Friday mosque was built by Abu Muslim.[28] Its area was 10 jarībs [about 10 hectares] and it had 1,000 columns. 60,000 people could pray there together. There were running streams and deep ponds in it. In its middle, they had built an icehouse which they filled with snow every year, and all through the summer, the sick and others were comforted by it, free of charge. There were pomegranate and mulberry trees there, most of them with several trunks, so tall were they. The mosque had more than a hundred servants and cleaners, and in one place, the building was elevated over six columns of marble and two other columns [of wood?], brought over from a forest near [the headwaters] of the Tigris, black and white, like [chess] pawns. Also four columns of plaster and baked brick. The ceiling and the columns were covered with gold, and the gold over the dome . . . was estimated to be 20,000 methqāls [94kg]. . . . In the whole of Khorāsān there was not a pulpit finer than the one Abu Muslim had erected there.[29]

Hākim's *History* would have been an important textbook for young Omar as he grew up, and it is likely that the following passage about how Nishāpur's first Arab conqueror had destroyed its main Zoroastrian fire temple would have angered the young Iranian patriot.

When Abdullah Āmer, may Allah be pleased with him, conquered Nishāpur, he began to destroy the fire temple of Old Castle to erect a mosque in its place. . . . The people of the former governor came and said: We have agreed to pay the *jizyah* tax so that our temple may not be destroyed. Abdullah designated them a place far from the mosque. That place is now called Fire Temple Lane.[30]

The implication is that even the later temple had been destroyed by Āmer's successors. More shocking still to Omar would have been the fate of the most sacred fire temple in the whole of Khorāsān, the temple of Borzin Mehr on Mount Rīvand near Nishāpur. It was said to have been built by Zarathustra himself some 1,400 years earlier. Its holy flame had been kept alive without interruption for all that time, and it was the scene of perhaps the most romantic love story in Middle Persian. As the story ran, Rāmīn, the prince of Marv, fell in love with the beautiful Veis. They married and lived happily until she died at the age of eighty-one, 'when the cedar of her height had bent over and her straight back resembled a horseshoe'. The prince ordered that a handsome tomb be constructed for her among lovely gardens in the hills beside the temple of Borzin Mehr. Then he gave up the throne to spend his last days beside her. He died three years later.

Borzin Mehr had also nurtured the most sacred tree in the Zoroastrian world, a cedar said to be 1,405 years old and planted, again by Zarathustra in person, to commemorate the conversion of the local king to his creed. It had survived the first wave of the Arabs, but was felled on the orders of the Caliph Motawakkil in 846 in a manner seemingly designed to hurt the feelings of the Zoroastrians as much as possible. Despite the passage of centuries, the story still irked the historian Beihaqi during Omar's early youth, even though Beihaqi was a committed Muslim:

They described the tree to Motawakkil and he wrote to the governor of Nishāpur to cut it down and send it to Baghdad. He ordered that all the branches be preserved and protected in felt so that carpenters in Baghdad could erect it again for him to see, before he used it to build a new palace. So the Zoroastrians all gathered and told the governor: 'We are ready to collect for the caliph's treasury 50,000 gold dīnārs of Nishāpur; ask him to let the tree live on; tell him it is a sacred tree; no one will benefit from such an act.' The governor replied that Motawakkil was not one of those kings whose commands could be denied him. So he appointed Amīr Attāb, the Sheibāni [Arab] poet to carry out the task and Amīr Attāb found a carpenter, a man called Hussein, who spent some time making a suitable saw, because the girth of the tree, as has been written down in books, was 27 horse whips. . . . They spent 500,000 dirhams to carry it to Baghdad and 1,300 camels were needed for the stem and the branches. But when they arrived within one resting place of Baghdad, Motawakkil's slaves murdered him that night and he did not see the cedar.

But life was not all a tale of woes, especially for the young. A happier passage in Hākim's *History* describes the famous climate of Nishāpur, together with its bounty:

A proof of the altitude of Nishāpur as compared to other cities near and far is that fruits do not last throughout the year in any city other than Nishāpur. For instance, pears, apples and quinces are available twelve months of the year, and for about nine or ten months, grapes and melons, crisp and fresh, may be obtained from markets or houses, by paying or asking; and they make beneficial drinks from those fruits. In the other cities of the east, if these aforementioned are to be found at all, they rot quickly. In Nishāpur they remain perfect, unless care is not taken in their preservation.[31]

*   *   *

How do we envisage young Omar's physical appearance as a schoolboy? Though one day his skull may be used to determine his precise racial type and personal appearance, for now we must resort to conjecture.

When the first Arabs invaded Iran in the seventh century, a nickname quickly spread among them for the people they had conquered. They called them the Yellow Moustaches, which suggests a people similar, perhaps, to the Russians of today – to whose language all the Iranian tongues are related.[32]

By Khayyām's time, racial mixing between the majority Iranians and the minority Arabs and Turks had not become a common practice. Some Arab tribes had migrated to Khorāsān in the early decades of the Muslim conquest, but their numbers had been small; some had been massacred in subsequent uprisings and some forced to flee. Now, inter-marriage between rich Tajiks (Iranians who had converted to Islam[33]) and Turks and Arabs did take place, but it remained rare. Most people married their cousins, close or distant, within their families or clan.

Proof for the claim may be sought in contemporary writings. For example, in a passage in *Norūz Nāmeh* (*The book of the New Year*) widely attributed to the poet himself, Khayyām describes Iranians and Romans as 'of the race of Afrídūn', the legendary forefather of the Iranian peoples. Furthermore, one old source says that Khayyām's family had migrated to Nishāpur from the north-eastern coastal areas of the Caspian sea, suggesting that they might be of Parthian[34] descent, rather than Persian. These two Iranian peoples were, of course, very similar in race and language, but, if anything, the Parthians were even more of a northern type than were the Persians. This is quite clear from the marble busts of some of their princes that have survived.

Young Omar was then, in all likelihood, a fair-haired boy with blue or green eyes and, judging by his remains today, tall for his age. We may also imagine that, because he later grew into a gregarious young man, he was energetic, keen to please and ready to rush away on errands for his father's pharmacy, a bright boy with a twinkle in his eye. 'Bright' here may, of course, be a huge understatement. His intelligence would have dazzled his family from the earliest childhood. In particular, as with all prodigies, his memory for names and numbers would have struck all who knew him.[35]

* * *

Omar's mother is not mentioned in the sources, but fortunately we have a brief profile of a woman of her class to give us a notion of the kind of status she would have enjoyed.

Beihaqi tells the story of a commander-in-chief of the army under Mahmūd, the Ghaznavid sultan, in the earlier part of the century.

The general's jealous rivals at court had persuaded the king that he was plotting rebellion, and they had resorted to the influence that the general's women exerted on him to provide the king with 'evidence':

> There was a widow in Nishāpur who was much accomplished and experienced, with a fair calligraphic hand and able to write Persian well. After the death of her husband, Hasan Mehrān, many a nobleman had asked to marry her, but she had refused them all. She had adopted as her daughter a young slave in the household of the general and this girl ran the whole of the general's household.
>
> At first, the courtiers had tried to get to the general through the girl. But she had turned them down. So they made contact with her adopted mother and told her: 'Poor general Ghāzi! The sultan is planning to get him and will be arriving here soon. Ghāzi will be captured on such-and-such night.' The woman told the slave girl and the slave girl told the general and he was frightened. She told him: 'Think of a way, for you are vulnerable. Do not let them take you by surprise, as they did so-and-so.' Ghāzi became anxious and told the slave woman: 'Call this noble woman here, that she may think on it. If the trouble passes, I will reward her.' The slave girl called the woman. She replied: 'I cannot come, because I am afraid. I shall write to you instead. You can read. Tell it all to the general.' The girl said: 'Very well.' So the widow sent letters and told the girl everything she heard. The sultan's people were experts at intrigue, and the poor woman was no match for them.
>
> So in the afternoon of Monday the ninth of Rabi' al Ākhir, 422 [4 April 1031], they told the woman: 'Tomorrow, as Ghāzi enters the court, he will be arrested.' They made up details and mentioned names. The woman immediately wrote a letter and the slave girl told the general and the general panicked.
>
> He ordered that, in utmost secrecy – so that even his chief of staff did not hear of it – horses be shod and the . . . treasury be opened and whatever was the lightest in weight of jewellery, gold, silver and clothes be loaded on to mules and fast camels. . . . Then he chose the slave girl, plus four other slave girls, and set off in the night for . . . the city of Balkh, far away from the sultan's palace . . .[36]

This particular story has a relatively happy ending as, in the end, the general lost only his wealth and his position. He escaped with his life and his 'slave wife'. But the story shows that the oppression of women was not total and universal. In a culture where women were not supposed to be seen or heard, and where even free men lived in constant fear of brutal princes and grasping officials, it occasionally happened that some noble-born women's formal property rights were respected and that the odd, enlightened father did not force his daughters to marry against their wishes. A few slaves, too, could hope to be adopted by noble families and win a measure of independence.

In the case of Khayyām's mother, it is quite likely that she enjoyed as much freedom and respect as was possible for women in the new Nishāpur of the Saljuqs. Away from the prying eye of the Arab clergy and Turkish soldiery, at home or on the family estate, in society gatherings or in the bath house, she would have been the respected matriarch of a wealthy household.

Altogether, then, it seems safe to assume that the Khayyāmi family enjoyed high status in the society of Nishāpur. It would be inappropriate to use the modern term 'nationalistic' to describe medieval people, but most Iranians of the time seem to have exhibited a strong pride in the achievements of their pre-Islamic forefathers.[37]

In any case, such was the public thirst for tales of romance and general escapism, that we may be certain that the Khayyāmis' possessed at least several instalments of Firdowsi's *Book of the Kings*, the *Shah Nāmeh*.[38] The tome of some 50,000 verses devoted to pre-Islamic Iran was not only the well-to-do Iranian's symbol of status, it provided the justification for his pride in his people's past. Its powerful, epic language and its tales of love and jealousy, heroism and treachery mesmerised even the Turks and Arabs, despite their being belittled in its pages frequently.

Certainly, the many references in the Rubāiyāt to characters in the *Shah Nāmeh* – combined with a total absence of Arab or Muslim heroes in the poems – suggests that Khayyām fell under Firdowsi's spell in his earliest, most impressionable years. His language also contains many ancient Iranian words that Firdowsi had borrowed from Middle Persian and incorporated into Fārsi or New Persian.[39]

* * *

It was 12 December 1059, and it was the twenty-eighth anniversary of his ascent to the throne as the twenty-sixth caliph of the House of

Abbāss. But instead of receiving courtiers to the cry of trumpets, al-Qa'im Bi Amrallah, Steadfast by the Command of God, found himself in a prison room in a dusty castle in Ana, in remote northern Mesopotamia. Nevertheless, as he thought about it – and over the past year of his captivity he had been able to reflect over his strange life endlessly – he could see that he had been one of the luckiest men ever to have lived.

In the first place, as the son of a Christian concubine from Armenia, no one in their right mind would have expected him to be chosen to succeed his grandfather as the successor to the Prophet of Islam – and without a single sword being drawn to challenge him. Secondly, for a supposed man of God, he had lived a life of unimagined decadence. He had never gone to bed except in the best silks of Marv, the stifling summers of Baghdad had been tempered for him by mountains of ice brought down from the peaks of Kurdistan to cool his underground pools, and the most beautiful boys and girls of all races had been brought to him in fresh batches every year to satiate his lust. Even now, in captivity in the hands of an uncouth Arab tribesman, that nonsense about his being of the holy blood of Muhammad still overawed the toughest of ruffians – in truth, especially ruffians. The governor of the castle had ordered that his every wish for worldly comforts be granted immediately. The normal treatment would have been to blind him before killing him slowly on the rack to extract every little secret he might have come across, especially the whereabouts of every little box of gold or silver he might have hidden somewhere.

In the past, despite being subject to the demands of heretical Persians and wild Turkomans, the caliph had never felt in real danger, unlike during the past 12 months. But, it now looked as if he would survive once more. Basāsiri, his 'slave' commander who had taken over Baghdad in the name of the caliph of Cairo, had no possibility of putting up a reasonable fight as Toghril approached the city with a huge force after defeating and killing his own rebellious brother, Yenal. The cursed former slave had made all the mosques of the capital to recite prayers in the name of the Shia usurper of Egypt and he had piled every insult possible on the House of Abbāss. Now, he was going to pay for it all, with his women and children taken into slavery by Toghril's savages. But even Basāsiri, who had been under pressure from Cairo to send him there in chains, had recoiled from committing such a blasphemous act. Instead, he had given him over to the custody of this sentimental Arab chieftain, Quraish, who was changing sides now and going over to Toghril.

Qā'im dreamt on. At the age of only fifty-eight, he would not be surprised if he became one of the longest-lived of all his line. As soon as he got back to Baghdad, he would refurbish all those dear, looted palaces to make them even more luxurious than they had been before. It would cost huge sums. But this superstitious simpleton sultan from the plains of far-away Asia could be relied on to do his duty. If only he could persuade him not to let his rude barbarians defile the beloved city once more.

*   *   *

Twenty-two days later, on 3 January 1060, the caliph's small family party catches its first glimpse of Baghdad on the horizon, and who should be there to welcome him but the mighty sultan himself. The Turk awaits in the path of the mule carrying the Commander of the Faithful and prostrates himself on the ground to kiss the earth in gratitude that Allah has once again saved the life of His anointed deputy in this world for the benefit of the whole nation of Islam. Toghril then stands up and takes the rein of the mule and leads it on foot for several miles into the city, all the time muttering the few words of Arabic he has learnt to thank Allah in an almost unrecognisable accent.

In the meantime, plumes of black smoke rise in the distance as the Sunnis of the city sack the houses of the Shias for supporting the Basā-siri rebellion, and Toghril's own Turkomans are busy, too. No one at all notices that one object of the looters and arsonists is a library, the library of Shāhpūr bin Ardashīr, the most learned of the viziers under the previous Persian dynasty, the Būyids.

Set up in 991 in the Karkh district of the city, The House of Books had acquired over 10,000 manuscripts on varied subjects and, in the six decades of its existence, some of the most able scholars of the caliphate had served as its chief librarians, while its sprawling reading rooms were open to all researchers. One of its most illustrious visitors had been the Syrian poet al-Ma'arri, and it exhibited works even by the enemy, the Fatimid Ismailis in Egypt.

In the next three weeks or so, Toghril's distraught Persian vizier, Kondori, will be able to reclaim 'a handful' of the books from the looters. But that will lay him open to accusations that he is stealing large numbers of the most precious volumes for his own personal collection.

*   *   *

A violent end to a violent life! Arslan 'the Victorious' al-Basāsiri, the former army chief of the Persian King Khosrow-Firuz in Baghdad, could now see his own head stuck on a pole to be presented to that child rapist, the Caliph Qa'im. He could accept that. He was an old man now and had shed plenty of blood of his own. But as he looked on his trembling grandchildren in the middle of that bleak desert near Kufa in central Iraq, he wished he had remained a simple Turkish slave in Basā in southern Iran.

Instead, ambition, energy and insight had taken him out of obscurity all the way to palaces in Baghdad forty years ago and his achievements had made him proud. But then, who would not have been proud in his position? He had marched up and down Mesopotamia at the head of a great army to pacify the land from brigands, and he had even defeated the king's brilliant brother. Afterwards, all the slave class in Baghdad, no, the whole of the region, had looked up to him to win them justice, and to stop that pervert Qa'im from handing over the land to the barbarian Saljuqs.

So he had sent secret emissaries to fellow Shias in Cairo to ask for help. Perhaps it had been a mistake not to send Qa'im to Cairo in chains. If he had, they might have sent him more money than they did.

Just over a month ago, as intelligence arrived that Toghril was approaching Baghdad at the head of a strong body of Turkomans and others, al-Basāsiri decided that he could not defend the city, not with those double-crossing Arabs, Quraish and Dubays, deserting him. Now his softly-raised offspring were going to be auctioned as slaves among Toghril's savages. For a moment he tried to imagine the scenes. He could not bear it. Nor would they be spared if he surrendered. He looked over the horizon for plumes of dust. Toghril's cavalry was closing in on him. It was 15 January.

*   *   *

It is right to be generous to the dead, within reason. Certainly, this is the policy of the great newspapers of the world in our time in their obituary columns. We are all creatures of our genes, eras and upbringings, and allowance ought to be made for those overpowering gods. Besides, to paraphrase a famous television advertisement for a brand of beer in the last decade of the twentieth century, forgiving refreshes those parts of the mind that avenging does not reach.

So how would, say, *The Times* of London today assess the life of Toghril, the Shah of Shahs, the King of the East and West, the Lord of all Muslims, and the founder of the Saljuq empire – one of the most successful crime families in world history – when he died on 4 September 1063, at the age of seventy-three, in the city of Rayy, near today's Tehran?

First of all, the length of his obituary would have to be set in proportion to his importance as a political and military leader. Secondly, attention would have to be given to the extent to which he had engaged – or enraged – the public's imagination.[40] On the other hand, allowance would have to be made that, on the day of his death, it was not clear whether his state would endure. So perhaps 2,000 words would be the maximum he would be allotted, as opposed to 15,000 allotted to Churchill or 3,000 to de Gaul. Here is how it might read:

> *In a later age, Paramount Chief Toghril of the Saljuqs, known in the eastern half of the lands of Islam as King of the East and West, would have become a hero far beyond the confines of his own realm. Emerging from among the impoverished nomads of a despised ethnic minority, he rose to capture supreme power and made his Saljuq tribe a major regional force. But, due to the absence of the means of mass communication and also a retiring disposition, very little was known about him outside his immediate retinue. He had little personal flare and, besides, for nearly all his seventy-three years, he was constantly on the move, capturing new regions and subduing old ones.*

Toghril, the son of Mikhail and grandson of Saljuq, whose adopted Muslim name was Muhammad, was born probably in 990 somewhere in Transoxania into a branch of the shamanistic Qozz Turks who had for some time been in close contact with Judaism and Islam. They had originally been natives of the region to the south and west of the Aral sea, but had been forced by an explosion in the population of the Turks in that region to migrate southwards and convert to Islam.

On account of their profession of the latter faith – which seemed at times to have been adopted for political reasons – the Iranian rulers of Transoxania allowed them to roam their livestock in the countryside. But after Mikhail was killed in fighting a neighbouring clan, Toghril, as the new chief, sought to take his followers into the region of Bukhara.

He was defeated and taken hostage to ensure the good behaviour of the Saljuqs, but he was rescued by his younger brother, Dāwūd Chaghri Beg, and their long march to supremacy began. Though often extremely cruel in their pillaging of the countryside, it was difficult not to sympathise with Toghril and his brothers, for they had the responsibility of finding pastureland for their herds of sheep. Their rivals and opponents were also extremely cruel, and treachery was normal practice.

The Saljuqs' greatest early achievement was the capture of the province of Khorāsān from Sultan Mass'ud, the Ghaznavid emperor. In 1040, Toghril's mobile nomads drew the sultan's huge army out of the city of Nishāpur and, helped by a severe drought that killed the bulk of the sultan's elephants, camels and horses in the central Asian desert, waged a war of attrition on him until he was forced to give up Khorāsān and flee to his eastern lands in today's Afghanistan and India, where he was killed by his own slaves.

Toghril subsequently left Khorāsān in the hands of Dāwūd, and turned his attention to the interior of Iran. His technique was to encourage bands of Saljuq nomads to devastate the countryside of neighbouring states in search of booty before moving in himself to negotiate or enforce a surrender. In this way, Toghril was able to enter Baghdad in Iraq within fifteen years of capturing Nishāpur and force the Caliph Qā'im to bestow on him the highest title in his possession, King of the East and West. Towards the end of his life, he forced the caliph to give him one of his daughters in marriage. Due to the avowed sanctity of the Abbāsid family, this had no precedent in history. But Toghril was deeply religious and yearned to combine the blood of the Saljuqs with that of Muhammad. Alas for him, none of his marriages produced a child.

Those who knew him well remember him fondly as a simple tribesman who remained true to his family and comrades, with his limited outlook reflected in his way of dressing. He wore an unadorned tunic, a cotton turban and felt boots. Always expecting an ambush, he was accompanied by at least several hundred armed guards even on festive occasions and carried a bow and an arrow in one hand, ready to shoot, while three more arrows hung by his waist.⁴¹ He could neither read nor write. He left the complexities of administering the state to his Persian viziers, the last and most able of whom was Abu Nassr Mansūr Kondori.

He never patronised any of the arts and was, in addition, the butt of many jokes among his more sophisticated subjects. It was said that after eating an almond cake for the first time in Nishāpur, he had announced: 'This is good, although it has no garlic in it'.

His last, controversial act was to appoint Sulaimān, one of his younger nephews, as his successor. This is widely regarded as the work of Kondori. It has to be seen whether it will be accepted by Toghril's eldest and most powerful nephew Alp-Arslān, the ruler of Khorāsān.

*   *   *

And so the sultan was dead and the unthinkable had happened. That wily old Kondori had persuaded the old man to appoint, not the natural choice, Alp-Arslān, the able and most powerful prince in the land, but Alp Arslān's little step-brother Sulaimān, to be his successor. In Nishāpur, Alp-Arslān's vizier Hasan Tūsi was not surprised by the news. His spies in Rayy had alerted him to the possibility ever since Sulaimān's mother had taken the boy there a year earlier and been received by Kondori in ceremony. Now it was clear what had to be done. Orders were issued to all mosques to mention Alp-Arslān as the new sultan in their Friday sermons.

By mid-September, messages were pouring into Nishāpur from various Saljuq princelings all over the realm to promise support. Tūsi made sure that Kondori's spies heard all, and the army was prepared in full view of the public for its forthcoming march on Rayy. It worked. The Grand Vizier, seeing that the forces at his command were no match for Alp-Arslān's, ditched little Sulaimān as quickly as he had picked him. He ordered that all mosques switch to Alp-Arslān in their sermons, but, unfortunately for him, he also committed a large mistake. He appointed Sulaimān as the new crown prince without consulting Alp-Arslān.

Eventually, a few months later, after first defeating one of his cousins who had seized central Iran and proclaimed himself sovereign, Alp-Arslān, with Tūsi riding beside him, entered Rayy in triumph. The Grand Vizier requested audience and pledged full loyalty, bringing with him 500 gold Nishāpur dinars as a gift. This was graciously accepted and Kondori was reinstalled in his position, for a month, until he made his next mistake. One evening, when he turned up for an audience with the sultan, he brought a small army with him and, when he left, the soldiers and their commanders made a point of leaving with him in a choreographed display of pomp and power. An exchange of glances between Alp-Arslān and Tūsi decided his fate. Kondori was still plotting, the glances said, and he had to be stopped. He was arrested the next day and banished to a remote castle 'over the river', in Transoxania, 1,000 farsangs to the north-east. There he languished for a year before Tū si, now Grand Vizier himself, ordered his execution. His severed head was delivered to Tūsi's tent during a campaign in the city of Kirmān in southern Iran.

Now it was time to think whether His Holiness the Caliph served a useful purpose. Yes, his Abbāsid ancestors had been on that throne in Baghdad for more than 300 years, but times changed, did they not? Everything changed.

* * *

The story of the Armenian nation is one of the most heartbreaking and yet also heart-warming tales in all history. It is a chronicle of tears, but also of dynamism and creativity, pride and joy, hopefully culminating now, after nearly 3,000 years, in a full sighting of the sun, a feeling that eternity appears assured at last.

The first fleeting glimpse of the Armenians in history occurs in the ninth century BC, in the mountainous kingdom of Urartu to the north-east of Lake Van, between the Caspian and the Black seas. We hear of a king by the name of Armé or Armu, the indication being that the dominant people of Urartu and the Armenians are merely different tribes within the same basic stock, like the other Indo-European newcomers to the region from the north, the Medes and the Persians. By 520 BC, the Armenians come into the light under their own name when we read in Herodotus that they have a semi-autonomous region beside that of the kings of Urartu and pay tribute to the Achaemenid emperors of Persia.

By then, they are already afflicted with their later, normal fate: to be 'a theatre of perpetual war'[42] between the great powers on either side of them. Their fertile plains attract the covetous eyes of their neighbours, and they are landlocked. Their valleys lead from east to west and allow rapid movement to rampaging foreign armies, making them a prize possession of the Iranians one day, the Greeks or the Romans the next. No sooner has the emperor of the Parthians installed his brother on the Armenian throne than the same man is taken to Rome in chains to proclaim eternal loyalty to Nero, or else be fed to lions.

Later on, in medieval times, the Arabs lure their nobility to a peace conference only to massacre them, while no better treatment is to be expected from fellow Christians in Constantinople. The Byzantines declare the Armenians heretics over their belief that Christ's divine and human natures merged into one another. Thus Armenian principalities are destroyed and, at one time, Constantinople even incites Muslim Turks in Azerbaijan to wage war on them from the east while they, the Byzantines, attack them from the west.

Despite the heavy odds, the Armenians not only survived, but are able to build some of the most beautiful buildings ever erected, such as the cathedral of Echmiadzin in AD 301, while their distinct alphabet, designed in 404 to express all the sounds of their language, gives them one of the oldest literatures in the world, including some of the most moving poetry ever written.

In yet another unhappy respect in the Middle East, the Armenians are unique. More than any other people in the region, they have suffered from the westward migration of the Turks that began in the eleventh century. This, more than any other catastrophe, pushed them to the edge of extinction and, had it not been for the imperial ambitions of Russia that saved a corner of their homeland, the Turkish campaign of annihilation waged against them in the opening decades of the twentieth century would have assured their total loss to mankind.

Turkish domination set in only a year after Alp-Arslan became the undisputed sultan of the Saljuqs. Having heard from raiding bands of Turkoman nomads that the Byzantines had neglected the defence of their Christian possessions in Anatolia, and keen to gain a place in Heaven – beside much gold and slaves – by pushing forth the western borders of Islam, Alp-Arslan led a large army into the Caucasus in 1064 and met little resistance, the locals having already been weakened by years of heavy taxation by Constantinople and exhausted by new nomads raiding from the east.

As if it were not painful enough for the poor Armenian king at the time, Bagrat IV, to watch the loss of countless young men and the raping and abduction of countless young women, he had to give up his own young daughter to the illiterate and uncouth chief barbarian 'in marriage' in the hope of buying a measure of safety for the rest of his people, though they would still have to starve every winter while they gave food and fodder to the Turkish soldiery stationed among them.

We shall hear more later of the wretched young princess who was plucked from the safety of her family to be thrown to the mercy of the wolves. For the time being, she will disappear into a Muslim harem, to be just one of hundreds of other nameless women who may, or may not, be summoned to the bed of the smelly lecher once or twice a year.

* * *

As we saw earlier, no record has survived in the Middle East of the visit of Halley's comet to the inner solar system in 1066, but there is no doubt that it would have frightened the overwhelmingly fatalistic people there, as it did all others elsewhere. A measure of such apprehension may be read into a contemporary account in the Anglo-Saxon Chronicles in the western extremity of the known world at that time. For the writer of the account, it was proof that the subsequent defeat of his people at the hands of the Normans at Hastings in October had been divinely ordained:

> In this year, King Harold came from York to Westminster at Easter, which was after the midwinter in which the King [Edward] died. Then was seen over all England such a sign in the heavens as no man ever before saw. Some say it was the star Cometa, which some men call the long-haired star, and it first appeared on the eve of Litania-Major, the 8th of the Kalends of May, and so shone all the seven nights.[43]

* * *

The visitation of Halley's comet in May 1066 seemed to contemporaries to have brought in its wake, in many places, events of special magnitude. One such event, though it would prove of historic importance, was not noticed at the time. It was a mental storm that traumatised a young man about the same age as Omar living several hundred miles to the west of Nishāpur in the city of Rayy.

His full name was Hasan bin Ali bin Muhammad bin Ja'far bin Hussein bin Sabbāh al-Hemyari, the son of a Yemeni immigrant. His father Ali had drifted to Rayy by a tortuous route. He had arrived by way of, among other places, the Shia or Shiite stronghold of Kūfa in southern Iraq and the Arab settlement of Qom on the edge of the great desert in central Iran. A historian who later inspected a captured copy of Sabbāh's autobiography in the castle of Alamūt and quoted from it extensively says that the son, Hasan, was born and brought up in Rayy.[44]

Around this time, young Hasan was pondering what turned out to be the central decision of his long and terrifying life. Until the age of seventeen, he wrote, he had 'no doubts about the truth of the faith of my ancestors, the Twelver Shiites'. Then there appeared in his life a mysterious older man by the name of Amira Zarrab, apparently another Yemeni immigrant.

Zarrab sought the boy's friendship and spent many seemingly idle hours with him. The two would argue 'hypothetically' about the validity of various religious concepts and the older man 'would suddenly decide to be provocative for argument's sake'. He would say, for example, that the Ismaili Shiites of Egypt had different views. This enraged the young man. He would reply, in his own words later: 'Oh, please do not mention them, for they are the enemies of all religion.' Ismaili Shiites believed that the line of true imams bearing the blood of Muhammad had ended with the twelfth imam.

After Zarrab had moved on, Hasan became dangerously ill for several weeks, during which he repeatedly re-examined Zarrab's arguments in his mind. He came to fear the possibility of dying and being plunged directly into the fires of Hell for having been offered – and refused – 'the chance to be directed on to the True Path'. Now, at the height of his illness, heavenly voices were offering him another chance, the possibility of redeeming himself by devoting his life to the service of God's true representative on earth. The Ismailis, Zarrab had implied, knew who he was. They were in contact with him, for he was no other than the great Fātimid caliph of Egypt in Cairo. If Hasan won their confidence and proved himself a loyal comrade, they would promote him inside their vast organisation. Perhaps one day they might even take him to Egypt. No, no, the line of the imams, the direct descendants of the Prophet through his daughter Fatimah and his cousin Ali had not died out. They were well and alive and would one day, perhaps soon, announce the Day of Judgement and the end of the world. On that day, only the true believers would be rewarded with eternal life in paradise.

The voices in Hasan's head told him, further, that even if he survived his illness, it would not be easy for him to prove himself. Much hard work lay ahead. The letter of the Koran and the Shari'a law were only for the uncouth and ignorant masses. The holy book's true message was hidden and became known only to the followers of the True Imam after years of instruction and devotion. At first, the initiate might even be frustrated at the slow pace of his progress. But then, one day, The Truth would come to him in a blinding moment of revelation. At that moment, he would attain the spiritual stature to be permitted into the secret circle of the few holiest men in the world, the dā'is or summoners of Ismaili Shiism, the men who were the confidants and companions of the Imam in Cairo.

Hasan also had to be brave. The Ismailis had captured Egypt a century earlier in 946 and set themselves up in opposition to the corrupt Sunni Abbassid caliphs of Baghdad. As a result, all those who leaned towards them in the eastern lands of Islam were regarded as enemy, opposed both to the Abbāsids and their new military protectors, the Sunni Saljuq sultans. The actual chances of becoming an Ismaili activist in Iran and surviving for long were small. By contrast, the Twelver Shiites, his father's people, though resentful of the Sunni sway over the realm, chose the coward's way. They had despaired of guiding mankind back onto the path of the Prophet and took care of their own interests only. They wanted to be left alone. Hasan would need to keep his new beliefs secret from his relatives. Not only might someone among them leak the intelligence to the authorities, but they themselves regarded converts to Ismailism as traitors. He would have to be very patient. In good time, perhaps, he might even lead them to salvation.

Since Sabbāh's autobiography was later largely destroyed by his Sunni enemies during the Mongol invasion of the thirteenth century, we do not know the precise details of what happened to him soon after his conversion. But we do know that another Ismaili missionary visited Rayy a few years afterwards and decided that the young man was sane and reliable enough to be received into the movement. Sabbāh was made to go through a standard initiation ceremony that lasted three days and three nights. As he did so, even he, surely, could not have dreamt that, one day, his command would be obeyed by a network of unassailable castles from central Asia to Syria, and that great Saljuq emperors, no less, would tremble at night in Isfahan at the thought of his agents watching over them in the uniform of the guards of the bedchamber.

* * *

Four days after the comet had disappeared from the sky on 14 May 1066, the Khayyāmi family celebrated Omar's eighteenth birthday – the marking of birthdays being an old Iranian custom that had survived the disapproval of Islam.[45] It was not a legal milestone, for the threshold of adulthood had been passed years earlier according to Islamic law. But, in practice, a young man of his age remained under the supervision of his father for many more years. Rebellions against paternal rule were rare and offspring carried on the family profession or trade as a matter of course.

In Omar's case, all indications are that his father, Dr Ebrāhīm, seeing his son's prodigious appetite for figures and concepts from an early age, had chosen a different path for the boy. He had spent considerable sums on the most renowned philosophers of the region to give personal tuition to his son, and young Omar had, in turn, dazzled his teachers with the speed with which he had picked up the most complex thoughts. The great Zoroastrian philosopher Abu Hasan Bahmanyār bin Marzbān, whose broken Arabic Omar loved to mimic, had been astonished frequently by him, and the other famous teacher in Nishāpur, Abu Hasan al-Anbāri, who had taught him

Ptolemy's astronomical manual, *Almajest*, including its introduction to trigonometry, had said that the boy would 'go far'. Indeed, he had, already. As we shall see later in the preface to one of his books on algebra, while still at school in Nishāpur, Omar had learnt the latest thinking of Indian arithmeticians and advanced them further in his first treatise, *Difficult Problems in Arithmetics*.

When the lad had been much younger, the question of his future had been less pressing. He had seemed happy enough spending many a hot afternoon playing in the street or else dreaming in the shade of the trees in the garden. But now the final decision had to be made, whether or not to put long-gestating notions into action.

Ebrāhīm had frequently discussed the problem with his wife. But in a patriarchal society such as Nishāpur's, the decision was formally his only. He dreaded sending the boy too far away. It took weeks for news from such cities as Samarkand to reach Nishāpur by the fastest of couriers. But Nishāpur was now only a shadow of its former self and lived off its reputation. Many of its men of learning had emigrated during the Saljuq takeover, and the subsequent recession in commerce, caused by back-breaking taxation and the ruination of the irrigation canals, had driven away most of the remainder.

By contrast, Samarkand offered what was needed. It had not been affected by a recent change of dynasties, its teachers were in contact with Indian mathematicians and they attracted students from as far as Egypt in the west. Furthermore, Ebrāhīm had a 'friend' there in the powerful chief judge and governor of the city, an aristocrat by the name of Abu Tāhir Abd al-Rahman, who would be glad to keep an eye on the boy. Abu Tāhir would probably even give the boy a job to enable him to earn his keep while he studied.

Not everyone in the family would have supported the idea. Some relatives would have thought Ebrāhīm overly ambitious and unfeeling.[46] We do not know how his poor wife felt, but we can imagine many a secret tear shed.

Preparations for the journey would have taken many months. Ebrāhīm would have wanted to find a suitable master in Samarkand to accept his son as a student, and he would also have wanted to book a place on a well-guarded caravan for him, together perhaps with enlisting a couple of poorer relatives or servants to accompany him. The efficient postal service that the caravans provided would have been used heavily for making these arrangements.

But it was not to be. Omar's eighteenth birthday on 18 May 1066, was the last such occasion at which Ebrāhīm was present. Within a few months, he died.[47]

*   *   *

The death of his father would have had predictable consequences. Eighteen-year-old sons were expected to take on their shoulders all the responsibilities of the head of the household[48] and, in his case, they would have been substantial. Beside the family's medical practice, he would have inherited several farms and orchards in the green ribbon that surrounded Nishāpur, if not a larger agricultural estate in the hills. At least a dozen people, including relatives, would have worked for him at the pharmacy or on the farms. We know that he had at least one sister, and there was his mother, too.

Far more onerous would have been the need to protect the interests of his family from the covetous eyes of the Turkish soldiery and Muslim clergy. We may assume that some of his father's old friends would have been influential magnates in the city's political hierarchy.

A lesser but still emotional loss followed a few months later with the death of Bahmanyār. The aristocratic-sounding Banmanyār bin Marzbān, who appears to have descended from a line of provincial governors in Sasanian times, was special in at least two respects. He had resisted pressure to abandon his ancestral religion for that of the invaders, and his books had earned him appreciation throughout Khorāsān. One of the most brilliant students of Avicenna earlier in the century, Bahmanyār had written on logic, music and cosmology. Omar would later routinely describe himself as 'a student of Avicenna', by which he really meant that he had inherited the learning of the great man through Bahmanyār.

Did Bahmanyār's death have any bearings on Omar's decision to leave the city of his birth for Samarkand? It is not inconceivable. Without his main master and mentor, Omar had one less authority to guide his further education.

Anyhow, leave he did, and we may assume that tearful promises were made to write regularly. The postal system was good, he would have said, and he could even try to visit once a year. The faster caravans took only a couple of months between Samarkand and Nishāpur and, in the meantime, he had full confidence in the managers who had served the family so well in the past.

Arrangements would have probably taken up to a year to complete, and there would have been the weather to take into account. Heavy snow, mud and slush made the higher mountain gorges impassable in winter and early spring, while turbulent currents made the crossing of the vast Oxus river between Khorāsān and Transoxania difficult to contemplate in April and May. Then came high summer, which meant that tackling the great Karakum desert, before the Oxus, would be suicidal. That left only autumn, the autumn of 1069, reasonably cool and everywhere fruitful, though still not ideal. The journey took at least three months by the bigger, safer caravans. If all went well, the party would arrive in Samarkand by the first frosts of late December, or in early January.

Everything had to be planned in detail. Several camels would be needed to carry his books alone, his most precious possessions. As all books were copied by hand and were expensive, they would not have been left behind in Nishāpur in the expectation of buying new copies in Samarkand. Some would have been rare, a few of them unique.

Omar was a youth of nineteen now, but medieval youths matured early. This was true particularly in his case. At his father's surgery, he had seen for years how precariously posed was human existence. Early death was a daily occurrence, such as that of women in childbirth, and, of course, he had been brought up on his parents' stories of tyranny and corruption by government officials, not to mention the horrors of the dynastic wars and famines of the 1040s.

Furthermore, as a Persian youth in a city under the spell of Firdowsi's patriotic epic, and educated at the feet of such a proud Persian as Bahmanyār, one theme would have regularly exercised his mind: the sad state of his people in recent centuries. From those idyllic scenes depicted by Firdowsi, where emperor and peasant ate together for two weeks to celebrate the New Year every spring, Iran had sunk to the slavery of savages from the deserts of Arabia and the steppes of central Asia. Why did God – if he existed – allow such injustice to come to pass? If only another Rostam[49] would appear from somewhere to liberate the Iranians once more! But there was no sign at all on the horizon of any such champion arising.

We can guess that suddenly facing the prospect of leaving his family and the city of his birth, perhaps never to return, would have caused the young man to brood. He would perhaps have walked for hours on his own in the fields around the city or climbed the heights above it, where the remains of abandoned fire temples and Sasanian palaces would have reminded him of what there had once been. We may speculate that, as the day of his departure drew close, busy though he was taking leave of friends and relatives, he cast mournful eyes about him. Graveyards of unloved ancestors suddenly became revered ground and every boulder beside every brook called for a lover's last caress. He was leaving behind a special city and a special people. Nishāpur was the wellspring of 'the Iranians' in the tribal myths of his forefathers, anointed by the person of Zarathustra, no less. His forthcoming journey into the unknown would take him into exile, far, far away.

CHAPTER TWO

The Libraries of Samarkand

When my Creator my elements planned,
They say He meant me for the Promised Land.
Lover, lute and wine by a field of corn,
Give me those three now: Birds are best in hand!

Silk Route caravans were slow coaches, and the larger they were, the slower they became. Travellers usually rode their own animals – on occasion up to 3,000 in tow – and these, despite the rigorous veterinary checks they had to pass, went suddenly lame, while carts and carriages lost wheels mid-journey. To abandon the stricken to their fates at the hands of bandits or nature was unthinkable – it would destroy at once the central ethos of the caravan, safety in numbers, and it would bring upon the head of the caravan captain the severest punishment at the court of the next prince on the route, for whom the traffic was a gold mine of tax and trade. So, in-between caravanserais, they travelled at the speed of the oldest donkey. To minimise that risk, the grandest of the captains always took along with them scores of spare mules and camels, and their guards included wheelwrights and vets, not to mention conjurors and storytellers to amuse the young during the numerous halts.

The larger caravans were elaborate institutions and often long-established businesses. They had offices in every town and way station on their route, and their methods and traditions had evolved over many generations. While their captains led their charges from the front, in order to send couriers to the next stop, they also had to hear of any emergencies in the body of the caravan immediately. To this end the guards carried horns or bugles for sounding coded messages.

These included: 'Stop, serious accident', 'Warning: possible bandits sighted' and 'Ambushed!'. Deputy captains were responsible for particular sections. In bushy savannahs, dense forests and tight gorges, drums were beaten to frighten off lions and tigers. It seemed at times that a caravan, like a troupe of actors rehearsing, stopped more often than it moved. Not knowing precisely what was happening made the dreary long waits even more frustrating.

This was, in all likelihood, young Omar's first long journey and, in particular, his first encounter with a great desert, though the caravan would have travelled north-easterly, partly along the edges of it. The Karakum or 'Black Sands', as the recently arrived Turks called it, had struck terror in the hearts of men since the beginnings of time. Its written history stretched into antiquity.

Omar would have probably read that no less a fiend of energy, ingenuity and courage than Alexander of Macedon nearly came to grief here, losing many of his horses and men to the endless sand dunes and the cruel sun before he reached the sweet, life-giving waters of the Oxus in the summer of 329 BC. More recently, in 1046, a couple of years before Omar himself had been born, it had taken the writer Nasser Khosrow forty-seven days to travel this first leg of the journey, in the opposite direction from Marv to Nishāpur. That was a mere 1½ farsangs or 8 miles a day, on average. The daily lives of caravans were accident-prone and their need to rest and recover from the hardships of the road at every caravanserai in their path was constant.

Almost certainly, Omar and his companions made their journey in the cooler, fruit-laden months of autumn and, before they reached the Karakum, they enjoyed the comforts of urban life in such highland cities as Tūs, the birth-place of Firdowsi. Omar would have rushed to visit the great epic poet's grave, for by then Firdowsi had already become a folk hero. We can imagine the ardent young Iranian approaching the gravestone with heartfelt reverence.

After a few days of rest in Tūs and another short stay in Sarakhs, the next big town just over the mountains, the caravan would have taken a long deep breath and prepared, mentally as well as physically, for the ordeal ahead. This always taxed even the most enthusiastic young men.

To spare the travellers and their beasts the worst of the sun, the caravan travelled only in the early morning and late evening. Nevertheless, overpowering heat and strict water rationing for days on end were inescapable, not to mention the stifling, flea-infested rooms in some of the more remote caravanserais or the menace of persistent desert flies whose only source of moisture – and life – was the eyes and mouths of passing beasts and men. Natural springs, unmanned wells and open pools, all rare occurrences, were marked on the horizon by artificial mounds of specific design to give advance notice to the traveller. Sometimes the water was saline and often polluted by animals. The more experienced journeymen resorted to long-established tricks, such as carrying small, fist-sized melons. Many such varieties of melon, often aromatic, have been bred in Khorāsān. For the long-distance journeymen, they were small enough to prevent waste and large enough to quench thirst.

Even without any major horrors, such as being ambushed by bandits, some of the scenes that Omar would have witnessed during this journey would have been 'character forming', in the words of a later age. Despite the best efforts of the caravan captain, some families would have had to be left behind at the hospices and caravanserais that dotted the 900 mile route between Nishāpur and Marv, and, worst of all, a number of travellers would have died and been buried in 'temporary' graves, their relatives knowing well that, despite their tearful pledges by the graveside, they would never return to reclaim their remains for reburial.

During the many hours of waiting, and even when the caravan moved slowly against the sand dunes in its seemingly futile chase of the horizon, Omar would have fought boredom in any manner he could, by tinkering with his arithmetical and algebraic theories or by reading the works of historians and geographers known to him. Some of these described Marv's chief attractions and told the story of its tremendous past. He would have been reinforced in his view that he was not headed for just any large city. It was going to be 'Marvé Shāhigān', Marv the Royal. Even when Alexander had passed through the region over 1,400 years earlier, 'Marg' had been prosperous enough for him to build a costly new castle for its protection. He had renamed the city 'Alexandria in Margiana', and it had been there, too, only about 400

years before his time that the last truly Iranian emperor, the tragic
Yazdagart III, had taken refuge in a mill from the invading Arabs. The
story of Yazdagart was a popular tragedy with the reading public and
Firdowsi's account of it was a particular favourite of the ladies and the
young in Omar's social class. In the second half of the seventh
century, the last Sasanian emperor had gathered many armies and
fought tirelessly to save his people, only to be slain in cold blood in
the dead of night by a miller for money. The Zoroastrian Iranians of
the city had so feared the invaders that the local Christian bishop had
had to take it upon himself to give the crowned head a dignified
burial. After that, Marv the Royal had become Marvé Doshman-
Khodā, Marv the Traitor (literally: the Enemy of God).

Marv was also the city of romance for Iranians. It had been there
that Shahrzād,[1] the heroine of the old Persian story book of the
Thousand Tales, had tricked her tyrannical husband of a king not to
kill her as he had every previous mistress every morning after the first
night. The Arabs had later confiscated the book for themselves and
had destroyed the original, but Omar knew the original name of it,
the *Hazār Afsāneh*.

Marv, of course, had seen numerous tragedies in its long history, but it
seemingly never tired of recalling them for the benefit of its young.
They hid embryonic truths about human nature. It was again there, for
example, that in 52 BC, over 10,000 captured Roman legionaries – most
of them recruited from among poor peasant boys from as far away as the
island of Pritannia on the western edge of the world – arrived in chains
to work on the construction of new buildings for the Iranian Parthian
emperor, Orodes II. None of the depressed and homesick men, as far as
we know, ever saw their families again. They were victims, with
countless other dead and wounded and captured, of the whims of a
cynical Roman politician who had broken his own pact with Parthia to
attack it merely because he craved military kudos to make him the
equal of his partners, Julius Caesar and Pompey, in the Triumvirate.

Whether the young Omar knew the history of Marv in such detail,
we do not know. But we may dwell, for a few moments more, on the
chain of events that brought those hapless captives from the hamlets
of Britain and Germany to Transoxania. It reveals the complex
cultural background to which he, Omar, was heir.

After the crushing defeat of Crassus's army in Asia Minor, where the 30,000 dead Romans included the emperor himself, his severed head was taken to Armenia to be presented to Orodes. Chroniclers tell us that, as the golden platter containing the Roman's head was brought in the Parthian emperor was, together with the king of the Armenians, watching a Greek play in the original language. And what play was it? It was Euripides's eternal masterpiece of a tragedy, the *Bacchai*, in which Pentheus, the young king of Thebes, is murdered by his own mother who has fallen under the spell of a cult.[2]

Orodes and Artawāz were tragic figures like Crassus and Pentheus. Orodes had assassinated his own father, Emperor Mithradites III, to seize the throne, and Artawāz would one day be dragged in chains to Egypt by Marc Antony to be executed there with the whole of his family. No wonder the folklore of Khorāsān is to this day so full of mournful songs, echoes of which, of course, we see in Omar's poetry.

* * *

Omar would have been expected to learn the following poem at school, for it is one of the most renowned of its age. It was written by Manūchehri Dāmghāni who had died in 1040, eight years before Omar's birth, at the court of Sultan Mass'ud. It is the kind of ode that Poet Laureates design for language classes in secondary schools: innocuous and accessible, yet stirring and romantic. Since it is about a caravan, can we allow ourselves to imagine that Omar would have recited it to himself sometime during this particularly long journey? I have translated only about half of it to leave out its local references, and I have not attempted to make it rhyme.

The Caravan

Hurry, tent keepers, dismantle the tents,
The Chief has mounted, his vanguard has left;
The First Drums now end,
The moon's rising high.

Oh, my love, so white, tall and slender!
Please go home, don't cry, my woes are not new.
Time carries parting in its womb and so,
Sooner or later, it would deliver.

As she gazed on me, on my broken face,
A rain of tears flooded her cheeks.
She rushed towards me, falling and rising
As if a poor beast, mortally wounded.
She raised her two arms onto my shoulders
And hung from my side, as she were my sword.
'Oh, tyrant!', she cried. 'A traitor, you are!
See to what low state you have flung me.
How can I be sure that this caravan
That takes you away, brings you back one day?
I thought you perfect in all of the arts,
Now I see in love you are not true.
The old Greek was right, his wisdom stands:
Love cures the young of their innocence.'[3]

I hugged her, kissed her, pleaded with her:
'So sorry I am, please forgive me;
I am not one who plays around with hearts.
But the old sages did also tell us
That the Stars stalk those who make plans.'

When at long last my love departed,
I resolved to make patience my creed.
I looked around me, where the camp had been,
No man to be seen, nor beast standing.
Only my faithful, my noble camel,
Tall as a giant, dark against the sky,
Stood beside me, motionless, silent.

I lifted his chains, his spirit soared
As if a caged bird had been set free.
I rode him westwards into a light wind,
The desert fell back behind us in haste.
The Seven Sisters gathered round the Moon,[4]
The night grew colder, Death was on the prowl.

Till at last a faint sound of bells I heard:
Could it be true? Hope in me stirred.
The caravan called its wayward brood,
The harbour beckoned, we were drawing near.
I patted my mount's proud, blonde mane,
And whispered softly into his ear:
'No more haste, my friend, brother, saviour.'

*   *   *

Eventually, Marv's outer fortifications came into view and the pulse of the caravan quickened. As it drew closer, the outlines of the tallest domes within the walls could be seen. This city, as other great cities, needed to impress friend and foe. For some of the travellers it was home, for others it held out the hope of a new life. For another group it was the prospect of a week or two of eating, drinking, sight-seeing and sleeping in fresh linen. Omar fell among the latter group. All reviewed their plans for arrival.

As the caravan similarly became visible to the city's watchtowers, groups of riders trotted towards it with fresh horses in tow for the more important personages and to collect the most urgent mail. Young men and women rode out to meet relatives simply because they could not wait any longer. Expectations were high on both sides. There were also some disappointed faces, for no one came out to greet them.

What did Omar and his companions find when they dismounted? Very little to surprise them, but everything to lift their spirits. The buildings were as grand as they had expected – many of them six or seven storeys high – and they bore a family resemblance to those in Nishāpur. Both cities were, after all, Khorāsānian, despite the great distance separating them, and they shared the same ancient Iranian descent. As with Sasanian Nishāpur, Marv, too, had three distinct parts, each with its own defensive walls, ramparts and guarded gates. They were the Castle, the City or Shahristān and the newer, brasher, Arabic-named Rabad, the residential and industrial town to which more and more governmental institutions were migrating as Marv continued its centuries-old move westwards along the great Murghāb's[5] shifting course. In fact, by now, the foundations of Alexander's castle were miles in the east and called Gabr Qal'eh, 'Zoroastrian Castle'. Nearby, on the edge of the new city, were the once-glorious mansions of the former Zoroastrian aristocracy, slowly crumbling into dust as a result of persecution and marginalisation. The new elite were Turkish soldiers and Arab clerics.

Still, the buzz of commercial Marv would be remembered long. Since it had fallen to the Saljuqs in 1037, the frequent clashing of its many Muslim sects had been brought under a degree of control, while the remaining working-class communities of Christians, Jews and Zoroastrians – the 'tolerated' communities who had to pay the heavy *jizyah* tax for their 'protection' – cowered in their walled ghettoes. The new, relative security of the roads enabled caravan traffic in all directions to thrive once more. According to one geographer, an elaborate system of canals took huge volumes of water from the river to gardens and orchards everywhere and a multitude of engineers and their workers monitored the flow and distribution of that water. They even included a team of divers.

The modern Shahristān or City was dissected not only by a number of such canals, but also by four main thoroughfares. One of them ran from north to south, while another stretched from east to west. Where the two met at the Square or Chārsu,[6] the intersection was crowned with a high dome that sheltered the traders and their customers from the sun. The maze of nearby, minor streets that served as specialist bazaars was in the usual form of arcades to keep them cool in summer and dry in winter.

The caravanserai where, in all likelihood, Omar and his possible relatives and servants stayed, would have probably been a more expensive establishment in the Shahristān, for middle-class men of his station paid for the comfort and hygiene to which they were accustomed. We can imagine him and his party deciding to familiarise themselves with the Shahristān and the castle for a day or two before sampling what the suburbs had to offer. They would have had their first meals in a mehmānsarāi, a 'guest house', overlooking a courtyard or busy square with fine monuments and dancing fountains.

*   *   *

Marv had a reputation for being a city of book lovers. We shall see later, in connection with the libraries of Samarkand, that scions of prominent families in all the cities of Khorāsān spent fortunes collecting rare or antique books, while their municipalities competed with one another in setting up public libraries. Given that Omar, the aspiring philosopher obsessed by the fast-developing new mathematics of algebra, had little time to waste in Marv, he would have rushed in all directions in search of any new writing on the subject. Conversely, the local mathematicians would have sought his company eagerly as, they too, were keen to hear of the state of their obsession in other cities.

What Omar may not quite have expected was the extent of Marv's love affair with the mulberry tree. Marv's very prosperity depended on it, to the extent that, to the south-west in one industrial district, a research institution had been set up whose sole function was to make the silkworm more productive. As a result, the city was the largest producer of silk in the whole of Iran and its silk was valued in Europe above China's. Where it could not compete with the original home of the silk thread was in cost. Labour was much cheaper in China and so, while princes and princesses in Constantinople would not dream of wearing any but the finest silk of Marv, the minor nobility and the middle classes there had to settle for second best.

Before he had left Nishāpur some six weeks earlier, Omar might have heard that the ordinary people of Marv were not enamoured of the grasping officials that surrounded their new Saljuq governor. In the previous year, the sultan had appointed his youngest son, Prince Arslan Shah, to the governorate and the decision had brought about no improvement at all. He was a mere boy and the fresh batch of officials who had accompanied him into the palace seemed as hungry as their predecessors.

Furthermore, there were rumours of war with the kingdom of the Western Qarakhanids in Samarkand and Bukhara. The country there was run by its able and popular Crown Prince, Shams al-Mulk Nassr, on behalf of his reclusive father, and he was unwilling to pay tribute to the Saljuqs in Isfahan.

For the time being, though, peace prevailed and the general air was complacent. Still, young Omar could surely not have imagined that in a couple of years' time, that distant and mighty king would choose him to be one of his drinking companions and become a guiding star in his life.

*   *   *

Based on the assumption that Omar's party had left Nishāpur at the onset of cooler weather in early September, he and his companions would have probably mounted their horses and camels in Marv for the next leg of their journey towards the end of October. But whatever the exact date of their departure, can we hazard a guess as to how Omar felt about Marv as he left it? At the very least, he would have been pleased that he had been there, for very few people had the privilege of travelling widely in those times, fewer still so early in life. The great majority of his people seldom ventured outside their own towns and villages, and, when they did, it was for a short visit to relatives in the nearby countryside. Furthermore, Marv's public buildings, tree-lined streets and shaded squares, its hospitals and libraries, its prominent men of letters and its famous observatory had not disappointed his expectations. They really did justify the city's jealous clinging to its former title, Marvé Shāhigān, Marv the Royal.

Today, none of Marv's splendour survives. In the whistling wilderness of sand piles and thorn bushes that remains of it, a heap of earth may be all that remains of a many-storied tower, and a trench may be the only trace of a deep moat that once protected a royal treasury.

Was it the Mongols, less than a century after Khayyām's death, who finally destroyed the old metropolis so thoroughly that it never rose again? They certainly were a terrible plague and massacred countless thousands in the city, as we shall see later. But Marv survived them. Some seventy years after their ravages, Marco Polo found Marv: 'a city with a great castle where a large market for corn is held, it being situated in a fine and fruitful country'. In the absence of firm historical evidence, the blame must be laid at the foot of nature. In the past 600 years alone, at least three catastrophic floods have changed the course of the Murghāb, each time forcing the inhabitants to move on to the river's new shores several miles away. The vast remains of the old city are now some twenty miles to the east of the new town of Mari and the gifted British writer Colin Thubron gives us a moving description of the ruins in one of his books:

> No ruined city I had ever seen – not Balkh nor Nineveh nor Ctesiphon – had delivered such a shock of desolation as this. It measured fifteen miles from end to end. Even in April the sun flailed down (and the temperature can reach 160 degrees Fahrenheit, the hottest in the old Soviet Union). A line of battlements rose and glimmered across the wilderness for mile after broken mile. Here and there, out of their wind-smoothed walls, a ghostly tower erupted; but more often they broke into separate chunks and seemed only to emphasise, by their vast and futile compass, the void inside them. Once or twice a fortified hill stood up naked and sudden, as if a great levelling tempest had burst across the oasis and inexplicably missed it.[7]

Whether or not Marco Polo, at the time of recalling his memories to a fellow prisoner in a Genoese jail, had full access to his notes or those of his father or uncle about their journey through Khorāsān, he has left us an evocative and convincing description of the countryside to the north-east of Marv around 1290. It is a brief account, but a telling one. It shows how the latest Turkic wave, the Mongols, had changed the demography of the region for ever:

> Leaving Thaikan* and travelling three days, still in a north-easterly direction, you pass through a well-inhabited country, very beautiful and abounding in fruit, corn and vines.[8] The people are Mahometans, bloodthirsty and treacherous. They are also given to debauchery, and to excess in drink, to which the excellence of their sweet wine encourages them. On their heads they wear nothing but a cord, about ten spans in length, which they bind around the head.[9] They are keen sportsmen, and take many wild animals, wearing no other clothing than the skins of the beasts they kill, of which materials their shoes are also made.[10]

The people whom Polo describes here in the steppe two centuries later are no longer the old Iranians who made up the bulk of the populace in Khayyām's time, but the Turkic ancestors of today's

* By this he can only mean Shāhigān, 'Royal'. The local popular pronunciation of the word was 'Shāigān'.

Turkmens and Uzbeks. As Omar and his new friends from the caravan passed through Marv's gates to meet outside the walls for the next leg of their journey, they had of course no reason to be preoccupied with omens for Marv's future, but a measure of the coming disaster would be that the city he was leaving behind would one day sink so low that some of its survivors would turn for solace to the student who once visited their streets on his way to Samarkand.

*   *   *

The Oxus was the largest body of water that Omar had ever seen. The Āmu Daryā lived up to its double-barrelled Turkish and Persian name, the River Sea, and tales of its great width and depth and man-eating 'whales' had reached his ears in his earliest childhood in Nishāpur. The storytellers had not themselves seen any such monsters, but they had all met someone who had been nearby when someone else had been pulled under the waves by the giant fish.

The river was now, in early winter, frozen over from shore to distant shore and that increased the fear of it in the hearts of the travellers. For while in summer, crossing was made by ferry boats, now there was no alternative to walking over it. If any man or beast happened to venture over thin ice, there was little hope for them. On the other hand, a local true story still lived on of how a Persian prince of the Samanid dynasty and 300 horsemen had crossed the river at full trot, aided only by felt shoes on the hooves of their horses to prevent them from slipping. Unfortunately, the prince's enemies caught up with him.

Sometimes the river froze as early as late summer. Now, only the horses and donkeys needed felt shoes, not the camels or the cattle with their broad, soft hooves.

After a short while, the reassurances of the caravan masters and the swagger of the more experienced travellers worked their effect and trepidation gave way to bravado on the part of the young, so that, before long, the 3-mile width of the water was traversed. The head of the caravan emerged into the thicker vegetation of the northern shore and got lost in the mist. What a contrast with the heat and dust of the Karakum desert several weeks earlier.

In fact, for a number of days even before the first, distant sighting of the River Sea, the diet of the caravan had suddenly improved. Fish and game had appeared at the caravanserais as well as a variety of late-ripening autumn fruit, particularly luscious grapes and pears and apples. Samarkand beckoned with greater delights still.

The rich, sandy loam underfoot continued for some distance beyond the river and gave rise mainly to brush and shrubs of many hues. Especially noticeable were the junipers and sweetbriers, buckthorns and oleasters, which gave way only slowly to willows and poplars and walnuts uphill. Animals abounded everywhere: boars, hares and foxes in the lower reaches, brown bears and red eagles in the higher. This was indeed the legendary hunting ground of many a crowned head in many an age past, particularly Bahram of the Wild Ass, the dashing Sasanian emperor who eventually gave his life pursuing the zebra.

*   *   *

It is the last day of December 1067 and while Omar's caravan approaches Samarkand, we are far away in the great city of Constantinople, where the air is tense with rumours of portentous events. Also here, if there is only one man alive who will in later ages epitomise the pejorative term 'Byzantine politics', it is Michael Psellus. He is a 49-year-old former 'monk of convenience' who has risen to become a king-maker and chief minister, the second most powerful position after the empress herself.[11] He says he is, at present, a soulmate to Empress Eudocia and he is the tutor of her two elder sons, the heirs to the throne. He is well-known – and well-hated – for intriguing against the army when the empire needs to inject every copper coin it can spare into bolstering its strength. Yet, his defenders claim that he harbours no personal malice towards anyone, though he exhibits irate Christian righteousness. He is steeped in the classical writers and is himself writing a history of recent rulers. In this respect, he resembles his Persian contemporary, Beihaqi, whom we met in the last chapter and who now lives on his estate near Nishāpur. As with that historian, he too seems to love nothing better than the political gossip of his peers but, unlike Beihaqi, whose days of closeness to his emperor are over now, Psellus is, at this moment anyway, the true ruler of Byzantium in partnership with the empress's brother-in-law, John Ducas, 'the Caesar'.

This December, as usual, the populace has been preoccupied with the festivities of Christmas, but for a small number of people with access to the latest intelligence, the times could scarcely be gloomier. After overcoming the fortifications of the grand city of Caesaria in Central Anatolia in the east recently and abducting thousands of Christian children for sale in the markets of Baghdad and Isfahan, roaming bands of Turkish nomads are making further incursions into western Anatolia, approaching closer to Constantinople itself, and there seems to be no power that can stop them. As a result, a clamour is gathering force among the population that the ruling family ought to be overthrown, and that the only saviour can come from among the ranks of young army commanders who have a record of valour and initiative.

Almost as alarming is news from Italy that the Normans – who say they have become Christians nowadays – continue their encroachments on the empire's last possessions there, while a host of other Turkic tribes, the Bulgars and the Pechenegs, are menacing the imperial lands in Russia and the Balkans.

In the middle of this historic catastrophe, perhaps the most depressed, and the loneliest, person in the city is the empress Eudocia herself, a woman in early middle-age who, outwardly, has everything and ought to be celebrating New Year's Eve with her children, family and friends. Instead, out of duty alone, she is about to finalise a decision that is tantamount to selling her body. She has sent for Psellus to tell him.

Later, Psellus commits his recollections to paper:

When we were alone, she began to speak with tears in her eyes. . . . 'The decision has been made', she said. 'Romanus, the son of Diogenes, has been invited to rule as emperor with me, in preference to all others.' These words filled me with terror. I could not imagine what would happen to me. 'Well', I said, 'I will give you my opinion tomorrow.' 'No, no, not tomorrow', she replied. 'Give me your support now.' I returned to the attack, with just one question: 'What about your son, the co-emperor, who will presumably one day rule the empire alone? Does he know?' 'Not all the details', she replied. 'But I am glad you mention him. Let us go to him now. He is asleep upstairs.' So we went up to him. How she felt about it, I do not know, but I was most agitated. A sudden fit of trembling came over me. She sat down on the edge of the bed and called the boy. 'My emperor, my best of sons, rise up and prepare to receive your step-father. Although he takes the place of your father, he will be a subject, not a ruler. I have bound him in writing to observe it.' Well, the young man rose from his bed at once and, although he looked at me suspiciously, I do not know what he was thinking. He left the room with his mother and immediately came face to face with the new emperor. With an expressionless face, he embraced Romanus as his new colleague and friend.[12]

Psellus has good reason to tremble. The army regards him as the evil genius behind the blindness to reality in effeminate, chattering, intriguing Constantinople that has, for decades, starved it of funds to satiate its own lust for luxury, pretending that sending imperial titles or other empty bribes to Turkish chiefs will fool them into becoming loyal subjects. This so-called Peace Camp, headed by Psellus and Ducas, now wants negotiations with Alp Arslan, even though everyone knows that he is not in full control of his plunder-crazed hordes, and probably does not even dare to be seen trying to curb the advance of Islam.

To his shock, Psellus has just discovered that other voices have been whispering into the ears of the mere woman. Who could they be? How did he allow himself to become so complacent and be taken by surprise by them?

Equally shocked will be another leader of the Peace Camp, Patriarch John Xiphilinus. Only last May, he was summoned to the bedside of the dying emperor, Constantine X, a Ducas, to witness a solemn oath by the empress never to marry after him. A few months later, he was tricked by the empress who told him that, in the interests of the Christian state, she needed a strong male presence beside her on the throne and that she had chosen his, the patriarch's, brother, to be that presence. The patriarch had thus declared that the late king had not been of sound mind and that his will could now be ignored to safeguard the empire. Now he could see that the empress never had the slightest intention of marrying a non-military man.

Although Romanus has just arrived in the capital after an arduous journey from the Balkans, so urgent is Eudocia's need for decisive military action that she will marry him tomorrow, New Year's Day, 1068, and crown him as her 'partner on the throne'. But Romanus is an angry soldier who has come to be a saviour. He has no intention of being anyone's partner in this temple of indulgence, let alone a woman's partner. But though an experienced commander and a suspicious man by upbringing, as he looks down upon the sleepy face of the boy Michael and embraces him this fateful night, even he does not suspect into what pit of vipers he has just lowered himself.

*   *   *

As the famous three layers of Samarkand eventually emerged on the horizon, probably with the lengthening shadows one late afternoon in early January 1068, the pace of the caravan picked up once more. Since the death of his father the previous year, young Omar had been in full charge of his life. He could have decided to remain in Nishāpur and live both in material comfort and public esteem. Instead, he had embarked on this expensive and arduous migration whose outcome none could predict.

Such thoughts, if they did occur to him at this late stage, would have been quickly banished by the excitement of the end of the road, the proof that all had gone right, the realisation that he and his party really had made it to the metropolis 'Beyond the River' whose descriptions had mesmerised Khorāsānians for generations unknown.

Tripartite Samarkand was built on two hills and a plain, on the southern shore of the Zarafshan River as it flowed from the snow-capped mountains of the Pamir in the east towards Bukhara in the west. The highest part, the Kohan Dezh or Old Castle district, was a self-contained village by itself, as all such citadels from old Iran were designed to be for times of siege. It had its defensive walls. It possessed all the essential offices of the local government, including a prison, and it had a few warehouses, deep wells and even fields to grow food. Alexander had to conquer it three times and eventually burnt it down.

The Greeks recorded its name as Marakanda, which is still a mystery to scholars, though it probably ought not to be. The second part of the compound word means 'settlement' in old Iranian and still survives in many places, such as Tashkent. 'Sar' means 'head' or 'on' in all Iranian languages, including the now-extinct Soghdian of the region, and 'Marq' meant 'meadow', often a whole side of a river valley where animals grazed. It is therefore likely that Samarkand began as Sar-Marq-Kent or 'Top-Meadow-Hamlet'.[†] In today's Persian and Kurdish, there are countless villages or towns called 'Sarāb' or 'Sarow', meaning simply 'On Water'.

The locals themselves call their city 'Samarqand'. The Chinese later gave up all attempts at accuracy and turned it into 'Samokian'.

The proper heart of the city lay on the lower hill and was again called the Shahristān, the City. Here lived the merchants and the officers of the state who required wide avenues and great squares as symbols of their standing in society, and they had their own protection, too, in the form of a moat that could be flooded on intelligence of a hostile army. The earth dug up in the construction of the moat had been piled up behind it to form a second wall for yet more protection.

Finally, at the foot of the City and stretching all the way to the shore of the river were the suburbs, where the majority of the bazaars, warehouses and caravanserais were built. Here, too, lay the housing estates of the poor and their workshops. The suburbs, in turn, were flanked on either side of the river by the numerous fruit orchards that made summer and autumn such pleasant seasons in Samarkand, producing the mulberries and cherries of June, the peaches and red grapes of August, and the melons, pears, quinces and white grapes of September and October. Those were the obvious delights of the year ahead that Omar could anticipate this late December 1067. Other delights, more important to him and less certain, needed discovering on arrival: in the libraries and colleges, in the company of the men of letters, in the hunting parties of his peers.

Abu Tāhir, the governor of the city and his late father's friend, received Omar well and apparently gave him a job in his own office. Mention is made in the sources of Omar's working in 'the treasury' in Samarkand, though no exact date is given. It may be that soon he progressed from Abu Tāhir's office to the king's treasury without

† This, however, is only my conjecture.

straining his friendship with the chief judge. But so rapid was his rise in the esteem of the new city that we must assume other factors were at work beside his genius as a mathematician. His respectable birth, good looks and powerful connections would have helped, of course, but they may still not explain the facts. Additional spurs might well have been his undoubted wit and his ability to play and sing, which were expected of a young man who, as we shall see later, had already written a book on music.

Samarkand took pride in its achievements in municipal organisation and engineering, and Omar would have wanted to see how the huge quantities of water were, since Sasanian times, brought into the centre of the Shahristān by a network of viaducts and lead-lined underground canals. In the first few centuries after the Islamic conquest, the system had been supervised exclusively by Zoroastrian engineers who had been exempted payment of the poll tax imposed on non-Muslims, to encourage them to stay. A tour of the waterfront would also have been among Omar's priorities. The Zarafshan, the 'gold sprinkled',[13] provided miles of riverside restaurants, kebab kiosks and drinking houses in the shade of poplars and weeping willows, although these really came into their own in the summer, still months away.

* * *

By about February 1068, Omar would have been settled in Samarkand, though still aglow with the excitement of arrival and still in awe of the great city with its luminous present and antique past. In particular, Omar would have made it one of his first tasks to visit the tomb of Rūdaki, the poet who had boosted the literary pretensions of New Persian in the previous century, a full hundred years before Firdowsi had raised it to be the nation's rock of defiance. Rūdaki, whom we shall get to know better in Omar's next city, Bukhara, was buried in the suburb of Rodak and attracted the more educated type of pilgrim. His power over his king had made him a legend and his long poem on the art of the winemaker remained a favourite of fair songstresses in every city of Khorāsān. As Omar approached the threshold of the mausoleum, he would have been aware of his own great good fortune to be there at all.

Much more than Nishāpur, Samarkand had maintained its old-Iranian air, even though Transoxania had often been only a vassal state of the Sasanians. A most evocative remainder of those times was an iron gate in the city wall that still bore Middle Persian script. Less obvious reminders of the pre-Islamic past were new buildings that replicated the architectural style of Zoroastrian fire temples.[14]

One living sage that Omar would, no doubt, have longed to meet was the famous traveller and poet Nasser Khosrow. But it is most unlikely that Khosrow would have remained in a region that was in the full grip of Muslim orthodoxy. He had by then become well known in Khorāsān as one of the main leaders of Ismaili Shias, with his followers as agents of the Egyptian caliphate.

Khosrow has left us a famous story of persecution that is not without humour. He was in a cobbler's shop in the city of Balkh when a tumult arose in a neighbouring street. The cobbler rushed to the scene of the trouble, but returned shortly afterwards with blood on his hands. On being asked what had happened, he replied: 'Oh, it was nothing. They'd found one of Khosrow's followers. We killed him.' Khosrow thought it advisable not to collect his personal belongings from his lodgings before fleeing the city.

The genteel man of ideas had survived many such perils, particularly during his seven-year journey to Cairo and back by way of Mecca and the Persian Gulf. His account of that journey, the *Safar Nāmeh* or *Travel Journal*, which remains a favourite of many to this day, would have almost certainly been bought 'under the counter' by Omar and enjoyed enormously. It was to be found everywhere, for two reasons. It was brimful with exciting facts about hostile places, and it was a short book that could be copied inside a week. Hence its surviving early manuscripts have proved a nightmare to scholars trying to decipher what the author actually wrote. Generations of playful schoolboys have inflicted unspeakable atrocities on this gem of a book while copying it.

Furthermore, Khosrow had acquired legendary status even among his fiercest religious opponents. It was rumoured that he had converted to Ismailism at the hand of the caliph of Egypt himself. Now Khosrow was probably already in distant Badakhshan in the Hindukosh mountains in the east. He would die there in 1088 in the castle of Yamkān which had been captured by his followers. The only time we can be certain Khayyām was in close physical proximity to him was in 1055 in Nishāpur, when Khosrow returned from his travels. Omar was then only a seven-year-old schoolboy.

* * *

Samarkand was the gateway through which the East gave at least one of its two most precious gifts to the West: paper. The other gift, the number zero, which brought an even greater transformation to the world, still needs its precise manner of transmission investigated. But both had their effect on the state of the libraries that Omar found in Samarkand on his arrival.

One of the most moving finds in the history of archaeology must surely be that of the sack of undelivered mail from possibly the fourth century near Dunhuang in eastern Central Asia. In the early twentieth century, the British explorer Sir Marc Aurel Stein found there, in a ruined watchtower, more than 30,000 letters and documents. The great majority were written in Chinese, but there were also some in Sanskrit, Soghdian, Middle Persian or Pahlavi, Uighur and Tibetan. In one letter, a homesick Soghdian merchant from Samarkand sends news to his family, showing that the use of paper had by then spread from the inventors, the Chinese, to others as far away as Transoxania.

The letter, now at the British Library and seemingly as fresh as when it was written 1,600 years ago, is untypical of Chinese paper in one significant respect. It does not contain bamboo and rattan, but is made of hemp and mulberry, both of which grow well in the cool, dry climate of Central Asia. More recently, paper samples just as old have been found as far west as the Caucasus in southern Russia.

It is believed that the technique of manufacturing paper was known to Buddhist missionaries in Transoxania even before the fourth century.[15] Though no samples of ancient paper have been found in Iran proper, it would seem inconceivable that the secret had not found its way to the heart of the Sasanian empire in Ctesiphon by at least the sixth century when that city became the centre of Greek learning due to the persecution of scholars in Edessa‡ and Athens by the newly dominant Christians. Surely among the thousands of books burnt by the Arab invaders in Ctesiphon in the seventh century,[16] there were many made from the newer, cheaper, more permanent material?[17]

This is important to point out because a later Arab myth has gained ground that the technique of making paper reached the west when an Arab army captured a number of Chinese technicians after the battle of Talas in Central Asia in the eighth century (751 CE). The same myth even claims that paper was taken into India by Muslims. Scholars, on the other hand, believe that paper-making must have been common in India by at least the fourth century, when, in its land of origin, China, it had become so cheap that it was being used for toiletry. If no samples of ancient paper have been found in India, the centre of Buddhism, it must primarily be due to the warm and wet climate. Alternatively, we have not been lucky yet.

Wherever paper arrived, libraries flourished, and Samarkand, as with the other large cities of Transoxania and Khorāsān, already had a long history of literacy behind it. Political turmoil and conquest, as well as accidental fires and economic decline, periodically inflicted their wrath on libraries there, as elsewhere, and historical records are incomplete or lost. For example, at the time of Khayyām's arrival, there is a noticeable absence of first-person descriptions of the libraries of Samarkand. For this reason, we will have to invoke reports on the libraries of neighbouring cities to give us a reasonable picture of what Omar found when he arrived, for Samarkand was the most advanced of all the centres of learning in Transoxania and Khorāsān.

Two accounts come to mind immediately. One is by Omar's idol, the philosopher Avicenna, and describes the royal library of Bukhara some eighty years earlier. The other is a comprehensive report on the libraries of Marv about eighty years after Omar's death; just before the Mongol invasion from the east devastated the whole region.

Sometime in the 1030s, in the city of Hamadan in today's Western Iran, an especially persistent student pressed his master and employer,

‡   Today's Urfa in eastern Anatolia or Turkish Kurdistan.

Avicenna, to give him a biographical sketch of his life. Avicenna, who was by then the Grand Vizier of the Persian Buyid state, beside being physician to the king, eventually agreed and, among the facts of his ancestry and career, provided the following recollection of a library in Bukhara that had made a lasting impression on him when he had been seventeen years old:

> The king of Bukhara was at that time Nūh Bin Mansūr. He became ill and his doctors could not do very much for him. As I was by then known to the doctors for wide reading, they mentioned me to the king and asked for permission to summon me. He agreed and I took part in his treatment with the doctors until he was well again.
>
> One day I asked him to allow me to use the royal library to study the medical books there. He agreed and they took me there. I saw a library large and wide, with many rooms and in each room cases stacked with books, neatly arranged. Each room was devoted to a specific kind of book. For example, they had given over a room to Arabic and poetry, another to law, others to the various sciences.
>
> The library also had a catalogue which I studied. I chose what I needed and began to read them. I saw many books whose existence I had not learnt from any other, nor seen them before myself. Some of them I never saw again afterwards.[18]

It is quite clear that the library was in the Greek style, not Roman. It had a large central hall where, presumably, the librarians sat at desks or on benches ready to serve visitors. The books were in rooms radiating away on two or three sides. This made supervision of visitors in the various rooms difficult. A lazy student bent on tearing off a leaf or two from a reference book to study at home or, even worse, a cheat intent on destroying the evidence of his plagiarism, could inflict massive damage on a library. By contrast, in libraries built in the Roman style, the books were on stacks or cases all around large reading halls where a single librarian could keep an eye on several suspicious characters.

Unfortunately, soon after Avicenna's visits, the library was largely destroyed when a bonfire to celebrate an ancient Iranian festival got out of control. The young physician's detractors spread a rumour that it had been started by him, but the authorities did not fall prey to the ploy.

For a description of the libraries of Marv just before the Mongol invasion, we are indebted to a Syrian scholar, Yaqut Al-Hamawi, who spent three years there in the 1210s. He has left us the names of ten of them and says that he used them 'with the avidity of a glutton'. At times, he claims, he had up to 200 expensive, leather-bound volumes lent to him to read or copy free of charge. He did not even have to place a deposit for loss or damage with the libraries:

> I remained in Marv three years and found no fault with it except that the people were afflicted by the Medina Worm [the water-born guinea worm *filaria medinensis*], for they were greatly troubled by it. Hardly anyone escaped it in any year. Were it not for the coming of the Tartars and the devastation of the city, I would not have left till I died because of the generosity of the people and their kindness and sociability and because of the abundance of reliable, basic books there.
>
> When I left, there were ten endowed libraries the like of which I had never seen. Two of them were in mosques and the rest belonged to *Madrasas* (a combination of theological school and vocational college). One of them, called the Aziziyah, was the gift of a man called Aziz al Din Abu Bakr, formerly a slave. In his youth, he had sold fruits and flowers in the market. Then he had become a supplier of beer to the sultan, Sanjar, and then a cup-bearer to him and was held in high respect by the sultan. There were 12,000 volumes in his library, all bound in skin.
>
> And there was the library of Sharaf al Mulk, the Chief Accountant. . . . This man died in 494 AH., (1100–1101 CE) Nizām al Mulk [the Grand Vizier and Khayyām's future patron] had also set up a library in his mosque, as had Princess Khatun in hers.[19]

Clearly Yaqut hopes to inspire his audience back in Syria to emulate the Iranians when he implies that anyone could borrow 200 expensive books from the libraries of Marv without any sureties. Native, less-honoured, citizens of the city itself would no doubt have had a different story to tell than the exotic visitor from the fabled, faraway land of Shām [Damascus] who suffered no shortage of powerful local sponsors. But he does give us an idea of the expansive book culture in Marv in his time and it is interesting to hear that most of the libraries were not attached to mosques. He says that two of them had departments specialising in the history and documentation of the Sāmānids, the consciously-Iranian dynasty who, from their capital in Bukhara, had proved instrumental in the flowering of New Persian; the royal library described by Avicenna earlier being only one of their achievements.

Yaqut's libraries were, nevertheless, conservative institutions in social terms. To read entertaining, not to mention scandalous, authors, people headed for their city's Bāzār-i-Ketāb-Forūshān, the Market of the Booksellers, where they could hire, as well as buy.

*   *   *

In the spring of 1068, brave Romanus Diogenes IV, the new co-emperor of the Eastern Roman Empire and consort to Empress Eudocia for the past couple of months, embodied everyone's hope that, at last, the onslaught of Turkish marauders into the Anatolian heartland might be stemmed. The recent fall of fair Caesaria to them had concentrated minds further on the plight of the empire, particularly in its eastern bastions which were now being raped and pillaged by savages from far-flung Asia. But as the co-emperor continued his furious effort to rebuild the army, he knew that for the time being, Anatolia might be kept Roman only by default. The new Turkish chief Alp-Arslan had been preoccupied with the threat he faced in Syria from fellow Muslims, the Fatimids of Egypt, and, furthermore, the mere mention of Constantinople's name still made every Saracen tremble. It invoked the memory of the crushing defeats inflicted on them by Basil II, 'Bulgar-Slayer', half a century earlier. The 'Rūmies' were not to be provoked lightly.

Or, at least, this had been the Turks' thinking under Alp-Arslan's uncle, Tangriplex§ who had been beaten back twice by Byzantine armies. The facts on the ground were changing rapidly. The Turkish hordes under the nominal leadership of Alp-Arslan had a mind of their own and did not always heed their sultan's advice. Their anarchic and egalitarian nature regarded all the newly captured lands of 'the two Iraqs', the Persian and the Arab, western Iran and Mesopotamia, as common tribal property and, what is more, their appetite for booty was constantly being refreshed. Even richer

§   The Byzantine name for Toghril.

Christian cities lay on the western horizon, they heard, and sheep grew fat on the great, green plains.

Tangriplex had been a simple chieftain, grateful to find himself master of Isfahan and Baghdad. His nephew needed to gain glory of his own and had already made his mark by conquering the Christian lands of Armenia and Georgia four years earlier. But he was apparently in awe of his ambitious and ruthless vizier who had risen from being the son of a humble Persian tax collector to become almost as powerful as his sovereign. What kinds of men were they?

So, over the recent weeks, Romanus had tried to separate fact from rumour by putting new vigour into the intelligence department of the foreign office. He had set spies on the heels of Alp-Arslan wherever he went. He had formed committees to study the Turk's personality, his current preoccupations, his health. He had ordered that every effort be made to penetrate the courts of both the sultan and the vizier with brave and tested agents who would not shirk from the greatest sacrifice in the service of Christ. But finding and training such heroes would take time.

Overtures were made immediately to the Shia ruler of Cairo for at least an unspoken pact against the common threat, but Romanus was not optimistic. The Fatimid caliph had not forgotten how Empress Theodora had offended him so unnecessarily. His Sunni rival for the religious leadership of Islam, the Abbāsid caliph of Baghdad, had asked for his name to be recited in prayers in the mosques of Constantinople instead of the Egyptian's. Theodora had agreed without demanding any concessions in return.

Even the remaining diplomats in the foreign office were mostly not worthy of the name. That snake Psellus and the other moving spirits of the reign of Constantine X had starved them of funds for so long that they had all but forgotten their skills, often having to earn their livelihood elsewhere. Psellus's men were still strong at the top of the department.

Romanus decided to see for himself the true state of the army. In his first few weeks, he had cut the salaries of a thousand dowager ladies, lawyers and other hangers-on to give the starving garrisons their unpaid wages, and he had promised the commanders new arms. Some progress had been achieved, he was told.

But as he arrived on the appointed plain in the province of the Anatolics after weeks of preparation, he sank into a deep depression. Many of the cavalry did not have horses. They had sold their mounts for food. Others rode sickly or lame animals. The infantry carried farmers' scythes and forks for arms. Flags were soiled and irreparable.[20] Worst of all was the lack of a glimmer of enthusiasm in the eyes of the soldiers. He detected even a sullen hatred towards himself in the faces of the many Armenian fighters he needed to motivate. Under Constantine, their church leaders had been persecuted as Monophysite** heretics and their ruling families had been exiled to the interior of Anatolia. To them, Romanus was just another Roman bigot, another despiser of their very existence, who made them promises he knew he would not keep.

*   *   *

The autumn of that same year, 1068, found Alp-Arslan in Georgia for a second time to extend his grip into the north-western Caucasus against the Kurdish kings of Arrān. The Kurds had not only overcome Hungarian rule over the Upper Kūr valley in the far north; they had now built a bridge over the Araxes River in the south to threaten Alp-Arslan's vassals, the Rawandid kings of Azerbaijan.

As Alp-Arslan conquered, Romanus's spies watched his every move and confirmed the emperor's analysis that the Turk was not interested in a war with Constantinople. Nevertheless, he could be seen to face a dilemma, depending on Romanus's next move. His tribesmen, constantly on the prowl for booty, slaves and fresh pasture, regarded him only as one of themselves, albeit the most powerful. What would he do if Romanus sent an army to the borderlands to stop the harassment? Not rushing to the aid of his people might give the impression that the sultan was not in charge, or did not care. But if he did go to their support, he risked defeat at the hands of the mighty Romans, or at least stalemate and a dissipation of resources. That would leave him weaker in his plans to conquer Egypt.

** Those Christians who believed that Jesus had only one nature, the divine and human combined.

Alp-Arslan had good reason to be wary. His uncle, the great Sultan Toghril, had twice driven into Armenia, in 1048 and 1053, and had even managed to sack the city of Kars, but on both occasions he had been beaten back decisively. Those Byzantine armies remained formidable, although, of course, times changed.

On his side, Romanus knew that the tide had to be stemmed and Caesaria reclaimed if there was to be an end to the deprecations of the hordes. Yet the army was not ready and, what was more, it would not be ready unless he won the political battle at court. The Peace Camp around Michael Psellus and John Ducas detested and feared him. Both sides needed the country's treasury, nearly empty though it was.

Romanus's spies reported heart-rending tales of the mistreatment of Christians at the hands of the Turks in the Caucasus. Four years earlier, poor Bagrat IV, the Armenian king of Georgia and a vassal of the empire there, had been forced to give his precious young daughter to Alp-Arslan 'in marriage' in the hope of buying safety for the rest of his people. It had not worked. The enslavement of the Christians had continued and the young princess had been thrown into a Saracen harem somewhere in Isfahan, just one more wretched female hostage among hundreds of others.

* * *

As Omar and his companions accommodated themselves to their new circumstances in Samarkand in the winter of 1068, they became aware of the intense forebodings with which the dominant Sunni clergy regarded the new king, Shams al-Mulk. For the past decade or so, the Prince had been the effective ruler of the western Qarakhanid empire, for his father had become a virtual hermit. Some said that the older man had become demented as punishment for the killing of a leading imam at the start of his reign. Others claimed that he had become genuinely religious after hearing voices telling him to repent. Now, true to his father's example, the new king also trod that path. He ignored the basic tenets of Islamic observance. He never prayed, he ate and drank openly during Ramadan, and he did not even draw back from humiliating the chief imam of Samarkand, the Sadr Ismā'īl bin Abi Nassr as-Saffār, in public. Some said that, despite his avowed profession of Islam, in truth he followed the shamanistic practices of his ancestors in the Turkish steppe. Most expected an eventual terrible clash between the court and the clergy.

But it took only a few months. Shams al-Mulk ordered the Sadr's execution for disrespect, or, as the clergy saw it, 'for daring to urge the king to observe the commands of the faith and to desist from the forbidden'. As also prevalent in western Europe at the time – where a fierce struggle for power had broken out between the church and the various royal houses – the execution of a chief cleric was one of the gravest crimes any ruler could commit. If unpunished, it would set a precedent for other rulers and here, in the western Qarakhanid empire, it did indeed set the tone for the relationship between the two sides for the whole duration of Shams al-Mulk's rule. As we shall see in greater detail later, Omar's present mentor, Abu Tāhir, was to lead a rebellion that would result in the execution of Shams al-Mulk's successor.

For the time being, though, neither the tension between the clergy and the court, nor even the execution of the Sadr alienated Omar from either side. He was probably too junior to be noticed, or perhaps the breach between Abu Tāhir and the king had not come into the open. So, despite working in the king's treasury, he succeeded in remaining on good terms with his father's friend, at least until the autumn of 1072, the entire duration of his stay in Samarkand. In that year, he was still able to dedicate his fifth and most important book, *Proofs of Problems in Algebra and Confrontation*, to Abu Tāhir without provoking the king. In the dedication, he mentions Abu Tāhir twice by name and describes him in the loftiest of terms, 'the Judge of Judges, the unique great lord, Lord Imam Abu Tāhir'. Gratefully, he acknowledges that if it had not been for joining Abu Tāhir's circle, he would not have been able to climb the heights[††] as he had done. Arrogant, certainly, about his status, but arrogance has often been a weakness of mathematical prodigies.

The preface is striking in an important respect. It is not at all polite and platitudinous. It is even shocking. Omar, the stranger, the young man and newcomer, denounces the established scientists and astronomers of the region as frauds and fools:

††   See 'Appendix IV, Khayyām's Mathematics and Other Writings'.

. . . and from the start I was keen to investigate all the remaining problems in order to distinguish the genuine among them from the absurd, for to solve difficult [practical?] problems, this is needed. But it was not possible to concentrate on the subject. In our time, few remain from the ranks of the true scientists, and those who are true scientists have to fight many obstacles if they wish to revive science by new research from the neglect of ages.

Most pretenders to science present falsehood in the robe of truth. They lay false claims to knowledge, and what they know, they use only for the fulfilment of their bodily needs. If they see someone who is sincere about seeking truths and unveiling pretentiousness and fraud, they belittle him and mock him . . .

And this was so until God Almighty led me to the court of our unique great lord, the Chief Judge, the Lord Imam Abu Tāhir, may God prolong his greatness and banish his enemies and those who are jealous of him, and all this, when I had given up hope of ever meeting someone like him, someone who has mastered all the practical and theoretical accomplishments and who combines a curiosity in the details of science with perseverance in action and pursuing the wellbeing of his fellows.

My heart soared meeting him and my name spread with his companionship. My affairs ascended through his generosity and his kindnesses gave me confidence. Then, so that I might be admitted to his High Council and make up for the setbacks that the hardships of the age had inflicted upon me, I determined on summarizing the philosophical truths that I had already investigated. This I began with a preparation [of a list] of the rudiments of algebra, for mathematics benefits from presentation . . .[21]

There are a number of other pointers to Omar's upbringing and his new position in Samarkand in these passages. Apart from being the work of a haughty, perhaps at times unlovable, young man with high connections, the passages suggest that he did not have sufficient wealth of his own when he arrived in the city to pursue his interests. He clearly needed a rich patron to provide him with the peace of mind in which to complete his researches, and he had given up hope of finding such a patron in his birthplace of Nishāpur. We are also confirmed in our previous conclusion that he had discovered his mathematical abilities early in life, perhaps up to a decade earlier, when still a schoolchild. We have seen that his father employed for him the renowned Zoroastrian philosopher and mathematician Bahmanyār as a teacher. But Nishāpur had fallen under the Turks and no longer appreciated scientists as it had previously.

Some of his phrases may sound as if Omar arrived in Samarkand in middle age, not as a youth aged nineteen. We can dismiss the notion. There are too many firm mentions of his dates. The preface is the work of someone who exaggerates the difficulties he has had to overcome in order to further glorify what he has achieved.

The question must be asked why he indulged in antagonising his rivals. Some of them had influential connections of their own and were even heads of prominent families or clans. While his remarks would have been seen as truthful by many, his admirers would not have been there to defend him if an assassin were sent to catch up with him one dark night in a narrow lane as he wound his way home. Why was he so abrasive? What gave him the confidence to breach the first rule of polite society in a place as honour-bound as Samarkand? Abu Tāhir would certainly not have approved openly. In the coming struggle with the king, the governor would need all the friends he could cultivate and some of those wronged men belonged to his own circle of friends and associates. Some were members of the same High Council of advisors to which he had elevated Omar.

Apart from telling us that Khayyām could be obnoxious as a young man, and that this trait would mean he made many more enemies in later life, there is only one safe conclusion we can draw from his behaviour: he felt secure in the power of his connections now, and those connections must have led to the very person of the king, no less.

Shams al-Mulk's official capital was at Bukhara, a week's journey to the west, but he spent much time in Samarkand, the chief city of his empire and the gathering place of the elite. In such a place, the presence of a dazzling scientist such as Omar would have been brought to his attention early.

The new treatise on algebra was Omar's third book to be published[‡‡] and caused his reputation as a mathematical innovator to spread quickly to all the learned circles of Transoxania, Khorāsān and beyond. It broke new ground by demonstrating solutions to several classes of cubic equations. It may be argued, plausibly, that without the breakthroughs being achieved at this time, subsequent

---

[‡‡] Which means that scribes were allowed to copy it for sale.

achievements such as the discovery of calculus by Newton might have been delayed.

Of Omar's other writings in these first years of his professional life as a mathematician, some have perished. But one chapter has survived from an earlier book: *On the Problems in Euclid's Book of Music* (See 'Appendix IV').

* * *

One of the most tragic dates in the history of Europe and the world is 26 August 1071. On that day a state that, for some 700 years, had preserved many of the cultural treasures of ancient Greece and Rome from destruction suffered a major defeat at the hands of an eastern horde and began its relentless decline until it fell eventually to that same people in 1453. The catastrophe resulted in the rapid loss of Asia Minor to western civilisation, and it led later to a threat to the remainder of Europe so serious that, had it not been thrown back by Polish and German armies outside the walls of Vienna in 1683, there might never have come into being what we now call the European Enlightenment that has improved and inspired mankind to this day. The defeat also altered the course of events in the new Saljuq empire and directly affected Khayyām's life, in particular his future relationships with several kings and princes.

When Romanus IV, son of Diogenes, arrived in Constantinople on 31 December 1067 and married the widowed Empress Eudocia the next day, he despaired in whatever direction he looked.

To the west, the Norseman upstart Robert Guiscard was intent on grabbing the empire's last possessions in Italy and had allied himself to the chief Christian heretic, the Bishop of Rome.

In the south, Italian merchants from Amalfi had bribed the Egyptian governor of Jerusalem and established a base there that would, again, undermine the ecclesiastical authority of Constantinople in that most holy city of the Christians to the benefit of Rome.

To the north, two older strains of Turks, the Pechenegs and the Bulgars, had lately become active and challenged the empire's borders above the Black Sea and in the Balkans. In the east, the newest wave of Turks, the Saljuqs, were threatening the very breadbasket of the capital in its heartland of Anatolia.

Every month news arrived of a new Saljuq atrocity committed against Christians and, indeed, Romanus's own family estates in Cappadocia. His relatives, friends and staff in Middle Anatolia now lived in constant terror. Many of the farmers with whom he had grown up had been killed in their fields and their flocks taken away.

This was largely the work of autonomous Saljuq warbands, out to grab what they could. If they could not breach fortifications, they settled for abducting thousands of farmers in the countryside for sale in the slave markets of Iran and Arabia. Their formal leader, the Sultan Alp-Arslan, worked more systematically. He was looting and holding the Armenian uplands further east.

Was this state of affairs terminal? Was the empire of Constantine at last nearing its fall? Or could a great general unite his people behind him, as Basil II had done only half a century earlier? It was not so much a lack of will on the part of his people, Romanus thought. They would readily risk their lives to safeguard their families. The trouble lay at the effeminate heart of Constantinople, the imperial court that put its faith in Christ and resisted any demand to curb its thirst for luxury.

As he celebrated his third anniversary on the throne on New Year's Day 1071, Romanus was able to boast of some successes. He had shut down many a high-sounding department of useless officialdom to divert their budgets to the army, so that today the eastern divisions were much larger, better equipped and more suitably trained. Furthermore he had in his first year led the army far into the east in the hills of Syria, around the metropolitan city of Antioch, to clear the Turks from the region, though they had now seeped back somewhat. The following year, he had taken to the field once more and captured a string of small fortifications in Armenia above Lake Van, only to be forced back by poor logistics; the problem of sustaining a large army in an impoverished land.

His enemies were less charitable. Romanus had failed to capture his avowed destination, the town of Khliat, north of Lake Van. The vipers such as Michael Psellus smirked. The hand of John Ducas, the late emperor's brother, had been strengthened.

Romanus's main problem was the inability of his cumbersome army to keep up with the lightly-armed Turkish horsemen who lived on a small sack of grain hanging from their shoulders and, when possible, food robbed from villagers. Time and again, their warbands broke through, and could even retreat back into Saljuq territory laden with booty. The old policy of maintaining a line of strong castles from Armenia southwards to Syria to intercept and destroy marauders was simply not working against the new enemy, even if morale could be bolstered among the squabbling ethnic contingents that made up the defenders.

In 1070, Romanus chose the humiliation of remaining in the capital rather than taking to the field himself. An expeditionary force he sent out into Anatolia was defeated, but when the officer returned with his former captor, a Turkish chieftain wanting to come over to the Byzantines and turn his arms on Alp-Arslan, so desperate was Romanus for a minor victory that he showered the defector with money and titles, even though the man had been deserted by his followers. So, as he celebrated his third anniversary on the throne, he knew that, politically, there was no alternative to risking life and limb again in search of a decisive victory against the elusive Saljuqs. Recently, they had even sacked one of the holiest sites of Christian pilgrimage in western Anatolia, the church of St Michael the Archangel in the city of Chonai.

In the summer of 1071, Romanus set off at the head of the army for the east with the hopes of the whole empire tied to his banner. Historians seem to have greatly exaggerated the size of his forces. It was probably no larger than 40,000 men, with the bulk of it made up of Anatolian natives, though it also included Frankish guards, Norman mercenaries, Pecheneg Turks and Ghuzz tribesmen of the same stock as the Saljuqs. The force would be strengthened in the field by contingents of Armenians.

Romanus had reason to hope for the loyalty of at least some of these peoples. The Europeans were far from their homeland and thrived only if the empire prospered, while the native Anatolians were defending their own towns, villages and estates. As for the Armenians, Romanus felt that the bonds of friendship and understanding he had forged with their nobility was now strong enough. He certainly did not share Constantinople's bigotry regarding their doctrinal differences. On his ancestral estate in Cappadocia, his father had often played host to Armenian noblemen who had settled there in exchange for their lands and titles further east. Most suspect was the loyalty of the various Turkic mercenaries, particularly the Ghuzz, who not only spoke the same dialect as the Saljuqs, but even dressed like them.

The route that Romanus chose this time to reach Armenia was different to the one he had tried two years earlier. Instead of approaching Armenia from the south, he headed for the shores of the Black Sea in the north and, to his surprise, captured the town of Manzikert easily. But he was continuing the same erroneous strategy of wanting to hold onto the great fortresses, and he was plagued by the empire's political and military weaknesses of recent decades.

After capturing Manzikert, Romanus sent a large section of the army to gain the fortress of Khliat while he himself camped with the remainder on the plain north of Lake Van. News arrived soon, however, that Alp-Arslan had arrived in the region at the head of his best troops. Romanus sent urgent message to the army at Khliat to return, but received no reply. On hearing that Alp-Arslan was leading the enemy in person and was intent on battle, the Khliat contingent had decided to flee westwards to the castle of Melitene, leaving its hapless commander, a Russian, to fall into Saljuq hands. Alp-Arslan ordered that the poor man's nose be cut off and sent as a present to Nizām al-Mulk in Hamadan in Iran.

When he had heard of Romanus's arrival in the east, Alp-Arslan had been in Syria laying siege to Aleppo and planning an offensive into Egypt to overthrow the caliphate of Cairo. He had abandoned this plan and rushed northwards, gathering some Kurdish cavalry on the way, west of lake Urmia. Muslim historians underplay the size of his forces at only 15,000, while they exaggerate the number of Romanus's men at up to 200,000. Whatever the truth, the Turks had mobility, fitness and recent experience of war on their side, while the Byzantine army was a ramshackle kaleidoscope of professional troops, mercenaries, palace guards and recently armed peasant levies.

Still, Alp-Arslan decided to sue for peace, fearing that he would be crushed by a headlong clash. Romanus sent message that they would make peace in Rayy, near today's Tehran, fearing that Alp-Arslan was merely trying to kill time to await reinforcements and to win over the Turkic mercenaries on the Byzantine side. Right or wrong, as battle was joined, the Byzantines got the better of the day until the late evening when Romanus decided on an orderly retreat for the night. He did not wish to subject his infantry to the mounted archers of the Turks in darkness.

This proved disastrous. The huge army was not sufficiently trained for the difficult manoeuvre of retreat when the role of the rearguard would become vital in defending the main body of the troops, and the commander of the rearguard was no other than Andronicus Ducas, the eldest son of Romanus's bitter enemy John Ducas. Fearing that a Byzantine victory would almost guarantee the succession of Romanus's sons with Eudocia at the expense of the empress's elder sons of the Ducas line, Andronicus spread the rumour that Romanus had been captured or killed, following which he fled with the rearguard.

The various ethnic contingents of the army now lost heart and Romanus saw no alternative to turning back with his own bodyguard to make a stand. It was not enough. He was surrounded, wounded and fell from his horse. He was captured and beaten and dragged in chains to Alp-Arslan who immediately struck the Byzantine emperor's bare, bloodied head three times with his horsewhip.

'Why did you not accept my offer?', the Turk shouted.

'Spare me the torment and do your worst', the Roman managed to reply.

'What would you have done to me if you were in my place?'

'I would have flogged you to death.'

Or at least, this is one account of the initial conversation between the two sovereigns that has come down to us. The man who had previously burnt towers full of Christian refugees for not submitting to him immediately is claimed to have quoted Jesus in advocating kindness. 'I will not imitate you', Alp-Arslan is said to have replied.[22] 'I have been told that your Christ teaches forgiveness. He resists the proud and gives grace to the humble.'

Whatever his motives, the Saljuq chief apparently took Romanus to his tent for eight days and treated him well. He freed all the captured Romans the emperor could name and he allowed them freedom of movement. The two then sealed a fifty-year peace treaty by which the sultan would hold on to the Armenian uplands and fortresses in addition to annual tributes in gold, without making any promise that Turkoman warbands would not continue to mount annual raids into Anatolia. It seems that Alp-Arslan was satisfied with the humiliation of mighty 'Rūm' and now felt free to return to overthrowing the Shia Fatimid caliph. If he achieved that, only his name and that that of his figurehead, the Sunni Abbasid caliph of Baghdad, would be recited in Friday prayer sermons all the way from Samarkand in central Asia to Tunis in north Africa.

The news of Romanus's survival shook the Ducas family, the traitors who had helped engineer the disaster. Fearing that the emperor, still popular with the army, would march on the city to reclaim his throne, they led the palace guard into an horrendously noisy demonstration which forced the empress to take refuge in a secret crypt. Shouting 'death to the traitor Romanus' and banging their swords on their shields, they carried the empress's elder son, Michael upstairs to proclaim him the new emperor. Michael then agreed to send his mother, to whom he had apparently been devoted, into exile at a remote monastery and to appoint his cousin Andronicus Ducas, the chief traitor, at the head of a new army to march east to capture Romanus.

Romanus made his last stand at the castle of Amasea with the help of the Duke of Antioch, an Armenian general he had previously promoted. But the rebellion collapsed after the capture of the Duke, and Romanus himself was seized. With his head shaven and forced to wear a monk's robe, he was taken to the presence of Andronicus who at first treated him well. But soon orders arrived from the senior Ducas, the Caesar, 'the deputy', Andronicus's father. Romanus was blinded, as had been his father, and then taken in chains to another remote monastery. There he died soon afterwards in the autumn of 1071 from his wounds and his torment. He displayed bravery and fortitude to the end.

* * *

In the event, Alp-Arslan's dream of capturing Egypt in the manner of Alexander was not to be. His empire was too vast and his hordes, including his own family, too unruly to let him concentrate on the plan in hand. His spies told him that his brother-in-law, the Qarakhanid king of Bukhara, was taking advantage of his preoccupation in the south-west. So Alp-Arslan decided to dispute the news that his sister, Shams al-Mulk's wife, had died of natural causes. Shams al-Mulk had murdered her for spying for her brother. Was the cunning Khorāsānian genius of his vizier, Ali Tūsi, now Nizām al-Mulk, the Order of the Realm, behind the ruse? The historians are silent on the subject, but it would be in character. After a little more fighting in Syria, the sultan and vizier had, by the early autumn of the next year, 1072, put together an army of some 200,000 fighting men with colossal catapults and other siege engines and crossed the Oxus into central Asia. But there disaster fell. It was due to a moment of madness on Alp-Arslan's part, probably due to excessive drink.

On Saturday, 22 November, he ordered that a captured chieftain by the name of Yusef of Khārazm be brought into his presence. He then ordered that the man's hands and feet be tied to four pegs on the ground so that he, Alp-Arslan, could shoot him. Yusef's only hope, perhaps, was to kiss his captor's feet and plead for mercy, humiliating himself and his people. But for some reason he burnt with rage, perhaps over the treatment of his family by the Turkomans. So he shouted at the sultan: 'Coward! Is this how you fight an enemy?'

Alp-Arslan put an arrow in his bow and told the guards to free the man. They did so and the sultan aimed at the man's chest. Yusef swayed from side to side to dodge the arrow. The sultan missed. Yusef leapt towards him and suddenly produced a dagger from under his cloak. It was too late for another arrow. Alp-Arslan ran. But he fell on his face as he jumped from the platform on which he had stood. Yusef fell upon him and plunged his dagger in his side. The nobleman then attacked the guards and wounded a couple of them before being killed by one from behind who brought down his mace on his head.

Alp-Arslan died four days later of his wound at the age of only forty-three, but he did have time to renew his will and to divided the empire among his sons and brothers. His body would be buried in Marv, where he had already erected a mausoleum for himself.

No trace of the monument remains, but Alp-Arslan did achieve one of his greatest dreams: he became a legend, at least among

Turkomans and zealous Muslims. To this day, many prominent families in Turkey and elsewhere trace their ancestry to him and, through his victory over the Byzantines a year earlier, he may be regarded as the true founder of the later Ottoman empire in Anatolia. How might an obituarist of our time sum him up? Probably he would write as follows:

Muhammad, the son of Prince Dāwūd Chaghri Beg, who became the paramount chief of the Saljuq Turks and one of their more illustrious sultans, acquired many titles during his life, including Alp-Arslan, which meant brave lion. He was a hardened nomad in the mould of his ancestors who had first become prominent in the previous century in central Asia and, more recently, brought to heel the mighty Ghaznavid empire in Khorāsān. A man of simple tastes, he had few interests apart from conquest and enjoyed being constantly on the move.

In appearance he was tall and athletic, distinguishing himself particularly in archery. He grew his moustaches so long that they had to be tied behind his head to enable him to shoot. This profusion of facial hair was due to his mixed parentage, for true Turks from eastern Asia were characterised by a scarcity of all bodily hair. They were also, as a rule, short in stature.

His precise date of birth was probably not registered, this not being a custom among the Turks as yet, although one account says that he was born 'just before the battle of 20 January 1029' between the Saljuqs and the Qarakhanid King Alitegin near the city of Balkh in eastern Khorāsān. The Saljuqs remembered his birth as a good omen for the next battle.

His education, if it may be called that, consisted mainly of horsemanship and archery, and he began to shoulder some of his father's responsibilities early, as Prince Dāwūd did not enjoy robust health in the last decades of his life.

Before succeeding his childless uncle Toghril as sultan in 1063, Alp-Arslan was fortunate to have the services of Ali Tusi, later Nizām al-Mulk, as his vizier or chancellor, and he had the wisdom to leave the daily administration of his state to the Persian man of letters. Furthermore, when he did succeed to the sultanate, he left the entire intricate diplomacy of the succession to Tusi. Otherwise, more blood would probably have had to be shed and more rivals created for the longer term. In the same vein, he let himself be persuaded by Tusi that for the entire length of his subsequent reign, he should not visit Baghdad, remembering the atrocities that Toghril's troops had unleashed there in 1055 during that sultan's supposed pilgrimage and coronation. Thus the caliphate was retained as a willing tool to legitimise the new empire.

As with most of the Turkoman chiefs who raided the Christian lands of the Caucasus and Anatolia, Alp-Arslan neither fully controlled his troops, nor himself desisted from committing extreme crimes in the service of spreading Islam and capturing greater wealth.²³ In at least one raid, he burnt down buildings in which Christian women and children had sought shelter, with great loss of life.

His biggest achievement was the capture of a Byzantine emperor for the first time since the rise of Islam in the seventh century, but here a great measure of luck assisted him. The Byzantines had allowed their armies to become enfeebled under a number of effeminate 'men of peace' and fatalistic empresses in recent times. That victory paved the way for the later overrunning of the whole of Anatolia and the Balkans by Muslims.

Towards the end of his short life, he gathered many potentates of the Saljuq ruling family to swear allegiance to his eldest son, Malik Shah, to reduce the chances of a great rebellion within the family over the throne. That rebellion, did, nevertheless, materialise immediately after his death when the administration was ousted from Isfahan by his elder brother Prince Qavurt.

So high was the esteem in which Alp-Arslan held his Grand Vizier that he divorced one of his most noble wives, the daughter of the Armenian King Bagrat IV, and gave her to Tusi to marry, thus elevating the vizier to virtual membership of the royal family. This has given Nizām al-Mulk the necessary prestige to guide the affairs of the state unhindered while the Crown Prince, who is seventeen years of age, grows to maturity.

The question most commentators now ask is what else the late sultan would have wanted to achieve if his life had not been cut short so unexpectedly? Almost certainly he would have wanted to resume his war against the Shia Fatimid caliphate of Egypt to unite the eastern lands of Islam with north Africa once more.

*   *   *

Ali Tusi, Nizām al-Mulk, Order of the Realm, Grand Vizier, was now in sole charge of an empire. A deeply religious man, for him little happened in the world that did not somehow reflect the hidden will and wisdom of the Almighty. As a result, when the funeral of the sultan was over in Marv and the throngs of relatives beating their chests and wives pretending grief had been sent away, at his first moment truly alone with himself, he could not help wondering why. The inner voice of a lifetime's experience of the unexpected urged him not to assume much for long. But it was true. His writ now ran from Marv to Mecca, with the two great cities of Isfahan and Baghdad in-between. The crown prince was still a mere boy and the empire had no challengers. He, Ali, the boy from the provincial town of Tūs, would now, hopefully for years, make the most vital decisions of this great realm all on his own, as lonely as any crowned head had ever been since Jamshīd of the legends.

How did it all happen? Who could have guessed it? Hard work, a helping of good fortune and being in the right place at the right time explained some of it, as did the wisdom of the late sultan who admitted openly that the Turks were not yet ready for administration and diplomacy. Still, the bulk of it must have been 'meant'.

*   *   *

Unlike his sponsor Abu Tāhir, for whom the execution of his chief colleague by Shams al-Mulk was a deep humiliation and direct threat, Omar must have been delighted by the news of the assassination of Alp-Arslan and the calling off of the Saljuq offensive. The Qarakhanid kings were an older strain of Turk who were on the verge of being Persianised, while the Saljuqs were new converts to Islam and paraded themselves as the new champions of the faith by sponsoring the Abbasid caliph in Baghdad. They also imposed religious austerity on their subjects to legitimise further their monopoly of power and their right to wage war on their neighbours, particularly Christians and Shias, in search of greater gold and land and slaves. They, themselves, of course, indulged in every crime and corruption imaginable.

Omar could now hope for at least a few more years of his new idyllic life. He was successful beyond expectation in his adopted land, to the extent that he had become a personal friend of the king. If the status quo was not disturbed, his position could only improve.

But change was in the air, and this came in the form of Omar's decision to leave the circle around Abu Tāhir in Samarkand for the royal court in Bukhara. It is not clear whether the decision caused an open rift with his mentor, or indeed, some of his friends, too, but it could not have been a comfortable one for him to take. The memory of the execution of the chief imam[24] was still fresh in their mind and they had nurtured Omar since he arrived among them as a stranger three years earlier. Now he was abandoning them for the gold and hedonism of the court of the chief murderer. No contemporary source has survived to explain the exact circumstances, but we do know that

Abu Tāhir would later fall out with the king to the extent that he complained to the Saljuq emperor Malik Shah in Isfahan of Shams al-Mulk's outrages.[25] Perhaps at this time relations between Abu Tāhir and Shams al-Mulk were still cordial on the surface.

It would appear that Omar moved to Bukhara either in the autumn of 1072, during the attempted invasion, or else in the following spring, after the death of Alp-Arslan, possibly as a result of an offer from the king that Omar could not refuse. His fame as a mathematician had spread throughout Transoxania and Khorāsān, yet he worked, we think, as a mere accountant in the treasury in Samarkand, not a fulfilling position. What might have the king offered him?

No word has reached us that the Qarakhanids had an astronomical observatory at the time, but the presence of such an institution can be assumed for a fact. In an intensely superstitious age, when astronomy was little more than a technique in the service of astrology, the ruler took few major decisions without first 'consulting the stars' for an approving omen. Furthermore, Shams al-Mulk, though his writ did not reach into the eastern half of the Qarakhanid Empire, was clearly the more endowed of the two kings. He possessed the wealth of Bukhara and basked in the prestige of learned Samarkand, equal, in his own eyes, to any emperor from China to Byzantium. It would have been unthinkable for him not to have an observatory or not to lavish money on the most talented scientists and engineers of his time to increase the standing of his crown in the world.

The court's need to consult the stars daily would have meant an observatory nearby in the capital, Bukhara, and that was the logical place for the most promising mathematician of Omar's generation to go. The move would lead to an extraordinarily deep friendship.

*   *   *

Among the hundreds of thousands, possibly millions, of people who took a secret pleasure in the news of Alp-Arslan's painful death was the young princess whom the dead sultan had extracted from her father, the Armenian Bagrat IV of Georgia, as booty six years earlier. We can imagine the extent of her misery as the 'wife' of the mass murderer of her people, and a wife who had later been discarded by her master to be given to his chief manager and accomplice in the vile crimes, Ali Tūsi, the self-centred ass Nizām al-Mulk. This had meant a small improvement to her. She now had a little son, Ziā', who was the only source of solace in her life. She did not lack a single luxury that her heart might desire, except the only one that mattered: the freedom to leave her savage captors to join her own family, to be a free Christian woman among Christians once more. She was allowed to send innocuous letters to her family in the Caucasus and received visitors from them once every year or two, but these only compounded her misery. The visitors told her that, despite her father now being an official vassal of the sultan, the Turkomans roamed like vermin throughout the land. They had penetrated even the remotest of the valleys and everywhere gorged themselves on blood and rape and plunder. Whole regions had been depopulated, with the few survivors often dying of cold and hunger in the mountains while the Turkomans turned their fields and orchards into pasture for their sheep.

Here in Muslim Isfahan, she had no rights of which to speak. She was a mere woman. Her meetings were monitored by eunuchs and no male visitors were allowed inside the mansion. None outside the harem knew her name and, if they knew of her existence, they referred to her as 'the Armenian lady'. More often, she was described only as 'one of the veiled ones of the Lord Nizām al-Mulk'.[26]

It would probably have taken less than a month for her to hear – by military mail – of the death of the sultan and the passing of effective power in the empire to her husband. It would have taken much longer for her to learn that her father had also died around the same time, that same November 1072. He had been only fifty-four years old, but he had aged prematurely due to all the stress and tragedies of his reign. His last words to his mother, Queen Mariam, had been: 'I grieve for you, Mother. We, your children, have gone before you, and now death awaits you all alone.'[27]

Grandmother's life, too, had been a vale of tears. Her husband, Giorgi I, had died at the age of thirty-one, leaving young Mariam to rule as regent on behalf of her nine-year-old, Bagrat, and suppress immediate challenges from a number of barons. Then she had had to confront the predatory armies of the Byzantines – at one time taking Bagrat to Constantinople for three years as a virtual hostage – and fend off the even more menacing Turkoman bandits who seemed to be as numerous as locusts. The most harrowing of all her experiences had perhaps been to watch her beloved granddaughter being given to the cruellest beast of all, Alp-Arslan.

Now she was too weak to play the prominent part that she had always played in the state. Bagrat's widow, Queen Borena, a princess of the Ossetians, would have to step into the fray and the future seemed bleak. The new king, Giorgi II, was too hesitant a character to be the saviour that his people needed.

How much would the nameless princess have loved to know that her people would not always be the downtrodden ones. In a hundred years' time, one of her relatives, Tamara, a woman, would turn the table on the Turks and establish an empire from the Mediterranean to the Caspian. She would even raid, in retaliation, all the cities of northern Iran as far as Nishāpur province in the east. In the longer term, the Armenians and the Georgians would even survive into the twenty-firstt century as sovereign nations, still Christian and still retaining their ancestral tongues.

CHAPTER THREE

The Throne of Bukhara

To drink, to laugh, is my religion.
Freedom from religion is my religion!
I asked Heaven about hers. She said:
Why, your irreligion is my religion!

Whether or not Omar had already moved to Bukhara when, at the
end of November 1072, news arrived that Alp-Arslan had been killed
a few days earlier and the invasion cancelled, we can be confident
that he would have joined in the general revelry. His friends and
patrons in the Qarakhanid government had escaped being
overthrown and who could say what would have happened to him if
those ferocious Turkomans had poured in to loot and to kill? Even if
the Qarakhanid army had succeeded in fending off the enemy, at the
very least a long siege and possible famine would have crippled both
cities.

As we saw in the last chapter, Omar had recently said in a book
preface that, thanks to the patronage of the governor and chief
judge of Samarkand, he had 'climbed the heights' there. That was
true. He had achieved unusual success through mathematics – and,
more importantly for a young man, he now enjoyed the company of
the great and the good – for which he had yearned. He felt
exhilarated by the fame that the publication of his treatise on
algebra was winning him throughout the region, even in distant
Isfahan and Baghdad, and the king's admiration for him had turned
into a personal friendship, or at least so he felt. If the kingdom
survived in its present shape, and if the Saljuqs did not mount
another offensive soon, fortune would continue to smile on him. On

the other hand, it was said that closeness to kings was best avoided. As easily as they chose you to be their favourite companion, they tired of you and dropped you. A passing anger on their part might even cost you your life. It was best to place some distance between yourself and the royal drinking chamber, to let the crown need you more than you needed it.

Omar was, in all probability, recruited to join the court observatory at Bukhara to study the stars, to predict what every new day might hold in store for the king, and to declare on what dates the most critical affairs of the state might best be conducted. As this is likely to have been a part-time job – and we shall see later that he did not believe in astrology – extra work as a part-time doctor of medicine or teacher of mathematics or music would have been essential.

Omar was, however, unable to follow the hard-earned advice of sages. Had he wanted to, his new fame as a man with a rare intellect, together with his charm and wit, would have made him quite wealthy as a physician and teacher of mathematics and music. But he was evidently a risk-taker, a seeker after excitement, a young man who filled his cup to the brim and damned the consequences. It is at this time in 1073 that he emerges in history for the first time as a close companion of Shams al-Mulk. A brief portrait drawn of him several decades later by his mini-biographer, Ibn Funduq, says that the king admired Omar to such an extent that he 'sat him on the throne beside himself'.

The 'throne' here cannot have been the royal throne from which Shams al-Mulk presided over the ceremonies of state. It must have been a raised platform on which he sat with close relatives, friends and ministers at dinner or during drinking sessions and theatrical performances. Even so, it reveals how high Omar's star had risen in the short few years after his arrival in Transoxania as a student in search of a future. Now he drank with a king and mingled with princes and viziers. These, in all likelihood, included the king's young daughter Terken Khātūn,[1] who was betrothed to the seventeen-year-old new Saljuq sultan, Malik Shah. Omar must at times have asked himself whether he was dreaming.

* * *

It was essential for Nizām now to rush back to central Iran. It was there that any challenge to the succession would be mounted and he was certain that it would be. He even knew the culprit. And so, whereas at the beginning of the month, it had taken the late sultan three weeks to take the army and its huge baggage train over the Oxus River alone, Nizām ordered the commanders to leave as much of the baggage and fodder behind as they could and recross the river at speed, in only three days if possible. There were other delays ahead, the biggest of them being the need to bury the sultan's body with full ceremony in the large new mausoleum he had built for himself in Marv. Then there would be at least another four weeks before Nizām could reach Nishāpur. Fortunately, the deepest frosts of winter had not yet set in.

As he watched the turmoil caused by 100,000 cavalrymen crossing a bridge of boats, he could surely not have helped being plunged once more into a reflective mood over the events of his life. Not in his wildest dreams as an obnoxiously ambitious young man had he ever imagined that he would one day be the effective ruler of a state, let alone an empire that stretched from the Oxus to the Euphrates, from Armenia to Oman. With the ousting of the Ghaznavids from Khorāsān by the Saljuqs, he and his father had become refugees for a time until someone had introduced him to the late, ailing Prince Chaghri. God had then smiled upon him again. The prince had recognised his abilities and recommended him to his son Alp-Arslan who had, in turn, promoted him rapidly through the administration of Khorāsān until, as his vizier, he was in daily charge of all civilian affairs while Alp-Arslan himself concentrated on the army. Afterwards, unexpectedly, Alp-Arslan had succeeded to the sultanate following the death of Toghril and, now he too, was dead, at the age of only forty-three, leaving Nizām in supreme charge, even of the imperial family.

In fact, he was now, at the age of fifty-four, a fully-fledged member of that family. As we have already seen, Alp-Arslan divorced one of his most prestigious wives, an Armenian princess, so that Hasan could marry her. It was true that the princess had been unhappy in the harem and had wanted a divorce, but what of that? She had no rights.

Nizām had already sent express messengers to the princes and governors all over the empire telling them that the crown prince had fortunately been on hand to take his oath of office immediately, to remind them that the succession was not in doubt. Six years earlier, he had himself persuaded the sultan to get all the possible rivals together to swear allegiance to Malik Shah as crown prince. In the same vein, he had got the sultan to allocate which of the other princes would succeed to which vice-royalties. Nevertheless, the sultan's assassination had changed everything. Malik Shah was only a boy and not every prince would accept him as the new master, specially that old associate of his own, that brave lion and hardened fox of the desert of Kerman: Prince Qavurt.

* * *

A hardened old fox as he was himself, and knowing Shams al-Mulk's bold nature all too well, Grand Vizier Nizām was not surprised when he heard news of an attack a few days after reaching Nishāpur on Friday, 29 December. As soon as he had seen the back of the Saljuq army, the Qarakhanid king had gathered up his forces from their defensive positions in Bukhara and Samarkand, crossed the Oxus and attacked Khorāsān. There followed daily reports of setbacks suffered by the Saljuqs. By the end of January, Shams al-Mulk had captured Termez and expelled the boy prince Ayāz from that other major city, Balkh.

It was painful news but the remedy had to wait. The setbacks in Khorāsān were now being eclipsed by the darker cloud arising within the empire itself which he had feared for some time. Prince Qavurt, the late sultan's elder brother, the virtually independent viceroy of Kerman in the south-east, was sending emissaries out to inform everyone that he would not tolerate the raising of a mere boy to the throne, in contravention of the old Turkish practice of succession by the most senior, competent male in the family. Even under Alp-Arslan, he had rebelled twice and submitted only to his younger brother when a great army under the sultan himself had appeared on the horizon. Long ago, commissioned by his uncle, the sultan Toghril, Qavurt had conquered the south-east, pushed eastwards in the direction of India and even captured Oman across the sea in Arabia from the Persian Būyids there. Now he was the clear scion of the

Saljuqs and his invocation of Turkish tradition, as opposed to the Persian practice of succession by the eldest son, was being applauded by many a Turkoman chief. Furthermore, as everyone knew, Alp-Arslan had willed on his deathbed that one of his senior wives marry Qavurt. Whereas this had been largely meant to mollify his elder brother, it had a powerful, symbolic force in many eyes.

A strong personal thread connected Nizām to Qavurt. The first time they met, three decades ago, Qavurt looked down upon Nizām from on high. The prince was the eldest son of Nizām's employer, the late Prince Dāwūd Chaghri Beg in Khorāsān, while Nizām was a mere scribe in the office. While Nizām had to spend many hours a day out of sight, pouring over letters and accounts, Qavurt made waves everywhere he went, accompanied by scores of horsemen as his bodyguard. Later, on conquest far away in the south-east and therefore out of his father's mind, Chaghri had given Khorāsān to his second eldest son to run, and the second eldest had eventually picked Nizām to be his vizier.

With such a history, then, Qavurt must have often reflected on the irony of a formerly humble servant of his own household having now become the most powerful man in the empire and, more importantly here, the main obstacle in his path to claim his rightful inheritance.

Apart from this clash of the two men's futures, did they also have a past score to settle? Was there, for example, a personal humiliation still festering in the former servant's bosom after all these years? We do not know. The original sources remain silent on the point. But we can be certain that Qavurt had good grounds for hating Nizām. Much of the wealth, and the diplomatic – and to a large extent – even the military success of Alp-Arslan had been due to this man's genius for administration, as well as his seemingly endless energy. For example, realising that the traditional backbone of the Saljuqs, the Turkoman tribesmen, were fickle in their moods, more attached to plunder than to principle, he had founded a professional standing army based on the Persian model, with a solid nucleus of permanent officers receiving generous salaries and regular training. Furthermore, that army now included other nationalities, such as Armenians, Greeks, Arabs and Slavs. Nizām specially valued Dailamis from the southern shores of the Caspian, Khorāsānians, Georgians and Kurds. The historian Rāvandi tells us that he would not allow the number of cavalrymen in the permanent army to fall below 46,000. Otherwise, long ago, Qavurt would have probably succeeded in grabbing the crown from his younger brother.

But Qavurt was popular among the non-Turkish bulk of the population. He had married several of his daughters to members of the Persian aristocracy in Kerman, built caravanserais and baths, installed markers alongside roads in deserts and even erected beacons to guide travellers in the dark. Beside whole sections of Turks in the army, several large Persian cities might well go over to him.

*   *   *

The struggle would prove one of the hardest in Nizām's long and eventful life. Many Turkoman chieftains did, indeed, go over to the senior Saljuq, and the man himself showed once again why he was a legend as a military commander. With seven sons in the field beside him, he swept into several garrison towns and almost sealed victory by marching into the capital. He bombarded Nizām with messages urging him not to endanger the lives of thousands of innocent people in a doomed attempt to save his ministry which would, in any case, be safe if he regained his sanity.

To his young nephew Malik Shah, he wrote: 'I am the eldest brother and you are a young son. I have the greater right to my brother's inheritance.' Nizām composed an equally firm reply on behalf of Malik Shah: 'A brother does not inherit when there is a son and designated crown prince.'[2]

On Nizām's side, finding new allies and making certain that the main treasury in Isfahan did not fall into Qavurt's hands were priorities. On a bright spring day in April in the south-western city of Hamadan[3], the two mighty armies clashed in one of the fiercest battles Nizām had ever witnessed.

After three days and three nights of hard fighting, God smiled on Nizām again. His new allies, Kurds from nearby Kurdistan and Arabs from distant Hilla in Mesopotamia, stood firm and, on the third day, turned the tide against the enemy. At one point, when Nizām's remaining Turkish contingents saw that the Kurds and Arabs had put

Qavurt's right flank to flight, they turned against their own side and plundered the baggage of the Kurds and the Arabs. It was too late.

At last Nizām's old acquaintance and adversary, ashen-faced, white-haired, utterly broken, was brought to him bound in chains. Malik Shah wanted his uncle pardoned. Nizām gave no quarter. Qavurt pleaded. If he were allowed to retire across the sea to Oman, he would be content for the remainder of his life. Nizām told Malik Shah his uncle had made too many such promises in the past to the late sultan only to break them as soon as he could. Qavurt was strangled that night with a bowstring, so that royal blood might not be shed.[4]

A few days later, the young shah's trauma had abated enough for him to see what a blessing his chancellor was to him, not only through his insights into the human soul, but also through his endless energy that put the young to shame. Over the past few months, Nizām had hardly slept and paid little attention to any matter other than preparing for the battle ahead. He ordered that all the land and revenue of the district of Tūs in Khorāsān be given in perpetuity to the chancellor. Tūs was one of the richest regions of Khorāsān, next only to Nishāpur which had been designated by the late sultan for Malik Shah's own office as crown prince. Furthermore, Tūs was emotionally important to Nizām. It was the land of his birth, and that of his ancestors. Malik Shah also commanded that the grandest of all possible titles in the Saljuq family be bestowed on Nizām, one that had never before been granted any man not related by blood to them. Henceforth, all courtiers and all countries would address the Grand Vizier as 'Ata Beg', Father Commander. Soon afterwards, the sultan himself would begin to address the old man simply as 'Father'.

*   *   *

It was not lost on observers, least of all on Nizām, that Shams al-Mulk had not gone for Marv, the nearest Saljuq-held city in Khorāsān, but for the two cities to the east of it, Termez and Balkh. Perhaps he thought that Marv was riddled with too much symbolism for the Saljuqs. Alp-Arslan had just been buried there, in a sumptuous mausoleum he had spent years and a great fortune to build. If he captured it, it might appear as if he were literally walking over the grave of his enemy – and former brother-in-law – when the corpse was still fresh.

We do not know. Few historical accounts of Qarakhanid affairs have come down to us. Other considerations may well have weighed on Shams al-Mulk's mind. Marv might have, for example, been better defended, or he might have expected it to fall to him once the other two cities had submitted. Perhaps he had information from within the city that it would rebel against Saljuq rule shortly. We know that two years earlier, Nizām had ordered the construction of a new wall to strengthen its defences, but that would take at least ten years to complete.

Shams al-Mulk was, by temperament, almost as restless and nomadic as any other Turkish ruler, including the Saljuqs. This was despite his Qarakhanid family having become established as a royal house for a far longer period. They had first come to prominence in Turkestan in western China in the 800s and had captured Bukhara from the Iranian Samanids in 999. They had long been subject to Chinese artistic influences and, more recently, to Persian, the very first book in Turkish having been written during the reign of Shams al-Mulk himself, though in Turkestan under his eastern cousins. As such, therefore, the family had softened their sharp desert edges some time ago. But the Turkoman tribesmen who made up the military backbone of their state were a constant headache of indiscipline, not to say rebellion, and Shams al-Mulk spent only the winters in the capital. Even when the military did not appear on the verge of rebellion, the king had to endear himself to them by visits to their tents in the steppe bearing gifts, or else hosting huge feasts for their chiefs in Samarkand and other cities.

The Qarakhanids were remarkable for their love of ceremony. The king was always preceded by a column of slaves bearing gold maces and followed by a courtier bearing a giant red parasol to mark the king's presence and shade his head.[6]

By the time of Shams al-Mulk, the initial genuine piety of the first Qarakhanids who, for example, abstained from alcohol, had given place to the indulgence of fine wines and the company of poets. Though no specific information has reached us to prove the point, Shams al-Mulk's earlier execution of the chief imam of Samarkand –

a bore of a fanatic – may owe itself to the king's open refusal to pray and fast. In other respects, the king has come down to us as a just and hard-working sovereign. At his own expense, he built several grand caravansaries for the comfort of travellers, many bath houses in cities and a cathedral mosque in Bukhara. No contemporary writer accuses him of levying heavy taxes on the populace.[7]

In this, he seems to have been similar to his father, Ebrāhūm, who became a hermit in the latter part of his life and abdicated in favour of Shams al-Mulk as his own father had done before him. Ebrāhūm is on record for his harsh persecution of thieves and his enforcement of fair prices in shops.

In one instance, a group of thieves in Samarkand wrote on the gate of the castle: 'We are like an onion. The more you cut us down, the more vigorously do we grow.' The king ordered to be written under the graffiti: 'And I am like a gardener. However vigorously you grow, I shall uproot you.' The threat did not work and the king had to adopt another strategy. He announced that he had learned from his mistakes and come to the conclusion that, in fact, he needed such proven 'men of action' to enforce the law for him. So he recruited the chief robber with four of his sons for the purpose, giving them big salaries and honouring them with colourful robes. He then commissioned them to recruit 300 others of their kind. When these turned up to be robed at the palace, he arrested and executed them all. 'Afterwards, not a dirham was stolen from the population in Samarkand,' claimed one historian.

*   *   *

When he left glittering Samarkand to start the next stage of his career in fabled Bukhara, Omar would have had to be among the most ignorant of his people not to have known by heart at least a dozen poems by Rūdaki, the most celebrated poet of the golden age of Bukhara under the Samanids a century and a half earlier. Furthermore, we may say with some confidence that the favourite among Omar's dozen poems of Rūdaki was 'I smell the scent of Mūliān Waters' in praise of Bukhara. Down the ages that poem, which once so excited a crowned head that he mounted his horse without his shoes to return to his capital, has been, and is still, daily recited by countless schoolchildren as a supreme example of the fluency of which any would-be bard might dream. Despite the passage of a thousand years, 'Mūliān' has acquired few rivals in the Persian tongue.

The following is my abridged translation of the story of the poem as relayed to us by Khayyām's future secretary, Nizāmi the Prosodist, in his *Four Discourses*:[8]

They say that in the time of King Nassr, son of Ahmad, who was the best of the Samanids, with prosperity ascendant, the treasury full, the army awesome and the nation obedient, the king spent winters in Bukhara and the summers in Samarkand or some other city in Khorāsān. One year it was Herat's turn and the entourage arrived in the region there in the spring, in a valley that is most green, with over a thousand streams, each enough for an army. There they rested and fed their mounts until these regained their weight and became fit again for battle and polo. Nassr then moved on to Herat and just outside it, at White Bird, set up his encampment. It was late in the spring now and the cool north wind blew and the fruits of Mālon and Karūkh started arriving. Few other regions produce such fruits, or if they do, not so cheaply.

And so the army rested there for the summer, too, for the air was good and the wind pleasant and the food various and the fruits many. Then arrived the festival of Mehrgān and the juice ripened[9] and the basil and the pyrethrum and others followed, one after another, and all took full advantage of the blessings of their youth.

That year, the autumn lasted and the cold did not gather strength until all the grapes had ripened, all 120 varieties of them, each more delicate and delicious than the other, thin-skinned, small-pipped, full of juice, some as black as tar while as sweet as sugar.

As the king sampled the autumn and its blessings and liked it very much, he moved the army to two villages by the names of Qūra and Darvāz and saw there houses as one might imagine in paradise, each with a garden and an orchard facing the [coo] north wind. He chose them for the winter and they brought him oranges from Sistan and grapefruits from Māzandarān. They passed the winter in great happiness, until spring arrived again and they took the horses to pasture. When summer arrived, with its fruits, the king said: 'Why should we leave? There's no place more pleasing? We'll leave in the autumn.' And when autumn came, he said: 'Let's enjoy Herat's autumn first.'

In this way he prevaricated for four years, season after season, for he could do what he wished. It was the height of the glory of the Samanids and the world was prosperous, the kingdom without enemies, the army obedient, luck agreeable. But the courtiers were miserable by now. While they wanted their families, their king had the fancy of Herat in his head and its love in his heart, wanting to spend that summer there, too.

It was then that the commanders of the army and the grand men of the state went before Master Rūdaki, for among the companions of the king there was none more dear to him and none more influential over him. They said: 'Master, we will present to you five thousand dinārs if you devise a trick to persuade the king to leave this land, for our hearts ache for our children and our souls long for Bukhara.' Rūdaki accepted, for he felt the king's pulse and knew his mind. He knew that prose would not soften him, only verse had any hope of doing so. He wrote a poem and waited one morning after breakfast. He picked up the harp and began to sing it:

> I smell the scent of Mūliān Waters,[10]
> I see the faces of beloved friends.
> Pebbles of Āmūy, roughness of the roads,
> Feel as soft as silk under my bare feet.
> Oxus's water rises joyously
> To carry my horse to its other shore.
> Bukhara city! Prosper, be happy!
> For the king returns, is pleased with thee.
> The king is the moon, Bukhara the sky,
> The moon is full now, and it rises high.

By the time Rūdaki reached this line, the king was so overcome that he could wait no longer. He left the throne and, without his shoes, mounted the duty horse and turned towards Bukhara. It took two farsangs for them to catch up with him to give him his shoes and riding trousers.[11]

Nizāmi adds that when the royal party reached Samarkand on its way to Bukhara, they counted the camels carrying Rūdaki's personal belongings and the number passed 400. Poetic license, we may be certain, no doubt encouraged by Rūdaki himself, for he was a self-aggrandising court jester, as well as a great poet, but it does serve Nizāmi's purpose in recalling the Samanids' patronising of Persian letters.

Other of Rūdaki's poems that Khayyām might have memorised and recited to himself on this journey are, by contrast, plaintive, particularly on the disaster of extreme old age and the loss of children. Another describes, exquisitely, the art of the winemaker. Here is a quatrain that is as defiant of the writ of the imam as any that Omar himself would write later:

> What good can there be going to the mosque?
> I love Bukhara, a girl from Tarāz![12]
> Our God[13] prefers whispering lovers
> To austere men prostrate in prayer.

That the ghosts of such great men as Rūdaki and Avicenna haunted Bukhara's public places for Omar, we can be in no doubt. But, above all, for him, the city was the former capital of the Samanids and, as such, the place that had given new birth to a pride in old Iran before it had fallen to the Arabs and Turks. It was the city where, through the Samanids' patronage of all things Iranian, obscure manuscripts in Pahlavi or Middle Persian had been acquired from Zoroastrian priests or impoverished former noblemen. They were then translated into the new vulgar tongue of the street to give 'New Persian' a prestige and a currency that the Arabs and their agents, the Muslim priesthood, had spent several centuries to wipe out. It was true that Firdowsi, the epic poet of the Shāh-Nāmeh, had claimed only half a century ago that he had 'revived old Iran with this Persian'. But who had produced Firdowsi himself, and the market for his verse? It had been here in Bukhara decades before him that lyric poets such as Rūdaki had been inundated with riches to inspire them to write more, and it had been here that the epic poet Daqiqi, a proud Zoroastrian, had been commissioned to make the first major attempt to render the fading memories of Iranian glory into the new language.

In this light, one of the first acts of pilgrimage for Omar in his new city would have been to visit the mausoleum of the Samanid kings, an exquisite building built before 943 that has, against all odds, survived arsonists, Mongols and Tartars to reach our time.[14] Experts describe it as 'a fire temple in Islamic dress', for it has the typical structure of a Zoroastrian hall of worship.[15] Should it be the reader's good fortune to visit Bukhara, he can emulate the steps of a 25-year-old young man who, long ago, approached that same doorway with reverence in his heart and, probably, tears in his eyes.

But Bukhara had many other pleasant surprises for Omar. The city had not declined physically in any manner from its peak of glory under the Samanids a hundred years earlier, but had, in fact, expanded and acquired new monuments, parks and palaces, the most glittering of which were in the district of Mūliān Waters, as we have seen. While the king's personal office, the treasury and the jailhouse remained inside the heavily fortified Kohan Dezh or Old Castle, it was in Mūliān that the royal family, the aristocracy and top statesmen had their palaces, mansions and rose gardens. As a friend of the king and as one of his most valued 'astrologers', Omar is almost certain to have been given a substantial house in this district, with its own stables and servants' apartments.

Here is one description of Mūliān that has survived to our time:

> Better than the heavenly district of Mūliān Waters there was none in the city. Everywhere there were mansions, rose gardens, parks, orchards, and clear streams and rivers to irrigate them rushing on in a thousand directions towards the fields, and anyone who looked at them wondered where they came from and where they went. One also wondered at the art of the architects and planners.[16]

Another writer, the Arab merchant Ibn Hawqal, has left us a general view of Bukhara:

> A more pleasant-looking and a more ornamented city I have never seen anywhere in the Muslim lands. As you climb the castle, the whole of the world is green as far as the eye can see, with the sky acting as a blue cover on top. In the midst of the green are numerous mansions, each one like a Tibetan shield or a shining star. Even in Transoxania itself there is no city whose buildings and gardens and parks and wide squares can compare with Bukhara's.

It would appear from the records that many of the poorer town houses were made of wood and this caused many fires. The poorer inhabitants' unremarkable health may also be guessed, for almost the only source of drinking water in the city was the Soghd River which came all the way from Samarkand. The river was diverted and divided, as we have seen, into numerous canals and streams to enable the populace to irrigate their gardens and parks.

Failing to be housed in Mūliān Waters, Omar might have been given another house in another district where the well-to-do also lived. This was called Magi Mansions, for it had originally been built by the Zoroastrian aristocracy of the city after their expulsion by the invading Muslims some 400 years earlier. The Zoroastrians had been expelled again later and now land was so expensive in Magi Mansions that even the new aristocracy complained.

* * *

The summer of 1073 approached and the afternoon heat began to tax young and old alike. But you did not have to leave Bukhara for the cooler hills overlooking Samarkand, as did the king in normal years. Almost invariably, the kind of house in which Khayyām would have lived, in either of the two wealthy districts of Mūliān Waters and Magi Mansions, had freshwater ponds with fountains in basement rooms to make summers more than tolerable. Grapes and cucumbers, cherries, apricots, greengages and peaches were chilled in the pool and so were jugs of wine and herbal infusions, plus, of course, that refreshing mainstay of the whole year, māst-ow, soured yogurt water, also known as dūq, the drink that characterises the region still.

This was the slow time of year. Time to read, to whisper, to doze and to dream. But, unfortunately, recently it had also become a time of suddenly starting out of your dreams with a cold sweat on the brow. The Saljuqs had now quelled the challenge of their sultan's uncle to his throne and were rumoured to be preparing to resume the aborted offensive of last autumn. The king gave every sign that he would resist the invaders as determinedly as he had last time but many people were secretly pessimistic about his chances. A deep animosity separated the two royal houses since the death of Queen Āisha, the sultan Alp-Arslan's sister, whose death the Saljuqs blamed on her husband. They said that Shams al-Mulk had poisoned her when he discovered she had been spying for her brother in Isfahan. Whatever the true reason for the Saljuqs' warmongering, this coming autumn would probably find the peoples of Samarkand and Bukhara under a cruel siege.

* * *

Back in April and immediately after the quelling of Prince Qavurt and his Turkomans in Hamadan, chancellor Nizām fixed his gaze on the unfinished business of Khorāsān and Transoxania. Balkh had already been recaptured from Shams al-Mulk, but Termez remained in his hands. Now he had to be punished in his own strongholds of Bukhara and Samarkand. Thus bribes and promises of support were sent to the king's cousins, the Eastern Qarakhanids in distant Turkestan, to resume their quarrels with him over their disputed borders, and secret emissaries were sent to the Sunni clergy in Samarkand and Bukhara to reassure them that the champion of the holy Shari'a law, the Saljuq sultan, would soon be on his way with the mightiest army in the world to release them from the restrictions placed on them by Shams al-Mulk.[17]

The problem for the Saljuqs was that at least two months of new recruitment and recuperation were needed before the army could leave Isfahan for the north-east. Then there would be the long journey itself of at least a month, probably two, before the walls of Termez came into sight. How long it would take to recapture the city was a matter of conjecture, though the intelligence looked promising. If it surrendered quickly, the army would have to remain there for the duration of the summer heat in July and August before tackling the sand dunes of the Karakum could be contemplated. Further delay would then arise from the difficulty of crossing the Oxus with a great army. Last autumn, it had taken the late sultan twenty days to build a bridge of boats sturdy enough for the horses and the baggage.

Ibn al-Athīr, the Arab historian whose *Annals of the Saljuq Turks* remains our main listing of events for these decades, is unusually vague about the date of this second Saljuq invasion of Transoxania. We therefore have to carry out some calculations of our own and these lead us to believe that the army reached the outskirts of Samarkand towards the end of September 1073. By then, the invasion of Shams al-Mulk's north-eastern territories by his Qarakhanid cousins had produced the result that Nizām wanted. Shams sued for peace and Nizām, pretending to mediate between the two sovereigns, his own and the Qarakhanid, dictated the terms of surrender.

To most people's relief, Nizām treated Shams al-Mulk well and, most importantly, he did not allow the normal systematic looting of the cities by his troops. After all, the two royal houses were related. Back in 1065,[18] Shams al-Mulk had married Malik Shah's aunt, the late Princess Āisha, and Shams al-Mulk's small daughter Terken Khātūn had been betrothed to the ten-year-old Malik Shah, then crown prince. Now here was a good opportunity to organise a sumptuous wedding for the benefit of the populace while the practical business of subduing the kingdom to the will of Isfahan proceeded in the background.

Nizām allowed Shams al-Mulk to remain the official ruler of the kingdom, but his coins would henceforth mention his name after that of Malik Shah and prayers would be recited in mosques every Friday for the health of the Saljuq sultan. The treasury would be largely taken over by the sultan's men as reparation, all ministries would have officials from Isfahan as deputies to monitor decisions and the Saljuqs could pick any poet, artist and scientist they wanted for the purpose of taking them to the capital to adorn the imperial court there.

* * *

Nizām could not remain in distant Transoxania for long, but he could not leave immediately either. First there was the business of making certain that Shams al-Mulk would not remain in charge of enough forces to enable him to invade Khorāsān once more. Then there was the task of finding the trusted agents who would supervise the various government departments, particularly the treasury, to ensure the smooth flow of revenue and information to the capital. Lastly, if there was time still, he would like to try in person to persuade the best of the poets, artists and scientists at the Qarakhanid court to move to Isfahan.

One of these turned out to be Omar, though we do not know whether he was at the top of the list prepared for Nizām by his advisors. We can only be reasonably confident that, given the idyllic life he had attained as one of the closest companions of the king in Bukhara, Omar would have not volunteered to leave for an unknown future under the Saljuqs who were, in any case, humourless new converts to Islam.

There is not the slightest historical evidence that the great chancellor and young Omar met for the first time in Bukhara, but

we know that Nizām tried, whenever he could, to enlist fellow
Khorāsānians, particularly the graduates of the schools of Nishāpur
– where he himself had been educated – for the highest posts in the
Saljuq administration. It can, therefore, not be ruled out that a
semblance of the following, totally speculative conversation took
place.

On his part, young Omar would have probably feared being called
to the presence of the man, the mere mention of whose name made
mighty kings tremble. A man of letters he might be, but Nizām al-
Mulk was also responsible for the execution of Sultan Toghril's great
chancellor, Kondori, the slaying of Toghril's brother Qutlomush and,
of course, the death of the most awesome of them all, the Prince
Qavurt, King of Kerman and Oman, earlier this same year:

Ah, Master Omar Khayyāmi?
(Omar can hardly speak and only manages to whisper his reply).
Your obedient servant, Sir.
*Please sit down. I met your late father once, all too briefly, though. Were you
there? I hear you're now a philosopher and a friend of royals. Amazing.*
(Omar tries to smile).
*Don't worry, don't worry, I won't hold it against you! I would have done the
same. These quarrels between kings are not serious. Especially these kings. One
moment they're fighting one another and the next they're jumping into bed with
each other's sisters!*
*(Omar's face breaks into a grin. Grand Vizier laughs, too. Then he looks down
at a piece of paper he's holding).*
I've brought you here because I have a proposition for you.
Your obedient servant, Sir.
*We're expanding the observatory in Isfahan and I need you there. We'll pay
you good money and you'll work on making the place the biggest in the world.
You'll work alongside the brightest men alive. You'll also work on the Persian
calendar. It's a mess. I want the New Year back at the beginning of spring. What
do you say to that?*
Your obedient servant, Sir.
Does that mean yes, or no?
Your obedient servant, Sir.
Yes or no?
Yes, Sir. . . . Do I have time to think about it?. . . Sir?
Why do you want to think about it? What is there to think about?
Well, Sir . . .

*I'll be leaving soon. Tell my men in a day or two. As I said, we'll give you
good money and I'll see to it that you get a good house near the palace. You know,
we Khorāsānians ought to stick to one another. I hear you studied under old
Bahmanyār, God have mercy on his soul. He taught me, too, didn't you know?*

He told me, Sir.

You may leave. I should be jumping in the air, if I were you.

Yes, Sir. (He bows slightly and begins to leave, walking backwards.)

*Are you reading Beihaqi's memoirs? He's just brought out his twenty-fifth
book.*

I read them at court, Sir.

Ah, good. What other languages do you have, beside Persian and Arabic?

I've got Pahlavi, Sir, of course, and some Greek.

*That's good, that's good. You'll need both of those. See you in Isfahan, then,
and be there soon, perhaps with the Khātūn's party.*

(Grand Vizier turns to one of his secretaries.)

Write his name down for the observatory.

* * *

The presence of Saljuq soldiers on the streets had sharply reduced the
socialising of the long evenings and people sought safety in numbers
behind locked doors. It was true, as a result of the peaceful surrender,
that there had not been widespread looting, but trespasses had still
occurred and the humiliation of the king, the harsh terms of the peace
dictated by Nizām al-Mulk and the confiscation of the treasury were
especially painful.

As for Omar, there seemed to be no alternative to bowing his head
before the inevitable. Exactly sixty-six years earlier in this same city,
the great Avicenna had decided to flee rather than risk being taken to
distant, dour Ghazna in the east by Sultan Mahmūd. But Avicenna
had somewhere better, more enlightened, to which to flee, the city of
Rayy, which was at that time under the Persian Būyids. Now all the
south was equally under the heel of the Saljuqs.

On the other hand, the chancellor was said to be tolerant of the
weaknesses of his fellow Khorāsānians and the large salary and other
incentives he had offered Omar suggested that he genuinely held him
in great regard. Perhaps if he did go to Isfahan, but kept discreet
counsel and concentrated on his work, he would fare well, despite the

harsh religious regime. In addition, he would surely be able to visit Nishāpur and even Bukhara every year or so, to do research and recruit colleagues. To work on expanding the Isfahan observatory to make it fit for the capital of the new empire excited him.

We do not know, but Nizām probably returned to the capital with the bulk of the army that winter despite the snows of Transoxania and the mud of Khorāsān and Rayy. The playboy sultan probably remained in the two fabled cities to exhaust their delights and indulge in their royal hunting preserves, as well as familiarising himself with his new relatives. On the other hand, it is possible that even the chancellor decided to rest for a while and spend the winter in Bukhara. The reputation of the Saljuq army was such now that no force, from within or without the empire, dared to cause its iron Grand Vizier to raise his eyebrows.

*   *   *

Hundreds of miles away to the south-west, in the illustrious city of Rayy, another young man was finding himself bound for Isfahan. We last caught up with Hasan Sabbāh there when he was a traumatised youth of seventeen having recently recovered from a prolonged fever. At the height of the illness, he had heard voices in the sky warning him not to die in a false faith, the Twelver Shi'ism of his parents. Just before the illness, he had been befriended by a stranger, who seemed to be a Yemeni immigrant like his own father, and the man had spoken to him of the beliefs of the Ismaili Shi'ites, the official creed of the caliph of Egypt. He had subsequently vowed to himself that, if he survived, he would devote his life to the spreading of the True Faith, available only to special souls, Allah's chosen. Later, he had been visited by a string of other Ismailis whose confidence he had won. One of them had even taken an oath of allegiance from him to the imam in Cairo.

Despite strenuous efforts, Hasan's secret was now endangering his life. His closest relatives had suspected the worst from the beginning. His father had groomed him from earliest childhood as a future Twelver cleric and spent a fortune on his education. Now he was seen too often in the company of secretive strangers who had foreign accents and seemed to have no visible means of support, certainly no jobs in Rayy. Furthermore, there were government spies everywhere, even among the Twelver Shi'ites. They worked for the fanatical Sunni state which looked upon all Shi'ites as heretics, let alone anyone beholden to the enemy state of Egypt. As a result, Hasan was forced frequently to deny his convictions. The practice was widespread among both wings of Shi'ism. It was called Taqiyah, dissimulation, denying your faith if it helped to safeguard the survival of it. The believer was even allowed to curse his faith in public.

But Hasan had never been happier. He had become one of the top Ismaili activists in the region with money to spend on his mission, and he had acquired true and upright men for friends who knew they had at last found the true path to eternal bliss. They were purposeful and joyful. They would travel, possibly even to Egypt, to see the ancient pyramids of the pharaohs, and there mingle freely without fear with the mass of the people who were all fellow Ismailis.

But Hasan knew something that even his closest colleagues did not. He had already been chosen to go to Egypt, and was even to be allowed into an exclusive audience with the caliph, Allah's Deputy on Earth, directly descended from the seed of Muhammad, Peace Be Upon Him. He, Hasan, would be allowed, as few men were, to see His Holiness's luminous face, to hear his life-giving voice, to be blessed by the Hand of Allah.

This was because, last year, 1072, in the spring, the chief Ismaili missionary in Iran had visited him in Rayy to tell him that he had chosen him to go to Cairo to be his representative there. Abdul Malik Attāsh, who lived secretly somewhere in a castle near Isfahan, had high hopes for the spreading of the faith in this great, but Sunni-blighted, land, from the mountains of Kurdistan in the west to the great rivers of Transoxania in the north-east, and Hasan had been chosen to be central to realising the dream. But he must first go to Isfahan.

Hasan thus knew that his destiny was to carry a heavy burden and witness great events. Even so, if someone had told him that he would one day be in charge of a string of castles from Transoxania to Syria which even the Saljuq sultans could not sack, he would have laughed. As for going down in history as the founder of 'the state of the Assassins', he would not have recognised the description at all.

CHAPTER FOUR

The Palaces of Isfahan

Girl of the light foot, rise up to the day,
Bring out the lute, a dance tune play.
It hates happiness, this Relentless Wheel,
This old parade of Dey succeedin Dey.[1]

'At the bride's entry into Nishāpur, a thousand male and a thousand female slaves preceded the palanquin (shaded litter) of the beautiful Samarkand princess, each carrying some costly present and scattering in her path musk, ambergris and aloes.'[2]

This is a description of Princess Terken's 'wedding' procession alongside her husband into Nishāpur. But it took place eight years before her real wedding to the Saljuq sultan. It describes the celebrations of 1065, when Malik Shah was only crown prince and only ten years old, the bride even younger. In that year, the two children were 'wed' – 'betrothed' is a better term – as part of a number of dynastic marriages between the two royal houses of the Saljuqs in Isfahan and the Qarakhanids in Bukhara. On account of the children's delicate ages, the symbolic union merely advertised the new alliance – and wealth – of their fathers to their enemies. Nor was little Terken handed over to her husband's relatives to be brought up by them in distant Isfahan. After a visit to Isfahan, she would have returned home until she came of age. But in the following years, as we have seen, relations between the two dynasties deteriorated until war broke out between them in the autumn of 1073, resulting in the total surrender of the Qarakhanids. Thus Terken grew up at her father's court in Bukhara.

Still, the royal couple's second and real wedding procession through Transoxania, Khorāsān and Rayy on their journey of two or three months to Isfahan would have been equally anticipated by the beggars and traders in every village, town and city on the way. The Saljuqs were now even more powerful and even more wealthy. To scatter gold coins on their new bride's entry into every settlement with an aristocracy to impress was an act of politics as much as it had been on the earlier occasion, and Omar would have, in all probability, been a member of the bride's party on account of his closeness to her father. It is equally likely that during Malik Shah's stay in Bukhara – as he familiarised himself with the Qarakhanids and their courtiers – Omar's youth, wit and musical ability turned him into a close companion of the eighteen-year-old Saljuq emperor, mimicking the process that had made him a favourite of his father-in-law's.

In the absence of contemporary records on this particular subject, we can only speculate how long Omar stayed over in the city of his birth, Nishāpur, on his way to Isfahan. Did he, for example, make an excuse of the need to find and recruit talented young mathematicians for the projected reform of the calendar in Isfahan to stay a little longer in Nishāpur with his family and old friends? In the event, Malik Shah's return to the capital would have been a leisurely procession, interrupted by meetings with local potentates to nurture the new sultan's standing among them. It is likely that Malik Shah, too, would have wanted to stay a little longer than usual in Nishāpur, the revenues of which had been allocated to his private office for the last few years by his late father.

Of one fact we can be reasonably certain: somewhere among the brightest students approaching graduation in the city's schools was a fifteen-year old boy watching Omar's high status enviously. In the years ahead, Omar came to dislike Muhammad ibn Muhammad al Ghazāli al-Tūsi wholeheartedly. The youth would one day become a favourite protégé of the chancellor and one of the most influential thinkers in the history of orthodox Islam. In the small intellectual circles of Nishāpur in 1073, the return of the prodigiously successful son would have not escaped Ghazāli's attention and Omar might even have given a lecture at the youth's school. The two men's stars would collide in Isfahan and Baghdad.

*   *   *

It has just passed midnight on 29 January 1074, and the city of Cairo is fast asleep, unaware of an event that will take it by surprise at sunrise and change its history. A column of horsemen commanded by an Armenian general approaches it under cover of darkness. Its arrival will prove a disaster for the city's military and civilian elite. Now that the normal pattern of the Nile floods has returned after a drought of seven years, the ruling bureaucracy hopes that the trauma of the dreadful famine will soon recede from memory and that the fabled era of plenty will resume. The drought had reduced the population to eating carrion, with instances discovered even of households lowering butchers' hooks into the streets to lift up children for slaughter.

But somewhere inside the strongest room in the strongest tower of the caliph's castle a few people are in full knowledge of the secret. They are awake and their hearts pound with anxiety, for their lives depend on the success of the venture. They include the Fatimid caliph al-Mustansir who, with a handful of his most trusted advisors, has invited the Armenian to take over the city and rescue him from the grip of his own supposed 'slaves', his Turkish royal guard who commit every crime and even choose his viziers for him.

The conspiracy will have ramifications far beyond Egypt. It will be studied closely in Rome, where strategies are being devised to supersede the authority of the eastern church in Constantinople; it will shake the rival Abbasid caliphate in Baghdad; it will be placed under the magnifying glass by the Grand Vizier in Isfahan; It will also alter the course of life of a young man who is preparing to leave his native city of Rayy for Isfahan before going on to Cairo to represent the Ismailis of the east at the court of their imam caliph there. That, in turn, will one day spell disaster for a twenty-five-year-old youth who has been summoned to Isfahan to help reform the Iranian solar calendar.

The general is called Badr al-Jamālī and is the governor of the city of Acre in Palestine. As a child, he was captured in a Saljuq raid on an Armenian town in Anatolia and sold as a slave to the Emir Jamāl ed-Din bin Ammār of Syria. He was given the Muslim name of Badr and became known as Badr the Jamāli, meaning that he belonged to the Emir Jamāl.

Young Badr's outstanding abilities soon caused his superiors to promote him rapidly through the army ranks, and he eventually defeated many challengers to the authority of the emir and became the most powerful military figure in the eastern region of the Fatimid caliphate. Thus when Mustansir sent a secret mission to him to ask for help, he replied that he would only go to Egypt if he could take his own Armenian forces with him. The caliph had no choice.

What Badr did next may explain why he had risen to the top of the pyramid. He was unpredictable. Instead of marching to Cairo by land, as any normal general would do in winter, he took the hazardous sea route. It paid dividends. The gales were in his favour and he landed at Damietta only a few days later. As he now entered Cairo in the guise of a family party, his men rushed behind him in the darkness and overwhelmed the guards at the gate. He secured the palace first and then allotted each one of the caliph's Turkish top tormentors to one of his officers. These then appeared at the castle in the morning carrying the still bleeding heads of their prey on platters.

*   *   *

It is 1 March 1074, and Gregory VII, the future St Gregory and the most pugnacious man ever to have sat on the throne of St Peter, has a big day ahead of him.

Born Hildebrand, in a workman's family of German origins in the Papal States of central Italy in 1020, he went to Rome as a child and became a 'singing monk', a chorister. He continued his studies in a church school for musicians which was also attended by the sons of the nobility.

His chance came when one of his teachers, Giovanni Graziano, became Pope Gregory VI in 1045 and took Hildebrand with him to St Peter's Basilica. There, only a year later, the new pope was deposed by the Holy Roman Emperor, Henry III of Bavaria. But Hildebrand, through a circuitous route of exile and return, rose to take his revenge. As a cardinal, he helped to found an influential circle of reform-minded bishops who would leave a permanent mark on the course of western history.

We met one of his peers, Cardinal Humbert of Silva Candida, when, on 24 July 1054, in the cathedral church of Santa Sophia in Constantinople, he formalised the chasm of the past 600 years between the two wings of Christendom. But causing schisms was not the group's aim. It longed primarily to rid the church of the yoke of the emperor, without whose consent no bishop could assume office. It also wanted to forbid 'simony', the practice of buying and selling clerical positions. Yet another aim was to banish the stain of concubinage among clerics who were supposed to be celibate.

Humbert died in 1061 when his turn seemed to have at last arrived to become pope, but Hildebrand survived a kidnapping by Roman noblemen to become the power behind the throne of Pope Alexander II, whom he succeeded a year ago.

Today, as he prepares to preside over a synod of his top cardinals to proclaim his plans for the future, he sees history sitting in judgment on him. If he succeeds, he will be seen as the pope who brought all temporal powers in Christendom under the umbrella of the bishop of Rome, Christ's deputy on Earth.

This urge seized the church after Henry's death in 1056, for the great man was succeeded by an infant son and widespread rebellion. The popes then started being elected by their own fellow clerics without the new emperor's prior approval, and without having to receive the symbols of their authority – the mace and cloak of office – from his hand. But now, Henry IV has become an adult and longs to regain his father's privileges. He started by deposing bishops sent to Germany and elsewhere by Rome.

Gregory, of course, means well. He can see that if the emperor, together with the kings of France and England and all the lesser tyrants, were made subject to the writ of the Universal Church, the common man would rest more easily at night. He has already seen the improvements that his own curbing of the powers of the petty nobility in the region of Rome has brought to the lives of ordinary people. How is he to know that combining divinely-sanctioned ideology and temporal government will bring even greater corruption upon the Church and end up in more wars, a mighty split and the Inquisition?

Among the set of reforms that Gregory will propose today and his cardinals will approve is a new departure. They will decide that Christians must no longer bear in silence the news of atrocities committed against their eastern brethren by savage new Asiatics. Too many Christian women and children have been burnt alive in their places of refuge by the Muslims and too many more have been taken into slavery. Now Constantinople itself is in danger. The kings and the nobility and the common men of Christ have the duty to prepare for a war of the Cross to march east and push back the tide of the enemy.

This new foreign policy, though sincerely held to be defensive, will prove even more successful than Gregory dreams. It will result in the establishment of a string of Christian states in the Holy Land and, here in the west, it will bring the new German emperor to heel in a most humiliating manner.

*　　*　　*

For Khayyām, above all, Rayy was the venerable city that had given its name to Rāzi, the great physician and blasphemer of the previous century. Abu Bakr Muhammad bin Zachariah, famous in the Greek and Roman world by his Latinised name of Rhazes, had been born and bred here and his tomb had become a minor place of pilgrimage for the subversive and the untrustworthy. While Muslims hated him, patriotic Iranians revered him covertly.[3]

And the city really was a venerable old lady of special sentiment for historically-conscious Iranians such as Omar. As Raghā or Raghāu, one of the two great cities of Media, it is mentioned several times in Zoroastrian scripture. The Avesta depicts it as a beautiful city that always remained faithful to Zarathustra. After all, Ahura Mazda had created it the twelfth most sacred place in the universe. Those references in the old book gave it a history of sixteen centuries at the time. It was probably much older. It was the meeting point of several ancient trading routes between China, Egypt, India and Europe.

Alexander had laid waste to it in the summer of 330 BC before one of his men had rebuilt it as 'Europos' in memory of his Macedonian home town, but the new name did not survive. The local Zoroastrians were too fond of their revered old town to bear the impudence for long. Similarly, the Iranian Parthians had later renamed it Arashkia, after their own clan, but again the insult failed. The Arabs destroyed it in the seventh century and renamed it Muhammadiya, but that, too, was forgotten. Zarathustra overcame them all.

Today, only a few ruins of its walls and institutions can be seen. They are to be found to the south of Tehran, where a branch of the snow-capped Alborz mountains protrudes onto the parched plain. When Omar passed through it, probably in the late spring of 1074, meltwater from the peaks watered its lush gardens and put lustre into it swaying fields of corn.

It is difficult to imagine that Omar on this journey would not have possessed at least a dozen books written a century earlier in this same city by its most famous son. Rāzi had written some 200 books, starting with music which had been his initial speciality. As a rich landowner, he had then studied medicine and become the director of the local hospital before his fame had caused him to be summoned to Baghdad to head the largest hospital there. He had always treated the poor among his patients free of charge, he had become a personal friend of many an Iranian prince of the Samanid or Sāmānian dynasty of Bukhara, and he had infuriated the Muslim clergy by denouncing all prophets as 'frauds'. Amazingly, he had survived, though towards the end of his life he had gone blind and been deserted by his royal friends. He had sought solace in the Greek writers and, according to Birūni, the historian, wrote poetry of his own in the Greek tongue. We may safely imagine that young Omar would have idolised him and visited his grave with deep feeling, perhaps even seeking out his heirs in search of a keepsake of his last years.

As time approached for him to move on, Omar could now boast that, at the age of twenty-five, he knew most of the great cities of Transoxania, Khorāsān and 'the Mountains', old Media of central and western Iran. Few peers matched his achievements in this respect. Furthermore, he was on his way to Isfahan, the capital, where he would work as an astronomer for the emperor. From there, professional visits to Baghdad and Damascus were inevitable. Shiraz and Kerman could be put on the agenda easily.

Contemporary sources put the number of Arabs living in Rayy at the time as 'insignificant', but, of course, we know that at least one pair of Arab eyes watched every group of travellers that passed through the city. They belonged to that youth of recent Yemeni extraction whom we met earlier. He had converted from Twelver

Shiism to Ismaili Shiism against the wishes of his family, he was probably being watched by government spies as a possible Egyptian agent, and he would soon flee the region – under a pseudonym – to familiarise himself with the court in Isfahan before going on to Cairo. If indeed Hasan Sabbāh did come across Omar, a couple of years younger than himself at this time, he would have been as polite as possible not to betray his inner turmoil and hostility, but he would have, nevertheless, appeared to Omar as somewhat dark and brooding. To Hasan, the younger man from Nishāpur would have appeared a collaborator, implicated in all the crimes of the Saljuq Turks, and all for money and momentary glory in this world. His hatred for Omar and all that he symbolised would have been palpable.

*   *   *

'Tell me the story of the Nasnās again.'

If indeed Omar accompanied the party of the newly-wed royal couple on their way from Nishāpur to Isfahan, we may imagine that, on some of the long, monotonous days of enforced idleness in her covered litter on top of a camel, the child-bride would have wanted to hear stories of wonder told with relish by a companion. A suitable candidate among those storytellers would have been Omar who had, only a few months earlier, been a confidant of her father's.

One such tale was that of the Nasnās and we can well imagine Omar telling it several times to Terken. Here it is adapted from the writings of Omar's future secretary Arūzi:

. . . it's a most beautiful animal. It stands upright, just like us, and it has hair like us. Also its nails are just like ours, wide, not like birds' talons. It loves humans and stands by caravan routes staring at our kind. If it finds one of us alone, it abducts him or her to keep as a mate. In Nishāpur, I heard Abu Reza, the son of Abdel-Salām, saying that he was once travelling in Turkistan in one of the deserts, going towards Tamqāch, [Terken's grandfather's birthplace,] and his caravan was several thousand camels strong. He said that he saw this most beautiful woman by the roadside, standing on top of a boulder, completely naked and as elfin as a cypress, with long hair, more pretty than the moon, just staring at the caravan. He

said: 'We spoke to her, but she wouldn't reply. Just stared. Then we tried to
capture her and she ran away, so swiftly that no horse could catch up with
her. Our porters were Turks. They told us the creature was called Nasnās.
It's the most noble of all the animals in the world. . . .'[4]

Back to the world of the adults, Khayyām's mind would have, at
times, examined the philosophical heritage of Rayy. Was Rāzi right,
for example, when he said that the contemplation of pleasure
presupposed the existence of pain? And was he original? Probably not.
Was not all philosophy Greek philosophy?

*   *   *

Surely this was the fairest city he had ever seen, and yet Isfahan was
embarking on even bolder architectural adventures, conscious that it
must use its buildings to flaunt its new military power and political
reach. Must not the centre of any empire also be its fairest city?

Whenever precisely it was in the early months of 1074[5] that Omar's
caravan arrived in Isfahan, and whether or not he was in the retinue
of the newly-wed royal couple, his first impressions of the city would
have lifted his heart. He has not left us a recollection of what struck
him most as he began to familiarise himself with the city that would
be his home for the next twenty-eight years, but one of his
contemporaries has. He is the traveller and Ismaili sage Nasser
Khosrow who arrived in Isfahan on 10 May 1052, after a seven year
journey from Bukhara through Armenia to Egypt and Arabia,
accompanied by his younger brother and a servant:

It's a city built upon a plain with a pleasant climate. Wherever you dig a
well to the depth of ten arms only, you'll find sweet and cool water. A great
wall, three-and-a-half farsangs long, surrounds it, with gates, strong points,
and castellated towers. Inside, every district looked prosperous. I never saw
any ruins. Everywhere, there were running streams and canals, and the
buildings were tall and handsome, with a large and beautiful Friday mosque
in the middle.

   There were many bazaars. I saw one bazaar belonging to the
moneychangers and lenders. There were 200 traders there. Each bazaar had
its own entrance and strong gate and the same was true of [residential]
districts and streets. There was one street called Kūtarāz with

50 caravanserais, all of them clean and smart, with many shopkeepers and customers. The caravan in which we travelled brought in 1,300 kharvārs[6] of cargo and we weren't inspected, nor did we go short of accommodation or fodder.

When the late sultan Toghril Beg Abu-Tālib Muhammad Bin Mikhail Bin Saljuq, may Allah have mercy upon his soul, took the city, he appointed a young man from Nishāpur over it, an able secretary with a beautiful [calligraphic] hand, a calm temperament and good looks. They called him the Lord Amīd. He loved cultured men and spoke well and was kind. The sultan had told him to demand nothing of the people for three years, and he was obeying his orders. The scattered ones had returned to their homes. . . .

In all the lands of the Persian-speakers, I never saw a city more beautiful or prosperous or self-sufficient. Some said its air had suffered somewhat after the wall was built around it [under the previous Iranian kingdom of the Buyids].[7]

Isfahan had improved further in the last two decades since the late sultan Toghril had transferred the centre of his administration there. Despite the heavy taxes that were now levied on farmers, shopkeepers and merchants by the Saljuqs, trade thrived in the new peace.

Omar's caravan from Rayy would have approached from over the mountains to the north-west and, from there, he would have seen a lush plain with the Zarrīn River meandering through the centre of the city.[8] On reaching the outskirts, he would have been impressed by the grandeur of riverside mansions, with their hordes of gardeners watering avenues of roses in the full exuberance of spring. Where was his new residence going to be?

It is likely that he would have been given temporary quarters in the palace or complex of mansions allocated to the young queen. It is important here to point out that the Turks at that time still largely observed their Central Asian tribal customs. They were not fully Islamicised and did not restrict their women – particularly high-born women – as did the caliphs in Baghdad. Young Terken, as we shall see later, gradually became a power in the empire and employed a large number of influential men among her courtiers in Isfahan. They became known as 'the Qarakhanids'. Unless, for some peculiar reason, Malik Shah decided to ban Omar from Terken's retinue, we have to assume that for years he remained close to her and, however erroneously, was regarded as 'one of Terken's men'. But we shall see that he became an intimate companion of the shah, too.

In the following few months, Omar would have wanted greater independence. His temperament was unsuited to living at court, with his every movement observed by security officials, coachmen, cleaners. Besides, we are told that his salary of 10,000 gold dinars was larger than the annual earnings of many a prominent minister of state. He could afford to buy or rent a substantial mansion by the river in either of the two affluent districts favoured by the new elite. These were the 'Shahristan', or 'City', the royal heart of Isfahan on both sides of the river, where the old town square in the north-east of Isfahan stands now, and the 'Yahudiyah', or 'Jews' Town', which was no longer confined to the Jews, but had grown to include merchants, army chiefs, administrators and minor nobility among its population. It was a suburb cut off from the Shahristan by several miles of parkland and orchards and, despite Omar's independent spirit, he would have probably not wanted to be too far away from both the intellectual hub of the city and his royal friends. Malik Shah's offices – as well as those of chancellor Nizām's – were in the Kohan Dezh or Old Castle district, a much fortified little town next to the Shahristan.

Apart from reporting his arrival to his new employers and settling how his salary would be paid to him – he arranged for some of it to be paid to his estate in Nishāpur, even though we do not know whether this began from the very start – what else is Omar likely to have done in his first few weeks in his new city? A visit to the great Friday mosque with its Sasanian crypt may well have been a priority. It had the oldest architecture in the city, and it remains graceful to this day. The mosque had been started in 771 on the remains of a pre-Islamic palace or Zoroastrian temple, and it had continued to be expanded in the next three centuries.

*   *   *

Was Omar married by this time? Probably. He was twenty-five years old and it would have been a social impediment if he were still single. Our guess must be that either in Samarkand or later in Bukhara, as he began to make a name for himself – and therefore a fortune – at the Qarakhanid court, he would have been wooed by any number of mercantile or even aristocratic houses as a potential son-in-law. Marriage, in turn, would have made it easier for him to continue to associate with the families of his royal friends.

As it happens, our knowledge of Omar's private life is confined to an image of him later in life as a patriarch in charge of a large household. We seem to have a description of his wife after his death, and we know that he also had at least one surviving son – as well as one who predeceased him – and at least one daughter. For the moment, we have to settle for the proposition that he was a normal young man on his arrival in Isfahan – normal, that is, by the standards of the privileged circles in which he moved; untouched by serious scandal and able to rise rapidly through both society and guild. As such, he would have been a young husband and father who spent much of his spare time in the company of other such families. At court, he would have been seen as an amiable genius with a great future ahead of him due to his rare access to the emperor and queen. But he was not interested in politics – unlike his hero, the scientist Avicenna, in this same city a century earlier. Omar seems to have been keen only in promoting his career as a mathematician and astronomer, hoping to be placed in charge of the future observatory that the chancellor was planning to build.

The Arab historian Ibn al-Athīr mentions Khayyām in connection with the Muslim lunar year 467 (from 27 August 1074 to 15 August 1075):

In this year, Nizām al-Mulk and Sultan Malik Shah assembled several leading astronomers who fixed the start of Nayruz [sic], at the starting point of Aries [i.e. the spring equinox]. Previously, the new year had been when the sun was halfway through Pisces. This initiative of the sultan provided the starting point for yearly calendars. At the same time, astronomical observations were started for Sultan Malik Shah. A group of astronomers gathered to carry this out. They included Omar Ibn Ebrāhīm al-Khayyāmi, Abul-Mozaffar al-Asfizāri and Maymūn Ibn al-Najīb al-Wā siti. A large sum of money was spent on this and the observations lasted until the sultan died . . . in 480 [sic], but they were discontinued after his death.[9]

Ibn al-Athīr is not always accurate in his dates, as he made his compilation around a hundred years after Malik Shah, and his assertions are sometimes couched in loose language. The calendar was not fully reformed in 1074–5, as he implies; only a set of astronomical tables had been drawn up and leap years reinstated as a preliminary step. Also Malik Shah died at the end of 1092, four years later than Ibn al-Athīr says. Nevertheless, the passage just quoted throws some light on Khayyām at this stage of his life. It tells us that the project for which he was recruited and taken to Isfahan was regarded by the authorities as crucial, as they decided to spend 'a large sum of money' on it. It also tells us that he was recruited to revive an important cultural institution of pre-Islamic Iran which had been corrupted by over four centuries of Muslim neglect and, at times, violent hostility. Malik Shah is thought to have been the first Saljuq sultan who could read, and it was Persian, not Turkish or Arabic, that he read. Culturally speaking, he was an Iranian, deeply enamoured of the romances in Firdowsi's Shah Nāmeh and fully identified with the Sasanian emperors who were held up to him as examples of wise kinghood.

Another document that may shed light on Omar at this time is a booklet of some twelve pages that is traditionally attributed to him. The *Norūz Nāmeh* or the *Book of the New Year*, is an investigation into the history of Norūz and its place in ancient Iran. It is the work of a specialist obsessed with his subject, inspiring enthusiasm in some and boring others.

Scholars believe the *Norūz Nāmeh* was finished in 1074, the year in which Omar began his work on the reform of the calendar. Certainly it would have made sense for him and his colleagues to have prepared a report on the date of Norūz under the Sasanians, and on how extra days had been added in leap years, to ensure the calendar remained in step with the natural seasons. The Persian text of the booklet chimes in with other examples of Omar's writing that have survived from these early years of his career. He is fond of using as pure a Persian as he can without becoming ridiculous; he likes to flaunt his knowledge of Middle Persian, the court language of the Sasanians, and he displays unusual self-confidence with his use of such terms as 'I heard' and 'We found'. Here is a segment:

And thus the Shah Jamshīd[10] called the day Norūz [New Day] and celebrated it. He ordered the people to follow him, to throw a feast every year as the month of Farvardin [the first month of spring] arrived. The day would be [the start of] a new era. . . .

Jamshīd was just and generous in the first part of his reign. People loved him and prospered under him. Izad,[11] Almighty, had given him intelligence and wisdom to discover many things in the world, so that the people came by gold and gems, fine cloths, perfumes and chattels.

But as some 400 years passed of his reign, evil found its way into his heart. The world became dear to his eye and he thought much of himself. He practiced grandeur and injustice. He gathered onto himself that which belonged to others. His people, who had loved him, mourned, and they prayed day and night for his downfall. His divine intelligence deserted him and his decisions all went astray.[12]

The late Iranian scholar and politician under the last shah, Senator Ali Dashti, thought that the booklet could not possibly be Khayyām's, for it read like 'the work of a fanatical Zoroastrian'. In my view, it does not, by itself, justify Dashti's conclusion. Any lax Iranian Muslim in the last half of the eleventh century who regretted the Arab takeover of his ancient homeland four centuries earlier might have used the same language to express his resentment obliquely. He would only need some courage to risk the anger of the clergy and he would have had to be a little arrogant. But both of these Omar possessed in large measure, and he knew that he had powerful friends.

*   *   *

On Wednesday, 2 April 1075, in Baghdad, the twenty-sixth Abbasid caliph Al-Qā'im at last departed this world for the other, where he could hopefully enjoy his accustomed luxuries without anxiety. He had for forty-four years been the final source of legitimacy for emperors and princes in the whole of the eastern lands of Islam. He had lived in utter decadence, eating, drinking and fornicating, but he had also mostly been a helpless puppet to other men's ambitions. Had it been a good life on the whole? Or would it have been better if he had been a simple farmer's son by the banks of the Tigris, living off bread, dates and buffalo milk?

Born to an Armenian slave girl seventy-four years earlier, Al-Qā'im
was proclaimed heir to his grandfather, Al-Qādir, when he was
twenty-nine, and he had inherited the mantle of Muhammad
unopposed a year later.

We last met him as a prisoner in the castle of Ana in upper
Mesopotamia in December 1059, just over fifteen years ago. One of
his Turkish slave commanders had banished him there and replaced
him in the Friday sermons of Baghdad with his rival Shia caliph of
Cairo. But another Turkish military man, this time a free warlord from
central Asia, Toghril the Saljuq, rescued him and returned him to his
palaces.

In the next fifteen years, Al-Qā'im's star rose somewhat. True,
childless Toghril forced himself on his daughter, hoping for a miracle
and wanting to mingle the blood of Muhammad with his own. But
then, Alp-Arslan returned his daughter to him, instead of insisting on
inheriting all of Toghril's women as his own. Furthermore, Alp-Arslan
never set foot in Baghdad. He was advised by that good Sunni, his
wise chancellor, Nizām al-Mulk, to avoid the complications of
Toghril's visits to the city. Nizām was still in power and reining in the
wilder fancies of the latest Saljuq ogre, Malik Shah, to abolish the
caliphate altogether. Hopefully, his son Moqtada as the next caliph
would have an easier time of it as Malik Shah grew up to see the
wisdom of tradition.

In Isfahan, Nizām proclaimed weeks of mourning for the passing of
the empire's spiritual head. Black flags were hoisted everywhere and
all merrymaking was banned. The clergy grabbed their moment to
flaunt their influence. Princes and potentates organised private
memorial services and competed to attract the best reciters of the
Koran.

The political class, of course, was privy to the gossip of Baghdad
and knew too much about the old devil to think him a man of God.
But politics had 'no father and no mother'. For the moment, to be
seen to be mourning was proof of piety, and so the caliph became both
the guarantor of Muslim unity and the gateway to paradise. For Omar
and countless others who were conscious of the disaster that had
befallen their people in the rise of Islam, the occasion posed a
dilemma. Should the Iranians be seen to be mourning the symbol of

Islam? The answer was 'Yes' if they, too, were of the political class. But they were determined not to appear keen mourners. They attended only one service at the Friday mosque and one or two in the mansions of their chiefs and mentors.

* * *

'In the year 469 I left Rayy for Egypt by way of Isfahan.' If ever there were a sentence that was economical with the truth, this was it. It is from the autobiography of Hasan Sabbāh, which was partly destroyed when his castle of Alamūt, the headquarters of the 'Assassins', fell to the Mongols several generations after him in 1256.

It is not quite the whole truth because on his 'way to Egypt', Hasan spent fifteen to eighteen months in Isfahan. He does not tell us why he stayed there so long, but he does not have to. It is understood. He was there to infiltrate the highest social and political circles of the Saljuq court to gain as much information and make as many contacts as he could before leaving for Cairo. His reception in Egypt depended on how much he knew.

As we saw a few years ago, while still in Rayy, he had caught the eye of the chancellor's men because of his strange associates, men with foreign accents and no visible means of support. Their suspicions led in only one direction. He was a dangerous heretic with his loyalties lying outside the Saljuq state. Unbeknown to the spies, however, we know that he had been chosen by the chief Ismaili missionary in Iran to 'go to Cairo to be received by His Holiness the Imam in Egypt' as the ambassador of the Ismailis of the east. Hasan would thus have been foolish to travel to Isfahan under his own name. He would have disguised himself as as some other type, most advisedly as an orthodox Sunni Muslim. That would have facilitated both his physical survival and his infiltration of the court for the duration of his stay in Isfahan.

The Islamic lunar year 469 to which he refers began in August 1076 and ended in July 1077, suggesting that he arrived in Isfahan either in the cool and dry months of autumn 1076 or else in the months of late spring 1077. The date of his arrival in Cairo we know precisely. He tells us it was Wednesday, 31 August 1078, his precision implying that his arrival was regarded by him as one of the greatest events in his life, which it certainly was. Allowing for his taking several months to travel by land and sea through Armenia, Mesopotamia, Syria, Mount Lebanon and the Mediterranean to reach Egypt, we can be certain that Hasan spent more that a year in Isfahan.

If he had merely wished to consult the secret leaders of the Ismaili Shia community in Isfahan before leaving for Cairo, he would not have had to remain there for more than a week or two. As he was already a wanted man, the longer he stayed there under the noses of the chancellor's spies – who might have had reports of his leaving Rayy – the more he would have exposed both himself and his fellow Ismailis in Isfahan to the severest of dangers: torture, to force them to betray their fellows, and execution. The conclusion must, therefore, be that he communicated with Ismaili leaders as little as possible while in the capital. He would not have wanted to be seen visiting them or even approaching their houses, for they were under constant observation. He would have contacted them through members or sympathisers who had infiltrated the establishment earlier. We know that some of them had attained high office and he might have been recruited by them into their departments. Hasan was well educated in Persian and Arabic, and he was brave, charismatic and intelligent. He would have risen rapidly in any office he joined.

The Ismailis themselves have written that Hasan rose so high in the treasury that Malik Shah commissioned him to report on the financial health of the empire, thus inciting the jealousy of the chancellor. This is, however, almost certainly a fabrication by his followers to enhance his reputation in history. The tradition claims that Hasan, Nizām and Khayyām had begun as schoolfriends in Nishāpur. It cannot be true. Nizām had probably had several children by the time the other two were born and, furthermore, there is not the slightest evidence that Hasan, a poor man of recent Yemeni migrant stock, born and brought up in Rayy – according to his own biography – could have been anywhere near Nishāpur in his youth.

However, the chances are high that Hasan and Omar had met in Isfahan in the twelve months or so that Hasan spent there in 1077 and 1078. They were approximately the same age and, as bright young men with seemingly brilliant futures ahead of them, they would have moved in a relatively small circle of young professionals. Government servants in the various departments of state did not, in medieval times, work as furiously as their counterparts do now. Outside office hours in Isfahan, they would have spent much time each week relaxing in riverside kebab houses. They might also have been invited to social functions in the homes of acquaintances.

But being of the same age and occasionally meeting by chance does not necessarily lead to friendship. Hasan and Omar were dissimilar in both their beliefs and their temperaments. Though Hasan seems to have been only a couple of years older than Omar, he was possessed by a single idea: to rise in the world through religion, and to guide the destiny of the rest of mankind. He had heard voices and seen visions. He would not have been endowed with much humour. The mere sound of merriment arising from a gathering of young people would have probably revolted him.

By contrast, gregarious Omar would have been the very heart and centre of any gathering he attended. His own earliest poems lead us to suspect that wherever he was to be found outside office hours or while networking to promote himself, there would have been wine and women and music and dance. He had, however, one attribute that would have made him attractive to Sabbāh to cultivate: his high connections made him a possible path to the royal family. For a man brought up in the tradition of Taqiyah, the religious permissibility of even cursing your religion if you wanted to promote it, lying came easily to Hasan. To befriend that trivial-minded youth from Nishāpur in order to stand next to Malik Shah and Nizām al-Mulk to bring about their destruction did not cause him any sleepless nights. Whether Omar would have allowed any such contrasting personality to come close to him is quite another matter.

*   *   *

The fun-loving youth would have settled smoothly into the daily routine of a well-paid professional devoted to astronomy while probably also earning good money as a physician and teacher: his special subjects, beside medicine, being mathematics and music. His astronomy had two aspects, one to his liking, the other not. He approved of recording the movements of the stars, predicting the next eclipse and calculating the date of the next harvest. Being told to determine an auspicious date and predict good weather for the emperor's next hunting expedition he detested, as we shall see later. But he was a government servant and had no choice. Even as a close friend of the emperor and his wife, he had to justify his salary.

A highlight of the social year for the young people of Isfahan was the spring festival of the village of Karina, just outside the city. It was a week-long excess of drinking, singing and dancing, men and women together, with a tradition reaching back into pre-Islamic times. Every household and business in the village paid a sum towards its organisation and was, in turn, rewarded by the spending it attracted. Folk wisdom asserted that a terrible fate would befall any king who interfered with it. But this particular king did not intend to meddle. He was young and rumoured to attend in disguise. Let the Mesopotamian merchant-traveller Ibn Hawqal take up the description:

> They adorn the bazaar profusely and have built places for drinking wine and eating food. . . . They organise functions and use the best musicians and dancers, men and women, and in the mansions and houses and gardens, they dance and sing all day and all night, joining dusk to dawn, with nobody bothering them, because the rulers and the officials let them be. . . . The food and drink are so cheap, you would think they gave them away. A mann of grapes costs only five dirhams and the pears, pomegranates, apples and other fruit are so delicate and aromatic, you would think them the best in the world.[13]

CHAPTER FIVE

The Boy Triumphs

The stars ruling far-flung skies,
Have come to belong to the haughty Wise!
My son, listen well to this, my finding:
The Wise themselves know they philosophise!

Their orders had sounded simple enough: 'Bring the Persian solar calendar back into step with the seasons, and don't worry about the cost; buy any buildings you need, find any books you want, order the best instruments wherever they might be made, just make sure your handiwork is not unwieldy: no irregular leap years, please.'

But there was an underlying expectation that would prove hard to meet. The experiences of any nation which had had a calendar for at least a thousand years would have to be collated and improved to devise the most accurate system there had ever been. Nothing less would satisfy the chancellor, nor the sultan, let alone the pride of the eight egotistic mathematicians and astronomers themselves. Some of them were mere raw youths, fired by wild flights of fancy and oblivious to the consequences of endangering the whole project through attempting too much.

The story of how the Persian calendar had been abandoned, then revived, then neglected to fall out of step again with the natural seasons, closely reflected the fortunes of civilisation itself in the vanquished country over the past four centuries. For the first 150 years of Islam, its rulers had shown little interest in building, only in destroying and looting. What the zealots of the world's latest triumphant sect did not understand, or thought they did not need, they demolished. Libraries and schools of philosophy were obvious targets, but even guilds of artisans and the houses of the nobility were regarded with hostility, unless they downgraded themselves to the level of the men of the desert. They were seen, rightly, as prolonging loyalty to the old empire and nurturing nostalgia for the old religion. Institutional reservoirs of memory even posed the danger of overcoming the minds of the Arabs themselves. What if they learned that the pre-Islamic past had not been as bad as the Koran portrayed it? In Khārazm, the conquerors killed all the natives 'who could read their script', wrote Bīrūni, the Persian historian, 'so that, afterwards, there was no-one who knew their history.'

The solar Sasanian calendar, with its resounding Persian names for the months, had been one of the first casualties of the Arab onslaught. But even where it had survived out of sight among Zoroastrians, social fragmentation had resulted in its corruption. Pockets of devotees of the old order had kept it alive for the observance of religious rites and as a reminder of their forefathers. But persecution and engineered poverty through the levying of back-breaking taxes on non-Muslims had severed links between their leaders in various regions and their mistakes in calculating leap years had accumulated to throw the system into chaos.

The new Muslim regime at first enforced the Arab lunar calendar. It fell short of the natural year by eleven days, and so constantly advanced against the seasons. But if it were good enough for the Prophet of Allah, it would be good enough for all.

During the reign of Muhammad himself in Arabia, no major problem had arisen. He kept the Arabs' lunar calendar with the minor innovation of instituting his own Year Zero to draw a line between the new Islamic era, beginning in AD 622, and what had been before, which he called the Age of Ignorance. But since he moved the beginning of the year from the first day of Muharram, the traditional first month of the Arab calendar, to the actual anniversary of his fleeing from Mecca in the third month, Rabī' el-Awwal, confusion set in. Some of his followers still counted according to the old system until his second successor, Umar the Orator, ended the anomaly by returning the start of the year to the first day of Muharram.

It has been said that Umar, who now found himself in charge of a vast realm due to his armies' lightning advances into the old Persian and Byzantine empires, also decided to adopt the solar calendar of the Persians as the parallel, civic calendar of the new Islamic empire. Even if this were true, it was never implemented or observed for long, for we find Bīrūni reporting that during the reign of the Umayyad caliph Hishām (AD 724–43) some landowners petitioned him to reform the calendar to ensure that the collection of taxes fell after harvests, not before them. Taxpayers' complaints continued during the early Abbassid caliphate also.

For the Arabs, keeping to the lunar calendar served a vital political function. It was a harsh message of force, a symbol of domination on display every day, lest the vanquished forget that the new order had been imposed on them by the sword and could be reimposed similarly if they rebelled, which they did frequently. It was also simple enough for a simple people, the Arabs themselves and those who had converted to their religion. Every Muslim family could keep a record of it for themselves by merely watching the moon, more or less accurately, even while scattered across the desert without coming across other human beings for months. All they needed to do was to watch for the appearance of the new moon and make a scratch on a bone. By this method they could celebrate their religious feasts approximately on time. Every now and then, the new moon took an extra day to appear or bad weather hampered sightings of it. In the next few days, the progress of the crescent into the full moon confirmed expectations.

It is not known quite how the measuring of time among Arabs had so fallen behind the practices of other peoples. Even the ancient Sumerians in that same region 4,000 years earlier had added the occasional month to the lunar year to keep their calendar reasonably in tune with nature. The Babylonians, Jews, Greeks and Chinese had learnt to do the same. The Egyptians across the Red Sea had given up the moon altogether, thousands of years ago, to be followed by the ancient Persians in the fifth century BC and the Romans under Julius Caesar in 46 BC.

The explanation perhaps lies in the absence of a large central state in Arabia before the rise of Islam, with the result that there was a range of practices in use there. For example, the names of some of today's Arab months, such as Safar, Yellow, suggest that they had, in at least some places, been kept in reasonable harmony with such annual phenomena as the colour of autumn. Elsewhere, in the Persian Gulf region for example, Arab navigators and merchants lived by the Sasanian calendar, while on the littoral of the Red Sea, they looked towards Hellenised Egypt and observed a version of the Julian Calendar that was in use among the Byzantines.

So the Islamic religious year of 354 days regressed – and still regresses – against the seasons rapidly. For farmers, the appearance of greedy tax collectors at their doors before the harvest presented a widespread problem, while, in the mercantile class, anniversaries of birth and death in the family soon lost all resemblance to their original circumstances.

But all began to change in the first quarter of the ninth century when a prince of the Abbasid clan, distant relatives of Muhammad, was put on the throne in Baghdad by a Persian army. The new dynasty were austere and holy at first, but quickly became fun-loving and Persianised, so that by the time of Ma'mūn, the seventh Abbasid caliph, the sovereign was not only born to an Iranian mother, he was also brought up in Khorāsān under a Zoroastrian tutor. Thus 'the son of the Persian', as he was called by his Arab enemies, was a virtual Iranian by sympathy, taste and culture, and he began to collect books from as far away as Constantinople.

Indeed, he was even more remarkable than that. He and his advisors invoked an ancient Greek philosophical concept to declare that the Koran had been created 'in time' and would therefore date with time. In other words, it needed to be ignored in places and superseded by new laws in others to bring it into line with the changing circumstances of the world. The clearly heretical reform movement Ma'mūn spearheaded became known as Mu'tazilism or 'withdrawal', meaning that its adherents no longer wanted to participate in the doctrinal disputes of the past 200 years of Islam. To this day, Mu'tazilism remains the only major attempt at serious reform in Islam.

A year before his death in 833, Ma'mūn gathered some of the most talented scholars of his empire in a Sasanian-style university – and by extension, an Athenian-type academy – which he called The House of Wisdom. He showered it with money in order that even more books could be bought to translate into Arabic, and he encouraged the setting up of an observatory. He had revived the Persian solar calendar to govern the civic affairs of the caliphate.

Of truly historic importance proved one of Ma'mun's less-noticed decisions, an order that a little book brought to the court of his grandfather Mansour by a delegation of diplomats from India be translated, at last. That little book gave the Islamic world – and later the whole world – our present system of numerals, which really ought to be called Indian, not Arabic. And so, almost overnight, scholars, accountants and engineers began to take advantage of the ease of use of the new system over its Roman equivalent. Very soon mathematics would be pushing ahead in leaps and bounds and decimal fractions would make accurate calculations possible, revolutionising astronomy in particular.

The observatory employed, among others, two geniuses whose feats gained for them the status of legend in their own age. One was an agnostic Iranian from central Asia and the other a heretical Arab of the Sabian creed from upper Mesopotamia.

The first hailed from Khārazm to the south of the Aral Sea in Transoxania and, as 'Al-Khwarazmi', would later give his name to the Latin term 'algorithm'. But he would do much more. He would write the first book on algebra, beside numerous other works, and he would, after two trips to Byzantium and India, raise the ire of the mullahs by openly espousing agnosticism. This, by itself, shows the extent of the enlightenment that Ma'mūn had brought with him from his former Khorāsānian seat of Marv, where Zoroastrians, Buddhists, Christians, Jews and even atheists had been welcome guests at his court. It also, in truth, reflects the absolute power of the autocrat at the top of the pyramid. Islam has always made intellectual progress only when the ruler has been a 'bad Muslim' and also strong enough to banish troublesome mullahs from his court. In Ma'mūn's time, there was even a fashionable club in Baghdad that openly preached the racial and cultural superiority of the Persians and Romans over Arabs and others.

The second genius of Ma'mūn's intellectual elite, Abu Abdallah al-Battāni as-Sābi, had reason not to love his master quite wholeheartedly, for Ma'mūn had treated his clan in the town of

Harran in upper Mesopotamia relatively harshly. He had given them an unpleasant choice: either convert to one of the 'religions of the Book', meaning Islam, Christianity, Judaism or Zoroastrianism, or be 'exterminated'. Al-Battāni's immediate family had chosen Islam and moved to Baghdad, while his relatives had argued that the Koran had mentioned their religion three times, with the implication that they, too, were one of the 'Peoples of the Book'. The act of extermination was suspended while the disputation continued.

Unfortunately for everyone, 'the son of the Persian' became entrenched in his own dogma of Mu'tazilism towards the end of his reign to the extent that he started an inquisition against those who stuck to traditional Islam. He flogged famous theologians and dismissed high officials. As a result, the philosophical school that promised so much did not survive him long. Under his heirs, the solar calendar also fell into abeyance for over sixty years. Then, during the reign of Al-Mu'tazid, two extra months were injected into the Zoroastrian year and the first day of the first month of Farvardin was transferred from the twelfth of April to the twelfth of May 895. This is curious. It ought to have been shifted backwards, not forwards. Since the reign of Darius the Great in the fifth century BC, the start of the new year had always been meant to coincide with the first day of spring in March.

But the heirs of Al-Mu'tazid, too, became preoccupied with other concerns which caused the solar calendar to fall by the wayside again. Yet another attempt was made, this time in central Iran around the year 1000, under the Persian Buyids. It never caught on, for the dynasty was toppled by the Saljuqs.

Now, three-quarters of a century later in the same city, Isfahan, the leader of the team of reformers was a middle-aged man by the name of Muhammad bin Ahmad Ma'mūri of western Khorāsān. 'The philosopher' – as he was usually called – had published a book on mathematics but, unlike Omar's, it had not made waves. His special attributes were management and a knowledge of the bureaucracy in the capital. Another Khorāsānian on the team of eight was Abbās Lokari, the chief of an old Iranian family, the Lokaris of Marv. He had studied with Omar in Nishāpur under Bahmanyār, as had the fourth Khorāsānian on the team, Mozaffar Asfizari, a noisy young man who seemed constantly engaged in a good-tempered quarrel with Omar. The eye of the team was on the latter two, the 'youngsters', whose close friendship would continue to the end of their lives, as we shall see later.

Did such heavy leaning towards fellow Khorāsānians merely reflect the chancellor's normal practice of favouring his own people for high office, or did it reflect the brilliance of Khorāsān's schools at the time? Both factors were at work.

The team's first decision was to halt immediately the further regression of the calendar. It now began on 26 February and would regress to 15 February in a year's time if nothing were done. If, on the other hand, the neglected eleven days of intercalation were added to the end of it, its further falling out of step with the seasons would be stopped until a final decision would be made on its future shape. This was accepted.[1]

Thus we can imagine these first few years of Omar's new life in Isfahan to have been a period of deep immersion in the works of the most imminent astronomers of the past. He would have had to digest many of the thirteen volumes of Ptolemy's great compendium on astronomy, the *Almagest*, which put the earth at the unmoving centre of the universe and wove around it a number of impressive theories to explain why the planets and the stars misbehaved. Omar and his colleagues would have also studied in detail the astronomical works of Khārazmi, Battāni, Avicenna and – another great idol of Omar's – Bīrūni, who had died relatively recently in December 1048, when infant Omar was seven months old.

While Ptolemy's compendium was available in Arabic, certain other relevant works were not. Furthermore, the translations were often second-hand through the medium of Syriac. They were often convoluted in style and mistaken in parts. How much better it would be to master them in their original Greek.

There is no direct evidence that Omar studied the language but the indications are that, at the very least, he read scientific texts in it. In his poetry and other writings, he displays an obsession with the classical authors and, as we saw in the last chapter, at least one of his idols, the scientist Rāzi, 'wrote poetry in Greek'. A leading astronomer and mathematician of Omar's stature would have been expected by all around him to have studied the mother tongue of all science and, to show that the concept was not far-fetched in his time, it may be mentioned here that one of his future students in Marv – if not one of his closest friends – the astronomer Khāzeni – was of Greek birth. He had been captured in Byzantium by the Saljuqs and then castrated before being given a first-class education by his master, the khāzen or treasurer to the sultan Sanjar. While Khāzeni was not, at this time, in Isfahan, the city had many such Greek-born residents to give tuition to Omar and his colleagues. In fact, we may well assume that studying Greek was normal practice and that, in his case, it would have been financed by his office if he did not already have the language.

*   *   *

It is early in the morning of Friday, 28 January 1077, and for the third day running after the dawn prayers, the pope, Gregory VII, stares through a window in the castle of Canossa in Tuscany at the freezing scene spreading out before him. He focuses his troubled eyes on the pathetic figure of a young man who has stood there at the gate shivering and pleading incoherently. Wearing a single shirt, the twenty-one-year-old king of the Germans has come to do penance.

The Holy Father is accompanied by his host, Matilda, the thirty-year-old Countess of Canossa and powerful ruler of Tuscany. Behind them stand several elders of the church and the majority opinion is that Henry IV's wishes be granted. The pope has excommunicated him and pronounced him deposed from his position as emperor of the Holy Roman Empire. As a result, there has been rebellion in the German lands. The barons have elected one of themselves as Henry's successor as king of Germany and the young man has seen the error of his ways. His pitiable sight affects all onlookers, particularly Matilda. What is Gregory to do?

The church's troubles with temporal rule had begun long ago. In fact, immediately upon Constantine's making Christianity the dominant religion of the Roman state in 313, some Christians whispered dark forebodings. It was wrong and dangerous, they said, to subject the church of the Son of God to the whims of military men with their oscillating political needs, and the doubters had been proved right soon afterwards. The nobility in each locality had now come to regard themselves as the final arbiters of all clerical appointments; symbolised by the ceremony of granting bishops and priests their robes and insignia of office. They demanded bribes from the clergy and expected unquestioning support for their behaviour. Ecclesiastical appointments regularly came on the market for sale to drag the church into further disrepute and, on occasion, even the papacy itself was traded.

But help was at hand from an unexpected direction, though no one noticed its nature at the time. The climate of western Europe had recently warmed to bring in its wake better nutrition and an expanding population. New towns were established where only forest had been. Trade flourished and the church spread its wings to become richer, more confident. Wherever there was a vacuum, it set itself up in rivalry with the barons and ate into their powers. It raised its voice against cruelty and corruption, and it became more popular, more influential. In 1049, Graf (Count) Bruno Von Egisheim Und Dagsburg, who had become a bishop at the age of only twenty-five, succeeded in getting himself elected to the papacy as Leo IX by the clergy and the people of Rome. His second successor, Alexander II, was not recognised at first by the German court.

The present clash came to a head in 1055 with the death of Henry III. When some German potentates refused to be subordinate to the late emperor's widow, regent for her child Henry IV, the Vatican decided that its time had come. It banned the investiture of priests by lay rulers, it denounced simony and declared the clerical practice of concubinage a corruption. As yet another sign of its growing confidence, the Vatican also began to dream of sending a Christian army to the east to liberate the faithful in Anatolia from the yoke of the new barbarians from the east and, in the process, reopen the old routes of pilgrimage to Jerusalem.

And so Gregory's heart was nowadays in the east, not the west. The whole of civilised Europe had come to accept his political and spiritual supremacy, and the success of the recent holy wars against the heathen Moors in Spain and Sicily had left him little else of importance to do here. He dreamt of personally leading an army of Western knights into Constantinople to expel the Turks from

Anatolia. The emperor of the Byzantines, Michael VII, seemed sincere in his appeal for the pope's friendship. Gregory's own legates had established that. But if young Henry turned out to be as treacherous as his father and rallied Germany against Rome once more, the dream of walking triumphantly into Jerusalem would disappear with the frost.

On the other hand, if Henry had really seen the error of his ways and finally thrown off the malign influence of his mother, he could be a source of strength for those who remained behind. The German barons, who were at that very moment expecting the pope to arrive among them for the anointment of Henry's successor, would surely understand.

Gregory turned to Matilda beside him and saw pain in her face. He looked back over his shoulder at his cardinals and read the same plea in theirs. Hugh, the Abbot of Cluny, was especially decided. After more heart-searching and more consultation, Gregory finally caved in and sent a message to invite the boy in to kiss his hands and have his excommunication lifted. But he feared he had made the worst mistake of his long, eventful life.

*   *   *

'Until the age of seventeen, I searched for knowledge, but I held to the faith of my fathers. . . . There had [previously] never been any doubt in my faith in Islam.'

What does Hasan Sabbāh, the future founder of history's first significant terrorist party, mean by 'Islam' here? Is he not supposed to be an Ismaili, and are the Ismailis not supposed to be Muslims? He clearly nurtures a secret in his soul. What is it? Can we hope to find out? We have time yet. The quote comes from his autobiography that, as mentioned earlier, the Mongols captured in his castle of Alamūt. But, as Hasan strolled in one of the riverside parks of Isfahan one evening in the autumn of 1077 and occasionally exchanged pleasantries with other young men, he was as troubled as he had ever been. This was despite his apparent confidence in all he espoused. He had from early childhood in Rayy been a 'searcher', a lone soul yearning 'to belong', and now he was planning to leave in search of final fulfilment on the most hazardous journey of his life, the long road to Cairo, the promised land of his adopted faith.

For the past twelve months or so, Hasan had survived living and working in the capital, even though the chancellor's numerous secret agents looked for Ismaili infiltrators everywhere. He says that he had 'fled' his city of birth, and that he had been chosen by the chief Ismaili missionary in Iran to travel to Egypt to be his envoy there. But why had he come to Isfahan, where the secret police were most alert?

There may have been at least two reasons. If he were to speak with authority in Egypt, he had to be familiar with the ruling establishment of the rival empire – its strengths and weaknesses, its zealots and saboteurs – to enable Cairo to better plan its enemy's downfall, and he also had to know the mind of the Iranian Ismailis' chief missionary, Abdul Malik Attāsh, who lived in secrecy near Isfahan. The capital had the largest concentration of Ismailis and he had to see for himself their overall plight, their readiness to fight, their expectations of the imam caliph in Cairo. In other words, Hasan had to spy on the leadership of the state, make friends among its elite, and learn how best the Ismailis' resources might be used in the coming war of destiny.

We may safely say that Hasan lived in the capital under a pseudonym – for he would later speak of his many *nom de guerres* in his autobiography – and it would have been logical for him even to alter his appearance for fear of being recognised by the police or someone from Rayy on the streets.

We have already seen that the story told later by the Ismailis about Hasan's stay in Isfahan can be largely dismissed. It claims that he was a schoolfriend of both Omar and Nizām, despite the huge gap in years between him and the chancellor, and that, in Isfahan, he became a rival to Nizām. But if the story has a germ of truth it must be that, in his disguise at the court, Hasan made rapid progress. He was educated enough to achieve the tasks allocated to him, and he was motivated enough to impress his employers with his diligence. By all accounts, he was extremely intelligent and charismatic. Whatever the extent of his success, however, after a year or so in Isfahan, it was eventually time for him to move on, to leave on a circuitous route for Cairo. He

himself says that he arrived in the Egyptian capital on 30 August
1078. Instead of setting off in the normal direction, westwards for
Baghdad and Damascus, he headed for the north-west, for Azerbaijan
and Armenia before turning south towards Kurdistan and Syria. On
the way, he says, he argued constantly with Sunni scholars about the
true doctrines of the faith, to the extent that he was ejected from one
town. In Damascus, he found that fighting between Saljuqs and
Egyptians in Palestine had made further progress by land impossible.
He boarded a ship instead, following in the footsteps of the Armenian
general Badr al-Jamāli, and arrived in Cairo without much trouble.
But a great shock awaited him there. The Armenian general was the
cause of it.

*   *   *

In October 1077, news reached Isfahan that Abul Fadl Beihaqi, the
historian and courtier of the Ghaznavid sultans, had died the previous
month in painful isolation in western Khorāsān. In the small
intellectual circles of the capital, the news spread quickly, for the old
man's thirty volumes of recollections and research on the decline and
fall of the Ghaznavids were favourite reading among them. They also
recalled the rise of the Saljuqs, and how it had felt to be involved in
decision-making in the very throne room of a mighty empire. Though
attitudes to writers and artists are shaped by many factors, we can try
to guess how Omar, who was himself no stranger to the companion of
the sceptred, might have reacted to the news of Beihaqi's final
passing.

   He would probably have been saddened, but not overmuch. His
generation enjoyed Beihaqi's frank writings and felt grateful for the
pains the old man had taken over so many years in corroborating his
information. It had also been instructive to see how, after much loyal
service to a dynasty of mighty sultans as secretary and advisor, he had
been thrown to the wolves for a minor indiscretion and his wealth
seized.

   But Beihaqi had his weaknesses too. Although he had written in
Persian, his language was strewn with an abundance of borrowed
Arabic words and, altogether, he had not shown any strong

attachment to the legacy of his own people. He had been a mere careerist who lusted after wealth and was drunk on closeness to power. Still, he had not deserved to be cast aside on what he called his 'rubbish heap of redundancy', intellectual isolation in his remote village of birth.

At some time in the next few days, in the privacy of his home, it is possible that Omar leafed through one of the old man's books in search of one of those entertaining, enlightening passages for which Beihaqi was famous. In the following, the historian detects the first signs of madness in Sultan Mass'ūd after the crushing defeats he had suffered in 1040 at the hands of the Saljuqs in Khorāsān:

> The king [back in his capital of Ghaznin in Afghanistan] told me: 'Go to his lordship's [the vizier's] house, and sit with him alone. Write down all he says I've said and commanded, and everything we've agreed. Bring it back with you by the next prayer for copying. Whatever you do and hear him say, keep it to yourself'. I said: 'I'll do that', and left.
>
> I accompanied the vizier to his house and we ate something and rested a little. Then he left [for his own room] and sent for me. He said: 'Know and beware that the king is terrified of these [new] enemies and no matter how much I urge him to show patience, it's no use. Something's happened to him beyond our [mortal] powers. He's certain Dāwūd [the Saljuq prince] will now head for here, now that Altuntāsh [the Ghaznavid army commander] has also been defeated. I reasoned this would never be. Without first capturing Balkh, why should they want to go anywhere else? Especially Ghaznin. Again, no use. He says: 'There are things only I know. Just prepare the army and leave for Parwān and Heibān.' I fear the moment I've arrived there, he'll leave for India. He hides it from me. He says: 'I'll stay a little while in Ghaznin. Then come after you.' But I know he won't. It's impossible to question him any more. I'm frightened. . . . He [the vizier] wrote the document in his own hand and took a long time over it. . . . This lord was a rarity. He was the most effective and the most intelligent of his generation. . . .
>
> I took it to court. The king sent for me and ordered that we should not be disturbed. He read the document and pondered it for some time. Then he said: 'How would you answer his questions? You worked under Abu Nassr Mushkān. You know how he would have replied in circumstances such as these.' I said: 'It's clear to me what the reply ought to be. If your Majesty approved, you would just confirm it [underneath] in your own hand.' He said: 'Sit down here and do it now.' I took the document and sat

down and replied to every question and read my replies aloud to his majesty. He liked it, changing only a few points. . . .

I returned to the vizier and gave him the document. He was very pleased. He said: 'You took great pains on my behalf today.' I replied that I was his lordship's obedient servant. If only I could do something to help. As I stood up to leave, he asked me to sit down again. . . . He said a few words in Turkish to a servant and the servant brought in a purse of gold and silver and some robes. I kissed the ground and asked him to forgive me for refusing his gifts. He insisted. He said that he had himself been a secretary once and knew it was unfair to ask of secretaries to do unpaid work. I accepted. It was 5,000 dirhams and five robes which my men collected. . . .

On Tuesday, the 12th of Moharram,[2] his majesty arrived at the Palace of Victories and sat on the lawn of the lower square – when, of course, that building and that square were still what they used to be. He had ordered a grand party and the prince Modūd and the vizier also arrived and sat down. The army now began to pass by [on its way to the front, under the prince and the vizier]. First came the prince's vanguard, with its animals and wide standards and canopies and 200 House Guards, all armoured. . . . [By the time the parade was over], it was approaching the time of the [evening] prayer and the king ordered his son and the vizier and the others present to go in to the dining hall for a sumptuous harīsa,[3] after which they said their farewells and left.

The king now said to Abdul-Razzāq: 'What do you say? Shall we have a few bowls?' Abdul-Razzāq answered: 'Well, if we don't now, then when? Your majesty's victorious and the prince has got his wish to go [to war] and we've had a wonderful harīsa!' The king said: 'Let's have it simple, in the gardens'.

Presently the servants took some fifty jugs of wine [to one of the gardens] and the bowl they put in front of each man was of the full half-mann size. The king said: 'We want justice. Serve everyone equally.' Soon, all was laughter and the musicians began to sing. Bul-Hasan drank five, succumbed to the sixth and lost his wits to the seventh. At the eighth, he vomited and the servants dragged him away. Bu-Alā, the physician, drank five and keeled over, when they took him out, too. Khalīl Dāwūd drank ten and Siā Pirūz nine. They took them [to their homes] in Dailamān Street. Bu-Na'īm fled after his ninth. The singers and the dancers also escaped before they lost their senses, leaving only the king and Abdul Razzāq still drinking. Eventually, his lordship said to his majesty: 'Enough! If they give me any more, I'll be rude to you!' The king laughed and nodded and Abdul Razzāq stood up and left, still in charge of his manners. But the king drank on, happily, until his twenty-seventh. Then he stood up and asked for water and a prayer rug. He washed his mouth clean and prayed, as if he had not drunk at all. Then he retired to the palace by elephant.

And I, Abul Fadl, saw it all with my own eyes. Alas, it was the last time I would ever see that great sovereign. May God have mercy on his soul.[4]

*   *   *

Do not speak ill of dead men! Alas, that is not possible of public men, and particularly of this man, one Michael Psellus: lawyer, classicist, fake monk, courtier, statesman, historian, diarist, philosopher, theologian, schismatic and Renaissance man before the Renaissance! He died the death of a disillusioned and unlamented man in his sixtieth year in 1078 somewhere in Constantinople. Born a nobleman, he had risen to be the grand chancellor of the Byzantine empire and the personal tutor of the heir to the throne, only to be defeated finally by a eunuch when his pupil was on the throne.

He was born Constantine Psellus in 1018 – the same year as Nizām al-Mulk, in fact – the heir of an ancient line of noblemen who had recently fallen on relatively hard times. The need to provide a good dowry for his beloved elder sister, who later died young, forced him to interrupt his education to become a judge's clerk in Anatolia for a time. But his personal charm, eloquence and intelligence combined with the affection of his fellow students to pave his rapid rise in society and the court. He was appointed professor of rhetoric or 'consul of the philosophers' at the new imperial university and became a companion to emperors and empresses. Thus Constantine IX 'admired his eloquence', Michael the Aged 'tasted the honey of his lips', Constantine X regarded his words as 'nectar' and Eudocia 'looked upon him as a god'.[5]

In 1054, he feared that Constantine IX might tire of him in their constant companionship. So he pretended that he suffered from an incurable disease and asked to be allowed to retire to a monastery. That is when he chose the baptismal name of Michael, which afterwards stuck to him. However, immediately on Constantine's death, Empress Theodora heard of his miraculous recovery and of his desire to serve the crown once more. To his credit, Psellus readily admitted to having lied.

Historians of Byzantium and the Renaissance admire Psellus for making the study of the classical Greek writers, particularly Plato, admissible in the church, claiming that Plato's theology was the precursor of the Christian. Specialists believe that this, in turn, caused some of the sparks that later started the European Renaissance of the fourteenth and fifteenth centuries.

True or false, Psellus has also gone down in the history books as one of a breed of notorious 'men of peace' who used their influence on the feeble-minded sovereigns of their time to starve the Byzantine army of funds in order to satisfy the greed of their courtiers for luxury and soft lives. In Chapter II, we heard him confess how terrified he had been at the end of 1067 to be told by Eudocia that she had decided to marry the army strongman Romanus Diogenes in the hope of recovering some of the lands recently lost to Turkish marauders in eastern Anatolia. Later, after the battle of Manzikert in 1071, when Romanus suffered an historic defeat due to the decades of neglect of the army, Psellus was instrumental in conspiring with the chief traitor John Ducas to depose him – and Eudocia, too – in favour of the latter's unprepared son Michael VII.

In this light, therefore, Psellus deserved it when Michael, his pupil and protégé of many years, suddenly banned him from court and gave full authority to a man Psellus hated, the eunuch Nikephoritzes. The reasons for Michael's action are unclear, but Psellus was opposed to Michael's attempt to reconcile the Greek Church with Rome in pursuit of a military pact with the pope, Gregory VII. This the emperor wanted for the purpose of being allowed to recruit more mercenaries in western Europe to fight the Turks in the east.

When, in March 1078, Michael was, in turn, overthrown in a military rebellion and sent to a monastery – where he heard of the indignity suffered by his young and beautiful wife, Princess Mary of Alania, who was forced to marry the leader of the rebels – Psellus sank into obscurity without trace. By then, nearly the whole of Asia Minor was lost to the Turks.

*   *   *

How could anyone in 1078 calculate the average length of the year to within seconds of what atomic clocks give us today, without the atomic clocks of today? In fact without any accurate clocks of any kind? The only time-measuring devices available to astronomers at the time were sundials, hourglasses, water clocks and astrolabes, and while these were adequate for many purposes in daily life, they were woefully insufficient for calculating astronomical values to govern calendars. Each instrument was a unique, handmade creation, its accuracy depending on its particular maker and on the eye of its user. Nevertheless, given patience and human ingenuity in mathematics, great feats could be – and were – achieved.[6]

That year was to be the busiest and most momentous of young Omar's professional life, for he and his seven fellow astronomers were nearing their deadline for devising the most accurate calendar there had ever been. By midwinter at the latest their handiwork had to be ready for submission to the authorities, for the state had to declare it, well ahead of the coming spring equinox, 15 March, as the new time scheme of the empire. On a precise second on that day, the sun would cross the fine line between the southern and northern hemispheres in the sky. How could anyone be certain where that line lay without any optical instrument worthy of the name?

A bright idea had occurred to the mind of a clever Neolithic Egyptian almost five thousand years earlier. He had proposed that they could count the number of days between the maximum flood levels of the Nile. Experience had then proved that although the year often seemed to be about 365 days long, sometimes it was a little longer or shorter, depending, no doubt, on the vagaries of the weather over the far horizon, the unknown land, in the far south, that gave rise to the river. The next step had been to collect figures for a number of years and then divide the total by the number of those years. That finally had confirmed the average figure of 365 days, which was more than good enough for farmers. They could now predict when the annual flood would begin to recede from their fields and the hard work start. Then the daughter's wedding could be planned, the date of the annual trip to market could be agreed and the dreadful tax man expected. Thus the Egyptians finally discarded the moon to give the world its first purely solar calendar.

Some 2,000 years later, the same Egyptians discovered the more accurate figure of 365¼ days for the year by counting the number of days it took between the first appearance of the Dog Star or Sirius over the horizon and its re-emergence in the following year. In this way, observant – but instrument-poor – mankind arrived within 11 minutes and 24 seconds of the true average length of the year, the time it took the universe to make one whole pilgrimage around us, Thoth's chosen people.[7]

We do not know whether the Sumerians who lived near today's southern Iraqi marshes found a similar pointer in the annual floods of the Tigris and Euphrates rivers, but it cannot be ruled out. They devised a solar calendar by adding the required number of days to the lunar year of 354 days to ensure the months were accurate to the seasons.

Now, in 1078, none of these previous models were sufficiently accurate for the team of astronomers among whom Omar served and new ingenuity was required, without any guarantee of success. So the prolific reading and writing and calculating had its anxieties as well as its excitements and rewards.

No descriptive account has survived of the practical conditions under which the team laboured. If any were written – and they must have been, at least in letters to colleagues, friends and family – they would have been circulated in small numbers and are likely to have perished in the later Turkic and Mongolian invasions. But information is available elsewhere of how such astronomers achieved their impressive results in medieval times.

Four of their main instruments were the sundial, the water clock, the globe and the astrolabe, with the most sophisticated of them being the latter, a Greek invention of the sixth century. In recent times, in the hands of Byzantine and 'Muslim'[8] astronomers, it had improved further.

In essence, the medieval astrolabe was a primitive, hand-held computer that reckoned time and measured the positions of the sun and the visible planets in their orbits with regard to the horizon and the meridian. The most widely used type, the planespheric astrolabe, was made up of a base plate, the mater, with a number of lines drawn on it to represent the main celestial coordinates. One or two upper disks that could be rotated around a centre pin, the celestial north pole, had holes cut in them and a map of the principal 'stars' imprinted on them. As the observer rotated the upper disk or disks round the pin, with a straight line pointing towards a particular object in the sky, a range of information could be read. The instrument could also be used to estimate, for example, the height of a mountain. But to be reasonably accurate, it had to be designed for a particular latitude.

The simplest sundial, which was probably invented independently in several places as long ago as 3500 BC, was a straight pole pointing towards the centre of the sky and casting a shadow on a line or semi-circle at its base. At noon in midsummer, the stick cast no shadow. The line or semi-circle on the base of the dial was divided into the hours of the day and further information could be etched onto it to enable more accurate readings according to the time of day or season. The 'hours' were not all equal, but 'temporary hours', with a number of arcs needed at the base to give more accurate figures in the mornings, afternoons, summers and winters.

The beauty of the sundial lay in its simplicity. It could be made and installed by a carpenter for individual households and some are still being used in rural Egypt. They could be enormously sophisticated, as for example in the Tower of the Winds in Athens. Constructed sometime between 100 and 50 BC, the 13m high (42ft) building still exists and has eight sundials with bases at various angles to the horizontal. Designed by Andronicus of Cyrrhus, it had a weathervane at the top and an extra water clock for night-time and overcast days.

The city of Rome constructed its first public sundial in 164 BC and Augustus Caesar erected his grand memorial dial in 10 BC, still to be admired in Piazza del Popolo with a grid of lines in stone at its base.

As for water clocks, it is surprising to learn how early in history they were invented, for they, too, are simple in principle. They were invented independently in both the Old and the New World and could be, in their simplest form, a vessel filled with water with a hole in its bottom. As the water ran out, marks etched onto the inner walls of the vessel for separate hours were revealed.

The Romans invented a much more sophisticated form that used water dripping at a constant pressure into a lower cylinder. As the water rose in the cylinder, a float with a pointer rose against a calibrated scale on the wall above to show the time. It could be reasonably accurate and it was a 24-hour system. It was used, among other places, in town halls to tell public speakers that they were stretching their audiences' patience. In Athens, water clocks were installed in theatres and raised Aristotle's eyebrows when some uncouth member of the audience glanced towards them in the middle of a play. 'A tragedy', he wrote, 'ought not to be judged by how long it takes. The plot ought to be allowed to take as long as it needs.'

So, under exactly what conditions did the team of eight astronomers work in Isfahan those years between 1074 and 1079? In the absence of a contemporary account, we have to depend on conjecture. Certainly no large-scale observatory was constructed for their purpose, as was the case in the life of the unfortunate prince Ulug Beg in Samarkand in 1428, to come up with the most accurate map of the sky that there had ever been. But the task here was to measure accurately the average length of the year and devise a calendar whose leap years could be remembered easily. Thus we can imagine a hive of activity in whatever building in the city that the team and their large supportive staff of librarians, scribes, messengers, accountants, etc. occupied. In periodic conferences, no doubt, each member of the team reported on the state of the research allocated to him. Decisions were then made on how to proceed further. Occasionally, one or more members were asked to travel to another place to make measurements at different latitudes. The resulting figures were then pooled and averages made to reach an agreed figure.

We can also be certain of the tensions, quarrels and even physical conflicts that are likely to occur whenever highly strung geniuses work together for more than a few days. Some of these might well have required a summons to appear before chancellor Nizām himself, no less, with him threatening a humiliating flogging if the nonsense did not stop. Too much money was being spent on the project to allow its failure. Less drastic clashes might have occurred along the line of the following imagined conversation between Omar and an older, pedantic member of the team during a lunch break:

'Why should the earth be unique, anyway? Why shouldn't it be a planet, like the others? Aristotle thinks it goes round the sun, and we do know it rotates itself.

And why can't there be living creatures on the moon or the other planets? I grant you that nothing can live on the sun. It's obviously just too hot. But why not on the moon? Why not on Jupiter? They're distant enough from the sun. They're lit by the sun, just like us? Why not?'

'Because, you pig-headed fool, the Almighty would have told us in the Noble Book. The stars are there just to light our way. Are you doubting the truth of the Koran?'

'No, no, of course, not. Hey, be careful what you say. Someone might hear.'

'Go and wash out your mouth, you blasphemer. No one will report you if you don't say such things.'

And that would have been the end of one friendship, if there had been any in the first place!

But while the obstacles were many and the means meagre, there was hope too and inspiration at hand in the nearby library. In the past, focusing on seemingly impossible puzzles and using figures from a variety of sources had enabled such legendary men as Hipparchus of Rhodes in the second century, Claudius Ptolemaeus or Ptolemy of Alexandria a little later, and fellow Iranian Khārazmi of the early ninth century to achieve breathtaking results. Hipparchus gave up his quest to measure the distance between the earth and the sun, but only because he realised it was too great a distance to be measured with his means. He actually said that one day future generations would succeed where he failed. As for Ptolemy, his thirteen-volume model of the universe, which young Omar knew almost by heart, seemed to tax one's reason at times but his genius appeared almost beyond imagination. Khārazmi, who coined the term 'algebra', championed the new system of Indian numbers and paved the way for more thorough calculations. For now, studying the rate of progress of the sun and the stars along the lines of the meridian appeared the best line of attack.

*   *   *

On Monday, 15 March 1079, at 5.33 a.m. in Isfahan,[9] the new calendar came into force throughout the Saljuq empire after five years of reading, measuring, consulting, travelling and calculating by the eight-man team of astronomers whose task it had been to devise it. It was – and remains – the most accurate calendar ever adopted by man. This is how the Institute of Physics in London describes it in the *Encyclopedia of Astronomy and Astrophysics*, Volume 2, 2001:

> Khayyām developed a calendar which had an error of one day in 3,770 years (superior to the Gregorian calendar with an error of one day in 3,330 years). It was based on his amazingly accurate determination of the length of the year as 365.242199 days. The length of the year is currently 365.242190 days, decreasing by about six units in the sixth decimal place over a century.

That Monday thus saw, for the first time in centuries, the coincidence of the first day of the solar calendar with the start of the natural year, the true Norūz, when the sun entered Aries and heralded the first day of spring. As we saw earlier, the newly gathered team of astronomers had, nearly five years earlier, temporarily halted the further regression of the calendar against the seasons. They had added the customary eleven 'intercalatory' days to the year and thus fixed the start of the new year where it was then, 26 February. Now another sixteen days were added to the outgoing year to shift the start of the year to Norūz day itself, as it had first been designated by Darius the Great, the Achaemenid, in the fifth century BC. Henceforth, a system of intercalatory annual days and leap years would ensure that the two never parted company again.[10]

The new scheme of arranging the days and months of the year was named the 'Jalāli Era' after one of Malik Shah's titles, Jalāl ed-Dowlah, Glory of the State, and the new calendar was flaunted as the newest jewel in the young shah's already glittering crown. Its implications went far beyond the practical. It was used to depict the Saljuq state as a civilising force in the history of man and to put Malik Shah in the exalted class of the greatest sovereigns there had ever been, of the ilk of Great King Darius and Caesar Julius. They too had deemed an accurate calendar the mark of an advanced people and had allocated to its production vast amounts of gold and energy.

Alas, no contemporary account of the celebrations has survived, but they must have been elaborate and spread over countless cities and towns from Baghdad to Samarkand. At the precise time of the transition at dawn, trumpets must have sounded and drums must have rolled. Great bonfires would have been lit the previous Wednesday for the young to leap over while they made wishes. This occurred every year according to ancient tradition and survives to our time despite the efforts of Islamists to extinguish it. That year, the bonfires must have been especially substantial, spread over many evenings and many places, including mountain tops, for all the peoples of the capital to see. The celebrations must have been accompanied, as usual, by the king's own musicians and singers. The shah and chancellor would almost certainly have been there, together with Omar's old friend from his days in Bukhara, the princess Terken Khātūn, now the senior of Malik Shah's two wives. Perhaps even the nameless Armenian princess of the Bagratid dynasty of Georgia, whom the sultan Alp-Arslan had given to Nizām, would have been present. She had now borne the chancellor a son who would later rise to be a power in the state. Perhaps her days of misery were over by now.

Omar would have received the bulk of the accolade from the king and all the great and good personally, for it is only in connection with his name and that of Malik Shah that the new calendar is recorded in the history books. The other seven astronomers are sometimes mentioned, but in supporting roles only.

Why is this so? We can only guess. Although the new calendar was the collective achievement of a team of eight men over five years, the youngest member of the team was by far so much more brilliant than the rest that he overshadowed them in his contributions. None could hide the fact from the authorities or the public.

The single most important part of the achievement, on which all the rest was based, was the accurate measuring of the average length of the year, and this was Khayyām's work. By expanding on the algebra of Khārazmi and producing solutions to three new classes of cubic equations, he had become the greatest living mathematician of his time. Henceforth, the carefree, hard-drinking young man known to everyone as 'Omar' would be Hakīm or Doctor Omar-e-Khayyāmi.[11] At the age of thirty he had finally grown up.[12]

To show the true extent of Khayyām's victory over the manifold obstacles in his path, a few figures may be given here in non-technical language about the average length of the year. According to the atomic clocks of today, it is 365 days, five hours, forty-eight minutes and fifty seconds. Khayyām calculated it to be four seconds shorter.[13]

However, that is not quite the whole story. The average length of the year has been getting longer – by about one second every century – ever since our planet came into being as the result of cosmic debris accumulating around the sun around 4½ billion years ago (Khayyām would have given his right arm to know this single fact!). Thus in the eleventh century, the average length of the year was about nine seconds shorter than today's, and Khayyām's true target would have been the figure for his own time, not ours. In this respect, his calculation was five seconds too long, not four seconds too short.

Either way, he truly does deserve a crater on the moon named after him – and how he would have loved to know that, too.[14]

The Jalāli calendar remains the official calendar of Iran, and much of central Asia and Afghanistan, with small modifications, though it has to be said that its arrangement of leap years is slightly complicated. Instead of having a leap year in every four years, it has one in every four or five years.

It is different in one more important respect. Its actual transitions from one year to the next are calculated to the second and require astronomers. But they do provide the populace with a more dramatic sense of time as every Norūz they gather in family groups to await the arrival of the magic moment over their particular horizon. Every locality has its own unique moment of welcoming in the New Year.

The team of astronomers – or probably Khayyām on his own – achieved one more great feat which is not short of astonishing: at a time when some powerful clerics were trying to extinguish all traces of Zoroastrian Iran, Malik Shah was persuaded not only to allow the Iranian names of the months of the year to remain in use, but also to revive all the Zoroastrian names of all the days of every month.

The scheme inevitably fell into abeyance later, for even in Zoroastrian Iran people had had difficulty remembering thirty or thirty-one names each month. The fact that an attempt was made to revive it at all, however, confirms the strength of Persian patriotic sentiment on the part of Khayyām – the one man among the team who was a close friend of the king – and the majority of his colleagues. It is also astonishing that Malik Shah, who was himself of Turkish extraction and probably spoke Turkish with his family, should have agreed to the proposal. He never learnt to speak Arabic.

What is not recorded is the attitude of the powerful chancellor. Though a Persian and a great admirer of the ancient Persian kings – as can be seen in his *Book of Politics* – he was also a stern Sunni Muslim and allied to the orthodox clergy. It is almost certain that he would have opposed the revival of the Zoroastrian day names as both unnecessary and provocative. But tension had already set in between the young shah and his honorary 'father'. The king had grown resentful of the overwhelming power and wealth of his chancellor and his sons. Tragedy was certain to follow.

CHAPTER SIX

The Vizier Regrets

Shouted at a whore a raucous mullah:
'Drunkard, faithless, a menace you are.'
She replied: 'My Lord, I am all you say,
But are you truly all you say you are?'

It is late March 1079 and Grand Vizier Nizām's chief officers are in a quandary. Should they be seen to be arranging his life according to the king's newly reformed Zoroastrian solar calendar, on which vast sums have been spent, or should they stick by the lunar calendar of Islam? The first would please their increasingly resentful sovereign, the second their allies, the clerical class.

The trouble is that a decision has to be made. Among all the leaders of the state, the chancellor's birthday comes up first, on the 21st day of the current month of Farvardin,[1] the first month of the newly inaugurated solar calendar. He will be sixty-one.

One way of escaping the discomfiture might be to reason, albeit weakly, that the chancellor had already celebrated his birthday in the month of Dhulqa'dah, in the previous, Islamic calendar, and although it was flattering that the new calendar made him two years younger, he felt it was too much of an indulgence to celebrate your birthday twice inside ten months.

In the event, we do not know what happened. Perhaps he opted for a private banquet only. Perhaps there was a function given in his honour by the king himself. But we can be certain that there would have been few genuine smiles exchanged between the two camps whenever they met. The chancellor had become strident in claiming that he was central to the survival of the regime, and he had even had the confidence to send a circular to all ministerial departments that no orders issued by the royal court be obeyed unless it was approved by his office. This had particularly incensed the 'Qarakhanid court' of the queen,[2] Terken Khātūn. One of the chancellor's sons had even killed the king's favourite jester and the son had in turn been assassinated, by the king's agents – or possibly Terken's.

On the symbolic occasion of his birthday, Nizām al-Mulk would have probably reflected on his life so far. In a rare quiet moment with himself, away from the neighing of horses, the changing of guards, the clamour of petitioners or the constant arrival of important couriers from distant cities, he could be forgiven for looking back on his achievements with wonder and amazement. From a destitute refugee at the fall of the Ghaznavids in Khorāsān, he had risen to be the chief administrator of the succeeding empire and had even married into its ruling family. In fact, everyone thought – no, they knew – that he was more powerful than the sultan.

Fortunately, most people approved. A wise and loyal chancellor was at the helm of the state while the young and brave sultan bore his natural frustrations in good grace and held the social fabric of the court and army together with his pursuit of hunting and other royal interests. As a result, the empire was continuing to expand into Anatolia and Arabia, while the cities busied themselves with building grand mosques and palaces, schools and public parks, basking in their new prosperity. It was only a matter of time, too, before that false caliphate of the heretics, the Shias of Cairo, would fall to Saljuq arms and the world of Islam would be almost wholly reunited.

But those same acute inner senses that had raised 'the old man' to the heights he now occupied told him that the wind gathering strength in the reeds augured stormy weather ahead. The assassination of his son was indication enough, and, as all the history books made plain, change could not be averted for ever. The boy king, who would be twenty-five in the summer, even betrayed signs of instability and, although able to read and write, unlike his forefathers, he suffered from the Turks' unbecoming and dangerous impatience to take up the reins of power in their hands early. As the boy had grown older, his habitual use of 'Father' to address him had become just that, a habit, and it had become less frequent. His Majesty often needed to be reminded forcefully of the importance of ruling according to the Holy Law and of the dangers of the autocratic, lawless ways of his ancestors in the Central Asian steppe. It was more than time the Saljuq state grew up, absorbed the wisdom of the ages and emulated the examples of such great and beloved emperors as Anūshīrvān the Just, whose praises were still being sung on the streets of Isfahan 500 years later. To this end, to show that the state ought to see itself as more than an instrument satisfying the various lusts of its princes, the chancellor planned to write a book of advice for Malik Shah, and he patronised the experts of the Ash'ari legal school of Sunni Islam. The state needed their diligence. Permitting fashionable interpretations to suit the political needs of the day made people uncertain. It encouraged demands for more concessions. But if commoners thought that the law was immutable and the sovereign as helpless before it as they were, they would relax. They would be obedient servants of their monarch and pay their long-established taxes without grumbling too much.

The following passage is from that book, which the chancellor would later call Siāsat Nāmeh, Book of Politics. We can be certain that many of its stories and examples had become tiresome to the young king even before he wrote them down, for ever since the late sultan Alp-Arslan had put the Grand Vizier in charge of his young son's education, the boy had frequently been lectured about them. This passage is from chapter six of the book, 'On Judges, Preachers and Inspectors, and on the Enhancement of their Work':

They say it was a custom of the kings of Persia that for the festivals of Mehrgān [in the autumn] and Norūz they gave open audience to the people. No one was barred. For days previously, they sent out town criers to announce the day and, on the day itself, the criers again appeared in the markets to warn anyone who might try to stop petitioners appearing before the king. They were told they faced harsh punishment at his hands. Thus the people placed their stories before the king and the king heard each man on his own. If among them, one had a complaint against the king himself, the king descended from the throne and sat on his knees on the floor before the chief Mūbad [the Zoroastrian patriarch], who was also called the Judge of Judges in Pahlavi. The king would then say to the Mūbad: 'Before all others, deliver justice to this man, without any thoughts for me, for no sin exceeds in the eye of the Almighty than the sin of princes. They must uphold the rights of their subjects and ward off the hands of criminals. If the king himself be a tyrant, the army will follow suit, God will be forgotten and, soon, the king will be swept away and the world will go to ruins. Oh, God-fearing Mūbad, take care not to seek my favours, for if God Almighty should one day question me on any trespass, I shall put the blame on your shoulder.' . . .

Thus the Mūbad would sit in judgement on the king and the plaintiff. He would announce in favour of the plaintiff if he were right, and he would punish him if he were a liar, for it is a grave crime to libel the king or the government. . . .

On such days, the king would sit those who were closest to him the farthest away from him, and those who were powerful he would treat as the weakest. This custom was upheld from the time of Ardashīr to the days of Yazdgerd, but Yazdgerd upturned the ways of his fathers. He started tyranny in the world and the people fell into suffering. They cursed him and prayed until, one day, a beautiful horse appeared at his gate, so beautiful none had seen its peer. All tried to capture it, but none could. Then the horse went over to Yazdgerd and stood still before him. The king took its mane in hand and stroked its face and back. The horse remained calm. Then the king ordered a saddle and bridle be brought over and the horse was saddled. But when the king tried to mount it, it kicked him in the stomach with his hind legs so hard that Yazdgerd died there and then. The horse now ran out of court and disappeared. None could find it ever again. All the people agreed that it had been an angel sent by God Almighty to rid them of a tyrant.[3]

What was Nizām to do to prevent the headstrong young man becoming another Yazdgerd? While there was still time, he, Nizām, must devise a strategy to make such an outcome impossible, and that strategy he based on the experience of his own predecessors, but in a perverse manner. He had not forgotten of course how he himself had been instrumental in bringing about the downfall of his immediate predecessor, the late Grand Vizier Kondori. That wily old fellow Khorāsānian had established for himself a great power base in the army and administration and tried to put his own client prince, Suleimān, on the throne after the death of the sultan Toghril in 1063. In the end, he lost to Alp-Arslan, with Nizām's men bringing his head to him on a platter as proof of final victory. Nizām also knew from the history books how the great Iranian family of the Barmakids 200 years earlier had devoted their lives to serving the Abbassid caliphs only to be rewarded with murder and confiscation by Harūn al-Rashīd. Harūn had actually grown up with one of them as his foster brother before making him his vizier. Yet in a drunken and jealous moment in the middle of one night, he had sent for his vizier's head, and it was duly delivered to him by a eunuch accompanied by a few knights.

Nizām determined not to repeat their mistakes, but he concluded that their mistakes had been not to make themselves powerful enough. All they had done had been to create the impression that they were untouchable.

All of Nizām's acts as guardian and vizier to Malik Shah point to this strategy having been nurtured in the most secret corner of his heart from the moment Alp-Arslan was assassinated, and it was a highly refined strategy. Not only would he develop an enormous network of patronage for himself in the army and administration, he would also make large segments of the dominant Sunni clergy dependant on him for their very livelihoods. They were in daily contact with the mass of the empire's common subjects and could whip them up into a frenzy. The experience of the caliphs in Baghdad and the story of the Qarakhanid kings of Bukhara and Samarkand proved how dangerous the common people could be.

We shall see later to what extent Grand Vizier Nizām succeeded in his plan. Certainly at one point he would become bold enough to tell his king that the empire was a 'partnership' between the two of them, not a personal possession of the crown, and that 'without this inkpot', all would fall down in the wind.

Returning to the calendar, it may be indicative of a fierce resistance to it that, while the new reforms with their resounding Zoroastrian month names survived virtually intact to this day, coins struck subsequently by the government continued to bear only lunar dates and no Saljuq building erected afterwards was allowed to bear witness to a solar calendar having been in existence. Can there be a truer measure of the vizier's triumph over his headstrong royal 'son'?

*   *   *

Just over a month later on 18[4] May 1079, it was Omar's turn to celebrate his birthday, his thirty-first, but the two celebrations would have born little similarity. While Grand Vizier was constantly in the eye of the world, Omar was merely a young professional with few cares on his mind. Furthermore, while Nizām al-Mulk had to be sober and sombre and censorious, Omar was loud and fast and rebellious. He was an exhibitionist who shouted his gains from the rooftops and, while working hard, played hard, too. He debunked authority openly and he drank himself silly frequently.

At this stage, Omar would have been only an irritant, But he would have to be watched by the chancellor's men, nevertheless. He had the ear of both the king and the queen any time he wished, all three being of the same generation, while Nizām's own second son, Mo'ayyad, often accompanied him whenever he visited Isfahan on a break from his studies in Baghdad.[5] Though thoroughly loyal to the state as a whole, Omar had a destructive element in his character, and his inability to keep quiet about the affairs of the great and the good made him a useful source of information. For a vizier who insisted on paying the wages of the boatmen of the Oxus in Transoxania through his own office and who believed that the state must have spies everywhere, an irreverent, decadent young man who had become the witty ornament of every high table at the heart of the empire could not be ignored.

Did Khayyām have a family by now? The answer must be yes, almost certainly. Some of the sources refer to him as Abu-Hafs, implying that he had a son called Hafs. But the usage remains in the minority and gives place later in his life to Abu-Fath.[6] As the firstborn son was always given priority in this respect, the conclusion must be that Hafs died in childhood. Omar appears to have also had at least one daughter, of whom more later. For the time being, we may imagine Khayyām and his wife taking their children to Isfahan's famous public gardens or the private gardens of other young parents like themselves on the warmer evenings of spring, summer and autumn. They would have passed the hours in small talk as their children ran around on the lawn or splashed in a pool.

As Khayyām had known Terken Khātūn since her childhood and as Isfahan was, by today's standards, a town, it is likely that his children and hers virtually grew up together.

*   *   *

In July 1080, Isfahan received news that Terken Khātūn's father, the king Shams al-Mulk of the Qarakhanids in Samarkand and Bukhara, had died and that, since none of his sons had survived him, he had been succeeded by his brother Hasan. No greater detail is provided by the sources and we have to resort to conjecture on what it might have meant for the queen or her supporters in Isfahan.

By all accounts, Malik Shah had continued to behave cordially towards his vanquished father-in-law over the past seven years. In return for the prompt payment of the annual tribute by Bukhara, he – or rather, his chancellor Nizām – had allowed the king to rule his kingdom largely as he wished and, as a result, Shams al-Mulk had remained popular among his subjects. In fact, the historians tell us that he was regarded as an ideal ruler: just, generous, cultured and firm.

He had also been a broken man. Gone was the dashing warrior king leading his troops in person to conquer Marv and Termez. His cousins, the Qarakhanids of eastern Turkistan, had stabbed him in the back while he had tried to fend off a great Saljuq army led by Nizām al-Mulk and Malik Shah. The result had been a humiliating peace agreement dictated to him by Nizām in Samarkand that had installed Saljuq officials at his side to watch his every move. He had subsequently consoled himself by building palaces, public baths, mosques, schools and caravanserais. In his will, he had stipulated to be buried at one of the latter, a resting place by a roadside in a wilderness.

We can take it for granted that a grand memorial service was held at Isfahan's cathedral mosque, the present Friday Mosque in Old Square in the north-east of the city, at which the shah and the chancellor attended with all the dignitaries of the state. At the very least, several private receptions would have also been organised by Terken Khātūn at which to receive the condolences of the nobility, the prominent clergy, the richest merchants and other influential peoples of the capital. She had by now locked horns openly with the chancellor about the influence he had over her husband, and one way in which she made herself visible was to indulge in ostentation of various kinds.

Was Khayyām beside her during those ceremonies? Perhaps not right beside her, for that might have raised eyebrows on account of their compatible ages and past association, despite the relative freedom that women enjoyed in Turkish tribal society. But it is difficult to imagine him not being among the hosts at all.

As one of her father's drinking companions in Bukhara in 1073, before he was snatched by the Saljuqs, Khayyām would have initially been a 'Qarakhanid', meaning a member of Terken Khātūn's court. Unless he had annoyed her severely over the past several years, we have to assume that he remained close to her. It would have been normal for him to remain loyal to her family in Bukhara and to be sympathetic towards her personal dilemmas in Isfahan. She received regular news of how overbearing and grasping were Nizām's men at her father's court and this no doubt contributed to her feud with the chancellor. On his part, the chancellor was openly complaining of Malik Shah being under the influence of 'women', meaning that he deferred too much to Terken's opinions. Her chief of staff, Tāj al-Mulk, dared to oppose Nizām al-Mulk and was sometimes pointedly, but inaccurately, called Terken Khātūn's 'vizier'. In the midst of such politics, she was under pressure to produce as many male heirs to the throne as possible. Her eldest child, a daughter, did not qualify and her son, Dāwūd, the heir designate, seemed delicate.

* * *

It appears from Khayyām's own writings that he began to have more time on his hand after March 1079, at least for a year or two. It makes sense. In that month, on the fourteenth, as we have just seen, the calendar that he and his seven astronomer colleagues had devised was formally adopted as the official civil calendar of the empire, and the team would have been given a break before embarking on their next big project, the building of a new observatory in Isfahan. Khayyām says in a preface to a treatise later that, in the Islamic year 472 – which fell between July 1079 and June 1080 – he translated a treatise by Avicenna from Arabic into Persian.

Fortunately the translation, which he made 'at the request of a group of friends in Isfahan', has survived to throw light on his mentality at this time. On starting to read it, the immediate question that invades the mind of the reader is: why choose this one? The title,

'On the Unity of the Divine', is safe and orthodox enough. But read on and the opening sentence declares open rebellion. It is almost pure Zoroastrianism. Furthermore, its Persian is so archaic – and so theatrical – that it is clearly meant to produce shrieks of laughter at the brazenness of the rebellion:

Oh, good one, oh, shah, oh, lord![7] Izad the Almighty, the god by whom all things began, that Izad is not essence that might change by accepting opposites. Thou must know that not all essences accept opposites . . .

Khayyām then quickly gives up the effort of writing pure Persian and takes on the normal style of theological discourse, though still with less borrowed Arabic words than might be expected. The opening salvo of anti-Arabism has already made its point. It has been so distracting that concentrating on the verbose and abstract concepts in the next passage becomes doubly difficult for the reader.

Curiously, we find some of the same exaggeratedly archaic Persian and the same Zoroastrian theology in the preface of a book of romantic verse by a poet who flourished earlier in the 1050s during Khayyām's childhood. But Fakhri Gorgāni had translated his love story of Veis and Rāmīn straight from Pahlavi or Middle Persian. He had good reason both to be faithful to the original and to indulge in theatricality. Khayyām did not.

One more immediate question on the mind of the reader is why Khayyām addresses the translation to the king. There is no such dedication in the text he is supposed to be translating. Does it mean that those 'friends in Isfahan' who asked him to translate the monograph included Malik Shah, who did not read Arabic and who would have enjoyed reading the controversial article by Avicenna in Persian without commissioning it openly? To be seen to have done so would have further annoyed the clergy. The previous year, the shah had allowed his astronomers not only to retain the Zoroastrian names of the months of the solar calendar, but even revive the forgotten names of all the thirty or thirty-one days in each month with their provocative invocations of Mazda and the lesser Zoroastrian divinities.

We can certainly imagine Nizām al-Mulk not to have been amused at all by Khayyām's latest irreverent act. He is quite likely to have seen it as mocking his authority and challenging his religion. He was busy not only patronising the most unforgiving school of law in Sunni Islam, Ash'ari Sunnism – against the Saljuqs' preference for the Shāfi'is – but also spending huge sums of his own money building mosques and theological schools in almost every important city, from Baghdad to Nishāpur. The institutions he was founding were called Nizāmiyahs after him and they made thousands of hard-line clerics beholden to him personally for their very livelihoods. Can we not imagine him sending one of his men to deliver a stern warning to Khayyām, to tell him how much Grand Vizier regretted to see such irresponsible behaviour on the part of a young man he had himself chosen in Bukhara to bring over to Isfahan for a great future?

Whether or not Grand Vizier himself sent any such warning to Khayyām, there is evidence that Khayyām soon found himself in deep trouble. A year later we find him in the city of Shiraz at the invitation of the governor of Fārs province – a surviving relic of ancient 'Pārs' or Persia – writing a treatise on theology which is so meek and orthodox as to be unbelievable. What was going on? For an explanation, see 'Appendix IV: Khayyām's Mathematics and Other Writings'.

* * *

It is 10 June 1081 and a mysterious stranger arrives in Isfahan. He is of southern Arabian appearance, slight, dark and lean, but speaks perfect Persian with a northern accent, as if from the city of Rayy. He exudes dignity and appears to be the kind that prefers his own company and only answers pleasantries if he has to. For the next few days he stays at a caravanserai of the middling classes, run by orthodox Sunnis, not to draw attention to himself. He tells the reception that he will be leaving the city soon, but makes furtive visits to certain low-class shops and businesses, after making certain no one follows him. Then, one night, he makes his way with a guide to a cottage in the poorest district of the city, through narrow lanes enclosed by high walls.

He enters the small courtyard and is embraced by an older man without exchanging a word. Both have aged visibly since they last met in Rayy a dozen years ago. The older man had told the younger to prepare to go to Egypt to be his envoy at the court there.

They enter a small room and a woman brings them refreshments. The younger man looks the older in the face and shakes his head from side to side. 'Phew', he whispers. 'What a calamity I found!'

'They wouldn't let you see him, would they?', asks Abdul Malik Attāsh, the chief of the Ismailis of Iran.

'Of course not', replies Hasan Sabbāh. 'They nearly killed me'.

Attāsh now shakes his head in disbelief:

> Attāsh: *Sit down. I'm sorry. I didn't expect it to be this bad. But we had to know.*
>
> Sabbāh: *Yes, we had to know. After months of trouble by land and sea, eventually I arrived in Cairo two years ago and immediately reported to the court. They wouldn't let me anywhere near His Holiness. So I went over to the prince and found only glum faces. The Armenian lets him see his father only rarely, and then only if his own men are present. They found out and locked me up. They beat me up and starved me. Eventually they put me on a Frankish ship for Morocco. But a storm blew us east and we were wrecked on the coast of Syria.*
>
> Attāsh: *So we can't expect any help at all from the brothers there?*
>
> Sabbāh: *None at all. His Holiness really worries about us and I was told he wanted to see me. But he's a virtual prisoner. The Armenian's just waiting for him to die so that he can put the younger prince, his own son-in-law, on the throne. Everyone fears for the crown prince's life.*
>
> Attāsh: *Here our situation has definitely got worse. Not a week passes without some of our people being killed by the Turks or those Khorāsānian lackeys of theirs. They're so tireless, so cunning. They've even turned some of our own people against us. They inform on us for gold . . .*
>
> Sabbāh: *We need a miracle . . .*

This particular meeting may, or may not, have happened. It is a fantasy on my part. But the date of Sabbāh's arrival back in Isfahan after an absence of two years, and the story of what had happened to him in Cairo, are based on his autobiography. He would have confided them in someone among the leaders of his community in Isfahan. What Sabbāh did not know at this stage was that the deliverance they all hoped for would happen, and soon. He would himself achieve such power that Saljuq sultans would hesitate entering their bedchambers for fear of the Assassins. Before that, great heartaches would befall them, and him, including a severe mental breakdown that would leave him scarred for the rest of his life. Let that Persian official of the

Mongols, Atā-Malik Juvayni, who retained for us some of the factual parts of Sabbāh's autobiography, take up the story:

> By the time Hasan Sabbāh returned from Egypt, his belonging to the Ismailis[8] had been discovered, so that those who worried on behalf of Islam and religion were looking for him, forcing him on the run. In Isfahan, he lived in secrecy in the home of a government official called Abul-Fazl who had accepted their call. He lived there for some time and each day this officer would go to him and they would share their sorrows.
>
> One day as they discussed their complaints against the age and the zeal of the sultan and the leaders of his government, Hasan sighed and said: 'If only I had a couple of men of the same heart. I would turn this kingdom upside down.'
>
> The chief Abul-Fazl thought to himself that Hasan had succumbed to stress and fear and dangerous journeys, so that he was going mad, for how could the kingdom of a shah, under whose banner and coinage lived a multitude of nations from the borders of Egypt to Turkistan, be overturned by a few men of a determined mind?
>
> So, without telling Hasan, the chief decided to try to cure him. He prepared for him aromatic juices and nutritious foods and sat down with him for every meal. But when Hasan saw the drinks and the food, he suspected the chief's inner thoughts and immediately left his house, not heeding the man's heartfelt pleas to stay.[9]

*   *   *

On 18 May 1083, Khayyām reached the age of thirty-five, a figure which deserved celebration unless, of course, the young family had suffered a recent death, for example that of little Hafs, who apparently never reached maturity.

For the next few years, Khayyām disappears from the records. Either little of importance happens to him or else, more likely, the records have been lost to us. What we can assume with certainty is that he lived in Isfahan most of the time and worked on building Malik Shah's new observatory. We are told by Ibn al-Athīr that the king had observations made for him continuously to the end of his life and that 'he spent large sums on an observatory which fell into neglect afterwards'.

In these years, Khayyām would have travelled to other major cities, probably as far north as Samarkand and Bukhara, certainly to Baghdad in the west, perhaps even to Damascus. He would have met other mathematicians and visited the workshops of renowned instrument makers for the new institution. He would have had large amounts of gold in his purse to spend, he would have travelled in coaches wherever the roads permitted it, and he would have stayed in the most exquisite of palaces with local governors and the shah's relatives.

He would have probably also written some of his quatrains to express his frustrations or else his joviality of the moment as his mood swung this way and that. We shall see later that, arranged in apparent order of youthfulness, the poems seem to tell the story of a whole life. They begin as the semi-puerile utterances of a conceited young man to become, a little later, the boasts of a successful and well-connected professional, believing himself to be untouchable:

> This jug was, like me, a lover distraught,
> His heart was by one cruel beauty caught.
> This handle you see around its neck bent,
> Round that beauty's neck many a night it went!

> Girl of the light foot, rise up to the day,
> Bring out the lute, a dance tune play.
> It hates happiness, this Relentless Wheel,
> This old parade of Dey[10] succeeding Dey.

*   *   *

As Pope Gregory VII lay dying a broken-hearted man in exile in Salerno in May 1085, he wondered about his past mistakes. He thought that his famous decision to lift the excommunication of Henry IV of Germany really had been the worst in his life. But then, what choice had he had? By that fateful day, Friday, 28 January 1077, the young, handsome and innocent-looking king had stood before the gate of his castle for three freezing days begging to be forgiven, and Matilda of Tuscany and Hugh, the Abbot of Cluny, had appealed to him to be the priest again, to show mercy. He had also thought that if Henry really did become a loyal Christian and joined forces with him, he could put his old dream for the east into practice. By then, the heathen Saracens had been expelled from Sicily and the rest faced defeat in Spain. He dreamt of personally leading an army of Christian knights to the east to rescue his brethren there from the ravages of the latest barbarians out of Asia, even perhaps going on to rescue holy Jerusalem itself. He had thought it feasible to open up the pilgrim routes to the Holy Land once more. Now all that hope had vanished to give place to gloom and, in the meantime, the plight of the eastern Christians had worsened.

Henry had reverted to being a true son to his father and, with the anathema lifted, had recovered from his hopeless position among his fellow barons. He had betrayed his promise to fight alongside the pope against the Norman warlord Robert Giscard in southern Italy and the pope had been routed in battle by Robert. To make matters worse, Henry had sacked Rome and imposed an impostor on the throne of St Peter, while Gregory had been rescued by Robert and become dependent on that barbarian's thin mercy.

When Gregory died eventually on 25 May, the papacy's fortunes in the world seemed at their lowest in recent times. In fact, altogether, the position of Christians in most places had worsened. This was particularly true in the east, after the disastrous battle of Manzikert in 1071. The leading families of Byzantium had fallen into civil war among themselves and, at times, made alliances with the heathen against their rivals. The emperor had, in addition, ensured more Turks penetrated the interior of Anatolia by withdrawing some of the native troops there to Constantinople to guard his palaces. Many a Greek town, seeing their chiefs seek safety in Constantinople, had then proceeded to throw their gates open to the Turks to be spared only to find that, before long, their womenfolk were being carted off as slaves and their lands seized. Now almost the whole of the interior and the southern and northern rims of Asia Minor swarmed with Turkomans. With the exception of Armenia and the region around Trebizond, where the leading Christian family had decided to remain and fight, the east could now be justifiably called 'Turkistan'.

*   *   *

In the same year, 1085, a decision noticed by few was made in Khorāsān that would later deeply and adversely affect Khayyām's life. While passing through Nishāpur on campaign with Malik Shah to put down a rebellion by Takesh, one of the king's younger brothers, the chancellor recruited a religious fanatic by the name of Ghazāli for the central administration in Isfahan. He would soon shower privileges on the twenty-seven-year-old theologian and give him free rein to denounce many a greater official than himself. Nor was he alone of his type. There were thousands of his ilk in the vast bureaucracy, the Nizā miyah, that the chancellor had forged over the years. The continued promotion of such zealots merely showed that the chancellor had no intention of retiring, making way gracefully for the king to take charge of his kingdom. Over the past few years, an undeclared war had raged between the Nizāmiyah, on the one hand, and the courts of the shah and the khātūn, on the other. Some of the chancellor's sons had engineered the deaths of prominent courtiers, while the Khātūn's court had contrived the assassination of one of the chancellor's most influential sons, as we shall see in greater detail later.

The firebrand's full name was Muhammad bin Muhammad al-Ghazāli and he was of Arab origin, born near Tūs, the vizier's own birthplace. He had become an orphan when still a child, but clerical relatives had given him a thorough education in Arabic and theology. He had then joined the Nizāmiyah school in Nishāpur which the vizier had placed under the control of an extremist exponent of the Ash'ari school.

As a schoolboy, Ghazāli may have watched from a distance Khayyām's rapid rise in the professional and social circles of the empire. When Khayyām's caravan had made a stopover in Nishāpur a dozen years earlier on its way from Bukhara to Isfahan, Ghazāli was fifteen years old. The colourful procession of the royal Saljuq court could not have failed to impress him. Khayyām might have even been received in ceremony at the school at which the boy studied.

Ghazāli would have a short but turbulent life, suffering nervous breakdowns, periods of doubt and a complete loss of faith, before returning to fervent belief once more and ending up in a Sufi commune. In the immediate future, fear of his censorious writings would force many a prominent scientist and philosopher to choose silence rather than risk the wrath of mobs. He would study philosophy under Khayyām for the secret purpose of subsequently revealing his master's heresies and he would even, at the height of his religious fervour, urge the abolishing of Norūz and all other Iranian festivals and customs that transmitted the memory of old Iran to future generations. This, above all else, would earn him an intense hatred in Khayyām's heart. Today, 'Imam Ghazāli' is revered as a saint by many Muslims, but Khayyām has millions more admirers all over the world.

CHAPTER SEVEN

The Shah Applauds

Lost to the wine of the Magus? I am!
Pagan? Zarathustrian? Haereticus? I am!
Every nation holds its notion of me.
I am my own man, whatever I am.

Malik Shah was the first Saljuq emperor who knew his precise date of birth. Before him, the date of birth of his father, Alp-Arslan, had been known only roughly and accidentally, because it had fallen between two victorious battles. Before him, his uncle, the first sultan, Toghril, would have probably been puzzled by the question. It was not a custom of the nomads to bother about such luxuries. He often told his Grand Vizier: 'We Turks are a simple people, Kondori. I don't understand what you're saying. Do as you wish.'

But by now the Saljuq sultan was a sophisticated man. He had been born in 1055 in peace and wealth, surrounded by Persian secretaries and tutors who had even taught him to read and write to an extent. He was, of course, mainly interested in the manly arts, horse and sword, and, therefore, not keen on being seen reading or writing, and he had not learnt to speak Arabic beyond pleasantries. Nevertheless, he took pride in putting a few scribbles under a document. That made him the very model of a modern sultan.

On 6 August 1085, the empire celebrated his thirtieth birthday with lavish banquets, military parades and street parties, and it had good reason to do so. The emperor appeared on course to surpass even his father to become possibly the greatest of the three sultans of the House of Saljuq. The empire was secure and prosperous, with a strong and healthy sovereign on the throne and no major challengers within or without.

The empire was, in fact, still expanding and was larger than any rival state in the region in memory, even larger than the great realm into which Grand Vizier Nizām had been born in 1018, the empire of the Ghaznavids under their greatest leader Mahmūd. The Saljuqs' authority ran from Samarkand and Bukhara beyond the waters of the Oxus in the remote north-east to Baghdad, that most magical name in the south-west; and from western Anatolia on the sea of Yunān in the far north-west, to Oman on the sea of India in the distant south-east. If the shah captured Damascus, Jerusalem and Cairo, as it seemed to be his destiny to do, his glory would rival that of the greatest of the Sasanians.

But everyone knew of the secret war between shah and vizier. That made the idyll extremely fragile. Two kings, as they said, could never rule in one country and most wise heads, keen to stay out of the fray, hoped for a natural death soon for 'the old man'. He was sixty-seven, with a white beard, and had already had a good life, nay, a glorious one. In such an eventuality, they hoped, Malik Shah, even though only thirty, would find it in his own interest to maintain the decorum by drawing Nizām's sons and retainers into the new administration. That would be ideal, but ideals were seldom achieved in the affairs of kings. It was best to expect the worst.

On this particular royal birthday – almost thirteen years into Malik Shah's reign – the monarch and his chancellor were still able to keep peace in public. They were campaigning in Khorāsān to put down a rebellion by Prince Takesh, the king's younger brother. In a couple of months' time, the rebel leader would be safely in prison in a mountain-top castle and all serious intrigues would be of the usual subtle kind, in lovely Isfahan itself.[1]

* * *

Just in case the chancellor's piety had not by now been shouted from every roof all over the empire, and just in case his building of numerous schools, caravanserais and hospices in all the major cities had not become universal knowledge, he decided on yet another grand gesture, the grandest of them all. He decided to build the largest dome in the Islamic world right in the heart of the capital.

'The Dome of Nizām al-Mulk' on the southern side of the Friday mosque is, today, the oldest large structure in Isfahan and one of the city's great glories. The grace of its exterior lines combines with the austerity of its interior to infuse the visitor with a serene peace which leads him to look beyond himself. Its unadorned brick walls, with patterns clearly inspired by Sasanian religious buildings, speak of the futility of temporary obsessions compared with the eternal pulse of life and death in the world. Its high round ceiling is a representation of the celestial heavens.

But whether at the time it achieved its main aim fully is to be doubted. It was meant to be seen as a non-political act of faith. But do politicians ever embark on any act of faith without having an eye on its possible earthly effects? It certainly told visitors just how wealthy – and therefore how powerful – the chancellor and his numerous sons and relatives were.

The Dome was opened, it seems, some time between the late spring and the middle of summer 1086,[2] and Nizām would have wanted its inauguration to be the focus of attention that year. The king and the senior 'queen', Terken Khātūn, would have naturally been in the front rank of the dignitaries gathered on the big day, with a large crowd of political rivals and high officials behind them. Somewhere in that crowd, there may well have been the infant prodigy of the science of the time, the khājah[3] Omar Khayyām, almost certainly not by way of an enthusiastic personal invitation from the chancellor, but by virtue of his office and closeness to the royal family.

Somewhere also in that crowd, but well towards the front, is likely to have been the chancellor's main rival, the queen's chief of staff Tāj al-Mulk, 'Crown of the Realm'. Compared to Nizām's sixty-eight years, he was only a stripling of thirty-nine. Rumours claimed that the shah was conspiring with him as the chancellor's successor. Whether true or not, he would have watched how the occasion was affecting the king for he, too, was engaged in a similar ploy. At the other, northern, end of the square, he was building a dome of his own. 'The Dome of Tāj al-Mulk' has also survived to our time and it, too, is beautiful. But it is more ornate, more of a peacock; a reflection of its ambitious, frenetic, gregarious patron. It would open in similar pomp the following year.

*   *   *

In the spring of 1087, we suddenly see 'the Khātūn', the princess Terken, in a new light: assertive, brave, tireless, a true daughter of her royal father, the late Shams al-Mulk of the Qarakhanids in Bukhara. We hear that 'at her insistence', Malik Shah has gone to Baghdad for his first visit since he ascended the throne fifteen years earlier, and we read that she has set down unprecedented conditions for the caliph, the spiritual head of the empire, to agree to, before he can marry her daughter.

Five years earlier, the caliph had sent his vizier to Isfahan to ask Malik Shah for the hand of the little girl, but the king had sent the man, together with Grand Vizier Nizām, to Terken, saying 'go and discuss it with the Khātūn'. In her turn, she had told the envoy that the sultan of Ghazni and both princes of the Qarakhanid royal houses in Transoxania and Turkestan had each offered 100,000 dinars for the princess's hand for their heirs: 'But if His Holiness the caliph offers the same amount, I have to obey. He has priority.' Eventually, she had settled for 50,000 dinars, but with some seemingly impossible conditions. 'His Holiness must renounce the right to sleep with any other woman', she had dictated to the envoy of Allah's Deputy on Earth.

If the Khātūn had hoped to make it unacceptable for the caliph to marry her daughter, unfortunately she had failed. All her conditions had been accepted and this year, 1087, the date had arrived for the dreaded act.[4]

Malik Shah's father Alp-Arslan had refused to visit Baghdad at all. The son, too, had been reluctant. The official excuse was that it might cause the kind of complications that arose when Sultan Toghril's large retinue of bodyguards entered the city with him in 1055, which included rapes, riots, and even the burning down of the famous library of Shapār Ardashīr. But perhaps the real reason was a dislike of Caliph Moqtada, together with an antipathy towards the protocol that ruled any audience with the spiritual head of Sunni Islam. To obey the protocol would humiliate the sultan. To disregard it would weaken the religious sanction of the monarchy. But the Khātūn insisted on his going and she won.

Thus on 8 May, the bride's procession set out from the royal palace in Baghdad towards the caliphal palace, with the caliph's mother and aunt accompanying the bride in solemn progress. We read that 130 camels in Byzantine brocades and seventy-four mules with gold harnesses were needed to carry the dowry, and that her jewellery and perfume alone required twelve silver chests. Thirty-three purebred horses of various origins were an extra gift.

Unfortunately, the sources are reticent about giving the bride's name, this being a recurrent problem with Muslim historians. They display a distaste for mentioning women by name, as if it might imply either a lack of modesty on the part of the women or else, indecent familiarity with them on the part of the storyteller. Women are untouchable, sacrosanct. Only occasionally women of especially forceful personality break through the cordon thrown around them, and this princess had not found her feet yet. It seems she was called Māh Malak, a mixture of Persian and Arabic meaning 'Moon Goddess'.[5]

Be that as it may, the ceremonies in Baghdad lasted several days and seven nights and involved banquets for the whole population. They began with an envoy from the caliph arriving before Terken Khātūn to announce that Allah Almighty – no less – had commanded her to convey 'the treasure in your trust to its worthy owner'. 'Hearing is obeying', she replied and then Grand Vizier Nizām and other statesmen, princes and princesses led the procession towards the caliph's palace holding lighted candles and beacons. The wives of provincial governors and army commanders participated too. The bride's golden litter was surrounded by 200 Turkish female slaves of her own.

None of this, however, was witnessed by the bride's father. A few days earlier, he had been received in the Holy Presence and acted correctly, kissing the ground several times before he arrived in front of his prospective son-in-law's throne. Then, for reasons best known to himself and a few close advisers, he chose to leave the city to go hunting in the desert south of Baghdad. He returned after the wedding and left almost immediately with Grand Vizier to return to Isfahan. The queen stayed behind to make certain all went well with the treatment of her daughter.[6] The indications are that, even at this early stage, both Malik Shah and Terken found some aspect of the personality of the caliph deeply disturbing, though none of the sources shed light on it.

Did Khayyām accompany the royal household on this trip to Baghdad? Most probably he did. Apart from his long history of intimacy with Terken Khātūn's Qarakhanid family and his more recent closeness to the king, he was now the royal family's chief doctor, as we shall see in greater detail later. Furthermore, Malik Shah was a superstitious man and took an astrologer with him wherever he travelled. As it happens, Khayyām's future secretary, Nizāmi the Prosodist, tells us that he did not believe in astrology, implying that he saw it as the profession of crooks and sycophants. But it would have been uncomfortable, even for the most famous scientist of his age, to argue with his superstitious sovereign that he saw the practice as beneath him. For all we know, however, the two men may have laughed about it too, to an extent.

One of the most famous stories regarding Khayyām says that the future sultan Sanjar harboured a lifelong grudge against him, for when the prince was a young boy in Isfahan some time in the late 1080s, Khayyām gave up hope of his surviving.

Sanjar was born in 1084 of Malik Shah's third woman, a concubine for whom he had obtained the title of Tāj ed-Dīn – Crown of the Faith – from the caliph. The boy fell ill with smallpox and Khayyām, after spending many nights at his bedside and trying every possible cure, eventually declared him beyond recovery. As Khayyām pronounced his verdict on leaving the prince's bedchamber, an Abyssinian slave heard him and later, perhaps years later, reported him to the prince.

The grudge could not have been as deeply held as depicted, for when Sanjar is sultan in the 1100s, we see him insisting on Khayyām acting as his personal astrologer and weather forecaster on an important hunting expedition.

The story implies that, beside being physician to the royal family, Khayyām would have also been in demand by all the great families of the city to attend the bedside of their most prominent ailing members. As such, therefore, medicine would have been the source of some of the great personal wealth he is known to have accumulated.

* * *

At a time when the fortunes of the western church seemed to have sunk to unspeakable depths, there emerged a pope who would be remembered for ever. On 12 March 1088, Otto of Lagery, a forty-six-year-old French bishop of noble birth, who had recently been a prisoner of the German emperor Henry IV, was enthroned in Terracina, south of Rome, under the name of Urban II. He could not enter the Eternal City to claim his seat at the Lateran Palace because, there, Henry had appointed his own puppet, Guibert of Ravenna, to the throne of St Peter. Furthermore, Henry had driven Countess Matilda, the true papacy's main supporter in northern Italy, from her lands in northern Italy, while in the south, there were not enough noblemen of worth to help the church even to keep up appearances. The pope had to depend on charity for his sustenance and was deeply in debt.

But Urban would spend the next few years in ceaseless movement wherever the power of the German emperor did not quite extend. He would use his unusual eloquence to win over the faithful to his cause, to such an extent that even the emperor's own son, Conrad, would desert his father for him. But, as if Henry were not enough of an adversary, Urban would also excommunicate Philip II of France for adultery and denounce many other powerful rulers, such as William the Red of England, for not obeying his orders. His support would come mostly from the Normans of southern Italy and Sicily, even though they were fighting among themselves, and from the vanquished Matilda.

But Matilda would eventually triumph over Henry, and Urban would conquer Rome, win over the faithful of France and Spain, and extend the Peace of God among his followers across most of western Europe. He would subsequently organise an army of knights to march on Jerusalem itself – that captive, enslaved and humiliated heart of Christendom – to rescue it from the Saracens. On the way there, Urban's knights would reopen the pilgrimage routes of southern Anatolia and give Constantinople a much needed respite from the rampaging Saljuqs.[7]

*   *   *

Could it be that a secret visit by a wandering 'troubled soul' to a revered sage in a mountain-top fortress in the western Himalayas at

Above, left: 1. This Nishāpur ceramic bowl dates back to around the year 1000, half a century before Khayyām was born. He would have been familiar with the style. *(Private collection, Bridgeman Art Library)*

Above, right: 2. These pillars in the crypt of the Friday Mosque in Isfahan are thought to be remnants of a pre-Islamic building, possibly a Zoroastrian fire temple. Khayyām lived in Isfahan from 1074 to 1092. *(Roger Violett Collection/Getty Images)*

Below: 3. This ninth-century mausoleum of the Samanid dynasty, under whom the Persian language flourished against the wishes of devout Muslims, would have been among the first sites young Khayyām would have visited on his arrival in Bukhara in 1073. Some experts describe it as 'a Zoroastrian temple in disguise'. *(Bridgeman Art Library)*

4. A Nishāpur gold dinar at the British Museum. It bears the name of Khayyām's friend Malik Shah who paid him 10,000 such pieces a year, as compared to the 7,000 dinars that made up the entire annual revenue of a fiefdom the sultan had given one of his uncles.

5. The dome at the far end of the Friday mosque is known as the Dome of Nizām al-Mulk. Khayyām would have been among the important personages to be invited by the chancellor to its inauguration in 1080, although by then he was firmly in the rival circle of Malik Shah and Queen Terken. (*Engraving by Auguste Guillaumot, 1856/Private collection/Bridgeman Art Library*)

6. This astrolabe, at the British Museum, is known as the Chaucer Astrolabe because it is dated 1326 and was minutely described by the English poet. Astrolabes, originally a Greek invention, were used daily by astronomers such as Khayyām to fulfil a number of functions, including timekeeping.

7. Ceremonious ancestors at Persepolis, 490 BC. Khayyām's poems abound with names and legends from ancient Iran, never from its more recent Islamic past. (*Bridgeman Art Library*)

8. The East Staircase of the Apadana palace at Persepolis, 515 BC. In 1080, Khayyām spent several months in nearby Shiraz. (*Bridgeman Art Library*)

9. The assassination of Grand Vizier Nizām in 1092 by an agent of the Shia schismatic Hasan Sabbāh caused the collapse of Khayyām's world and paved the way for the First Crusade. This drawing made for the author by the British artist Bob Moulder accurately reproduces a faded and partially defaced painting from the early 1300s, now in Istanbul. The assassin had lain in wait in the village of Sahneh, the author's place of birth; hence the addition of the river and mountains there today as the background.

10. The next caravanserai after Sahneh was the hamlet of Behistun, where Khayyām would have rested during his many journeys to Baghdad. The above inscription is carved on a great rock overlooking the hamlet and is an account by Darius the Great in the sixth century BC of how he quelled many rebellions, including one in Babylon. The flying creature above the captured kings is Darius's Zoroastrian guardian angel or 'Farr', granted him by almighty Ahura Mazda himself. Alas for Khayyām, he lacked the skills of the young English envoy Henry Rawlinson who decoded the script in the 1830s. *(Bridgeman Art Library)*

11. As the Saljuq Empire tore itself apart, largely due to the rash actions of Khayyām's former friend Queen Terken, the Western church saw an opportunity to send an army to the east to avenge the atrocities inflicted on Anatolian Christians by the Turks and, in the process, impose its authority on the eastern church. In 1095 in Clermont, France, Pope Urban II declared a 'War of the Cross' in which every Christian fighting man was expected to bear arms to reopen the pilgrimage routes and liberate Jerusalem. (*Sebastien Mamerot de Soissons, c. 1490/Bridgeman Art Library*)

12. In January 1094 Khayyām was back in Baghdad, after a forced pilgrimage to Mecca, contemplating how to cross war-torn Iran to reach safety in faraway Nishāpur. A visit to the ruins of Ctesiphon, the summer capital of the Sasanian emperors, would have been one last farewell to the glories of ancient Iran. This engraving by an unknown artist shows the Audience Hall of Anushirvan the Just as it stood in the nineteenth century. The east wing has collapsed since then and the rest remains vulnerable to vandals, some of them motivated by Islamic fervour or Arab nationalism. (*Mary Evans Picture Library*)

13. In 1962, the late Shah of Iran built this mausoleum for Khayyām a short distance from his old grave, which had become part of a Muslim shrine. But the Islamic regime in 1979 cut off the supply of water and electricity to the building and the trees were saved only through the private efforts of the citizens of Nishāpur. (*Photograph by Talinn Grigor kindly provided by the Aga Khan Visual Archive at MIT, Cambridge, Massachusetts*)

14. Edward FitzGerald as 'photoed' [*sic*] for the first time a year before his death in 1883. 'Unexpectedly complimentary', he noted. (*Private collection, Bridgeman Art Library*)

15. FitzGerald's grave in Boulge churchyard, Suffolk. The rose at the foot of the grave was brought over as seed from Khayyām's graveyard in Nishāpur and planted by the Omar Khayyām Club in 1893. (*Author's photograph*)

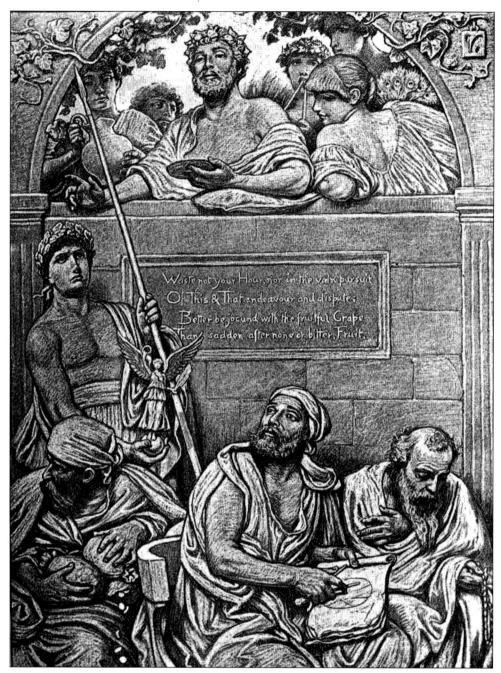

Waste not your Hour, nor in the vain pursuit
Of This & That endeavour and disputes;
Better be jocund with the fruitful Grape
Than sadden after none or bitter, Fruit.

16. The distortion begins, as it had long ago for poor Epicurus. In this early illustration for the fourth edition of the Rubáiyát in Boston in 1884, the artist E. Vedder portrays Khayyám as the Roman poet Lucretius preaching to the soldier, the merchant, the scholar and the priest that all their lives are in vain: 'Waste not your Hour, nor in the vain pursuit / Of This & That endeavour and dispute; / Better be jocund with the fruitful Grape / Than sadder after none, or bitter, Fruit.'

about this time prove to be the inspiration for one of the most audacious acts of piracy in the history of the world a few years later?

Mighty oaks do, indeed, grow from little acorns and, the oak tree in this case, would become the scourge of both Saracens and Crusaders in the region for two centuries. But no commentator has, to my knowledge, previously investigated precisely what the inspiration was for the founder of the movement of 'the Assassins' in his chosen method of taking over castles belonging to the government in order to use them as a fortified mini-state against that same government.

We last met Hasan Sabbāh, the future leader of the Ismaili rebellion in Iran, in June 1080 in Isfahan, when he returned a disillusioned man from his secret pilgrimage to Cairo, the seat of the Ismaili caliphate. In his memoirs he hints that, unlike his previous visit to Isfahan, when he worked there for a year or so before leaving for Egypt, he did not stay there long this time, but went on travelling under a variety of pseudonyms all over Iran, visiting the isolated and oppressed communities of his fellow Shi'ites, telling them of his meetings with their other leaders and strengthening their morale. His own account of his prolonged wonderings is rather vague, but he does say that he stayed in the Khorāsānian town of Dāmqān for three years. He adds that he sent missionaries to the mountains near the Caspian Sea and ventured eastwards, including the region of Chenāshak, near today's border with Afghanistan. Did he then venture further east to the valley of Yumqān in the upper reaches of the Oxus to meet the greatest and most revered of all the leaders of the Ismailis in the east, the poet and philosopher Nasser Khosrow? He would have longed for such a meeting, for the older man had also visited Cairo and the two would have had much to say to one another. Meeting Khosrow, who died at the age of eighty-five in 1088,[8] would have also bestowed additional prestige on the ambitious younger man, while for Khosrow, who constantly complained of intellectual isolation on his remote mountain, the company of the much-travelled and well-informed Hasan would have been more than a breath of fresh air. Khosrow had lived there in exile since his flight from the city of Balkh in Khorāsān in 1061.[9]

But even if Sabbāh, the professional missionary of the faith, never visited Yumqān, he would have certainly heard in detail how the Ismailis had captured the castle there and how they managed to live in reasonable harmony with their immediate neighbours, so that when the inevitable Saljuq army arrived, they might survive a prolonged siege.

However, to capture and hold a fortress on the edge of the Himalayan ice was one thing, to achieve the same at the centre of the empire quite another.

* * *

Terken Khātūn's apparent misgivings about allowing her little princess to enter the clutches of a lecherous autocrat were to be proved well founded, even though the man was the spiritual head of Sunni Islam and the bearer of the Prophet's mace. As we have seen, Caliph Moqtada had promised Terken that he would not sleep with any other women after his marriage to Māh Malak Khātūn, but he dishonoured his pledge from the start and even stopped calling on his bride as soon as the girl was pregnant. We are not told the precise reason. The girl may well have been miserable, pining for her mother and siblings in Isfahan, while her huge retinue of protective officials and 200 female slaves alone may have irritated her husband. However, the iron lady of the Qarakhanid royal house did not accept any excuses.

What was it that gave Moqtada the courage to behave so unwisely, given that every police officer in Baghdad was appointed by the Saljuqs and took orders from the girl's mother? He may have believed that Malik Shah, who himself had three wives, thought Terken Khātūn's stringent conditions unreasonable. Furthermore, the caliph's advisors may have told him that the sultan would never depose him, nor undermine the dignity of the caliphate, the only institution that gave religious sanction to the empire.

The caliph was right at one level and wrong at another. He was right to count on the support of the chancellor, 'a monarch all but in name',[10] but wrong to underestimate the determination of the sultan. At one time, Nizām himself had contemplated abolishing the caliphate, but he had changed his mind. As his relationship with Malik Shah had deteriorated in recent years and his need for allies increased, alienating the caliph and the huge clerical class would not have helped his position. So he had begun to shower some of the wealth of the state – and even some of his own – on the caliph. But Malik Shah, urged on by his domineering senior wife, was devoted to his children and resented the treatment of his daughter. Also, perhaps even more decisively, an idea had taken hold of his mind. The caliphate could be preserved without the caliph needing to live in Baghdad. That great city, so near the ruins of Ctesiphon, the winter capital of the Sasanians, would make an excellent winter retreat once more, this time for him and his heirs.

Once the idea of a winter capital gripped him, it became an obsession, and he would go down in the history books even more assuredly if he were to be the one ruler who expelled the last of the Arabs from Baghdad.[11] After all, 'Bagh Dād' seemed to mean 'Park of Justice' in Persian, implying that it had been the location of a court of law under the Sasanians. Would not the return of a shāhanshāh to the region be an act of poetic justice?

This was indeed a drastic change of mentality on the part of the Saljuqs from the days when Malik Shah's own father Alp-Arslan would not even set foot into the holy city so that the caliph might be spared the slight embarrassment of hosting Saljuq soldiers on his estate. As we have seen, even Malik Shah himself had visited Baghdad only once, and that had been at the insistence of Terken Khātūn for the wedding.

So, after the homesick little princess Māh Malak and her baby son Ja'far left for Isfahan on 30 May 1089, escorted by two of the highest-ranking military commanders of the Saljuq army, Malik Shah gave notice to Moqtadi to vacate the seat of his ancestors. He could go anywhere he liked, he was told. Baghdad was now wanted by the emperor himself.

Malik Shah's position had been made stronger by the birth of the little boy to his daughter a year earlier. He now thought that if he deposed the caliph quietly and replaced him with his own grandson, both temporal and spiritual power would come to rest in his hands alone. He plunged himself into frenetic activity. He employed a host of architects and managers and held numerous meetings with them to rebuild the institutional centre of the venerable city of the Abbasids. The caliphal palaces were too small for a sultan's grandeur and they were not to his taste.

But tragedy would raise its head in his family again, and soon. Six months after her return from Baghdad, the unhappy little Māh Malak died of smallpox. She was probably no older than fifteen years of age and left her baby son for grandmother Terken to bring up. A little earlier – it seems, for we do not know the exact date – an even greater tragedy had struck. Terken's eleven-year-old son and crown prince, Ahmad, for whom the emperor had devised four pompous titles, died in the city of Marv in the north-east. Malik Shah, who may have been present on the scene as he campaigned in the region in the spring, summer and autumn of 1089, is said to have been so distraught that he tried several times to take his own life. In Baghdad, to appease the sultan, the caliph ordered that no horses be ridden for seven days, while the inhabitants of the district of Karkh 'blackened the doors of their shops' to show that they shared the sultan's grief.

But hope was not completely lost for Terken. Despite being a grandmother, she was herself still young, almost certainly younger than her husband's thirty-four years. She had recently produced another son, Mahmūd, and kept alive the possibility that the sultanate would still pass on along her Qarakhanid line. This was apparently also Malik Shah's preference, though it had its difficulties. His other wife, his Saljuq first cousin Zubaida Khātūn, had a son who was eight years old. Even the two sons of his mistress, Tāj ed-Dīn Khātūn had priority over newborn Mahmūd. We may imagine the grief for the past and the anxiety for the future that must have afflicted Terken now, compounded by the glee on the face of her enemies.

*   *   *

In the late spring of 1089,[12] Khayyām's old mentor, the chief judge and governor of Samarkand, Abu Tāhir bin Alak Abdul-Rahman, bursts upon the scene once more, but this time to make mischief. We read that, at his secret behest, Malik Shah and Nizām have led an army back into Khorāsaān and Transoxania and overthrown their vassal, Terken's nephew Ahmad, as king or khān of the western Qarakhanid kingdom. We read that young Ahmad had behaved 'wickedly' by imposing heavy taxes on the population, but we need not believe this wholly. There are indications he had ignored the clerical class, led by aristocrats such as Abu Tāhir, in their championing of strict Shari'a law – and their own lucrative part in enforcing it. The same allegation was levelled against Terken's father, the late king Shams al-Mulk.

Whatever the real reason for Abu Tāhir's enmity with his king, we read that he made his case to Malik Shah and Nizām al-Mulk sometime during the previous autumn when he passed through Isfahan on route to Mecca on the hajj pilgrimage.

Did he also meet Khayyām during his stay in Isfahan? He may well have done so, but did he confide in him his real purpose? That seems unlikely, for although the 'Khājah', the Lord, Omar Khayyām, would have been a substantial personage worth lobbying, his sympathies would have lain with Terken. In fact, Abu Tāhir would have met with the king and the chancellor in the greatest of secrecy in the hope of not alerting 'the Khātūn'.

The invasion raises an intriguing question about Terken Khātūn's influence on her husband. Why did she fail to prevent it? Even if she had come to disapprove thoroughly of the behaviour of her nephew in Bukhara, she would have surely known the danger for the region of a military invasion by a Saljuq army, even if she herself accompanied her husband. Ahmad Khān might resist tenaciously – which in fact he did, angering Malik Shah to such an extent that he might end the rule of the whole family – which is again what happened. Even some of her innocent relatives might die in sieges and sackings. It would seem safe to conclude that she had exerted herself on both sides for a peaceful outcome. It must be assumed that as Malik Shah became more experienced as a ruler, Terken's influence over him weakened.

The prospect of capturing new riches and imposing heavier tribute on the vassalage cannot be ruled out as the shah's primary motive. An additional motive may well have been to push forth beyond Samarkand and Bukhara into the eastern Qarakhanid kingdom. That kingdom was ruled by Terken's distant cousins who had rarely been on good terms with her family. As such, she would not have cared much whether they stayed or fell. But the possibility of making history through the conquest of that distant and legendary land on the borders of China, which happened after the overthrow of Ahmad Khān,[13] would have been a most powerful lure for Malik Shah, even discounting the treasures that would flow from it.

Returning to Abu Tāhir, the clash of mentalities between him and Khayyām is revealed starkly a couple of years later in the autumn of 1091 when Abu Tāhir died in Baghdad. In a laudatory message for his funeral, Nizām described him as 'the most abstemious of holy men'. Nizām excused himself from walking behind the coffin on account of 'my advanced years', while Malik Shah later visited Abu Tāhir's tomb.

Anyhow, it was probably on their return journey from Bukhara in the autumn of 1089 that the chancellor thought up a ploy to boost Malik Shah's morale for, despite the recent conquests, the emperor was still in need of constant entertainment to forget the recent deaths of his two eldest children with Terken Khātūn. Once the great army had recrossed the Oxus to start its long trek towards Isfahan, the numerous local artisans and boatmen who had helped in building the bridge of boats asked to be paid. The chancellor issued them with money drafts payable only in the Syrian port of Antioch on the Mediterranean coast. Needless to say, the poor people suspected bad faith. Let the historian Rāwandi[14] take up the story:

> One day there was a minor disturbance outside the encampment, when the boatmen who had helped transport the army across the river petitioned Malik Shah about a great injustice. The chancellor had issued them papers to claim their wages in the port of Antioch in Syria. They gathered at the foot of Malik Shah's throne and shouted: 'We are a poor people. If a young man among us sets off for Antioch now, he'll return an old man.' 'Father', Malik Shah asked the Grand Vizier, 'What explains this? Are we so poor, here, that we must resort to Antioch?' Nizām replied: 'My Lord, there's no need for them to go anywhere. Our men will buy their papers back with gold. I did it for you and our state, so that the chroniclers will write it down in history and the world will know the true extent of our realm and how far your commands carry.'

Another of Nizām al-Mulk's subterfuges during this trip was supremely arrogant, as it was cruel. Again with an eye on what the chroniclers might say of the new extent of the empire, for which he was himself largely responsible, he insisted that a Byzantine emissary accompany the army all the way from Isfahan to Transoxania 'so that the annual tribute from that power' might be seen to be received there. Whether the poor envoy enjoyed the arduous, though picturesque trip is not recorded.

* * *

Whereas we have several snippets of reportage and gossip that link Khayyām directly to Malik Shah as a close companion, there is none that connects him personally to the vizier. Readers who have accompanied us on this journey so far will not be surprised. Indeed, we should not be surprised if, by now, in the first months of 1090, Khayyām had come to harbour a deep dislike for the chancellor, and not only for private reasons. Nizām al-Mulk's extended family could justly be described as a large network of 'organised crime'. His dozen or so sons and thousands of retainers behaved abominably, encroaching on other people's rights and even daring to kill one of Malik Shah's courtiers, his favourite jester, and, what is more, Nizām himself pretended that everything he did was in total obedience to religious law. He had also recently promoted Khayyām's most vehement critic, the fanatical and unstable bigot Ghazāli over the heads of good men and moderate clerics and would soon even send him to Baghdad to head an important department in the Nizāmiyah teaching institution there.

It has to be said that the aversion would have been mutual. The grand statesman who had, many years ago in Bukhara, picked the virtually unknown mathematical prodigy and brought him to Isfahan to work on the reform of the calendar, would have been disappointed in his protégé's refusal, as he saw it, to grow into a pious and respectable pillar of the state. Worse still, he had sided with an ungrateful king who was plotting the downfall of his 'father', the chancellor who had guarded the empire and expanded it for him.

One of those stories that link Khayyām personally to Malik Shah has Khayyām himself for its source. His mini-biographer Ibn Funduq, says that the great man once told his father that he and Malik Shah were one day talking quietly when the young son of a nobleman was brought in, apparently for his first audience with the emperor. Afterwards, Khayyām expressed surprise at the child's refined manners but Malik Shah, either in a flippant mood or else in a foolish vein, said that he, Khayyām, ought not be surprised: 'He's like the chick of a domestic hen', he said to Khayyām. 'When it emerges from its egg, it knows how to pick seeds without having been taught, but it can't find its way back to its nest without guidance. And a baby pigeon, when it hatches, can't pick seeds, but [later], it flies from Mecca to Baghdad without being guided.' Khayyām had added that he had been surprised at Malik Shah believing in such an absurdity.

On another occasion, someone had reported to Malik Shah the gist of a conversation between Khayyām and the lord treasurer, the Khāja Kāshāni.[15] Khayyām had gone to the minister to say that part of his salary had not been paid. The minister had asked how much he received each year from the emperor and how much was still due. Khayyām had replied that his salary was 10,000 gold dinars, upon which the minister had expressed amazement. 'What do you do for the sultan that he pays you 10,000 gold dinars?', he had asked. Khayyām had lost his temper: 'What do I do for the sultan? If you must know, there is only one man like me who can do what I do, whereas I could pick men like you by the dozen from each village in your own home region of Kāshān.' On hearing the story, Malik Shah had laughed raucously and said: 'By God, Khayyām is right'.

The story supports other accounts suggesting that Khayyām suffered from a short temper and could be extremely arrogant at times, making him many enemies within – and without – the court. But if a man in his position had only a single friend left in the land, and that friend sat on the imperial throne, surely he need not have feared enemies.

Indeed, some of the early writers describe Khayyām as one of the 'malāzim' of the sultan. The Arabic term is the plural for 'necessity' and may be translated as 'bonded' or 'constant' companion. Even more precisely, it seems to have been a strictly defined rank of courtier, applying to those who had been told always to be ready to pack up to leave with the monarch on any hurriedly decided venture away from the capital.

CHAPTER EIGHT

The Assassin Stalks

Sober, I cannot face the dawn, alas.
I cannot pull forth this tired carcass.
I long for that breath when the maid offers
One more cup to me, but it has to pass.

As Nizām al-Mulk had ordered Abu Muslim of Rayy to take me alive to him and as Abu Muslim was trying hard to find me, I could not visit Rayy. I wanted to go to Daylamān,[1] to which I had sent missionaries. So I went to Sāri. There I took the Damāvand road to Khwār, bypassing Rayy, and from there went to Qazvīn. In that city, once again, I sent men to Alamūt Castle, which was then run by an Alawite[2] called Mahdi for Malik Shah. Alamūt is from 'āl āmūt', meaning 'eagle nest', as eagles nested there.[3] Some in the fortress accepted the [Ismaili Shia] Call and asked the Alawite also to convert. He did, but only verbally. He deceived those who had accepted the Call and one day sent them down from the mountain, only to close the gates on them. He said that the castle belonged to the sultan, not him. After long negotiations, he let them in again, but this time they were determined never to leave by his command.

This is another excerpt from Hasan Sabbāh's autobiography. The Iranian official, Juvayni, who read the original complete work for his Mongol lord before destroying the bulk of it, adds an elaboration of his own that seems remarkably fair:

By pretending extreme piety, Hasan had attracted many people in the region to his side. Then, on the night of Wednesday 6 March 1090, he sneaked into the castle. He spent a while there in secrecy under the name of Deh-Khodā.[4] When the Alawite found who he really was, he was helpless. Hasan gave him a letter addressed to Chief Mozaffar of Gird Kūh [Round Mountain] and Dāmqān [in Khorāsān], who had secretly accepted his call, ordering the chief to pay the Alawite 3,000 dinars. Hasan wrote extremely short letters to pretend holiness. This is what he wrote: 'Chief MZ to pay Alawite Mahdi 3,000 dinars. Peace be upon the Prophet of God and his people.'

The Alawite took the paper, but thought to himself: 'Chief Mozaffar is a great man. He is deputy to the emir Dād, the sultan's commander [in the region]. Why should he honour the order of a man such as Hasan?' Later, in Dāmqān, he found himself in diminished times. He took the script to Chief Mozaffar to try it. Chief Mozaffar kissed the script and delivered the gold.

As Hasan – may Allah quash his soul – became established in Alamūt, he sent missionaries abroad and spent his time darkening the beliefs of simpletons. . . . His people called his movement the New Call and they believed that every divine revelation had an interpretation and every [Koranic] statement a hidden meaning. . . . He shut completely the door on education and training. He said that theology was impossible through reason and opinion. Only the imam could teach it, for most of humanity are mature people, yet they differ in their religions. If finding God were possible by reason, all would have come to agree with one another. . . . Thus every age needed an imam to teach its people the true religion. . . . Hasan said that he had disproved the religions of all other peoples, but this is not so. . . . It is as if someone says that the imam is so-and-so, and the proof of it is that I say so. . . .

Hasan worked hard to bring all of Alamūt's neighbouring districts under him. He tried persuasion first and, if that failed, he resorted to intimidation, war, killing. He captured all the fortifications he could, and wherever he found a rock, he built a fort on it. . . . The sultan Malik Shah had an emir in the region by the name of Yuron Tāsh.[5] He rode to Alamūt repeatedly and wherever he found people who had accepted Hasan's call, he killed and robbed them. And as Alamūt had not accumulated sufficient supplies yet, its people became desperate and migrated, leaving the castle to a few unattached men to defend. Hasan now claimed that his imam Mustansir [the caliph of Egypt] had sent him a prophesy that the castle would not fall. His men kept their position and bore many hardships.[6]

Given the extreme hostility of his masters to Ismailis, Juvayni has to pretend a visceral hatred of them himself, but he is conscientious with his facts. He tells us that Sabbāh had previously been thorough in surveying and infiltrating the area in person before choosing his mountian and his people. The warlike inhabitants of the region to the south-east of Caspian Sea had never been captured by Islam, but had converted to the Twelver Shia branch of it slowly over several centuries. Still, they included large pockets of Zoroastrianism and even their Muslim rulers exhibited a strong pride in ancient Iran as exhibited in their old Persian names. Before the Saljuq Turks, one of their leading families, the Būyids, even ruled over Baghdad and made a plaything of the caliphs. As the Būyids had been overthrown only recently by the Saljuqs, hatred of the Turks was particularly raw in the region Hasan had chosen to be his springboard.

As for the mountain on which the castle perched, Juvayni gives us a description that, of course, still stands: 'It resembles a kneeling camel with its neck lying on the ground'. It has a flat expanse at the top, some 200m above the surrounding gorges, on which crops could be grown and rainwater harvested in times of siege. Above all, it can only be reached on one side and even that side is guarded by a torrential river, named after the castle. It is now a major tourist attraction some eighty miles in the highlands to the north-west of Tehran.

And so, despite the brutal harassment of the sultan's local commandant, Sabbāh and his devoted sectarians worked hard for the remainder of 1090 and the whole of 1091 to dig deep into the top of their rock to construct water reservoirs and food stores. Whenever possible, his supporters in the neighbouring villages and forts took him extra supplies. This he was able to do because Isfahan, for whatever reasons, did not at first take his threat seriously. Nizām would have, of course, been disappointed to hear the news. An infamous fugitive, whose capture he had demanded of provincial governors, had defeated the elaborate network of espionage he had worked hard to set up over two decades. But a proper army could be sent to Daylamān in the spring and the fort captured quickly, he would have hoped. In the meantime, the failure would be an irritant at court, for it would be used by his enemies, particularly the men around Terken Khātūn, to undermine him. So he would play down the importance of the setback for the time being and declare that the focus of the little rebellion was too far from Egypt to enable it to receive any substantial aid in weapons or gold from that quarter.

But Sabbāh was more ambitious and more cunning than even Nizām al-Mulk suspected. Within only a year of his capturing the castle, he repeated his success in a large area south of Khorāsān. Some time in 1091, he sent his most able agent, Hussein Qāyeni, to Kūhistan (the Highlands), to the north-east of the central Iranian desert to capture a number of strong forts there, too. Hussein had been the man who had befriended the ruler of Alamūt and then secretly converted his underlings until, one day, the poor Alawite had found that none among them was obeying his orders anymore.

What did Khayyām think when he heard that Sabbāh had stolen a whole castle from the sultan? He would have chortled, certainly, at the incompetence of Nizām's spies and governors, but if he had met Sabbāh in 1076 or 1077, he would have recalled the mysterious and intense young man and asked himself whether he had thought of him as unusual. Sabbāh had lived and worked in Isfahan in disguise, for he had fled his native Rayy after harassment by the chancellor's agents, with his mission as yet undiscovered.

* * *

And so, in the summer of 1091, the Grand Vizier probably no longer raised objections to Malik Shah's longing to transfer the court to Baghdad in the autumn to make his first use of that city as his new 'winter capital'. In fact, the sojourn to Baghdad had an important attraction for the chancellor. The shah's mood would hopefully lift as he supervised his ambitious rebuilding of the city centre, and the two men would have time to talk at leisure again, perhaps to re-establish their old special bond as 'father' and 'son'.

As a result, in September 1091, the huge caravan of the court, with its several thousand cavalrymen in the van and rear, left Isfahan. The heat of summer had moderated and snow had not yet blocked the passes in the Zagros mountains in the region of Hamadan and Kermanshah. It was bad news for the bazaar in the capital as the lucrative business of the court would not be back in town till the spring, but it set abuzz most of those chosen to accompany the sultan and the chancellor, especially the young for whom it would be their very first visit to fabled Baghdad.

For the king himself it would be only his second visit, and he was full of ideas and plans. But some of those plans might have unpredictable consequences. What would, for example, be the attitude of the Sunnis of Baghdad to the eviction of the caliph?

If Nizām still hoped to change Malik Shah's mind about Moqtada, he would soon find how wrong he had been. When the caravan arrived in Baghdad in November, neither sailing and drinking on pleasure boats on the Tigris, nor chasing herds of gazelle on the wide open plains nearby, nor even the smiling faces of his architects busy at work on a new, dazzling royal palace persuaded Malik Shah to adopt a more conciliatory, more politic, attitude to the caliph. For the entire duration of their stay till after Norūz in March the sultan did not grant a single audience to the Prophet of Allah's Deputy on Earth, and everyone knew who was to blame: that headstrong khātun, the princess Terken, whose young daughter had been humiliated by the conceited Moqtada. The sultan was indeed a great and brave monarch, but for some unknown reason, he tended to listen to women in matters of state.

Among the other statesmen who accompanied the sultan on that winter sojourn to Baghdad was the man who hoped to succeed Nizām, Terken's chief of staff, Tāj al-Mulk. This could not have helped the chancellor's mood, especially as he saw that Tāj al-Mulk was also allowed to build himself a new residence in the city as sumptuous as the mansion he himself was building.

On this trip, Khayyām was not acting as astrologer to the sultan. The historian Ibn Athīr gives the astrologer's name as Bahrām, an Iranian named after a Sasanian emperor. The conclusion must be that either Khayyām had by then succeeded in excusing himself of the practice of which he disapproved, or else he had not accompanied the royal party.

*   *   *

As news of Hasan's actions spread and the atrocities against the nearby Muslims became known, the sultan Malik Shah sent the emir Arslan Tāsh against him and this emir laid siege to Alamūt in the late spring [1092]. Hasan's men by then numbered no more than sixty or seventy, and they had little supplies. They had to combat hunger and a hundred other hardships, until there arrived salvation in the shape of one of Hasan's missionaries, a landowner by the name of Bu Ali, who lived in Qazvīn. One night that autumn, he and 300 of his men, together with some of the local people who lived outside the castle, fell upon the sultan's army and, as Allah saw fit, destroyed it. The survivors reported to the sultan and he worried. He began to make new plans.[7]

But Malik Shah's plans still did not include marching on Alamūt at the head of a greater army, or at least certainly not that coming winter. Heavy snowfalls would soon make the Alborz mountains north of Rayy impassable and, in any case, the rebellion could not spread rapidly. It could wait another few months. As a result, the decision was made not to interrupt the winter sojourn in Baghdad. The new royal palaces and public institutions there were still not completed and the sultan's personal supervision of the architects was essential. Winter months were ideal in Baghdad for building work and the hunting was superb, too.

* * *

One day in September 1092, as the time approached for the court to set off for Baghdad again on its, by now, annual retirement there for the winter, Grand Vizier Nizām called in the treasury's Copyist of Special Books on a personal mission. As Muhammad Maqrebi was led by guards through a series of antechambers to enter the chancellor's private office, he tried to guess the nature of the task that awaited him. He did not know that it would change his life for ever.

The Grand Vizier was friendly enough and even smiled a little. He gave the scribe a bundle of notes in several hands with last minute corrections. Writing many years later in the reign of Sultan Muhammad, Malik Shah's second successor, Maqrebi recalled his moment in history:

> Nizām al-Mulk had first dictated [to secretaries] forty but one chapters, but they had been short ones. Then he had thought again and, because of that disappointment with his government's opponents, he added eleven more chapters and expanded the previous ones. At the time of his journey to

Baghdad, he gave them to me [to copy and bind]. But then, as that fate befell him during the journey, I did not dare to show the book to anyone until now, when the reign of the Sultan of the World [Muhammad] has again established justice and strengthened Islam. May God Almighty by His grace and mercy protect this government to the Day of Judgement.

The book, *Siāsat Nāmeh or Book of Politics*, has now become one of the treasures of Persian literature, but it is also an oblique commentary on the politics of Isfahan and the Saljuq empire at the time. We may try to guess what the humble civil servant Muhammad Maqrebi thought, as he immersed himself in the notes that had previously been seen only by the great vizier himself in totality. Here are some of the passages that would both have amused the scribe and alarmed him – in case some of the late chancellor's powerful enemies traced them to him:

And so this is the book we have written on governance. The Lord of the World [Malik Shah] had told me to make a collection on the matter and at some time I dictated thirty-nine chapters. When I sent it to the exalted chamber, it was judged well. But it was much too short. Later, I added more chapters to it and expanded the previous chapters, in clearer language. When it was time for us to leave for Baghdad, we gave it to the Copyist of Special Books, Muhammad Maqrebi, and commanded that he should copy it in a clean hand. If this humble servant should not survive the journey, he [Maqrebi] should take it to the Lord of the World, that he may read it constantly to the benefit of his exalted reign, that he may listen to his own inner voice, for he will not find this book tiresome. It is not all advice and wisdom, but also stories, commentaries on the Koran, history of the Prophet, peace by upon him, and the ways of just kings. It is the story of those who have been and the inheritance of those who will be. Yet, it remains short, and worthy of a fair king's court.

Chapter 43, On the Veiled Ones and Regulations Concerning the Commanders of the Army and Underlings: . . . Kings must take care that underlings do not gain the upper hand. Great damage will be born of it, and the king's glory will dim. Women, especially, lack full wisdom. Their purpose is to prolong the race. The more noble they are, the more suitable they will be, and the more hidden are they, the better will be they. If women come to command a king, they will reflect only the interests of the men of ill will around them. Corruption will spread, the people will suffer, statesmen will become estranged.

Whenever in history women have reigned, the result has been dissidence, corruption, calamity. When Adam obeyed Eve and ate of wheat [the Koran's version of the forbidden fruit] he was expelled from paradise. He wept for 200 years before the Almighty took pity on him and accepted his repentance.

Chapter 33, On Admonishing the Elite for their Mistakes and Sins: . . . They say that Muawiyah [the fifth caliph after Muhammad] was a most tolerant man. One day, as he received public petitions, a bold young man came to him and sat down without permission. 'Oh, Commander of the Faithful, he said, today I have a matter of importance to put to you. I am a stranger here and have no woman of my own. You have a mother who has no husband. Give her to me as Allah will be pleased with you.'

Muawiyah replied: 'You are a young man; my mother is old. She has not a single tooth in her mouth. Why have you chosen her?'

The man said: 'I have heard she has large buttocks and I like large buttocks.'

Muawiyah said: 'My father married her for the same reason and died of regret. She has no other art. Still, I will give her your message. If she agrees, I shall raise no objections.'

Chapter 17, On Companions and Confidants: . . . Some kings have chosen physicians and astrologers among their closest companions. Physicians keep an eye on their health and judge what foods suit them, what their nature requires. Astrologers determine the time and the hour for them, tell them of omens and what not to do.

Some kings deny it all. They say that physicians forbid us delicious meals and high pleasures, and they give us medicines without our being ill. Astrologers, too, deny us enjoyments and stop us from taking urgent action.

It is best to call upon physicians and astrologers when the need arises for them. But in all cases, it is best to choose companions from among those who have seen the world and have been successful. If they have previously served the nobility, that is better, and when the common folks want to learn of their sovereign's temperaments and habits, they will judge them by their companions. Each companion must be given a designated rank. Some ought to be able to sit with the king, others stand only in his presence.

Chapter 41, On the Hierarchy of Titles: . . . They say that the sultan Mahmūd complained to the caliph that he had received only one title from him, whereas the caliph had granted three to the khān of Turkistan, even though the khān was a vassal to Mahmūd. The caliph replied: 'You are too

noble and too well known to need any more, but the khān is an ignorant
Turk and has no knowledge of the world. That is why we agreed to his
pleading.'[8] Mahmūd was not satisfied and struck upon a ruse . . .[9]

*   *   *

In this same summer of 1092, while Sabbāh and his fewer than one
hundred devoted sectarians battled to keep Alamūt from falling into
the hands of Arslan Tāsh and his Saljuq army that besieging it, he also
dreamt of the success of a masterstroke he had planned, one that
would change the history of the region.

His spies at the court in Isfahan had reported to him the exact date
of departure of the royal caravan towards Baghdad and the exact route
it would take. Sabbāh could not arrange an ambush, for the caravan
had several thousand archers and cavalry in attendance, but he
possessed a new weapon the like of which none suspected. He had
bred a number of young men who would readily give their lives at his
command to avenge their community and advance their cause. He
had convinced them they need not fear death, but welcome it joyfully,
for they would be transported instantly to paradise where throngs of
beautiful angels awaited them with the blessing of God to sustain an
everlasting life of pleasure.

Some of the details have been lost, but we know that when, on 14
October, the caravan reached the hamlet of Sahneh[10] in a fertile
valley in the Zagros highlands of western Iran, a handful of Sabbāh's
men mingled with the locals curiously watching the splendid horses
and carriages and litters.

The Grand Vizier is said to have declared that Sahneh was a holy
place, for some of the bravest soldiers of the second caliph Omar had
lost their lives there fighting the locals during the Muslim conquest of
Iran. He did not suspect that his own blood would soon mix there in
the soil with that of his heroes.

It was after the evening prayers and Nizām, at seventy-four years of
age, had just broken his Ramadan fast. As his servants began to carry
his litter 'towards the tent of his womenfolk',[11] a youth in the robe of
a Sufi aesthete approached and asked to be allowed to submit a
petition to him. The guards may well have been reluctant to let the

man come too near, but anyhow he was granted his wish. As he reached forth to put his letter into the vizier's hand, he suddenly produced a long knife and plunged it into the great man's heart.

The assailant tried to run away, but he stumbled over a tent peg and fell, before being cut down in a rain of sabres by the guards. We do not know for how long afterwards he or Nizām remained conscious, for one to confess and the other to hear who stood behind the crime. But Nizām's supporters immediately suspected the hand of Tāj al-Mulk, Terken Khātūn's chief of staff. Some thought that even the sultan himself might be implicated, for he had long appeared to be grooming Tāj al-Mulk for the vizierate.

The highway alongside which the caravan would have camped was hemmed in by dense forest to the north and the Gā Māsi Ow[12] River to the south. It would have taken some time for all the travellers to learn of the assassination. Malik Shah rode to the scene immediately and kept the army calm. But we may be fairly certain that he felt the loss of the old man in such a tragic manner deeply. He would have wanted to find out who the culprits might be and whether they planned other assaults. On reflection, the tragedy gave him a new freedom of action and saved him the embarrassment of dismissing his 'father'. As for Tāj al-Mulk, he would have been forgiven in thinking that it meant his time had come at last.

Terken Khātūn would have immediately thought of the practical implications of the murder. As for Khayyām, whether he was present or not – for he was the royal family's chief doctor, as well as confidante – he would have been apprehensive knowing as he did, of the chaos in Khorāsān that had scarred the lives of his parents around the time of his birth. It is likely that he would have tried to see Nizām's senior son, Mo'ayyad al-Mulk, who had been a personal friend since their youth in Isfahan in the mid-1070s, as soon as he could.

Everyone who was anyone at the court, though, knew that the rivalry of recent years between Malik Shah and Nizām was unsustainable. The king had now grown into a confident leader in his own right, and he was alert in mind and vigorous in body. It was quite likely that, given the enormous wealth and influence of the sons and family of his old guide, who suspected him of complicity in the murder, he would go to extremes to placate them by renewing their governorships and fiefdoms. It was even possible that he would push aside Terken Khātūn's objections and appoint Mo'ayyad to his father's vacant seat.

*   *   *

But none of that was to be. While the body of Nizām al-Mulk was sent back to Isfahan for burial in an elaborate ceremony, Malik Shah appointed Tāj al-Mulk to the vizierate a few days after they reached Baghdad on 30 October. This turned out, it seems, to be the gravest mistake he could have made. For, a week or two later, he was taken ill with a violent fever. He had gone hunting and had eaten substantially of the game he had killed. It was claimed that the meat had got infected.

His doctors, who almost certainly included Khayyām, bled him, though not drastically, and they tried every known remedy and every nutritious food and drink. But his decline could not be halted. He died on the evening of Friday, 20 November at the age of only thirty-seven.

Was he poisoned? That is the general opinion of the time and it has to be said that none of the known, natural 'fevers' of the age, such as malaria, killed so quickly, particularly such a healthy, sporty and well-nourished man in middle life; while the game that would have been served to the king would have been the freshest. The whole hunt lasted less than six days and, even if, on the last day, he had been fed some of the game killed on the first, the chilly weather of late November in the Baghdad area would have prevented the meat from becoming badly infected. In any case, on one of his previous hunts in the same area, it is said that the number of birds and beasts killed exceeded 10,000. Any stale or smelly meat would have been thrown to the dogs, not fed to the king.

The majority opinion of the time declares that he was poisoned by the 'Nizāmiyah', the private court and army of the late Grand Vizier, in revenge for the king's suspected complicity in their patron's murder. One name mentioned as directly implicated in the poisoning is 'Khardak, the Eunuch' on behalf of the Nizāmiyah. But it is surely equally likely that Malik Shah's estranged son-in-law was behind the crime. As we have seen, Malik Shah had ordered Moqtada to vacate Baghdad as the seat of the caliphate and had lately even planned to depose him completely. Furthermore, the caliphal palace had a long family history in devising deadly potions and administering them to rivals through their own servants.

Malik Shah seems to have been a good man, relative to the norms of his era, that is. Unlike both his father, Alp-Arslan, and his guardian, Nizām al-Mulk, he had only three women in his life, and two of those had been chosen for him while still a child. The only woman he chose for himself was his concubine, Tāj al-Dīn Khātūn, Crown of the Realm, upon whom he showered titles and wealth.

It is said that, in his later years, he felt so guilty after hunting wild animals that he gave a dinar to charity for every living creature he and his companions had killed. After one such hunt near Baghdad, he gave away 10,000 dinars.

In matters of religion, he was a rationalist, as was his boon companion, the hard-drinking, lute-playing, Greek-loving astronomer. A cleric, al-Jurjani, confided in the historian Ibn Aqīl that Malik Shah had once shocked him by revealing how much his notion of God – if he believed in a deity at all – differed from that of Allah in the Koran. 'What is God?', he had asked Jurjani. 'To what are you referring when you say "God"?'[13]

In matters of state, he was wise enough to defer to Nizām al-Mulk, whom his father had appointed over him as guardian. In recent years, Nizām and his numerous, arrogant sons had stretched his patience to its extreme limits. Yet he had borne their trespasses in relatively good grace, at least in public, thinking always of what might happen to the state if he dismissed the architect of his reign's triumphs.

One of the most telling stories about the two men's recent tense relationship occurred in their last year, 1092. After one of Nizām's sons, the governor of Marv, had imprisoned Malik Shah's representative there, Malik Shah sent a delegation composed of Tāj al-Mulk and some other top statesmen and military commanders to Nizām with the following message: 'If you are my partner in this realm, that's a different matter. But if you're my subject, why are you allowing your sons and servants to commit so many crimes? Do you want me to send soldiers to take away your pen and inkwell?'

Nizām took special exception to the king's ingratitude. He replied: 'Tell the sultan that if he doesn't know I'm his partner, he better learn it now. Ask him if he's forgotten that I defeated his challengers and conquered new lands for him. Tell him this inkwell and that crown depend on each another. If he takes away this inkwell, that crown will be swept away also.'[14]

Anyhow, a Qarakhanid princess without a social base in the extended Saljuq family now found herself in charge of the instruments of power at the heart of the empire. What would she do next in a system that would not allow women openly to hold public office, even if they were the daughters or widows of mighty emperors? Yet taking urgent and pre-emptive action was vital. Her sole surviving son, Mahmūd, was only four years old, while her rival Zubeida Khātūn's son, Berkyaruq, was a whole seven years older. Berkyaruq had the greater legal right to be the next sultan and he had been favoured by Nizām al-Mulk and the whole Nizāmiyah establishment. The caliph, too, was on Zubeida's side due to Terken's visceral hatred of him. So was the whole of the clerical class. The only hope lay in the army.

CHAPTER NINE

The Queen Turns

It is best today few friends to seek;
It is best with folks from afar to speak.
The one for hard times to lean on I chose:
When I needed her, she[1] sang with my foes.

Malik Shah's illness lasted less than two weeks. Though, by this stage, no longer necessarily fond of her husband, the headstrong Terken Khātūn would have prayed desperately for a recovery. She was not ready for the consequences. But as the king's condition deteriorated and his doctors began to worry seriously, she would have started to plan her next moves. It must have been at that moment, probably a few days towards the end, that she decided to hide the news of his death for as long as she could. To succeed, she must have gradually stopped the stream of dignitaries who came to visit the dying king. If she had stopped the visitors suddenly on his death, it would have virtually amounted to her confirming it.

Did Malik Shah on his deathbed nominate any of his four remaining sons to succeed him? The assumption must be that he did. His own father had declared him crown prince when he was only nine years old and it was as vital now as it had been then to minimise the chances of a civil war breaking out. The assumption must also be that he nominated his eldest surviving son, Berkyaruq, by Zubeida Khātūn, his Saljuq cousin. To do otherwise would have guaranteed trouble. Berkyaruq had the superior legal right and, in any case, the Nizāmiyah would not accept any son of Terken Khātūn's. They would look for any excuse to rebel. If Malik Shah had kept his wits, he would have told Tāj al-Mulk, the new Grand Vizier, to forget his lifelong loyalty to Terken and submit himself to Berkyaruq in the greater interest of the family and the state.

But if indeed the emperor did make such a will, it must have been suppressed by both Terken Khātūn and Tāj al-Mulk. There is no trace of it in the sources, who otherwise give us graphic images of the king's last days. Terken could not contemplate letting the sultanate slip into Zubeida's lap, and Tāj al-Mulk knew that the 'Nizāmiyah' would never forgive him his former rivalry with Nizām, let alone their suspicion of his complicity in the great man's death.

Terken claimed vehemently that the late sultan's last words had been to nominate little Mahmūd as his heir. But she did not have the testimony of any respected religious, political or military official to back her assertion. Furthermore, in the absence of such proof, she needed religious sanction of the highest kind for her act, and that blessing could come only from a man who detested her as much as she detested him – her estranged son-in-law. But Caliph Moqtada argued that Islam did not allow toddlers to be declared monarchs and, in any case, Berkyaruq, at eleven years of age, was much older. Eventually, after much coming and going, with threats and blackmail always to the fore, the caliph obtained his pound of flesh, literally. Terken Khātūn would hand over to him his little son, Ja'far, her own motherless grandson, in return for his agreement to proclaim Mahmūd the new sultan. This was done formally on Friday, 26 November, six days after Malik Shah's death. On that day, mullahs in dozens of mosques in Baghdad proclaimed Mahmūd the new temporal ruler of the caliphate, and messengers were sent to the clergy everywhere else to do the same, from Mecca to Damascus, from Isfahan to Samarkand.

With his son back in his custody, Moqtada now knew that no future Saljuq ruler could depose him as caliph to put the little half-Saljuq boy in his place. He also squeezed other concessions out of Terken Khātūn. All political, administrative and financial decisions would be made officially by Grand Vizier Tāj al-Mulk, though 'sitting before the Khātūn', and the command of the army would be in the hands of her main military chief, Unur. Islam forbade the mention of a woman's name as the ruling power in the land.

That was only formality, of course. Now, truly and for the first time, Terken could be described as a real queen. She was sovereign in the state and possessed enough military power to crush any potential rebellion. She had made the top army generals swear loyalty to Mahmūd and her health was good. Though afflicted by neurosis as a result of all the personal tragedies of recent years, she was only in early middle age.

Nevertheless, she took every other action deemed advisable to strengthen her position. Before the news of the sultan's death was released, she sent one of her emirs to Isfahan with the sultan's signet ring to take over the castle and the treasury there. He would immediately arrest Berkyaruq and all his champions in the city, including his mother Zubeida. This was achieved swiftly enough, though it caused bewilderment among officials in the capital that the sultan should order the imprisonment of a son of his who was as yet so young. Bewilderment quickly gave place to shock when the rumour spread that the boy had been blinded to disqualify him in the succession.

*　　*　　*

We do not know the precise understanding behind the arrangement that Malik Shah had made for Khayyām to entitle him to the huge salary of 10,000 gold dinars a year. It makes sense to assume that it required Khayyām not only to supervise the building of the new observatory in Isfahan, but also act as the chief physician to the royal family. Beyond that, the arrangement would have been an acknowledgement that, as one of the sultan's closest friends, Khayyām needed a large income to enable him to keep up appearances with the princes and statesmen among whom he mixed at court. Another part of his job as supervisor of the observatory, which was to remain unfinished on the king's death, was to keep accurate time and calendar for the needs of the state, as well as to supply astrologers to the court to determine auspicious moments for the king's every action. This would have been done by his office, without much need of daily intervention by him.

But whether he was in Baghdad at the time of the sultan's death on 20 November or else, he had remained at the observatory in Isfahan, Khayyām is likely to have disapproved strongly of Terken's clear disregard of the law, and shocked by the ease with which she reverted to the normal behaviour of warlords in pursuit of a crown. As doctor to the whole family, too, he would have known the other royal wife, Zubeida, and her son Berkyaruq well. The very thought of the boy being blinded would have sickened him, as it did many others. Though he had always kept out of politics and tried to remain on friendly terms with all, Khayyām would have immediately tried to find out whether the rumour was true.

The overnight transformation of Terken from a royal, though domineering, wife into a ruthless tyrant would have also terrified him. Rebellion was assured. Even if Berkyaruq were blinded, there were still two other royal sons for the Nizāmiyah to champion. Terken would not now lift a finger to protect Khayyām from those fiends, the fatwa-wielders, who had yearned for his blood for years. No, it was worse. She would willingly throw him to the wolves herself if it helped her to woo them to her side. He was now a sacrificial lamb at the gate of the slaughterhouse, for all the factions wooed the clergy and needed the common, superstitious, volatile mobs of the streets, not him, the 'Greek-loving' scholar, the 'drunkard' writer of blasphemous songs.

* * *

In actuality, Berkyaruq had not been blinded in Terken Khātūn's prison, nor hurt in any other respect, except of course psychologically, before the Nizāmiyah rushed the jail in early December and freed him. The rebels also raided an armoury belonging to the late chancellor and armed themselves. They were joined by the populace in widespread rioting and Berkyaruq was declared the rightful sultan. When Terken Khātūn and her army returned in late December with Malik Shah's coffin, Berkyaruq was already on his way north to Rayy, where the governor, one of Nizām's sons-in-law, had joined the rebellion. Some other divisions of the army in the north now joined the rebels. It is said that the clergy of Isfahan refused to lead mourning ceremonies for the dead sovereign. Certainly, there were few public expressions of grief for him. The prevailing opinion was that his death did not compare in importance with that of the late chancellor.

Even worse news arrived soon afterwards. A more deadly threat had raised its head in the far south-east. Malik Shah's younger brother, Totosh, the battle-hardened viceroy of Syria, had declared himself to be the new rightful leader. Totosh was invoking Turkish tribal custom, the practice of the Saljuqs' ancestors, not the recently-adopted Persian practice. According to that custom, the succession went to the next eldest male member of the family, not necessarily a son of the dead chief. Such resort to ethnic Turkish sentiment endeared him to the military, he hoped. But the military, at least in his own region, really judged him by his past record. He would 'walk over the women', they thought.

As for the headstrong Qarakhanid princess, there was no going back. To encourage her troops, she showered on them what remained of the cash and treasure that Nizām al-Mulk and Malik Shah had accumulated over the years, and she promised them even more if they won the upcoming struggle. They were then dispatched under her tried and true servant, Grand Vizier Tāj al-Mulk, to pursue Zubeida's army in January.

The two sides clashed near the western town of Borujerd. The fighting proved hard and bloody, but several emirs defected to the eldest son. Terken's supporters were defeated and withdrew to Isfahan. Tāj al-Mulk was captured some days later hiding in a village. To buy his life, he volunteered to become Berkyaruq's vizier. He offered the Nizāmiyah 200,000 dinars if they would agree. They did, but not all of them. While laying siege to Isfahan in the following month, a younger group among them swore that nothing but the severed head of the man they held responsible for their setbacks would satisfy them. They rushed his tent on 12 February and cut him to pieces before parading his head on a pole. He was only forty-five years old[2] and had enough intelligence, intuition, energy and determination perhaps to have become a worthy successor to Nizām al-Mulk, had Malik Shah lived.

*   *   *

As Zubeida's – or, nominally, her son Berkyaruq's – army now besieged Isfahan, news reached Alamūt that the hated Saljuqs were indeed now fighting among themselves like packs of wild dogs. Alamūt's own siege had been lifted last October, when, as we saw, 300 peasant fighters and some other Ismaili irregulars fell upon an army sent by Malik Shah at night and routed it, capturing much needed supplies in the process. Now the inhabitants could rest in peace, confident in the knowledge that the Turks would not be back for some years. In the meantime, Sabbāh's devout followers, whose faith in him had strengthened manifold as his predictions came true, began to harass more of their neighbours and gained more castles, far and wide. Before long, they could claim convincingly that they possessed a state of their own, though it was not geographically contiguous. It dotted the map as a series of allied towns and principalities from Khorāsān in the north-east to Kurdistan in the south-west.

A story has survived from this period which throws light on the morale in Alamūt and, particularly, on the mood of Sabbāh himself.

It says that his old friend, the chief Abul-Fazl, who had in 1081 given him shelter while he was a fugitive in Isfahan, went to visit him in Alamūt after the death of Malik Shah. Sabbāh, as we saw earlier, had left the chief's house in disgust when he found that he was secretly being treated for a nervous breakdown. As the two men now met in much happier circumstances, Sabbāh said to Abul-Fazl: 'Do you remember you thought me mad when I told you I would turn the Turks' empire upside down if I had a couple of like-minded men?' Abul-Fazl apologised and confessed that a few like-minded men had, indeed, destroyed the great Saljuq empire.

*   *   *

Some authorities[3] say that Zubeida captured Isfahan and crowned her eleven-year-old son there. If so, she could not have conquered the whole city or its castle, for we find Terken's government in place soon afterwards, when Zubeida has left the capital to confront Totosh in Azerbaijan, to the north-west of Isfahan. It is unlikely that they came to an agreement to divide the capital between them. This little corner of Saljuq history will probably remain confused for the time being.

What we know for certain is that Zubeida scored a clear, though temporary, victory over her brother-in-law two months later, in May.

Two of Totosh's most prominent emirs defected to her and the prince thought it prudent to withdraw back to Syria to gather more troops.[4]

In the meantime, desperate for allies, Terken had struck upon a brilliant idea: she would propose marriage to Zubeida's elder brother and Malik Shah's cousin, Prince Ismail, the governor of Azerbaijan. She sent him envoys to encourage him to believe that he would be regent to little Mahmūd and, therefore, the real ruler if her camp won the struggle. As a result, he gathered a sizable force and offered battle to his sister, but he was defeated and fled to Isfahan with his surviving troops. There, Terken, still hopeful of his potential, received him with open arms and ordered that his name be recited in the Friday prayer sermons after Mahmūd, and that coins be struck in his name. We are told that the proposed union proceeded well at first, but her own army chief, the emir Unur, suspected Ismail of having his eyes on the crown for himself. Terken agreed and so Ismail departed for his sister's camp in north-west Iran. There he was forgiven, but was found soon afterwards trying to persuade the military to join him in overthrowing her. Her top emirs murdered him one late summer night in his tent. She 'kept her peace' with them, says Ibn Athīr.

Earlier in Isfahan, in late June or early July, Terken had heard that her six-year-old grandson Ja'far had died. He had lasted only seven months in his father, Caliph Moqtada's, custody in Baghdad. With him dead, she now had only Mahmūd left in her bloodline in the warring empire – if it could still be called an empire at all.

*   *   *

In the middle of this turmoil, all trace of Khayyām's history is lost, but he was safe enough, somewhere, trying to remain undiscovered by the clergy and the gangs of criminals who always roamed the streets in times of trouble to look for rich civilians to hold to ransom or to sell. Where might it have been safest for him to live in the winter of 1093?

All the lands to the west of Isfahan had descended into chaos as the main battleground of the contending princes and princesses. Nor would Khayyām have thought of seeking protection in peaceful Baghdad, for Ghazali, his venomous enemy and Nizām's protégé, held sway there among the top mullahs. Furthermore, though the caliph had now attained a degree of independence due to the death of Malik Shah, Baghdad remained largely in the grip of the Nizāmiyah.

There is a famous story about Khayyām and Ghazāli that, although almost certainly exaggerated, is worth recalling. While vehemently denouncing Khayyām and all the other scientists or philosophers of his time as heretics, Ghazāli had secretly been studying those very subjects as a private student at Khayyām's home. Khayyām found this intolerable and so one morning, as Ghazāli left the house, Khayyām gave a signal to a drummer he had stationed on the roof to start his tumult. Neighbours threw open the doors of their houses only to see the famous advocate of strict Shari'a law leaving, meekly, the home of the controversial philosopher.

Khayyām would not have behaved in such a cheap manner, but Ghazāli is said to have claimed that he studied under Khayyām, in Isfahan, so that he could all the more convincingly show up Khayyām's heresies in his subsequent book, *The Destruction of the Philosophers*.

Ghazāli certainly once humiliated Khayyām – some might say himself – badly in a gathering of the elite. He asked Khayyām a technical question on astronomy[5] and Khayyām tried to give an accurate and adequate answer, suspecting that Ghazāli would report whatever he said as heretical. As he elaborated his answer, the muezzin of a neighbouring mosque called the faithful to prayer. Ghazāli stood up and declared pompously: 'Truth has arrived to put falsehood to flight.'

Anyway, at the height of the frost in the winter of 1093, travelling northwards towards his native Nishāpur in Khorāsān would not have been advisable, even if Omar were, for example, disguised as a pauper to escape the clutches of his pursuers.[6] Furthermore, the crisis had just burst upon him and collecting his thoughts would have taken some weeks. It is likely, therefore, that he spent those months hiding in a series of houses belonging to friends in Isfahan itself. But his friends would have been highly uncomfortable with his presence, while he would have hated having to depend on them.[7]

Ironically, following the death of Tāj al-Mulk in early February after the battle of Borujerd, Terken chose Khayyām's old friend, Mo'ayyad al-Mulk, as her new Grand Vizier, to appease the Nizāmiyah. The assumption can be made that Khayyām – if indeed still in hiding in

Isfahan – would have sent a plea for help to Mo'ayyad. But it is quite clear that, despite the strictures imposed on Terken Khātūn by the clergy that a woman could not hold office in an Islamic state, she was the real power in the state, not her vizier or army chief. Whether or not Moayyad wanted to help Khayyām, he would have had to seek permission from 'the Khātūn' to extend protection to their mutual friend. Thus, ultimately, we have to hold Terken Khātūn's political priorities as responsible for the collapse of Khayyām's world. The quatrain in which Khayyām complains of betrayal by a friend may well refer to her.[8]

Under such circumstances, it would have made sense for Khayyām to go back to Khorāsān as soon as the weather in the northern mountain passes lifted, in the early spring of 1093. While a rebellion had erupted there too, Khorāsān had not become a battleground yet, and the rebel leader, Prince Arslan Arqūn, had the limited aim of seeking autonomy for his own province only, rather than seeking the sultanate in Isfahan. For the time being, Arslan Arqūn was safe in vast Khorāsān and would not have had to bend to the will of the local clergy to prosecute a fugitive philosopher.

As for Mo'ayyad al-Mulk, it is worth mentioning that soon all three main rivals for the sultanate would have a son of the late Nizām al-Mulk as their Grand Vizier. Such was the prestige of the family among the populace that while Terken chose Mo'ayyad, Zubeida chose Izz al-Mulk – 'the best-looking of men and the kindest', according to Ibn Athīr – and Totosh opted for Fakhr al-Mulk. Almost certainly, Khayyām would have known the other two brothers too, besides Mo'ayyad. Indeed, yet another son, Diā al-Mulk, the son of the Armenian princess from Georgia whom Alp-Arslan had once given to Nizām, would also climb the heights in the future and, in one way or another, the descendants of the legendary chancellor would hold high office in the region for the next hundred years and more.

CHAPTER TEN

The Pilgrim of Babel

This world, this ancient caravanserai,
This resting place of the low and high,
How for fair Shīrīn does it still grieve,
How for brave Farhād does it still sigh.

Omar Khayyām was the sage of Khorāsān, the leading learned man of his age and a master of the sciences of Yunān [Greece]. He advocated physical exercise for the cleansing of the self, and supported civil policies according to Greek thought.

Lately, Sufis have claimed him for their creed. They fall for the gloss of his poems and discuss them in their congregations, but in truth his poems are snakes on the body of the holy Shari'a law and overflow with treacherous hatred of it.

When people revealed his secrets and condemned him for his beliefs, he feared for his life. He reined in his tongue and curbed his pen. He went on the hājj pilgrimage, not out of conviction, but to save his life. When he reached Baghdad, the followers of his way and of the old sciences sought him out. But he shut his door on them, in the manner of a repentant man. . . . After the pilgrimage, he returned to his home city, attended places of worship and kept secret his inner beliefs.

He was unique in his time in astronomy and philosophy, so that they cited him as the infallible authority in those subjects.

His hair flew about in the air, revealing the root of every strand at his temples. Among his poems are: . . .[1]

The writer of these lines, Jamāl ad-Dīn Sheibāni al-Qifti, flourished a century after Khayyām. He was born in Upper Egypt and died as a vizier in Aleppo, Syria, in 1248, at the age of seventy-six. Clearly he had access to information that has now been lost to us. He is the only one of the contemporary – or near contemporary – sources who reports on Khayyām having made a pilgrimage to Mecca.

Qifti's assertion that the pilgrimage was only a pretend one obviously found ready acceptance at the time and it is one with which we can agree today. If Khayyām were alive in our time, we would describe him as a freethinker – or a 'passionate sceptic', as the philosopher Bertrand Russell was described by a biographer – and freethinkers do not make pilgrimages to holy sites. Furthermore, the man of substance that Khayyām had become under his friend, the equally sceptical Malik Shah, owed much of his popularity at court to precisely his readiness to speak his mind. His friends and admirers would have been shocked if he had really suddenly decided to become a 'hāji', an orthodox adherent to the rites of Islam; his actions were clearly determined by a real fear for his life after Malik Shah's sudden death.

What can Qifti mean precisely when he says the 'people revealed his secrets and condemned him for his beliefs'? He can only mean that the leading clerics of his time staged a formal investigation into Omar's writings and found some of them – particularly his secret poems and songs that had leaked outside Isfahan's elite circles – clearly refuting several of Islam's most basic precepts. The mullahs were right. The quatrains openly question the claims of the Koran that Allah is a merciful God and that another life awaits us when we die. In a series of sharp points, Omar implies that if there is a creator at all, a deity who is responsible for our existence, it would not be a jealous and selfish being who resembled ourselves and became enraged if we did not bow before him five times a day. Furthermore, in the absence of any direct evidence to prove the existence of such a creator, it was a waste of time to be preoccupied with the subject. Better to be kind to those around us while we lived, for our fellows were, like ourselves, vulnerable to suffering.[2]

Organised religions, particularly Judaism and its two major derivatives, with their rich priests and precise dogmas of Creation, Heaven, Hell and Prophesy, have naturally felt threatened by such thinking and, whenever able, have pronounced the same anathema – fatwa, in Arabic – that enemies of society must repent, or else . . .

Famous parallels to the treatment of Khayyām stretch to our time. In 1989, almost 900 years after Khayyām's troubles started, the novelist Salman Rushdie was pronounced a blasphemer by mullahs because of his book *The Satanic Verses*. Muslim zealots all over the world sought him out to kill him. After many months of hiding under the protection of British police, he announced that he had 'seen the light of Islam' after all, and re-embraced the faith of his forefathers. It was a ploy advised by friends to mollify the assassins, but few people believed him, including myself. I was, at the time, a commentator on the affair for *The Times* newspaper in London and many western broadcasters. The mullahs smelt blood and Rushdie lost many admirers who accused him of cowardice.[3]

Yet there is another assumption about Khayyām after the loss of his royal protector that we can make with a degree of confidence. It is that his pilgrimage to 'Arabistan' was made as soon as possible. This would have been to prevent the news of the fatwa from spreading far and wide. The accused had to be seen to refute it visibly and immediately. In fact, it would have been best for him to set out for Mecca in December 1092, while Terken Khātūn and her army were carrying the coffin of Malik Shah back to Isfahan for burial. War had not yet broken out between the dead sovereign's heirs and, by coincidence, the hājj fell on the last few days of the following month, January 1093, the cool season in which to tackle the deserts of Arabia.

This is possible, but unlikely to have been the case. It would have taken several months for the mullahs to complete their formalities, for the enormity of the threat to Khayyām's life to become clear to him, and for him to assess his plight and to collect his mind. So, probably, he went on the next hājj, in January 1094.

In the meantime, he would have been advised not to remain in Isfahan, or at least to go into hiding there. To remain in the public eye in the place where he was best known would have been suicidal, as it was the bastion of the clergy who were condemning him and who had, for years, growled at him on the streets as a 'Corruptor of the Earth' and a malign influence on no less a personage in the land than the sultan. They had longed for the moment when they could inflict the wrath of Allah on the swaggering dog.

I believe I have found among the writings of Khayyām's contemporaries in Isfahan an example of the admonishments that he must have suffered even before Malik Shah's death. It is by the pen of Mo'ezzi, a fellow Nishāpurian a little younger than Khayyām himself who was Malik Shah's part-time poet laureate. It is mild and anonymous, as you would expect from a courtier wary of angering his suzerain, but the recipient of its 'bouquet of barbed wire' would have been clear to everyone. Apart from Malik Shah himself, whose sceptical tendencies were kept a state secret until after his death, there was only one prominent personality in the capital who did not hide his disdain for 'revealed' dogma. Here is a short excerpt from the poet's satire:

> How do you explain this great Rolling Wheel,
> In whose blue sky shines that bright fire?
> What do you think of the two birds in flight,
> One as dark as tar, one of feathers white?
> What say you of all the races of man,
> Each one emblazoned with a different hue?
> How is it that your 'Zarathustra's House',[4]
> Has come to praise Muhammad's view?
> How could we exist without a Maker,
> An ultimate Will that brought us forth?
> Think of the day when Allah summons you,
> To judge you harshly by your present deeds.
> Sow the kind of seeds that might bear you fruit
> That Day of Trial, that Promised Morn.
> Praise Him, for to Him praise is due,
> Only through His Grace will your dreams come true.[5]

It has to be said that Allah did not, in the end, look as kindly on pious Mo'ezzi as he did on wild Khayyām. Mo'ezzi died, painfully, at the hands of Malik Shah's youngest son, Sanjar. When Sanjar eventually became sultan – and sought Khayyām's company, as we shall see later – an arrow shot by him in pursuit of game lodged itself in the poor poet's chest and, although he lived on for some years, he did not recover fully. The arrow could not entirely be removed from inside his breast. We do not know what Khayyām thought of the plight of his old acquaintance.

Mo'ezzi had an even more serious shortcoming in Khayyām's eye. To dispel any suspicion that he was nostalgic about pre-Islamic Iran, he sprinkled his writing with Arabic words and even sometimes imitated the style of Arab poets. He would have been a pillar of the Nizāmiyah Sunni establishment in Isfahan, rather than in Malik Shah's camp, and though Khayyām could not have avoided him in the small circles of the literate in Isfahan, we may assume that he could not stand the ignorant, almost traitorous, little pedant.

Back to Qifti now. As he does not give us the date of Khayyām's expedient pilgrimage to Mecca, and as there are no traces of Khayyām's whereabouts in the immediate years after the death of Malik Shah, we have to resort to a little detective work to point us in his direction. His best option would have been to flee Isfahan as soon as he could for his own homeland, faraway Khorāsān, as that region never became a battleground between the various claimants to the sultanate. He had family there, perhaps even a whole clan, and he was rich enough, in all likelihood, to have bought already at least one, and possibly several, large agricultural estates in the hills overlooking Nishāpur. Investing in the countryside was the universal practice of his peers, for it guaranteed survival in times of war and famine and, of course, it also provided a pleasant pastoral life and a grand style of living. There, on one of his estates, among his own tenant farmers, gardeners, shepherds, servants and bodyguards, he could sleep in peace and be safe from the volatile mobs of cities until, most probably, mid-autumn of 1093, when the first hājj caravans would leave Nishāpur for 'Arabistan'.

In the meantime, however, he would have lost any properties he had in Isfahan. Immediately upon the fatwa being issued against him, they would have first been looted by frenzied crowds and then confiscated by clerics 'for the benefit of orphans'. The losses would have been considerable. As we have seen, his salary of 10,000 gold pieces a year from the sultan astonished the Lord High Minister of the Treasury. But he would have earned extra sums as a 'second Avicenna', the most esteemed physician of his time. He is likely to have invested in a string of prestigious properties in town. They may have included shops, public baths and even whole caravanserais. In one instance we know, one rich man made a gift of a caravanserai in Baghdad to Nizām al-Mulk.

One last – and exciting – point about Qifti's short passage on Khayyām is that it gives us the only, if too brief, description of Khayyām's appearance. He says that his 'hair flew about', obviously as he moved or gesticulated so wildly that you could see 'the root of every strand at the temples'. This is indeed what we would expect of a poet and a sage who lived in the world of the philosophers of ancient Yunān, classical Greece. Combined with what he himself says about his long beard on his seventieth birthday, these descriptions enable us to envisage a 'Socrates' of a figure with long flowing hair and white beard in a long robe holding a lute in his lap and a glass of wine in his hand looking into a book of verse from which to sing to his companions by a tumbling stream:

> Today, I will shed my robe of restraint,
> Let trails of red wine my white beard taint:
> No more piety; I am *seventy*.
> If not dance now, when might it then be?

It is good to know that he lived for many years after his seventieth birthday and that he was able to dance and sing with his friends to his heart's desire.

* * *

Three foreign ministers were excited by the news of Malik Shah's sudden death at the height of his powers, particularly as it happened only a month after the death of his legendary iron chancellor Nizām al-Mulk. The foreign ministries were those in Cairo, Constantinople and Rome; their respective rulers were Badr al-Jamāli, the Armenian-born general who was the effective ruler of Egypt, Alexius Comnenus, the vigorous young emperor of the Eastern Romans in Constantinople, and Pope Urban II, the ambitious new leader of the western church in old Rome.

Their spy chiefs told them that Malik Shah's great empire could now fall into the most horrendous of dynastic conflicts, as it had after the death of his father, Alp-Arslan, in 1072. If Nizām had survived him, there would have been few ripples disturbing the pond. The old man would have, if necessary, ordered the arrest of Terken Khātūn and put the sultan's eldest son, Berkyaruq, on the throne. Few would have dared to contest his decision, as the army would have remained united. But now, with both men dead, the Qarakhanid princess would surely not give up the throne to the son of her rival, Zubeida Khātūn. Ever since her own little Mahmūd had been born in the spring of 1087, she had pressed Malik Shah to disqualify Zubeida's son in favour of hers. She would not give up her dream now, especially since she had physical possession of the treasury, not to mention Malik Shah's corpse, and she held a knife to the throat of Caliph Moqtada in Baghdad, her former son-in-law, whom she had forced to sanctify her son's accession.

The Ismaili caliphate of Cairo had recently been preparing itself for a head-on Saljuq invasion immediately after Malik Shah had completed his palaces in his new winter capital, Baghdad. But suddenly it seemed that a hurricane had levelled the whole world of the East. Even if Terken Khātūn killed Berkyaruq, surely her war-hardened brother-in-law, Totosh, the viceroy of Syria, who had captured Jerusalem and pushed the Fatimids back to the borders of Egypt itself, would not rest until he was sultan in Isfahan. This would give the beleaguered Fatimids a few years' respite.

Though General Badr had succeeded in expelling Totosh from outside the walls of Cairo, he knew that the Saljuq was possessed by strong ambition. Capturing Cairo would give him a prestigious empire of his own and winding up the heretical Ismaili Shia caliphate would bestow on him historic prestige in the eye of the whole of sunni Islam, making him the equal of his father Alp-Arslan.

The aged caliph, Mustansir, was approaching the end of his life rapidly and Badr had installed Mustansir's younger son Afdal, his own son-in-law, as the new crown prince. As Totosh's forces would now be withdrawn from Syria and switched to central Iran, Badr would consolidate his family's hold over Egypt further and then perhaps even pounce back on Jerusalem and Damascus. But nothing was predictable. The worst outcome for Cairo would be for Totosh to become supreme sultan in Isfahan. He would quickly afterwards inflict his revenge. On the other hand, there was the chance that he might disappear altogether in the coming internecine war among the Seljuq princes. That would be excellent indeed.

Across the Mediterranean in Constantinople, the leadership of the Byzantines had in the past dozen years been in the lap of a young aristocrat, Alexius Comnenus, who was proving a cunning diplomatist and a lucky, though also courageous, general. A man of genuine kindness and pleasing manners, he was capable of cruel decisiveness when the interests of the empire were threatened. A reputed lover of Michael VII's wife, the Caucasian princess Maria of Alania, 'the most beautiful woman of her time', he had fought loyally for the ruling Ducas family despite his own family's enmity towards them. However, the overthrow of Michael VII – who gladly retired to a monastery – had set in motion a series of other rebellions that, in turn, had forced Alexius to take over the helm himself before he was thirty years old. Now he had an empress of his own, a member of the Ducas family, though Maria's burning hatred for her was proving a constant irritant.

Alexius had been, to some extent, fortunate in his foreign enemies. His most formidable foe in the west, the Norman warlord Robert Giscard, died in 1085 as he led an assault on the empire, and this forced his sons to withdraw from Greece to fight among themselves over their inheritance in Italy. Alexius was defeated in the Balkans by the Turkic nomads, the Pechenegs, from beyond the Danube, but another Turkic people, the Cumans, were tempted by his bribes and promises and came to his rescue.

To the east, in Anatolia, Alexius had entered into an alliance with a Saljuq warlord, Suleiman, who had sent him 7,000 troops against the Normans. In return, Alexius had recognised the new Turkish ownership of the bulk of the former heartland of the empire. However the Turks had continued to raid and intimidate what had remained nominally in his possession. In the lands formally given away, countless Christian peasant communities had been forced to flee, while others had been massacred or taken into slavery. Many more had been forced to convert to Islam.

After the disappearance of the Norman threat – and despite his alliance with Suleiman and his successor, Kilich Arslan, a vassal of Isfahan – the Byzantine state had suffered more humiliations at the hands of another Turkish foe. He was the phenomenal Chaka[6] of Smyrna. By employing Greek experts, he had built up a formidable navy and made himself master of the Marmora Sea. He had also captured the islands of Lesbos, Chios, Samos and Rhodes and put together a federation of Turkish emirates in the interior of Anatolia for an assault on Constantinople itself. But by taxing his subjects in Greece and the rest of the Balkans pitilessly, Alexius had rebuilt the navy and defeated Chaka at sea before persuading Chaka's son-in-law, Kilich, that Chaka plotted against him. As a result, Kilich had murdered his father-in-law at a banquet. Now, with the empire more secure than it had been for a long time, Alexius felt he could give his full attention to the east. The removal of both Nizām al-Mulk and Malik Shah would help greatly. It would create a vacuum in Syria and Mesopotamia which was bound to suck into it the energies of Kilich.

Still, Alexius knew that the exhausted and demoralised polity under him, suffering as it did from heavy taxes and conscription, could not take on the task of dislodging the Turks from their strongholds. The Turks now had strategic reserves deep in Anatolia and Iran and the cumbersome Byzantine army would soon run into trouble if exposed for long to mobile and persistent bands of Turkoman horsemen. Alexius needed help and for that he decided to look westwards, towards the newly invigorated and rich church of Rome under its leader Urban II. This pope seemed genuinely aggrieved over the suffering of his Christian brethren in the east and wanted to reopen the pilgrimage routes to the Holy Land. So Alexius sent envoys to persuade Urban of the great new opportunity that Christ seemed to have offered his flock by the removal both of Nizām al-Mulk and Malik Shah within weeks of one another.

Urban was even more responsive than Alexius's envoys and spies hoped, for he had his own reasons, besides Christian ones, to want to become involved in the East. To begin with, since his childhood in the French province of Champagne, he had idolised those Christians who had taken up arms to recapture Spain from the Moors. Some of them had been fellow Frenchmen who had answered the call of their local bishops and returned laden with gold to bask in comfort and glory for the rest of their lives. He was predisposed to the idea of a 'crusade', though that term would only come into use centuries later.

Furthermore, the new pope was now the effective emperor of western Europe, and if he did not help the eastern wing of the old Roman empire, who would? He had ousted the usurper pope, Guibert, from the Lateran Palace by force of arms, he had isolated and marginalised Henry IV and crowned his son Conrad as the new king of the Germans, and his excommunication of Philip of France had been successful.

Urban could see that the heart of Europe now beat more vigorously, though quite why it was so would become clear only much later, with the birth of the new science of geology in the nineteenth century.

It all goes back to what we now call the Cretaceous period of the Mesozoic era in the history of the earth, a period that lasted from about 144 million years ago to the disappearance of the dinosaurs around 65 million years ago. The continent of Europe had not been formed yet, but consisted mainly of a series of low-lying islands in a tropical sea. The armour-plating of miniscule dead plankton sank to the bottom of the sea in countless numbers to form the future chalky hills of today's western Europe that, in turn, enable France to grow more wheat than the whole of Canada.[7] As north America slowly drifted away from 'proto-Europe' to turn the narrow stretch of water between them into today's Atlantic Ocean, yet another piece fell into place, allowing the future continent to remain relatively warm, even though the earth was cooling down. In the new oceans and seas, a massive current of warm water would flow from the tropical coast of south America towards north-western Europe – the Gulf Stream.

But just as crucial to the creation of Urban's Europe had been a man-made factor, European feudalism, for which, if we have to choose a single human face, we could do worse than to choose Clovis. He was a Germanic tribal chief who founded France, unintentionally, of course. He gave away so much of the vast lands he had conquered to his underlings that in the end, when he died in 511, he was himself left with little more than his private estates around his new capital, Paris. He gave away the lands in return for oaths of loyalty, and his vassals, in return, gave land to knights under them in return for taxes and military service. The system extended to the lowest member of society, the landless serfs who no longer had the freedom to take their loyalty elsewhere. They were tenant farmers and shepherds. They were tied to the land that they exploited on behalf of their master.

This hierarchy of noblemen that had come into being to replace the Roman Empire had its advantages. It brought greater stability which, in return, resulted in greater prosperity. Populations increased, new towns were set up where only forest had been, the old Roman roads were repaired, trade in wool and agricultural products increased, and ideas travelled rapidly. Thus the iron plough and the windmill became familiar features in the countryside, increasing production significantly. The resultant surplus in wealth in turn created a new class of leisured men in the universities, while monks spread out in every direction, taking their superior skills to new monasteries. Oxford and Cambridge started as monasteries in malarial lands no one else wanted and gradually became prestigious towns with industries.

But in the eleventh century the increasing population had created a new problem: a surplus of noblemen without the means – land of their own – to be noblemen. These were the younger sons of knights and feudal lords who found themselves as the losers in a system that gave all the family's acres to the eldest son. So warfare had increased and the Peace of God movement had suffered.

Launched a couple of centuries earlier to ban fighting on certain days and against certain persons and properties – the clergy, unarmed civilians, churches, monastic lands and businesses – the Peace of God movement had spread steadily and proved highly useful in clipping the wings of the knightly class, the class from which Urban himself hailed. But now younger nobles were becoming brutalised. They fought over patches of ground and badges of honour, and even land and property owned by the church were not immune.

If the attention of Christendom could be focused on the rampaging Turks in the east, and if in particular the younger noblemen could be recruited into an army of Christ to rescue the eastern wing of His kingdom, Europe would become more peaceful and the church would become more popular.

It was a superb idea. No one knew better than Urban and his colleagues the religious fervour that gripped the western populace. In this particular century, for example, over 1,500 new churches had been built in France alone, giving rise to the Latin phrase, morbus aedificandi, 'church-building disease'. But, because of that very fervour, Urban and his advisors could not be explicit about their aims. Rescuing the Byzantine heartland in Asia Minor would not, by itself, motivate enough volunteers, while if they proclaimed Jerusalem to be the final goal of the effort, the response might easily get out of hand, there could be no going back. The march would have to continue until the knights liberated the Holy Sepulchre from the grip of the heathen and covered the tomb of Christ with their tears. Any lesser victory would be seen as a defeat.

So the answer to Alexius's envoys was a private promise to make a sincere attempt to recruit an army of Christian knights to send to Constantinople in the next few years. They were told that no public proclamation to the effect could be made as yet. However, the great chasm of 1054 was certainly forgotten and, in the greater interest of Christendom as a whole, bygones would be bygones.

As they lobbied and negotiated, the ambassadors noticed that Urban's intelligence regarding the state of affairs in Jerusalem, Antioch and all the other holy places east of Constantinople was as good as theirs. Though pilgrimage east had become virtually impossible due to war and brigandage, with each Muslim emir demanding his own ransom from the pilgrims to let them pass, a trickle of hardy men – and women – still got through and reported both to Constantinople and Rome. But the western church also had access to Italian mariners and even monastic orders whom the Saracens regarded as friends. A dozen years earlier, for example, the Knights Hospitallers had bribed their way into establishing a base in Jerusalem.

* * *

If my intuition is right, that Khayyām wanted to act as soon as possible to defend himself against the mullah's charge of apostasy, and if it is right that the most visible method of defending oneself against the charge of apostasy in Islam is to go on a pilgrimage to Mecca, he would have set out from Khorāsān in the early autumn of 1093. The next hājj was in January 1094. To have delayed his departure to the last possible moment, say late autumn, could mean spending weeks cooped up in overcrowded and disease-ridden caravanserais on mountain passes in Rayy and Kurdistan waiting for the snows to melt. He would have also preferred to be part of a special hājj caravan, for if he travelled privately it would be easier for any mullah who recognised him on the route to order his arrest or, even worse, for a mob to lynch him as a special service to Allah. There are too many recorded instances of such killings by mobs in his time for him to have ignored the possibility. Far better to surround himself with the orthodox aura of pious Muslims, some of whom would not survive the hardships of the road, and much better to let every town and way station ahead of arrival to expect pilgrims, rather than a mixed bag of all kinds, including criminals and Ismailis.

This is not to dismiss the possibility of his taking the extra precaution of travelling under a pseudonym. He would have known from the autobiography of his hero, Avicenna, that he once fled from Hamadan to Isfahan disguised as a pauper, and if Avicenna, who had been a Grand Vizier and familiar to multitudes, had succeeded, why not he?

But travelling in disguise had its own risks. The hājj caravans from Khorāsān passed through such cities as Rayy, Isfahan and Hamadan, where Omar had known many people. Even if he grew a long beard, avoided the nobility and imitated the dialect of distant Samarkand, a degree of personal contact with strangers would have been inescapable and someone might always recognise his voice, his eyes, his manners. His ruse would then raise questions and alert the authorities as to why he had resorted to it.

For the moment, therefore, let us assume that he felt safer to travel under his own name, but among pilgrims and making sure his arrival at the next station was not expected.

However he travelled, he would have seen the horrors that the 'war of the women' had inflicted on the formerly ordered life of both city and countryside in central and western Iran. Villagers, even if not left destitute by plundering armies or forced into military service, would have complained of brigandage, and in each district of each city people had to organise their own militia to defend them against gangs of armed criminals. Everywhere there would have been shortages of food and fodder, and extremely high prices. All would have dreaded the arrival of the next army.

By the end of autumn 1093, when Khayyām's hypothetical hājj caravan would have climbed the passes around Hamadan before starting its descent towards the plains of Iraq, the armies of Terken Khātūn and her two main rivals had all suffered some reversals and Khayyām would have picked up the latest intelligence of his former friends' fortunes at each caravanserai. The news would have inevitably been confused and even contradictory, but he would have heard that the Egyptians were on the rampage in the far south-west, taking advantage of the vacuum left behind by Totosh. As we saw in the previous chapter, the prince at first made rapid progress through Kurdistan and Azerbaijan in the spring, but then two of his emirs defected to Zubeida and he withdrew to Allepo back in Syria to regroup. As a result, Jerusalem and Tyre had fallen to Badr, the Armenian.

More recently, Zubeida had been preparing to take the battle to Totosh in Syria when she had been distracted by one of her own generals over a trivial matter. Her spies had told her that the emir Yalband had insulted her in a conversation. She had ordered his return to base and executed him.

For the traveller Khayyām, a poignant moment would have been his caravan's arrival at the small way station of Sahneh, the green hamlet halfway between Hamadan and Kermanshah, where Nizām al-Mulk had been murdered by Sabbāh's agents. There, regardless of how alienated he had become in recent years from the late vizier, Khayyām is certain to have reflected on the peace and prosperity that had been the old man's main gift to the land over the past several decades. The descent into war and chaos after his death had shown how much the stability of the polity had depended on the continued beating of that single heart. The exact spot where the chancellor had been slain had become a little shrine. Khayyām would have paused longer than most others to review his memories of him.

In the evening, at the rock of Bhistun, he would have had reason to fall quiet and become emotional once more. As his fellow travellers sat down eagerly by the stream that gushes so suddenly out of the mountain before joining the Gā Māi Ow, waiting for overworked waiters to attend to them, Khayyām would have gazed at the cliff high above him in admiration of the long, carved inscription by Darius the Great. He would have seen the majestic figure of the great king of ancient Persia receiving the submission of his Babylonian enemies and he would have wished to know what the writing beneath the figures said.

The next day, at around noon, the caravan would have arrived at Shahpūr II's summer capital at Kermanshah, where, at the source of another underground river that emerges from another mountain, the mighty Sasanian emperor has had himself sculpted on a stallion receiving his crown from Mazda. Both the statues and the wall carvings around them had been badly damaged by the Arabs four centuries earlier, but so solid were they that they still radiated the confidence of a past civilisation. He would have wanted to be alone, for any sign of reverence for the old people and the old religion would not have been expected of a hājj pilgrim.

*   *   *

When he [Omar] reached Baghdad, the followers of his way and of the old sciences sought him out. But he shut his door on them, in the manner of a repentant man . . .

What exactly does the phrase 'in the manner of a repentant man' mean? Qifti is a notoriously vague writer and likes to play with words to impress his reader. In fact the whole phrase is: 'in the manner of a truly repentant man, not that of a friend'. The second part seems completely redundant and he uses it merely because the Arabic words for repentant and friend – nādim and nadīm – are similar.

Qifti seems to want to say that Khayyām told his admirers that he had seen the 'Truth of Islam' anew, that he was now a new man, sincerely ashamed of his past association with them and of the ideas they had shared.

He would, of course, have found being forced to repel his well-wishers extremely painful. His heart would have gone out to them and yet he had to 'shut his door on them'. Whether he apologised secretly to some of them if he thought they would keep his confidence, we do not know. Some, perhaps even the majority, would have understood, aware as they were of the bigotry of the men such as Ghazāli. Khayyām had no private army of his own, nor a bodyguard lent to him by an enlightened monarch to protect him from a lynch mob.

But at least the city in which he had arrived was a relative haven of peace. The constant tension and the occasional rioting between its

Sunni and Shia districts that sometimes resulted in whole streets being burnt down and hundreds killed meant, as usual, that some districts were out of bounds to strangers, but otherwise the city was not affected drastically by the war.

Some people would have complained that the city's economy had been affected somewhat by the death of Malik Shah. The extensive building programme that he and his ministers, relatives and commanders had started, to turn the city into a winter capital had come to a halt and, moreover, Terken Khātūn had taken with her every spare soldier and official she could. With them had departed their spending power and prices had plummeted. The only people who were happy were Caliph Moqtada and his court. The bearer of the mantle of Muhammad had suddenly found a new freedom that his ancestors would have envied.

As for Khayyām, another painful part of his stay in Baghdad was to meet the orthodox clergy to convince them that he had truly repented of his errors and genuinely sought Allah's forgiveness. Among them would have been Ghazāli, who, despite being a young man still, had been promoted by Nizām al-Mulk to head an important department at the Nizāmiyah school. The local endowments that the late chancellor had put in place for the school enabled it to function still. Ghazāli's smirking in the face of his former master's discomfort would not have been a happy scene to behold.

We have to take Qifti's word at face value that Khayyām actually completed the pilgrimage to Mecca. If so, at least it was a good time for it. He would have left Baghdad around the start of December 1093 to arrive at the Ka'ba early in the following month, so there was not a shortage of fresh water in the long desert journey ahead. Nor was it unbearably hot. The flies, too, would have been at their lowest numbers, just tolerable. But Omar's sole confidants would have been, perhaps, his own servants.

* * *

If there were only one place in the whole of Iraq and Arabia to which Khayyām went on pilgrimage willingly – longingly, even – it was here in the region of Baghdad. What remained of the ruins of the city of

Ctesiphon,[8] the winter capital of the Sasanians, was to be found on the right side of the Tigris some twenty miles to the south-east of Baghdad. We may assume that Khayyām had visited it on several occasions in the past – as he also had the ruins of old Babylon, 'Bābel' in Persian. But this time was likely to be his last. It was going to be a farewell, a leave-taking of those beloved stones that had once cradled such heroes as Anūshīrvān the Just and his philosopher of a vizier, Bozorgmehr, the man who had given the world one of its noisiest and most sociable board games, backgammon.

Khayyām would have arrived back in Baghdad in February, too soon to set out immediately on the journey home to Khorāsān. It was advisable to remain in Baghdad for an extra month or two to avoid arriving in the high passes in western and northern Iran before the snows had cleared towards the middle of April, and it was advisable to wait a little longer in the hope of receiving intelligence from friends in the interior of Iran as to which routes might be safer for him to pick. So, he had time on his hand to kill.

The centrepiece of the ruins was the great coronation hall of the palace of Anūshīrvān, one of the most important architectural trailblazers in history. It is said to have the largest single-span brick arch ever built and once stood in a sea of greenery, with gardens and fountains and even a deer park for the king's sport. Today, with much of its stone looted by prince and pauper alike for humbler dwellings and deserted by the Tigris River, which has changed course, the hall is surrounded by desert, infested with thorn bushes and in danger of complete collapse.

Khayyām saw it as we see it today – a shell of baked brick and concrete – only much larger. After its fall to Muslims in the seventh century, it was looted of the curtains of silk, the best carpets of Persia and the most expensive furniture of Constantinople, not to mention crowns of diamond and thrones of gold. By Omar's time the plaster had fallen in and the walls were the scurrying ground of lizards.

As he wandered from hall to hall alone and in silence, he would have tried to imagine it abuzz with the gossip of imperial power and the chatter of exiled philosophers from Athens after their expulsion by the newly dominant Christians. It was where emperors watched ancient Greek drama in the original language and judged debates between Zoroastrian mūbads and Christian bishops. It was where the classical music of today's Middle East developed formal shape, and where Norūz brought together emperor and peasant in feigned fellowship for a few days at the start of each spring. Even three reigning queens ruled over it, in turn, before the great catastrophe, the Arab invasion, struck.

Khayyām might well have recited in his mind – or even sung in the wilderness – some lines from Firdowsi about how that disaster came about:

> From drinking the milk of camels and the flesh of lizards,
> The Arab has risen to dream of the royal crown of Persia.
> Cursed be you, Rolling Wheel of Time, cursed be you.

Is it possible that the germs of some of his saddest quatrains came to his mind as he touched the stones of that forlorn hall? We have no proof, but a handful of the Rubāiyāt do depict heroes associated with the place. One example adorns the top of this chapter. Shirīn was the graceful Armenian queen of Khosrow Parvīz and it was here in this same hall that the prince Farhād fell in love with her. The emperor told the young man that he could have her if he carved a highway through the mountain of Behistun. The young man agreed. But when, several years later, he approached the completion of his task, he was sent the false message that Shirīn had died. Farhād threw his axe high in the air and stood underneath it to die instantly. The legend was well known in Khayyām's time, but whether the quatrain was inspired by Ctesiphon or not, is really immaterial. It is a measure of Khayyām's nostalgia and reverence for the vanquished empire symbolised by those stones.

                              *   *   *

That February in Baghdad, the rumpus of thousands of pilgrims returning from Mecca was rivalled by the arrival of a Saljuq army. It was led by Zubeida, who had gained dominance in western Iran. She wanted the caliph to reverse his earlier decision to sanction Terken's child as the new sultan. Zubeida had in tow her own boy, twelve years

old now, and Caliph Moqtada complied willingly. Any enemy of
Terken Khātūn was his friend. Thus all the city's numerous mosques
proclaimed Berkyaruq as his father's rightful successor.

The next day, however, celebration gave place to mourning. It was
announced that the caliph had died. It was said that he had died
immediately after signing the certificate that ratified Berkyaruq's right
to the throne. Was he poisoned? This is how his female attendant,
Shams an-Nahār or Light of Day, described his demise:

> After he had signed the investiture certificate and eaten some of the food I
> had given him, he said: 'Who are these people who've come here without
> being asked?' I turned round and saw nobody. I knew he was not himself.
> Then his arms and legs went limp and he fell to the floor. I loosened his
> shirt buttons as I thought he had fainted. But there was no sign of life in
> him any longer. He passed away immediately.[9]

It sounds as if he had a stroke, but he was only thirty-seven years old
and apparently fit. Furthermore, the new competition among Malik
Shah's heirs for his religious blessing had strengthened his position.
He was immediately succeeded by his young son, Mustazhir,* born to
one of his concubines. Moqtada's own mother had been a slave, too,
known only as Umm Walad, 'Mother of Child'.

The news of Zubeida's political triumph in Baghdad would have
depressed Terken in Isfahan. But at least the death of her detested
former son-in-law was good news. As for her military position, it was
becoming daily more precarious. She was confined with her army to
the region of Isfahan alone. But she had a plan.

* 'z' and 'h' are here pronounced separately.

CHAPTER ELEVEN

The Recluse of Nishāpur

To a potter's shop did I go last night,
To my eyes his art made a soothing sight.
Suddenly murmured a tall jug of clay:
'May to December, December to May'.

After the hajj, he returned to his city [of birth] . . .

Again, we have to take this statement by Qifti at face value. No one
else reports it, but every account of Khayyām's life leaves out some
point that other sources think important, including Qifti's. In this
case, circumstantial evidence supports the assertion and, given the
level of threat to Khayyām's life after the death of Malik Shah, it
would have made sense for the fugitive to seek safety in the city of his
upbringing in distant Khorasan. The cities of western and central Iran
remained in the chaos of war and, in addition, in the grip of the clergy
who had condemned him to death. In particular, he would have
wanted to bypass Isfahan. There, Terken was becoming desperate and
would, at the very least, continue to refuse to intervene on his behalf.
She needed the mullahs more than ever.

By contrast, in his native province of Nishāpur in distant Khorāsān,
one of Malik Shah's uncles, while no particular friend of Khayyām's,
had declared himself independent and remained untouched by the
war. More importantly, from Khayyām's point of view, the new king
was established deeply enough in power there not to have to pander
to the local clergy.

After he had put the rock of Behistun behind him in eastern
Kurdistan, his caravan of pilgrims returning from Mecca would have

divided into two halves. One would have taken the Harsīn branch of the fork towards Nahāvand and Isfahan, while the other would have taken the left route towards Sahneh – that by now infamous reminder of the assassination of the chancellor that had brought down the empire on everyone's head – to go on to Hamadan, Rayy and Nishāpur.

In this manner, Khayyām would have arrived back 'home' towards the middle of May, in time for his forty-sixth birthday, no doubt with several camels in tow carrying gifts from Baghdad for his family and friends. It would have been relief of a kind, mixed still with sorrow for that which was lost. Also, he had been forced to humiliate himself and renounce what he believed in. Gone were the days when he could stand up proudly in public and advocate 'civil policies according to Greek thought', as Qifti puts it. He had had to confess before some of the worst bigots in the world that he had been wrong in his view of the universe while they had been right all along. He had also had to turn away from his door some of the most caring and intelligent people he knew in order to placate the ignorant and the ignoble. Now, even if there were to be no further organised attempts on his life, there was always the possibility of some lone fanatic jumping out of a crowd somewhere to plunge a dagger in his heart. For the rest of his life, he would need to live under armed guard.

It is at this phase of his life that the sources describe him as 'ill tempered' and 'unwilling to teach'.[1] Friends would have understood. He was a wealthy man and did not need to earn money anymore. Though he would have lost a great fortune in Isfahan to looters and fatwa-wielders, his fortune in the Nishāpur region remained safe. Part of his huge salary had been paid there, out of Malik Shah's own private fiefdom. We know from his future secretary Arūzi that he had a 'noble residence' in the city itself and, as we have seen already, all wealthy men invested their extra cash in farmsteads and even whole villages outside. We also know that he was routinely addressed as a 'khājah', a lord, and none became a lord in any land without land, and a great deal of it. In the absence of information to the contrary, we can also assume that his father's old surgery of herbal physicians still functioned, bringing him yet another income, even if he himself did not attend it. He needed only to make as many influential friends as he could in this time of trouble.

But why should a previously dedicated teacher give up the pleasure of teaching the brightest of the young, merely because he did not need the income from it? The answer must be that, after the fatwa, he would have been expected, even in Nishāpur, to teach only what was regarded as orthodox. The usual description for it was – and still is – 'the Islamic sciences', at best meaning whatever did not clash with the Koran and the stories handed down about the sayings and practices of Muhammad. In other words, any subject that might increase, even indirectly, the prestige of the pre-Islamic eras – which the Muslims call the 'Jāhiliyah' or Age of Ignorance – automatically made its adherent suspect in the eye of the law. Although Omar evidently felt safer now, rather than suffering the pain of teaching what he regarded as falsehood, he gave up teaching altogether.

As a general guide to the politics of his survival over the next decade or so, we have to go back to Qifti's account: 'He returned to his city, attended places of worship and kept secret his inner beliefs.' The sentence implies that, at the very least, he would have had to be in Nishāpur on important religious occasions, when it was expected of prominent men to be in the van of worshippers at their regular mosque. Other requirements of pretended faith would have been to be present at prayer sermons led by famous clerics from abroad. One of those attendances he would have found particularly painful was a visit by Ghazāli. His unstable former tormentor returned to Nishāpur almost every summer from his hot base in Baghdad, and he later retired there. His knowing smirk as he saw his old teacher sitting in the crowd at his feet would have been almost unbearable to Khayyām.* We can imagine Omar's inner disgust, his desire to stand up and shout 'Bigot! Fool! Traitor!', as the fanatic urged his audience to make sure their children did not celebrate Norūz or read a word of Firdowsi that might strengthen their pride in pre-Islamic Iran. Instead, poor Khayyām had to nod approvingly.

Beginning immediately on his arrival in Nishāpur, he would have wanted to make a highly visible trip to Marv to visit the newly-declared 'Sultan of Khorāsān', Prince Arslan Arqūn. One of Malik

---

* We shall see later how Ghazāli goes through intense doubt on the existence of God and then somersaults back to end up as a Sufi saint.

Shah's uncles, he laid no claim to the heartland of the late sultan's empire, the so-called Two Iraqs, western Iran and most of today's Arab Iraq. Instead, he wanted to be left alone to rule Khorāsān as an independent kingdom.

Evidently, the prince had harboured an old resentment against his late nephew for years. He had been given a fiefdom in Khorāsān whose annual income was only 7,000 dinars. When compared to Khayyām's salary of 10,000 dinars, his resentment becomes understandable. Now he had taken over all the cities of the vast region and the mosques recited his name in Friday prayer sermons. Coins were struck in his name and he had mustered an army. A visit to him would have told the clergy that, even though Khayyām had been abandoned by his former friends in Isfahan, he continued to have friends in high places here, where it mattered now. On his part, Khayyām's stories about his former life as a companion of Malik Shah, as well as his reputation as the greatest physician of his age, would have made him a welcome visitor to the court of the new king any time he cared to call.

To the general public, Khayyām probably appeared now as a man with no inclination to spend time on social niceties, give lectures, attend weddings, etc. This must be the source of his reputation for ill temper.

To sum up, Khayyām would have spent as much time as he could away from crowded Nishāpur in a country estate to the north-west, or the south-east, of the valley. There, on the cool heights overlooking the city, he could busy himself – in a similar manner to Tolstoy 800 years later – reading and writing, supervising his herds of sheep, cattle and horse, inspecting the irrigation canals after the spring floods, attending to the medical needs of his tenant farmers as best he could, and keeping abreast of the latest news and gossip from the now distant worlds of politics and war.

*　*　*

It is surprising to learn how much information flowed from continent to continent when the fastest means of communication for ordinary people was the slow camel caravan. From the gossip of the court of his old friend Terken Khātūn to the news of preparations in farthest-flung western Europe for an assault on the world of Islam to reclaim the lost lands of Christianity, it all filtered through sooner or later.

Assuming that my intuition regarding the date of Omar's forced pilgrimage to Mecca is well founded, Khayyām would have heard on arriving in Nishāpur in May 1094 that Terken had sent an army to the city of Kerman, in the south-east, to force Turanshah to pay tribute to her. The prince was a cousin of her late husband, whose father, Qavurt, had been executed by Malik Shah and Nizām after a bloody rebellion. To Khayyām, the news would have suggested that Terken felt secure for the moment in Isfahan, as her rival Zubeida Khātūn had sent her army towards Syria to vanquish Totosh, their brother-in-law.

A little later, in the early summer of 1094, news would have arrived that contrary to expectations, Totosh had scored a crushing victory over Zubeida in Kurdistan, forcing her to run for safety at the court of – guess who? – Terken in Isfahan. Totosh had been so emboldened that he had subsequently swept all before him in Kurdistan and Azerbaijan to reach Hamadan. From there, he had sent an envoy to Baghdad to ask the new caliph, Mustazhir, to declare him the new sultan. Many more such delicious – or tragic – twists and turns would amuse the khājah Omar Khayyām in the years to come as he lived the life of a near recluse to await the passing of the storms.

* * *

Zubeida and her twelve-year-old son Berkyaruq did reach Isfahan safely to seek refuge under Terken, only to find that Terken had just died. She had left the city for Hamadan a little earlier to meet Totosh with a marriage proposal to unite their two realms. She had accepted that she could not defeat her brother-in-law. She would therefore recognise him as the new ruler, but on the condition that he would proclaim her little Mahmūd, now seven years old, as his heir. He had evidently agreed. But before she could reach her new husband, she was taken ill, was rushed back to Isfahan for treatment and succumbed. She only had time to obtain a promise from her emirs that they would not abandon Mahmūd.

So when Zubeida and Berkyaruq arrived outside the walls of Isfahan, confusion reigned inside. For three days the royal mother and son were kept waiting, until it was decided to let them in and arrest them. It was then decided to blind young Berkyaruq in order to disqualify him for the sultanate and, hopefully, please his uncle Totosh. But the doctor, Amīn al-Dawla ibn al-Tilmiz, who would presumably have had the ghastly task of maiming the poor boy, had a better idea. Little Mahmūd had just contracted smallpox, he said. Why not wait to see whether he survived. If he did, the blinding could go ahead. If he did not, they would put Berkyaruq in his place and strengthen their position in any negotiations with Totosh.

This was agreed on by the commanders of the army – of which only some 10,000 fighting troops now remained – and Mahmūd did die, paving the way for Berkyaruq to gain the throne.

Despite the ruthlessness that Terken Khātūn had shown, Khayyām is likely to have been genuinely grieved by the news of her death in early middle age. He had known her since she was a little girl in Bukhara in the early 1070s, had then accompanied her – as far as we can tell – to Isfahan as Malik Shah's first wife, and had there, for many years, been her friend and doctor. He had tried to console her at some of the worst moments of her life, when she lost child after child. Though refusing to take up a political post himself, he had been close enough – for long enough – to both Malik Shah and Terken to understand why rulers could not be sentimental, why friendship and crown were seldom permanent companions. But he was also aware of Terken's personal weaknesses. If only she had listened to the advice of some of her wiser friends to give in gracefully to the superior claim of Berkyaruq, the bulk of the old army would have remained together and, under Moayyad or any other of Nizām's senior sons, the empire would have survived.

What Khayyām did not know at the time was that his old friend Mo'ayyad, who had been Terken's vizier, was on his way to join Totosh and would, in a couple of years' time, personally strangle Zubeida Khātūn. That, however, would not be the end of orphaned Berkyaruq. With the help of another of Nizām's sons as his vizier, he would triumph over his uncle Totosh and kill him. He would also kill – by drowning in the Euphrates – yet another of his uncles, the blinded Takesh, the old ruler of Kerman. Then he would go on to inflict revenge on Moayyad by torturing him to death personally. On becoming supreme sultan over the exhausted shell of the empire, Berkyaruq would finally, in 1098, recapture Khorāsān without a fight and appoint as governor his youngest half-brother, Sanjar, the boy whom Khayyām once gave up, as virtually beyond hope, to smallpox.

* * *

It is Tuesday, 27 November 1095, and we are in Clermont, central France. For the past eight days, a conference has been held at the city's cathedral by the pope, Urban II, who has summoned some 300 of his top clerics from France and the neighbouring lands to examine a whole range of issues facing the western church; from the old problems of simony and clerical concubinage to the current adultery of the king of France.[2]

For today, Urban's throne has been taken outside the city gates and placed on a platform in an open field. Word has gone out that he is to make an historic appeal to the faithful and crowds larger than the capacity of the cathedral are expected.

When the appointed hour arrives, the 53-year-old pontiff is visibly emotional. He has been planning this speech for months. He struggles to make himself heard in the open. He devotes almost the whole of his speech to the plight of eastern Christians: how they have been massacred, uprooted, forced to renounce their faith or taken into slavery by wicked heathen invaders from the remote plains of unknown Asia. Now it is time for their brethren in the civilised west to rise to the task of rescuing them. Not only that, Jerusalem and all the other holy places of the faith must be reconquered for Jesus. Only in that case will His Second Coming be made possible:

> An accursed race, a race utterly alienated from God, . . . has invaded the lands of the Christians and depopulated them by the sword, pillage and fire. . . . They circumcise the Christians, and the blood of the circumcision they spread upon the altars or pour into the vases of the baptismal font.
>
> When they torture people to a base death, they pierce their navels and, pulling out the extremity of the intestines, bind them to a stake; then with flogging they lead the victim around. His viscera having gushed forth, he falls prostrate upon the ground.

Others, they bind to a post and pierce with arrows. . . . And what shall I say of the abominable rape of the women? To speak of it is worse than to remain silent.[3]

What comes next elates the crowd. An army of knights, under the command of the church itself, will be set up and leave for the east as soon as possible. Emperor Alexius has asked for it. Furthermore, some great lords here have already promised to contribute troops, money and arms. All the warriors will have the punishment of their sins forgiven them, even if they have broken the Peace of God, and all those who die in the cause will be granted absolution by Christ in Heaven. The church guarantees it.

Part of the crowd is now hysterical. 'Deus le volt, Deus le volt', it shouts, 'God wishes it, God wishes it.'

Adhemar, the bishop of Puy, as powerful as any lay prince, leaves his seat and kneels before the throne. He begs to be included in the holy mission. He walks determinedly, for he has had weeks to rehearse his response. It will emerge later that he has been chosen to be the official commander of the army. Another bishop, and yet another, comes forth and kneels and, before long, many hundreds of priests and peasants, too, have volunteered.

As we have already seen, Urban, the former Otto of Lagery of the province of Champagne, comes himself from a noble family and it is clear that he wants the army to be made up of experienced warriors, especially the landless younger sons of the nobility who might otherwise be a source of trouble to the church. But the response to his speech comes from all sections of the crowd, rich and poor, young and old; even the infirm who seek salvation in the pilgrimage. This worries him. In a letter sent a year later to the people of Bologna to thank them for their enthusiasm, he says that the old and the infirm ought to be discouraged, that priests must have the permission of their bishops to volunteer, and that newly married men must have the permission of their wives. This is curious. What about the wishes of older wives?

We have four extant reports of Urban's speech at Clermont that late autumn day in 1095, but although they all seem to be later recollections and cannot be regarded as accurate verbatim reports, they all have the gist of the above passage in common. They also all report that the personal belongings of the volunteers would be placed in safe keeping with the church, ready for them to reclaim after their return, and that no taxes would be imposed by any government on their properties during their absence. A dispute arises on whether Urban immediately distributed crosses of red cloth that each volunteer was to sew on the shoulder of his robe or tunic as his badge.

As the movement subsequently gathered pace, with the pope's emissaries journeying far and wide to spread the summons, more restrictions became apparent. All volunteers would have to aim at going as far east as Jerusalem. If they broke their vow and returned mid-journey, they would be excommunicated. Any land they captured that had once belonged to the emperor – while granted to the warriors as their personal property – would remain part of Romania (the Byzantine empire).

Only a few days after the speech, on 1 December, while Urban was still in Clermont, messengers arrived from the great Raymond of Saint-Gilles, Count of Toulouse and Marquis of Provence, that he and many of his vassals had decided to devote their persons and earthly belongings to the cause. The implications was that the pope had already discussed his plans with Raymond a month earlier during his procession through southern France. The fifty-five-year-old count had previously distinguished himself in the war against the Moors in Spain. He clearly hoped to be the real military commander of the expedition.

Other magnates soon followed. They included Hugh of Vermandois, a brother of the king of France, and Robert, Duke of Normandy. The latter leased his lands to his brother, King William the Red of England, for 10,000 silver marks to finance his journey.

More indicative still of the fervour was the fact that noblemen attached to Urban's enemy, King Henry IV of Germany, also came forward. They included Godfrey, Duke of Lower Lorraine, and his two brothers Eustace and Baldwin.

None of the reigning kings risked absence from their kingdom. But Philip, the king of the French, sent a message that, in addition to sending his brother Hugh, he would submit fully to any punishment for his recent adultery that the pope saw fit to administer.

It was decided that the bulk of the volunteers would set off after 15 August, when the harvest had been gathered, and that they would gather together in Constantinople, where the emperor would feed and house them during the winter, before venturing into the territories now held by the infidel.

It is said that, apart from risking military catastrophe at the hands of the Turks, the pope also risked the spiritual predominance of his own throne in the west. What would happen if Jerusalem were liberated? Would it not become a rival for the See of St Peter and become, eventually, the new spiritual centre of Christendom?

But Urban evidently did not perceive the venture in that light. He was genuinely aggrieved by the suffering of the Christians of the east, and he saw great advantages to be reaped immediately in western Europe. The surplus nobility would be sent abroad to fight a worthy cause, instead of quarrelling among themselves, and the troublesome Normans of southern Italy would stop harassing Constantinople if they were diverted to the Holy Land.

*　*　*

The Palazzo Ducale in Venice, the spectacle of pink and white marble that overlooks the historic lagoon and, beyond that, the Mediterranean sea, has a main balcony where the doges once saluted their fleets and soothed their subjects. The palace represents the wealth that Venice achieved in the Middle Ages, and its former power is symbolised by that balcony that seems almost celestial, almost as high above earth as the Eagle's Nest of Alamūt. Very few people, if any, know that there is a link between the two.

The present building was begun in the twelfth century, after the great naval victory of the Venetians over the forces of Egypt off Ascalon in 1123 had made them the undisputed rulers of the Mediterranean. It was meant to reflect the new grandeur of La Republica Serenissima, as well as to house an expanded administration with its dungeons and torture chambers in the basement. But an earlier, smaller palace occupied the spot before it, and that too had a balcony for the same ceremonial purposes. It was from that eyrie that, during the autumn of 1096, warships and merchant ships, newly built in the city's arsenal a few miles away, were seen off, taking some of the best warrior knights of Italy and northern Europe to Constantinople for the first War of the Cross. Alamūt had played the decisive part in giving that war its chance to succeed.

But Venice was not the leader of the naval wing of the First Crusade. The Republic of Genoa, Venice's deadly enemy which had recovered Corsica and Sardinia from the Muslims earlier in the century, had grabbed that prize. The pope had granted it, Genoa, the main contract for the provision of warships and transporters, so that, in a single undertaking in the autumn of 1096, it dispatched twelve galleys and a freighter, although it delayed implementing the contract until it made certain the mobilisation was serious. A whole string of other, lesser ports, too, from as far north as Scotland and Denmark, played their part. The whole of Christendom seemed to have come together against the common enemy, roused by reports of Urban's speech the previous autumn, but also propelled by western Europe's own internal economic and social needs.

We have already touched on some of the more long-term factors, most of which arose from a warming climate. They included a rapid increase in population, expanded wealth through trade, the revival of the old Roman routes, the rediscovery of ancient Greek science,[4] the growth of Latin literacy, the inspiration that resulted from inflicting defeat after defeat on the Muslims in the re-conquest of Spain, Sardinia and Sicily, and, not least, the Peace of God movement that had restricted the freedom of the knightly class to wage war on the church and within itself.

But over the past couple of years, despair among the poor had also become a powerful motivation. Whereas most of the great lords, particularly the Normans of Italy, were suspected of lusting after land and glory in the East, many of the peasant volunteers simply wanted to run away from their miserable lives. Devastating floods and pestilence blighted last year, 1094, while a severe drought and famine afflicted this year. Moreover, as small-holdings could not be subdivided into even smaller units, many farmers' sons and daughters faced destitution. To make matters worse in an age of omens and miracles, unusually prolific showers of meteorites had terrified the populace in April this year. If the Second Coming were to happen soon, as those natural calamities seemed to promise, one had better rush to die in Jerusalem to improve the chances of one's sins being forgiven.

The melancholy among the poor saw the rise of Peter the Hermit and Walter the Pauper, two visionaries who toured France, Flanders and Germany together to promote the Crusade to the wretched. Peter, a squat and swarthy man about sixty years old whose long face resembled the donkey he rode, had apparently been humiliated several years earlier by the Turks in Asia during a failed pilgrimage to Jerusalem. He would not eat bread and meat, though he ate fish and drank wine, and the aura of mystery that surrounded him made him – and his donkey – objects of reverence everywhere. His companion was a fellow Frenchman, Walter Sans-Avoir. By the time they reached Cologne in the spring of 1095, they had gathered an 'army' of some 15,000 people, mainly untrained peasants and including old men, women and children, who had sold whatever they had to fill Peter's money chest for the journey. Their numbers soon rose above 25,000, and they managed to attract some minor landowners. Some of these decided to linger on to gather even more volunteers, although that was only part of the reason.

Walter left with several thousand people immediately after Easter, and Peter followed with some 15,000 on 20 April, at the height of the meteorite showers. Both chose the northern land route alongside the Rhine, the Neckar and the Danube into central Europe and the Balkans.

Walter's contingent of the 'People's Expedition' was given every possible help by the king of Hungary to pass through his lands, and not too many clashes occurred with the locals. But when, towards the end of June, Peter's horde reached the town of Simlin on the eastern border of Hungary with Byzantium, a dispute over a pair of shoes ended in a riot and the Crusaders massacred some 4,000 locals. Subsequently, the Crusaders built barges out of timber from local houses and crossed the Save River into Byzantium before the Hungarians could retaliate. Everything had been seen by the inhabitants of Belgrade on the other shore and they decided to take no chances. They took to the hills. The Crusaders pillaged what remained behind and set fire to what could not be carried.

Despite these atrocities, there was some sympathy among the populace for the cross-bearing marauders, and the Byzantine governor supplied them with food and a police escort. But his forces were soon attacked by Peter's Germans and Italians, forcing him to deploy his garrison against them. Peter fled into a wood and thought that no more than 500 of his followers had survived. Eventually it was found that about 15,000 had.

* * *

Soon after the Hermit and the Pauper had left Germany some of their associates, who had remained behind to recruit more supporters, announced that the war for Christ began at home. They decided that, while Muslims were wicked enough and deserved punishment, they were only killing Christians, not Christ himself. His murderers were another group of people, and these were present in Europe itself as infiltrators. Thousands of Jews had grown rich on usury at the expense of poor Christians and rumour had it that they even drank the blood of Christian children to sanctify their religious rituals. At the very least, why should they not finance the Crusade? It would serve to expiate their sin of being born Jewish.

The problem for the holy mobs was that the Jews of Europe, who had never been persecuted seriously except under the Visigoths in Spain, were under the protection of Henry IV, and many of the great lords followed his example. The bulk of high churchmen, too, were often well inclined towards their local Jewish community. They regarded them as loyal and industrious.

While this shielded the Jews in many places, with lords and bishops warning the mobs and sometimes sheltering the vulnerable in their own palaces, in too many places the barriers could not hold. By the time the slaughter was over some 8,000 Jews had lost their lives and many more their livelihoods.

The worst culprit was a psychopath and minor nobleman with military experience. Count Emich of Leisingen in the Rhineland began by claiming that the imprint of the cross had miraculously appeared on his body, and went on to attract a host of fellow noblemen to his side. At Spier, near his home, the local bishop put the town's Jews under his protection and cut off the hands of some of the criminals who had slain a dozen of them. Emich turned his attention to Worms and incited a riot against the Jewish quarter. The bishop let the Jews take refuge in his palace, but the doors were broken and some 500 Jews were massacred inside. A few days later, on 25 May 1096, it was the turn of Mainz. The locals opened the gates to Emich's forces and he attacked the archbishop's palace, to which the Jews had fled. The archbishop and all his staff escaped. Some 1,000 Jews were put to the sword. Others threw themselves into the Main River and drowned. Lesser atrocities were committed in dozens of other places, some by preacher commanders who were already on their way east.

But almost all of them met their just deserts eventually, at the hands of Hungarians. Emich's forces, for example, reached the Hungarian border towards the end of July and were refused permission by King Colman to enter on account of the misbehaviour of the followers of Peter the Hermit. But Emich's followers included many battle-hardened knights and they built their own bridge to cross the river, a branch of the Danube at Wiesselburg. They laid siege to the latter and seemed about to capture it when they heard that the king was closing in on them. They panicked and the garrison within fell upon them. Emich and a few of his knights fled back to Germany on their swift horses. The bulk of his followers were massacred:

> The collapse of Emich's Crusade, following so soon after the collapse of Voklmar's and Gottschalk's Crusades, deeply impressed western Christendom. To most good Christians it appeared as a punishment meted out from on high to the murderers of the Jews. Others, who had thought the whole Crusading movement to be foolish and wrong, saw in these disasters God's open disavowal of it all. Nothing had yet occurred to justify the cry that echoed at Clermont, 'Deus le volt'.[5]

* * *

When the two wings of the People's Expedition eventually united in the suburbs of Constantinople on 1 August 1096, Emperor Alexius was not impressed. While feeding and housing them and allowing small groups of them to enter the city to be dazzled by the splendour of its streets, palaces and cathedrals, he urged Peter to wait for the arrival of the main army before setting out for enemy territory. Peter was convinced but, by then, his influence over his followers had waned. They had chosen several separate factional leaders. To make matters worse, they continued robbing the locals, including the mansions of the nobility. They even stripped church roofs of their lead. There was no alternative to letting them go. Only six days after their arrival, the emperor shipped them across the Strait of Bosphorus to be stationed at a camp he had earlier prepared for his own English mercenaries. It was called Civetot and it would soon become synonymous with tragedy.

There they settled down to a daily routine of pillaging the nearby Christian villages and, in mid-September, they raided the suburbs of the city of Nicaea, which was the capital of Alexius's uneasy Saljuq ally, Kilich Arslan. Those villages, too, were still Greek Orthodox and yet the Crusaders of the People's Expedition showed them no pity. From the point of view of the self-appointed champions of the liberation of Jerusalem, all that mattered was to be richly fed by all bystanders, to enable them to reach the Holy Land as soon as possible.

At the end of September, a German contingent under an Italian lord called Rainald, captured a rich castle by the name of Xerigordon beyond Nicaea, and his success excited the French back in Civetot. They began to mobilise for a similar effort when news arrived that an army sent out by Kilich had massacred all the several thousand Germans in Xerigordon after first cutting off their water supply. Only Rainald and some others who had agreed to become Muslims been spared. Even they had been sent into captivity, as far away as Khorāsān.

The 15,000 or so Crusaders at Civetot panicked. Peter was in Constantinople to lobby for more money from the emperor to buy back his influence. Walter the Pauper urged that the Crusaders stay in place until Peter returned. But he did not and, meanwhile, intelligence arrived that Kilich's army was on its way to Civetot. After much deliberation, it was agreed to go out to confront it. But an ambush had been laid for them in a wooded pass a few miles out. The knights' horses were shot down under them in the vanguard and those who survived reared back on the infantry. Only a few hundred made it back to Civetot, pursued by the Turks. There the women, and children too, were put to the sword, the exceptions being the prettiest and blondest boys and girls who were captured to sell as sex slaves in the bazaars of Baghdad, Isfahan and Nishāpur. Walter's corpse was among those that littered the countryside. It was 6 October 1096. Some 3,000 stragglers took refuge in an abandoned castle on the seafront, from which a naval force sent by Alexius disarmed them and took them back to Constantinople. The main army of knights had yet to leave central Europe.

* * *

Godfrey de Bouillon, the Duke of Lower Lorraine, was the first great lord to leave for the East. After seeking the permission of his liege, Henry IV, he left in mid-August 1095, as stipulated by Henry's enemy, the pope. He was accompanied by a whole host of equally impressive names, including his brother Baldwin of Boulogne who would one day succeed him as king in Jerusalem. But Godfrey was not the first of his kind to arrive in Constantinople. That title went to the French prince Hugh of Vermandois. Whereas the latter had shipped his small army across the Adriatic, Godfrey's forces had been too large for a sea crossing. Despite wanting to avoid the Hungarians and the frost of the Balkan winter, he had chosen the northern land route and promised King Colman to assert strict control over his troops. This the Hungarian king had accepted, on the condition that Godfrey hand over his brother Baldwin as hostage.

Thus all that autumn, winter and spring, a constant stream of bad-tempered, impatient and dangerous western warriors arrived in the suburbs of Constantinople demanding to be fed and housed. Alexius, who had only asked for a few thousand mercenaries to help him against the Turks, had no choice but to honour their leaders and feed their men. But while he flattered their leaders with expensive gifts and displays of ancient pomp, he also put them under virtual house arrest – when necessary – until they agreed to swear an oath of loyalty to him. They had to promise to return to the empire any of its former lands they rescued from the Turks.

Some of them found it difficult to agree to this. They feared that it would turn them into Alexius's vassals. Godfrey refused several invitations to visit the palace and twice confronted the imperial troops, and even laid siege to one of the imperial palaces. But when Alexius's patience ran out and he let his troops loose on Godfrey's, the latter had to accept defeat and swear as he had been ordered to.

The most stubborn of the Crusaders proved to be Raymond of Toulouse, the richest of them all, whom the pope wanted to be the overall leader of the war. But Alexius took advantage of Raymond's rivalry with Bohemund, the Norman who was hard at work endearing himself to the emperor in the hope of being appointed commander-in-chief. Raymond settled for a compromise formula that did not depict him as a vassal of Alexius. Ironically, he was the only one who remained true to his oath. Some of the other great lords were Count Robert II of Flanders, Duke Robert of Normandy and Count Stephen of Blois, Duke Robert's brother-in-law.

Alexius's formidable organisation ensured that most of the armies were shipped across the Bosphorus and assembled on land by the end of April. By the middle of May, they were laying siege to a great prize, the city of Nicaea.

Nicaea was important to the Crusaders on several accounts. Some of the earliest councils of the church had been held there, it was strategically placed at the heart of a network of roads, it was immensely rich, it was still largely peopled by Christians, and it was the seat of Kilich, the Saljuq 'Sultan of Rūm'. Kilich himself was not there at the time. His recent annihilation of the 'armies' of Peter the Hermit and Walter the Pauper had convinced him that his presence was more useful in the East, fighting fellow Turks. It turned out to be a huge mistake, especially as he had left his family and all his treasure in Nicaea. But it is arguable whether his absence made any difference in the longer run. The new Christian fighters were of a stuff the Turks had never seen before.

The city had 240 towers built by Justinian and it was bound by a lake on one side. It was also defended by a large garrison of Turks whose cruelties made certain they would be massacred if they fell, and fall they did, despite Kilich rushing to their rescue. As the sultan tried to break through the siege to relieve his capital on 21 May 1097, he was blocked by the heavily armoured knights of Raymond of Toulouse. He could not break through. Soon the pitched battle was joined by Robert of Flanders. The sultan fled to the mountains to lick his wounds. In his camp, the westerners found the ropes that he had brought along to tether them to one another as prisoners. 'For the first time the Crusaders had proved that if they could catch the Muslims in a pitched battle the tremendous impact of their heavily armed knights could give them victory.'[6]

But many of the westerners were soon to be disappointed. Kilich's flight was followed by the arrival of a Byzantine naval flotilla, sent overland and assembled on the lake to complete the siege. Apart from practical help, it was a message from the emperor that the westerners would find life difficult without his cooperation. The appearance of the Byzantines on the scene worked its magic. When one morning the Crusaders woke up, they saw the imperial Byzantine standard flying over the city. During the night, the garrison had surrendered to Alexius's navy through his admiral Manuel Butumites. It had feared an slaughter of its Muslim population and the Byzantines did not want their city back in their hands in ruins. Kilich's family were taken to Constantinople in dignity and released to him. The other Turks were allowed to buy their freedom.

The 'Varangies' or Franks were shocked by the Byzantines' leniency, seeing it almost as treachery. They also felt cheated out of the great riches that would have otherwise been theirs. But they had to be realistic and it was only the beginning of the war. They had promised to return all the emperor's captured territory to him, and he did reward them with much of the treasure he had captured. At least one of them was elated. Stephen of Blois described his share of the gold as 'a mountain' and wrote to his wife to give her the tremendous news. 'At this rate', he wrote, 'we shall be in Jerusalem in five weeks, if, that is, Antioch does not prove an obstacle.'

*   *   *

It is not possible, within the scope of this work, to describe the progress of the Crusaders through Asia Minor in the summer and autumn of 1097; only the impact on the Muslims of the more traumatic defeats inflicted on them as the Crusaders closed in on Syria and Palestine. Let it be said here merely that the fighting was hard and the environment even harsher. The Turks subjected the slow-moving columns of western knights and infantry to a rain of arrows wherever they could ambush them, while their practice of burning the villages and fields on the route caused the deaths of thousands of horses, sometimes slaughtered for food. At times knights rode oxen and carts were pulled by men. Nevertheless, in that long season of trial, city after legendary city fell back into Christian hands as ripe apples fall to the ground. These victories were made easier in many places as the Christian populations flung their gates open to their liberators with ecstatic zeal. Thus Philomelium was followed by Iconium and Caesarea by Edessa. In the latter city, the Armenian ruler, who had been paying tribute to the Saljuqs, adopted Baldwin as his son and heir in a farcical ancient ceremony in which father and son wore the same robe. A few weeks later, the 'father' was murdered – some said with the connivance of the 'son' – and Baldwin became king of the first Crusader State to come into being. He found the position so much to his liking that he decided to remain where he was, forgetting that it was Jerusalem that was the main objective of the new War of the Cross.

By the end of October the westerners stood before Antioch, once the third city of the old Roman Empire. There Stephen de Blois, who was said to have more castles in France than the year had days, suddenly saw how prophetic he had been, unfortunately. The city's 400 towers, again built by Justinian, meant that every yard of the formidable walls was within bowshot and these walls, as with the Great Wall of China, were stretched along the crests of steep hills to the tops of mountains without obvious points of weakness. A spectacular castle stood 300m above the city, outside the walls. The Saljuq garrison, both inside and out, would be certain to fight on to its last breath. Furthermore, there were fields and orchards within the walls, and the Turkish emir, Yaqi-Siān, had had months to accumulate vast stores of food. He had also expelled the bulk of the city's Christian population to minimise the risk of sabotage.

The siege lasted nine months, and it almost failed. A freezing winter and a dearth of food turned some of the Crusaders into cannibals. Some Flemings, survivors of Peter the Hermit's rabble, became notorious at the practice. They fought at the front line against any armed sortie that the Turks sent out, stalking the fattest among the enemy with special relish. Desertions became rife. At one time, even the Hermit deserted and had to be brought back by force.

Eventually a disgruntled commander inside the city, an armour-maker with the pre-Islamic Iranian name of Firūz, agreed to let some of the Normans under Bohemund to scale a turret under his control one night, and some of the city's remaining Christians led the knights through the narrow alleyways to their targets. Every Turk who could be found was slaughtered, including the emir. But only a day after their apparent triumph, the Crusaders found themselves trapped in a city that had run out of food. A Turkish army, headed by the emir of Mosul, arrived and the former besiegers became the besieged. However, inspiration was close at hand. A visionary preacher of humble origins dreamt of, and dug up, the True Lance, the weapon that the Romans had supposedly used to pierce the side of Christ, buried in the floor of a church. The forgery was attached to a banner and after many hysterical prayer sessions, the Crusaders marched out on 28 June 1098 to take on the Turks. It proved easy. The emir's overcautious tactics trapped his cavalry and friction broke out among contingents from Damascus and Aleppo. Much food and gold was captured by the Christians. Disaster had been avoided once more.

* * *

The troops now wanted to march on to Jerusalem, but were told that they could not do so. Rivalry had broken out among their leaders and no one wanted to leave Antioch to Bohemund, the restless eldest son of Robert Giscard, the late Norman conqueror of southern Italy. Bohemund wanted Antioch to be his, and he threatened all-out war on his fellow Crusaders if they did not agree.

After a summer and autumn during which most of the great lords dispersed to avoid a plague, and after a plea went out in vain to the pope to come to Antioch to settle the dispute, the bulk of the army asked Raymond of Toulouse to be its commander-in-chief. The date of 13 January was set for the departure. In the meantime, foraging expeditions to neighbouring towns and regions were mounted with increasing frequency, with the city of Ma'arra suffering horrendously. Most of the population there was put to the sword and their houses torched. Tales of the barbarities multiplied – as bands of refugees spread throughout the Islamic lands – and reduced grandees to tears in the mosques and palaces of Baghdad, Isfahan, Nishāpur, even as far as Samarkand and Bukhara.

Raymond set out on the appointed day, somewhat theatrically. He walked barefoot at the head of the army, in pilgrim robes, to remind the others of the religious nature of their venture. There were some setbacks. The siege of Arqa, an important town, had to be abandoned after three months, and a decision was taken to bypass the port city of Tripoli, which seemed impregnable. Many petty rulers on the way, together with the emir of Tripoli, sent gifts and provisions to the westerners in the hope of being spared, sometimes in vain. Bohemund stayed behind in Antioch but as news arrived of town after town falling to his rivals he hurried after them.

The Crusaders crossed the River of Dogs, north of Beirut, on 13 May 1099, and formally entered Egyptian territory. This had until recently been Saljuq land, but the vizier Afdal, the Armenian-born strongman of Cairo, had at last despaired of reaching an alliance with the Crusaders and thought it best to confront them with 'facts on the ground'. For a time, unsure of their further progress, the Crusader leaders had toyed with Afdal's proposal to recognise their conquest of northern Syria – including Edessa, Aleppo and Antioch – if they would agree not to attack southern Syria. He would also guarantee the freedom of Christian pilgrims to travel to the Holy Land whenever they wished. But the Crusaders' vague answers, and the secret letters he had received from Emperor Alexius in Constantinople revealing that he had no control over the Franks, prompted Adfal into pre-emptive action. He had captured Jerusalem after a short siege from its Turkish garrison and then proceeded to pacify the other strongholds on the way to Beirut. Thus it was Egyptians now who ruled over the vital port and city of Tyre. Not for long. Afdal's local vassals fled or were slain in quick succession. On 9 June 1099, albeit nearly three years after the knights of distant north-western Europe had left their castles to answer Pope Urban's summons to rescue the City of God from its heathen occupiers, the Crusaders climbed a hill that overlooked Jerusalem. They cried with joy and called the hill Montjoie. Just over a month later, they would be the city's new masters.

*   *   *

It is the afternoon of Friday, 19 August 1099, and we are in the great Friday mosque of Baghdad. Worshippers from all over the city are drifting in for the weekly sermon that includes important announcements concerning the state.[7]

This building has gone through many memorable occasions, some utterly joyous, others traumatic. One joyous day in its memory, for example, occurred in 1064, when the caliph announced that he had granted the sultan Alp-Arslan new honours for his sweeping victories against the Christians of Anatolia.[8] The Saljuq emperor had uprooted hundreds of thousands of the infidels from their villages, taken tens of thousands more into captivity for sale, and he had burnt whole towns for not surrendering immediately. Allah's praise was sung through the length and breadth of the Dār al-Islam for granting it such a valiant champion.

Today, by contrast, it is going to be a time to beat one's breast and search one's soul – why has Allah seemingly deserted his people in favour of those same infidels?

Some of the worshipers have noticed that a group of strangers have entered the mosque bareheaded. Not only that, they have shaven their heads. As they gather around the visitors to enquire after their news, suddenly a leader of the strangers takes a loaf of bread and starts to eat it. Shock registers on the faces of the natives. It is Ramadan, the month of fasting. Some shout that the man be arrested. But as more worshippers rush to the scene and form a crowd, the man starts to speak in the manner of a learned leader of the faith. He introduces himself as Imam Abu Sa'ad al-Harawi, from the Khorāsānian city of Herat, who is now the chief Islamic judge of Damascus. He has come to the faithful people of Baghdad, the city of the Abbassids, to shake them out of their shameful slumber. Just over a month ago, Jerusalem became yet another Muslim city that had fallen under the hooves of the unclean. Now the very rock from which the Prophet, Allah's

Blessing be Upon Him, flew to heaven on the wings of the Archangel
Gabriel, is daily desecrated by the presence of the Prophet's enemies.
For how long will Muslims bear in silence the atrocities being
committed against their brothers?

Some of the strangers begin to wail. They are survivors from
Jerusalem, from Tyre, from Ma'arra. Knots of men begin to gather
around each one of them as they begin to tell their stories. They are
urged to go to the palace to let His Holiness the caliph know what has
happened.

Before the day is out, the visitors' voices become hoarse. The
whole of the ruling class in Baghdad is traumatised. The imam Abu
Sa'ad is received by high officials at the palace and told that His
Holiness already knows about the situation. He has sent messengers to
Khorāsān to tell the sultan Berkyaruq and every effort is being made
to see what can be done. In the meantime, could the imam please
keep his voice down? His Holiness has just received his new bride,
the sultan's sister.

*   *   *

Khayyām is said to have been a keen hunter. It seems credible. He
probably developed a taste for it in his youth as a companion of King
Shams al-Mulk in Bukhara, and then continued to indulge in it in the
company of Malik Shah in Isfahan. The latter had a particular
weakness for the sport and went hunting almost immediately on
arrival in any new location which had good game. The foothills of
Nishāpur, Khayyām's old and new home, were ideal for horse and
hound. Furthermore, the gregarious sport went well with his
gregarious temperament.

His inclination towards hunting is found in the *Tarab Khāneh*, the
first anthology devoted entirely to his poetry and completed in 1462.
The author, Yār Ahmad Rashīdi Tabrīzi, gives it a short passage:

> The philosopher had a thorough fondness for hunting. Once in a village
> near Astar Ābād, he sent a young hound after an animal in the forest.
> Suddenly a wild boar appeared and killed the dog. The philosopher
> declaimed the following quatrain:

What a waste, this hound, that brimmed with life,
With whom only storms could hope to keep up.
Alas, one weakness proved the end of him:
He loved bones too much, even a boar's tusk!

We may assume that Omar's last years in Isfahan, with their lack of daily chores, would have left him with more time to indulge in pleasurable pursuits, and what pursuit could be more pleasurable than spending time with close friends riding in forests, hunting gazelles, deer and wild pigs with hounds, and enjoying an evening roast under a summer moon on one's private estate?

A mention of Astar Ābād is made in the above passage. According to one tradition, Khayyām was born in that eastern Caspian region. There is no evidence for it and it is contradicted by more reliable sources. Yet it may contain a grain of truth. Why was he in a village near Astar Ābād,[9] far from Nishāpur? Is it possible that his ancestors had originally hailed from there, previous to moving to Nishāpur? The fact that Omar hunted there strengthens this possibility and suggests that either he had inherited an estate there or he was visiting close relatives who had remained there.

Let us now catch up with events in Khorāsān since Omar's return there after his world collapsed in 1092.

As mentioned earlier, one of Malik Shah's less favoured uncles, Arslan Arqūn, took advantage of the family war and expanded his impoverished little fiefdom in Khorāsān to include most of the vast region. But he had an extremely short temper and harsh temperament, to such an extent that even his own servants disliked him.

To make certain that the main cities, Nishāpur, Marv and Balkh, would not rebel, he destroyed their walls and citadels, leaving them open to invasion by others. Eventually, in 1096, Zubeida decided it was time to recapture Khorāsān. She appointed young Prince Sanjar to the governorship of Khorāsān and herself led an army in its direction with her son Berkyaruq and his Grand Vizier Mo'ayyad in attendance. Fortunately for all, before the army reached Nishāpur, several of Arslan Arqūn's servants killed him one night after one of his drunken tantrums.

Thus when the Isfahan army arrived, it received a genuine welcome in Nishāpur and the other cities. Khayyām would have been in the front rank of dignitaries receiving the sultan, his mother and his Grand Vizier. All three would have, otherwise, noticed his absence immediately and have interpreted it badly. All three had known him in person, particularly his old friend Mo'ayyad.

But poor Berkyaruq did not enjoy the fruits of his valour long. Contemporary accounts describe him as a kind and handsome youth, as well as courageous and tireless. Perhaps it was the pressure on his nerves of constantly pursuing his enemies that eventually exhausted him at the age of only twenty-five. He died of tuberculosis and was succeeded by his half-brother, Muhammad.

It is in the third year of the reign of the latter prince, 1108, that Khayyām emerges into history once more. Arūzi tells us that the sultan had previously consulted his astrologers in Isfahan on whether leading an expedition to Mesopotamia to put down a rebellion by the Arab king Sadaqa would succeed. The astrologers had not been able to agree among themselves on the appropriate signs. So Muhammad had turned to a Jewish soothsayer in the bazaar of Isfahan who had predicted a great victory for him. When the sultan returned from the expedition, having killed Sadaqa, he admonished the court astrologers in March 1108 and they begged his forgiveness. They said that the signs had been confusing: 'If you do not believe us, send for the lord Omar Khayyām in Khorāsān.'[10]

The story suggests that Khayyām's rehabilitation was now complete, that he could move back to Isfahan to live at court once more as one of the leading figures of the state, if he wished. At the age of sixty, he enjoyed vigorous health and the glitter of Isfahan would have still had its attractions. But he would have none of it, and not only because, as Arūzi reminds us, 'he did not have the slightest confidence in astrology'. He had seen too many horrors in his companionship of kings, the latest example being Berkyaruq's personal execution of Mo'ayyad in revenge for the vizier personally strangling his mother. No. Khayyām was now much happier living as a private citizen in the company of his family and friends in the province of his birth.

CHAPTER TWELVE

The Sage of Khorāsān

This garden, this park, these broad skies,
Hillocks, waterfalls, flowers, butterflies.
Do send for my friends, those tingling wits
Who lighten my heart, who brighten my eyes.

Starting in 1112, we see a new flurry of activity in Khayyām's life. He hunts with princes, forecasts the weather, mixes in intellectual circles and travels to faraway cities in the other parts of Khorāsān – and he never glances back towards Isfahan.

This cannot be due simply to the chance survival of the memoirs of his acquaintances from this second decade of the twelfth century, while nothing survived from the previous decade. We can only conclude that, in the first decade, he still lived largely out of sight of society as a near recluse, appearing in public only as a silent witness on important religious and state occasions in the company of the orthodox and the powerful in order to rehabilitate his image. In other words, he did not draw attention to himself. By contrast, from the start of the second decade of the twelfth century, a new confidence seeped into his behaviour. He could be himself again to some extent, taking precautions only to reduce the chances of any heretical poems leaking outside the circle of his confidants.

We saw in the last chapter that in March 1108, the royal astrologers of Isfahan described Khayyām as the authority of the age in their profession, astrology. It is unlikely that the sultan Muhammad sent for Khayyām to go to Isfahan to settle the dispute between him and the astrologers. But the incident suggests that, by then, at least some people believed that the disgraced old thinker had been sufficiently rehabilitated in the eye of the public to travel to the scene of his former shaming.

Whether Khayyām would have gone to Isfahan if he had been summoned forcefully by the sultan is not known. But an instance of his refusing to intervene in public matters is documented, apparently early in the second decade of the century. The revered mystic, Sanā'i Ghaznavi, had been accused by one of his servants of receiving the proceeds of a robbery, 1,000 gold dinars from a moneychanger's shop in Nishāpur. Sanā'i, who had fled to Herat, but was being pursued there by the moneychanger's agents, wrote to Khayyām to ask him to use his influence with the authorities in Nishāpur to exonerate him. The letter is long and pompous. It quotes passages from the Koran at every turn and resorts to verbal fireworks every other sentence, indicating how deluded Sanā'i was in thinking that Khayyām would be impressed. But it shows in what high esteem the governor of Nishā pur must have held Khayyām by then.

The glimpse of his life that is preserved from 1112 portrays him as a vigorous 64-year-old enjoying travel and the company of intelligent friends, as well as good food and wine. We owe it to Arūzi, of whom we shall gain a fuller profile later in this chapter. He tells us that in that year, probably in the autumn, when the air was cool and the grapes were ripe, Omar visited the city of Balkh and stayed with his old friend and astronomer colleague, Abul-Mozaffar al-Asfizāri. We read that, one day, the two old soulmates go to lunch at the home of the regional governor, the emir Abu Sa'd Jarrah, in the Street of the Slave Sellers.[1] Despite the unfortunate name of the thoroughfare, it must have been the best location in the city, for otherwise the governor would not have had his mansion there.

Arūzi tells us that as the wine flows and the china tinkles, his master becomes especially expansive. He boasts that he has chosen the precise plot of land in the cemetery of Heira, the burial place of the great and good of Nishāpur, where he will be buried. It is a spot, he says, where 'every spring scatters flower petals on it twice', knowing that he will immediately cause inquisitive looks on the faces of his friends.[2]

We meet him next a year later, back in Nishāpur. His future mini-biographer, Ibn Funduq, tells us that in that year Khayyām visited his father and was asked, presumably during a bored moment, to test the young boy's knowledge of Arabic.

Judging by the later, adult Ibn Funduq, his father must have been an equally dry and humourless Muslim – Persian by language but Arab by mentality – for Khayyām emerges from the recollection as stern, unsmiling, unwilling to teach. He is in the company of the wrong people and wishes to leave as soon as it is polite to do so.

Khayyām emerges in the full glare of history once more a couple of years later, in the winter of 1115. Here, let Arūzi, who seems to have been present, indulge in his own expansiveness:

> I did not see in him the slightest belief in astrology, though I witnessed his [issuing of astrological] verdicts. Nor did I see any of the [other] great ones believing in the truth of astrology.
>
> In the winter of 508 H [the opening months of AD 1115], in Marv, the sultan sent men to the great lord Sadrud-Dīn Muhammad with the message: 'The lord Omar is staying with you. Ask him to see when we could go hunting soon for a few days without its raining or snowing.'
>
> The great lord sent for him and told him the story. Lord Omar retired for two days and then went to the sultan himself to mount him on his horse at the auspicious hour. But as they rode a while, clouds appeared, a wind began to blow and it rained and snowed. People started laughing and the sultan wanted to return. Lord Omar told him: 'Your majesty must not worry. The sky will clear this same hour and there will not be a drizzle for five days.' The sultan rode on and the sky cleared and no one saw even a cloud for those five days.[3]

How Khayyām must have sweated in those two wintry days when he was expected by Sanjar to forecast good weather for a small army's outing for a full five days, and all without satellite photographs showing the direction and temperature of air flows. Yet he had to comply with the demand of a capricious sultan and disguise his verdict, in which he had not the slightest confidence, as a message from Heaven. He was lucky, indeed, and he must have told the story to the raucous laughter of his friends for years afterwards.

A little puzzle arises from Arūzi's report. The sultan he mentions may not have been the reigning sultan Muhammad, who had his seat in Isfahan. Unless Muhammad was visiting his younger brother Sanjar in Khorāsān at the time, the reference must be to the latter, who had been viceroy in the province since 1096. Sanjar did not succeed Muhammad as sultan until 1118, but some contemporary texts do address him as 'sultan'. In practice, he was independent of his elder brother and had once even rescued him from Berkyaruq.

It is said that Sanjar 'never liked Khayyām', since the latter, as the family doctor in Isfahan in the 1080s, had despaired of the infant's life. But quite a different image emerges from the above event, probably witnessed by Arūzi in person. Sanjar evidently regarded Khayyām as an honorary uncle and revered him as a sage, to the extent that he thought being directed by the philosopher to mount his horse before a hunt a blessing. Khayyām also felt so relaxed with Sanjar that he invited himself to accompany the sultan for the duration of the hunt.

Nor was he honoured only by Saljuq – and earlier by Qarakhanid – princes. The story above suggests that a whole tier of lesser nobility and officialdom regarded a visit by him as bestowing moral legitimacy on their courts.

Among the glimpses that we have received of Omar's life in the latter third of his years, perhaps the most delightful is revealed by himself. The following quatrain must have been written on – or immediately after – his seventieth birthday on 18 May 1118, for it has the air of a birthday resolution about it:

> Today I will shed my robe of restraint;
> Let trails of red wine my white beard taint.
> No more piety: I am *seventy*.
> If not dance now, when might it then be?

Here is a man who has decided he no longer fears the accusing finger of the mullah or the raised fists of the mob. He has protection in the highest places.

But, alas, the poem also reveals that Khayyām knows time is running out on him. His nearest and dearest friends are, one by one, falling by the wayside, 'having drunk from the same cup'. No apologies need be made, therefore, for throwing a great party. A seventieth birthday has a hidden message in any life. The precious moments deserve to be savoured by then. Write a new poem for it, to be sung to the gathering beside the pool after the wine has begun to flow.

Finally, in a booklet written before March 1122, we read of an unpleasant encounter between Khayyām and the pedantic commentator on the Koran, Abul Qāsim Zamakhshari. This man, some twenty-six years younger than Khayyām, says that he met 'The lord, the master, Khayyāmi'[4] a couple of times in a learned gathering in the city of Marv, and that on both occasions he and Khayyām disagreed on the correct reading of two Arabic passages.

Two points emerge from the recollection. One is that Zamakhshari adopts a mocking tone, implying that his own Arabic was superior to that of Khayyām's. While this is possible, we can deduce that Khayyām would have taken an instant dislike to the man for his Islamic militancy. We have Zamakhshari on record elsewhere as saying that Allah had given Muslims two great weapons, the Koran and the sword. Apart from Khayyām seeing the man as almost worse than vermin, their personalities were totally opposed. Though born and brought up a Persian, Zamakhshari had spent many years in Mecca and Baghdad and had become a virtual Arab. He wrote some of his books in his native language, but argued for the need to discourage the observance of Iranian customs and history in order to turn Iranians into better Muslims.

The second point emerging from Zamakhshari's recollection is that Khayyām knew of the poetry of Abu Alā al-Ma'arri, as one of the passages on which he disagreed with Zamakhshari was from a poem by that Syrian sceptic. This does not prove that Khayyām was fully conversant with the scope of Ma'arri's scepticism, but it does suggests it. Nor do we know at what time in his life Khayyām became familiar with Ma'arri. If he had come across Ma'arri in his earliest youth, before he began to write the quatrains, he may well have been affected by the humanism of the rationalist of Ma'arra.[5] Otherwise, it would be true to say that both men, as with Rāzi and others before them, were under the spell of the classical philosophers of Athens. See Appendix III, Omar the Greek.

*   *   *

How did an intellectual without independent means make a living in twelfth-century Khorāsān? With great difficulty. How about his equivalent with a fortune of his own? He did not have to. Khayyām's two 'mini-biographers' illustrate the above truths: poor Arūzi had a hard time of it, while Ibn Funduq did not.

We first come across Ahmad Nizāmi Arūzi Samarkandi in 1110 in his city of birth. He was a young man with literary ambitions trying to make a name for himself by collecting anecdotes about the great poet Rūdaki. Two years later, as we have seen, he is with 'the Lord Imam Omar Khayyāmi' who is visiting the emir Abu Sa'd Jarrah in Balkh. In the next dozen years or so, we find him hunting for jobs in the cities of Herat, Nishāpur, where he complains of poverty and joins the office of Khayyām as a secretary – apparently not for the first time – , and Tūs, where he is introduced to the sultan Sanjar, probably clutching a letter of recommendation from Khayyām. He praises the glory of Sanjar's court in second-rate poetry and finds a position – and happiness – in the Department of Letters.

But alas his bliss does not last. He leaves for, or flees to, the court of the Qūri kings of Herat until they are scattered by Sanjar and he has to flee for his life. We do not know why. Perhaps he had satirised Sanjar to endear himself to his new lord.

By contrast, Zahīr al-Dīn Abul-Hasan Ali bin Zeid bin Funduq al-Beihaqi is born, around 1100, with a silver spoon in his mouth, to the extent that when he is appointed the chief judge of his birthplace of Sabzvār or Beihaq, he quickly tires of the chores of the job and resigns. Instead, he writes books few people ever buy, some seventy of them, before he dies around 1170.

Interestingly, Ibn Funduq, who has left us more information about Khayyām than any other source, describes the great man as a 'dastūr'. This old Persian word, borrowed by the Arabs, usually meant 'chief minister' or 'chancellor', or at the very least a minister of government. It is not clear why. But we have to take it seriously, for both Ibn Funduq and his father knew Khayyām personally. Does it mean that Malik Shah sent Khayyām on diplomatic missions to other rulers? Ibn Funduq describes Khayyām as one of Malik Shah's 'nadīms', closest friends. The notion that Khayyām might have been influential in a political sense is also supported by Qifti's report that 'he advocated civil policies according to Greek thought'.[6]

Ibn Funduq himself served the sultan Sanjar in a similar capacity. He says that once the Christian king of the Georgians sent a mission to Sanjar with some theological questions in Arabic and Syriac. Sanjar asked Ibn Funduq to prepare suitable answers and he did so, in both languages.

Finally, why is Ibn Funduq's tone, when mentioning Khayyām, negative on the whole? We have examined his description of Khayyām as bad-tempered and miserly in imparting knowledge to others. The crucial fact here may well be that the Ibn Fuduq's family proudly traced their descent to one of the companions of Muhammad and preferred to write in Arabic, not Persian. Though by outward appearances they were Persians now, Khayyām may well have looked upon them as Arabs who had forgotten Arabic, as he might also upon today's religious Iranians if he were alive.[7] He would have distrusted the loyalty of the young man and want to avoid any closeness with him.

*   *   *

A universal truth is that, in the last decades of our lives, our energies recede and visiting old friends becomes more taxing, eventually impossible. In those days of long and gruelling caravan journeys, this applies even more cruelly.

Who were his remaining friends in the 1120s, when he disappears from history before making one final dramatic appearance on his last day? Some of his oldest friends would have still been vigorous enough to write, and he would have received regular news of distant events such as the continuing conquests of the cities of Syria by the 'Farangis', the inventions of wondrous new devices from Rūm to Chīn, and the fluctuating fortunes of the numerous sons of Nizām al-Mulk who now ran several warring Saljuq kingdoms as viziers and whom he remembered from their childhoods in Isfahan.

Among his dearest and wittiest friends was 'Moz', Mozaffar Asfizāri, his fellow Khorāsānian and colleague at the observatory at Isfahan who 'died of grief' in 1121 or a little earlier. It is said that Sanjar worried that some of the precious metals in his treasury were being turned into similar-looking alloys to cheat him. Mozaffar recreated the scale of Archimedes to separate them. But the treasurer broke it and, indirectly, killed poor Mozaffar. It is a tall tale. From our earlier glimpses of Asfizāri's life, we know he was a gregarious and noisy character. In 1112, Khayyām stayed with him in Balkh for several weeks. Could one of Khayyām's most moving quatrains be about his death?

> Agreeable friends, where did they all go?
> At the feet of Time, all of them fell low.
> For a while we feigned brave defiance:
> None triumphs over this Vale of Sorrow.

An undated story speaks of Khayyām's talent as a sculptor. It is said that at a village near Nishāpur, the inhabitants complained to him of too many pigeons soiling their public places. Khayyām sculpted and then painted a large owl and installed it on a wall overlooking the village square. It was so realistic that the pigeons fled, at least until they wised up to the owl's lack of appetite.

The tone and contents of the story suggest strongly that Khayyām was in a position of lordship over the villagers, that their village was part of an estate he owned. This is only to be expected, as he was one of the wealthiest men in the whole of Khorāsān. Such men primarily invested their gold in agricultural estates. One such country landowner I knew in my childhood in Iranian Kurdistan owned fifty-three villages.

It would have been necessary for such landowners to spend hours each day riding around their estates. They would have visited points at which irrigation water was divided among farmers, for disputes often arose among them to whether they were receiving their fair share, and they would have had to inspect orchards in the spring to assess the likely harvest and agree the landlord's share in the autumn. In Khayyām's case, he no doubt would have also held regular meetings with his vineyard managers to choose new varieties of vine to improve the quality of his favourite drink in the years to come. In the remainder of the day, he would have attended as doctor to some of his peasants, whether or not they brought him a goat or a hen for a fee, he would have received visitors. If there were still time, he would have indulged his grandchildren. He would not have been bored.

One piece of news that would have interested Khayyām particularly was the death of the man who caused the collapse of his world in 1092 with his assassination of Nizām al-Mulk. Hasan Sabbāh, the lord of Alamūt Castle, died in his bed in 1126. By then, in fact, he had come to control a string of castles, each a little kingdom, all over the former empire of Malik Shah. From the icy mountains of the Himalayas to the hot plains of Syria, his 'Fedāyin' or 'Sacrificials' were ready to put their lives down for him immediately on receiving his command. Such was the reputation of his infiltrators now that the sultan Sanjar in Khorāsān feared falling asleep in the privacy of his bedchamber, in the most secure part of his castle. In Cairo, the city to which Hasan had gone as an envoy and which had expelled him, the new caliph and the new vizier were convinced that his men had infiltrated their bodyguards, with the vizier Afdal having been assassinated by an agent of his in 1121. Such was the fear of the Egyptians of Hasan that the names of every journeyman who approached the country were written down in the Mediterranean port of Ascalon and sent in advance to the next city, Bilbeis, to make certain that no strangers joined the caravan on the way. Anyone who was not known to the authorities would not be allowed to enter Egypt at all.[8]

In a war of words between the Ismailis of the east and west, the Egyptian caliph had declared that the followers of Hasan acted under the influence of cannabis. In a circular, he called them 'the Hashishiyah', thus coining a new word that would later be distorted through the medium of Latin to become 'assassin'.

In his faraway Khorāsān, though, out of sight and out of mind, Khayyām need no longer worry about the intentions of the mysterious stranger from Rayy he seemingly met many times in Isfahan when the two were young men about town. Hasan had had much bigger quarrels to settle lately and Khayyām no longer mixed with princes. He no longer mattered.

* * *

We must thank Ibn Funduq[9] for our final glimpse of Khayyām. It is of the last day of his life and it is a heavily distorted image, distorted by his son-in-law for the ear of a researcher who is known to be a rigid Muslim proud of his Arab descent. The son-in-law clearly knows that, in the eye of the clergy, his family are seen as the heirs of a sinner and blasphemer, a notorious doubter and philosopher, and a man who regarded the Muslim invasion of Iran as probably the greatest catastrophe in his people's history. Thus we have to push aside the layers of mist so deliberately thrown at us to reach, as best we may, the few neutral facts that unwittingly emerge.

But first, the passage in its entirety:

> His khatan,[10] Imam Muhammad Baghdadi,[11] told me: 'He was cleaning his teeth with a gold toothpick and [at the same time] reading [Avicenna's] *Divinity* in the book of *Shifā*.' When he reached the section 'The One and the Many', he inserted the toothpick between the pages [and put the book aside]. He told me: 'Call the household together that I may tell them of my will.' He told [us] his will and then stood up and prayed. Then he did not eat or drink till the next prayer, the evening prayer. Then he prostrated himself [in prayer] and as he did so, he prayed: 'My God, I have tried to know you to the limit of my ability. Forgive me, then, [if I failed], for I could reach you only through my reason, through knowledge.' And he died.

What are the neutral, incidental facts that emerge from the passage? They are very few, but significant. One is that Khayyām died in relatively good health for an 83-year-old man, both physically and mentally. In particular, he remained in full control of his mind, able to read and to make his will. Furthermore, he was at peace with the world. He could give his attention for extended periods to a book, and concentrate on complex subjects, including theology, metaphysics, medicine.

All the other claims, I am afraid, are man-made fog. They are designed to turn a sceptical philosopher into a holy man who could even bring about his own death by merely willing it. What else can one deduct from the claim that he made his will and then abstained from eating or drinking from the afternoon till late evening before dying there and then? Such claims were made routinely in medieval Iran and elsewhere for mystics and divines. Khayyām regarded them as crooks. He would have had, in particular, a low view of holy men who talked to God loudly for all to hear.

Yet there may be another significant fact detectable. The prayer that his relative puts into his dying mouth is a confession. Khayyām is depicted as saying to Allah that if there were controversies during his life for his doubting His justice or even existence, it was merely the failure of a frail human. He was, all the time, humbly trying, to the best of his ability, to get closer to 'The Compassionate, The Merciful', by the only method he had been taught: questioning and reasoning, seeking more and more knowledge. We may well envisage 'Baghdadi' subsequently spending large sums of Khayyām's money on an elaborate funeral in one of Nishāpur's most orthodox mosques and then receiving visitors at the old man's town house there for at least a week, offering everyone a sumptuous lunch or dinner to the accompaniment of a mullah reciting from the Koran.

We have indication elsewhere that Khayyām in his last years was nowhere near the repentant, Allah-seeking soul that his family pretended he had become. The writer of the *Tarab Khāneh* says in 1461 that in Beihaq he saw the following unpublished note in Arūzi's hand recalling his visit to Khayyām's grave four years after his death:

> [Then] I went to his noble residence. I saw the old lady [Khayyām's wife] sitting there. She recognised me and asked after me. After expressing my condolences and asking how she was, we talked of the past and of my news, as he had been my master. She said that after his death, on the ninth night, he appeared to her in a dream. He was very happy. 'What is there to be happy about?', she asked him. 'I used to pray day and night to God to forgive you. But Omar became angry and recited a quatrain that admonished me for not knowing about God's mercy. This is how it goes [the quatrain]'.

Towards the end of the passage, we can see the hand of the ambitious Arūzi clearly at work, trying to safeguard his future by indulging in pieties. He even makes up a bad quatrain about God's boundless compassion towards blasphemers and attributes it to Khayyām as he had appeared in the dream to his wife. But the earlier confession of the wife herself that she had prayed day and night for God's forgiveness for Omar the blasphemer rings true, as we recognise it from the portrait of Khayyām's middle years.

In fact the cover-up in which the son-in-law and Arūzi indulge can be seen today to have been shamelessly brazen. As we saw in the

report of the archaeologists who opened his tomb in 1962, it was a
Zoroastrian-style burial chamber in which he had been buried, not the
usual Islamic trench with earth poured over the corpse.[12] We know
that he had chosen his precise place of burial years before he died.
Had he gone further still and also built the chamber? If so, was
Khayyām trying to tell future generations that he was, emotionally at
least, a Zoroastrian, a true Persian still identifying with the old,
vanquished civilisation, and a man who believed that you could not
be a true Iranian and a Muslim? Does his famous quatrain telling his
persecutors to leave him alone hint at the rock on which he leant?

> Lost to the wine of the Magus? I am!
> Pagan? Zarathustrian? Haereticus? I am!
> Every nation holds its notion of me.
> I am my own man, whatever I am.

*   *   *

For a broader view of Khayyām's life, for a summing up, we may do
worse than turn to a comment on his own turbulent existence by an
illustrious successor of his from our times, a fellow mathematician and
fellow philosopher who admired Khayyām deeply and who died in
Wales in 1970:

> I do not know who my biographer may be, but I should like him to report
> 'with what flourish his nature will' something like this: 'I was not a solemn
> stained-glass saint, existing only for purposes of edification; I existed from
> my own centre, many things that I did were regrettable. I lied and practiced
> hypocrisy, because if I had not, I should not have been allowed to do my
> work. I hated hypocrisy and lies: I loved life and real people, and wished to
> get rid of the shams that prevent us from loving real people as they really
> are. I believed in laughter and spontaneity, and trusted to nature to bring
> out the genuine good in people, if once genuineness could come to be
> tolerated.'[13]

The Story of the Rubāiyāt

And when Thyself with shining Foot shall pass
Among the Guests Star-scatter'd on the Grass,
And in Thy joyous Errand reach the Spot
Where I made one – turn down an empty Glass![1]

Barbarians burning down great libraries were never the most lethal enemies of books in ancient times. Mice, civil wars, fire, famine, poverty and damp were bigger menaces. They caused the more numerous, smaller collections to crumble into dust, vanish into puffs of smoke or be scattered. When the descendants of a scholar or enthusiast fell on hard times, their precious heirlooms were readily sold to pay for a pilgrimage to a saint's shrine to pray for the recovery of that beloved daughter and, in times of war, a single week's food and shelter for the family at a distant caravanserai easily outshone the value of an ancestral memoir. To the buyer, the books seldom had any sentimental worth.

Thus it may have been that the dozens of complete and autographed collections of Khayyām's quatrains that must have existed in his own possession or in the households of his closest friends and descendants became dispersed in the next wave of Turkic invasion from the east. That disaster fell upon Khorāsān barely a generation after Khayyām's death in 1131, when his friend, the sultan Sanjar, was taken prisoner by his distant kinsmen, the Ghuzz Turks, in 1153. The Mongol blight of the following century compounded the catastrophe.

Juvayni, the Persian high courtier of the later Mongols and their official historian, says that they were not satisfied with merely killing all the inhabitants of Nishāpur 'man and beast alike' whom they could capture. They also razed the city to the ground and then diverted its rivers to flood the ruins to make them unrecognisable. If the confession is to be believed, then we owe the survival of Khayyām's grave to the failure of the invaders to accomplish their task fully. Some people evidently survived months or years of refuge in the hills, returning after the deluge to honour their city's landmarks anew.

As for personal recollections of Khayyām, there must have been a considerable number. The men with whom he associated were, in the majority, highly literate men who wrote down their memories for their descendents, if not for history. Only a fraction have survived and even fewer mention Khayyām. That is, however, entirely understandable. The writers were responsible officials and had to guard themselves against accusations of heresy through association. Owning up to a friendship with a man who had been condemned to death for heresy endangered their positions. We are lucky to have received the material that we have of him.

These include at least a hundred of his own quatrains and some of his articles and theses (see 'Appendix IV'), plus some descriptions of his life in textbooks or histories. They may well have reached relative safety in such far off cities as Damascus and Cairo before the Turks or the Mongols could destroy the society that preserved them; and they only survived the teeth of mice, the ravages of fire, the vagaries of the weather and the grasp of looters because many copies were made of them.

Although it cannot be proven for lack of evidence, I have a feeling that one of the hundreds of thousands of refugees who found safety away from eastern Iran after Khayyām's death was no less than a great-grandson of his. His name was Shāhpūr Khayyāmi Nishāpuri, and he is buried in the Mausoleum of the Poets in the Azerbaijani city of Tabrīz in north-west Iran. We find him active at the court of an aristocrat and regional governor there around 1180, half-way between the second time the Turks had overrun Nishāpur and its total destruction by the Mongols. Judging by the fragments of Shāhpūr Khayyāmi's best poems that have survived, his talents left much to be desired, strengthening the possibility that he owed his place at court to the fame of his ancestor.

Apart from his two family names, Khayyāmi and Nishāpuri, his personal name of Shāhpūr also directs us towards the sage of Khorāsā n. Khayyām, as we have seen, lived under the spell of Firdowsi and was strongly attached to the heritage of pre-Islamic Iran. He used, whenever he could, the purest Persian to help preserve his ancestral language against the wishes of the pro-Arabic clergy, to the point that he was suspected of being a secret Zoroastrian. As we have seen, there is good evidence for the latter suspicion, not in doctrinal but in emotional terms, in his poems and other writings. He is nostalgic about pre-Islamic Iran and tries to revive Zoroastrian day names in his calendar. In the case of *The Book of Norūz*, which he appears to have written for Malik Shah, he has been described by one modern commentator, the late senator Dashti, as 'a fanatical Zoroastrian'.[2]

It would thus seem reasonable to assume that the boy Shāhpūr was named after one of those Iranian emperors in yet another gesture of defiance, against what the Khayyāmis saw as the religion of the invaders.[3] It is probably also no coincidence that the emperor chosen was the one who founded Nishāpur.

Yet another reason to suspect a link between the second Khayyāmi and the first is that at least three, perhaps all five, of the later large-scale compilations of the Rubāiyāt originate in Azerbaijan, where the second Khayyāmi died, even though the bulk of Azerbaijan's people were not Persian speakers. I shall discuss this matter in greater detail a little further in this chapter.

Unfortunately we do not know the date of birth of the second Khayyāmi. But we do know that he died in 1203–4. Assuming that his lifespan was similar to that of Khayyām's eighty-three years, he could have known his ancestor for at least a dozen years before the great man died in 1131. And, if my suspicion is justified, then it becomes easy to imagine that at least one complete collection of the Rubāiyāt, even perhaps one in Khayyām's own hand, was in existence in Tabrīz as a family heirloom up to seventy years after his death.

A question that has exercised some scholars is why no contemporary writer, including Khayyām's own secretary Arūzi, referred to the great man writing poetry. Arūzi, for example, devotes one of his discourses in the *Chahār Maqāleh* to the art of the poets and yet he includes Khayyām among the section on astronomers and astrologers. I have briefly alluded to a possible explanation earlier and shall try to elaborate presently, but Arūzi would have had a ready-made, formal answer at hand. Quatrains or ruba'is did not qualify a man as a poet. Real poets wrote long poems and published collections. They also wrote poetry to eulogise their noble sponsors at court and delighted in displaying their talent by indulging in verbal fireworks. By contrast, almost anyone could – and often did – try their hand at short two-liners to amuse friends at parties or boast of an education.

Still, as one studies the works of contemporary and later scholars, historians and theologians concerning Khayyām, the universal impression is that they all thought of him as a writer of ruba'is, although one who was primarily interested in writing them as a vehicle for his philosophical beliefs. The picture emerges obliquely and gradually. The earliest of such men tells us – in 1122, during Khayyām's own lifetime – that Khayyām was familiar with – that is, he knew by heart – the poetry of Abu Alā al-Ma'arri, implying immediately that the great man shared the Syrian poet's disdain for the established religion. The imam Abul-Qāsim Mahmūd Zamakhshari, although of Iranian birth, had spent many years in Arabia and was, like Khayyām's outright enemy, Ghazāli, a fierce critic of all memories of ancient Iran. Both were adamant that if Islam were to plant permanent roots in Iran, they would have to be forced to abandon their languages for Arabic and stop practicing their ancestral customs, including of course Norūz and the solar calendar that Khayyām had spent years to reform and promote.[4]

Our second witness is not far behind, though he only alludes to Khayyām writing quatrains. He is none other than the faithful servant and secretary, Arūzi, who tries to keep Khayyām's secret safe. As we saw earlier, Yār Ahmad Rashīdi Tabrīzi, the compiler of the Tarab Khāneh, writes that during a visit to the Khorāsānian city of Beihaq – today's Sabzvār – presumably to research his life of Khayyām, he saw an account in Arūzi's own hand that expanded on his visit to Nishāpur in the spring of 1135, 'four years after the death of his lordship'. Arūzi recalled that, after he had paid his respects at Khayyām's grave, he went to his home and met 'the old lady', and gave her his condolences. There, 'after recognising me and asking after me, she said that nine days after Omar's death, he appeared to her in a dream, but appeared very happy. On being asked why he was laughing when she used to pray day and night to God to forgive him, he became angry with her and recited a ruba'i to the effect that God's mercy was greater than she knew.' While we may suspect that crafty Arūzi himself composed the verse to embellish yet another of his stories, the implication is clear: neither he, nor Khayyām's wife, were surprised that the old man was writing ruba'is in the other world. He had been in the habit of writing them in this.

Our third witness may, or may not, have met Khayyām, but he is the first man who says, explicitly, that Khayyām wrote poetry. Writing in Arabic around forty-six years after Khayyām's death, Emād-Eddin Kātib Isfahāni, 'the Scribe of Isfahan', says: 'In Isfahan, they recite his verses.' He then proceeds to quote the three Arabic poems by Khayyām that have survived. Though they are not in the form of quatrains, they are in the same spirit (see 'Appendix IV').[5]

The first attribution of a quatrain in Persian to Khayyām we owe to a man who died in 1210, ten years before the Mongols devastated Khorāsān. He is a Koranic commentator by the name of Fakhreddin Muhammad Rāzi, from Rayy, who quotes one of Khayyām's most rebellious quatrains to illustrate the existence of rival views to the teachings of the Koran. His chosen verse is:

> Mighty Lord, when He the world did ordain,
> Why did He often from ideal abstain?
> Who can be at fault if the tower leans?
> If it does not lean, why start again?

The fact that the theologian does not condemn Khayyām may indicate perhaps that he was himself secretly sceptical of religious dogma, and that he wrote his books merely to earn money. That, as we know, is an old, old story.

The next – and most moving – emergence into history of a quatrain by Khayyām owes itself to a circumstance of unimaginable sorrow, the destruction of Marv by the Mongols in 1220. Juvayni, the Persian servant and historian of the Mongols whom we met above, tells us that after Marv was sacked and the Mongol army had left to raze another place, a group of survivors returned to bury the dead. Let him take up the story himself:

> And the lord Ezz ed-Dīn was one of the great seyyeds, known for his asceticism and generosity. It is written that as he and others counted the dead for thirteen days and nights, beside those they could not find in tunnels and holes and in the countryside and villages and wildernesses, they reached the figure one thousand thousand [1,000,000] and three hundred thousand and a fraction. At that moment, he recited the following quatrain by Omar Khayyām, for it described well how they felt:
>
> > A vase of China, exuding charm,
> > Even drunkards do not wish to harm.
> > Yet these lovely heads, these delicate hands,
> > Who could hate them so? No one understands.

That even a professional man of religion could recite Khayyām by heart almost a hundred years after his death shows how popular his short little poems must have become by then. Juvayni's source for the story has been lost. Was it Ezz ed-Dīn's memoirs?

The third ruba'i is one of the most profound of all the Rubāiyāt and sees the light of day only three years later, in 1223, at the hands of a Sufi bigot by the name of Najm-ed-Dīn Rāzi, known as Dāyeh. He advocated that all philosophers and 'naturalists' be put to the sword. He wrote:

> Omar Khayyām is one of their sages, famous among them for wisdom and intelligence, but he is so lost in darkness and ignorance that he admits it himself:
>
> > This Circle in which we ebb and we flow,
> > Neither beginning, nor an end does know.
> > The Riddle stands as posed long ago:
> > Where do we come from? Where do we go?
>
> The wondering fool does not see that Almighty God has worshippers who, following in the path of the First and the Last Lord [Muhammad], have crossed all the Heavens and risen above this elliptical dome to find how all things emerge from the depths of oblivion onto the plane of existence and how they will do so to the end of Time. They know the purpose of each creature's life and foretell the end of each class of creature. . . .[6]

Other quatrains emerge in a similarly slow fashion in the next few decades, some from memory, others from the margins of books, etc., but they are all in the same sceptical and humanistic vein. They show not only why Khayyām found himself in trouble with the guardians of received dogma, but also set the criteria down the centuries by which scholars might judge as to which quatrains might, or might not, be his, both in philosophical content and poetical style.

This is not the place to amass more such facts about how all the quatrains that we now regard as almost certain, or at least highly likely, to be Khayyām's came to light. It should be enough to state that, with the passing of time, as the dead poet became less of a threat to the established order, more and more of his poems reached open circulation in professionally-made copies for sale. In the sources that have survived from before 1350, only fifty-eight quatrains are attributed to Khayyām and very little happens for another hundred years. But suddenly an eruption occurs in the middle of the fifteenth century, with one new 'collection', the *Tarab Khāneh*, gathering together over 600 quatrains under the name of Khayyām, the majority of them unfortunately laughably poor in poetics and even contrary to their supposed author's core beliefs.

Interestingly, however, three of the four new collections appear almost together, in the middle of the fifteenth century. They are the manuscript at France's Bibliothèque Nationale, known as 'the Paris'; 'the Bodleian', after the great library of that name in Oxford; the *Tarab Khāneh*, of which we have several copies; and the so-called 'Nakhjavāni' manuscript in Tehran. They are respectively dated 1449, 1461, 1463, and 'fifteenth century'.

One more interesting fact is that the two most significant among the four, the *Tarab Khāneh* and the 'Nakhjavāni', originate in Azerbaijan. Add to them the last batch of discoveries from the previous century, the twenty-six quatrains that were unearthed by Khalīl Shervāni of Azerbaijan in 1331, and it immediately becomes clear that Turkish-speaking Azerbaijan played a disproportionate part in the new scholarship centred on a long-dead Persian poet who never even visited the region.

As far as we know, 'the Paris' may have also hailed from Azerbaijan, and the compiler of 'the Bodleian', Sheikh Mahmūd Yarbudāqi, may

well have travelled there before he started his small anthology in
Shiraz. Though the *Tarab Khāneh* was completed two years later than
'the Bodleian', we may assume that the two men worked
independently of one another. The *Tarab Khāneh* is larger and also
contains original research material on the life of Khayyām.

Can the Azerbaijani connection be a coincidence? We might have
thought so, were it not for the dates. Something must have happened
that sparked the new flurry of activity, and that could not have
happened in several unrelated places at the same time. It would need
a centre, a place of origin. And could the event itself be the discovery
of a manuscript from the former library of Shāpūr Khayyāmi, Khayyā
m's apparent descendant?

I have described 'the Bodleian' manuscript as insignificant. This
may disappoint FitzGerald aficionados, but it ought not to. It was not
his only source. Furthermore, he was remarkably able – for a non-
Persian speaker – to distinguish the wheat from the chaff. Of the 158
quatrains in the small volume, I was myself able to classify ninety-
three as 'unlikely', 'highly unlikely', or 'laughable', leaving sixty-five
worthy of consideration, and of these, according to my notes, all had
been collected by the author of the *Tarab Khāneh* or earlier
researchers.

As for the *Tarab Khāneh*, I have said earlier that the bulk of its 600
quatrains are also spuriously attributed to Khayyām. However, it still
contains many that are new and which scholars accept as likely to be
authentic. Furthermore, its compiler Yār Ahmad travelled far and
wide in Iran, including Khorāsān, to unearth documents on the life of
Khayyām that were still extant, but which later disappeared. Thus
despite the many noises of dismissal against him, Yār Ahmad seems to
have had genuine affection for Khayyām, the rebellious thinker, and
he rendered the great man a unique service.

The subsequent centuries do not deserve examination, as far as
Khayyām scholarship is concerned. In particular, the past century-
and-a-half, since FitzGerald made Khayyām the inspiration of millions
of people, have given birth to what we might call 'Khayyāmania'.
Unscrupulous 'collectors' in British India and forgers of quatrains in
Iran imitating Khayyām's style hoodwinked wealthy westerners and
caused some genuine, if hasty, scholars to waste much of their time.

The only consolation is that a new generation of scholars has recently begun to wipe the dust off Khayyām's much-abused face to give us a much clearer view of him.

* * *

Edward FitzGerald was a boy who never truly grew up. He was lonely all his adult life and longed for love, often trying to buy it with money, for he had inherited a fortune. But he need not have worried. By all accounts he was a witty and loyal friend, adored by all around him. He was also a poet, although he thought himself as having only moderate talent. Others did not agree. Some thought of him – and many more still think of him – as one of the immortals of English literature. Certainly, without him, millions of people all over the world would not have heard of Khayyām. In this sense, as the man who gave new life to Omar Khayyām, he may justifiably be called 'the second Omar', and he did himself sometimes sign his name as 'FitzOmar'.

He once wrote to a friend: 'I have what Goethe calls the "Barber's talent" of easy narrative of easy things – can tell of Barton and Chesterton Inn, but not of Atreus and the Alps. Nor do I pretend to do so.'[7] In fact, even if he had been convinced of possessing a great talent, he was brought up as too much of a gentleman to lay claims to it, and his innate modesty, his lack of ambition and preference for anonymity made him all the more loved by his closest friends, who were themselves such luminaries of London literary life as Thomas Carlyle, William Thackeray and Lord Alfred Tennyson, the poet laureate.

Thackeray and Tennyson would have had greater obstacles to overcome if 'dear Fitz' had not subsidised their lives with regular substantial donations when they were young.[8] Just as importantly, he was an emotional pillar to them when they were older. He once lived with Thackeray for three months after the latter's wife had suffered a nervous breakdown, and he was a frequent visitor to Carlyle's unhappy household in Chelsea at the height of that writer's dark moods. They would lie down on the carpet beside a log fire into the small hours and smoke pipes, with Carlyle replying only in grunts and 'smoking indignantly'. In the knowing, polite language of Victorian society, Fitz was 'a confirmed bachelor' and did not have to report to a wife in the evening. The son of hugely rich parents, neither did he have to report to an office in the morning.

He was born at one of his family's grand country houses, The White House, between Bredfield village and the town of Woodbridge in Suffolk, on 31 March 1809, the seventh of eight children and the youngest of three sons. His parents were first cousins and hailed from rich landowning families in Ireland. His mother, Mary, was the only child of John FitzGerald, a descendant of the first earl of Kildare, and inherited her family's wealth in 1818. Her husband, John Purcell, a country gentleman who would later lose a fortune in a coal mine near Manchester, changed his name to hers because of its greater history and standing, although, in a roundabout way, he was a FitzGerald too. Young Edward thought his father's act 'disgusting' and hated snobs for the rest of his life. He also resented his mother's remoteness. She often left the children to the care of nannies in the country to preside over her salons in London and Brighton. His biographers have invariably seen in this the roots of his notorious preference for exclusively male company.

Edward was educated privately in Suffolk and France and was thought 'a beautiful dancer' before his teens, but he soon discovered a love of the classics when he was sent to a grammar school in Bury St Edmonds. At Cambridge University's Trinity College, he fell under the spell of 'the Apostles', the secret society of the supposedly cleverest students who also called themselves 'the Convesazione Society'. Erasmus Darwin, the elder brother of Charles, was a member, Alfred Tennyson another. Edward never achieved full membership.

Due to his parents' chilly relations – Mr FitzGerald kept a mistress in London, as had his father before him – Edward was later chosen by his mother to be her escort to parties or to the opera, though he disliked it. Despite maintaining Boulge Cottage in the grounds of the family residence in Suffolk, he lived separately in lodgings. Although his mother was proud of her beauty and was painted by Sir Thomas Lawrence, Edward sometimes referred to her as 'the Duke of Wellington'. But he remained an attentive son till she died, aged seventy-six, in 1855. Afterwards, he kept a portrait of her in a cupboard in Suffolk, claiming that he did not have enough room to put it on a wall.

A year later, when he was forty-seven, FitzGerald married Lucy Barton, the destitute daughter of his late friend, the Quaker poet Thomas Barton, but he realised his mistake even before they were wed. He had previously helped her to become a published author by editing her father's poetry and writing a preface to it in her name. Now he offered her money to forego marriage, but she was offended. The union lasted, in effect, only a few weeks, though much longer than poor Tchaikovsky's single night. Afterwards FitzGerald provided Lucy with a pension of £300 a year – the price of a good house – for the rest of her life.

Earlier, aged twenty-two, FitzGerald had published an anonymous poem in two literary magazines. It had attracted praise from Charles Lamb, among others. But a lazy – some might be kinder and say reflective – temperament stopped him from writing many more. He thought that artists should create only if they could produce extraordinary work.

The crucial meeting of his life – from our point of view – came in the late autumn of 1844, when he was thirty-five. At the home of a Suffolk gentleman farmer, he met a youth of eighteen who had lately taught himself Persian and Sanskrit, as well as Greek, Latin, Italian, French, German and Old Norse. He had even already published translations of Persian poetry. He was exceptionally handsome, too, and exhibited, as well he might, remarkable confidence in society. Within a year, the boy was the true master in the relationship, the older man the pupil. Despite their close relationship, there has never been any hint of an interest on the boy's part in men as sexual partners. In fact, at that very first meeting with FitzGerald, he fell under the spell of his future wife, Elizabeth Charlesworth, with whom FitzGerald had also earlier imagined himself to be in love.

The youth's name was Edward Cowell and he, also, formed an instant high impression of FitzGerald. In a letter to his mother, he wrote: 'he is a man of *real* power, one such as we seldom meet within the world. There is something so very solid and stately about him, a kind of slumbering giant, or silent Vesuvius. It is only at times that the eruption comes, but when it *does* come, it overwhelms you!'[9]

Cowell first inspired FitzGerald to start learning Spanish, so that he could read Calderon. The result was translations into blank verse of six plays by the dramatist that would eventually earn FitzGerald a medal from the Spanish Royal Academy. He published them in 1853, and they bore his name to distinguish them from another man's effort that would appear at about the same time. That was the only instance in his life he allowed his name to appear in connection with any of his works.

The plays were not literal translations, but contained English near-equivalents of mood and message. They were criticised for it. FitzGerald defended himself: 'A Thing must *live*', he wrote, 'with a transfusion of one's worse Life if one can't retain the Original's better. Better a live sparrow than a stuffed eagle.' The principle would prove even truer in his later, much greater work.

Pushed by his new wife, Cowell went to Oxford as a mature student, despite pressure from FitzGerald and another friend not to do so, on the grounds that it would interrupt his pursuit of Sanskrit and Persian. But the wife won. So did FitzGerald, though in a manner he could not have foreseen, for it was at Oxford's Bodleian Library a few years later that Cowell discovered an old manuscript of a Persian poet called Omar Khayyām. As FitzGerald had by then made good progress in Persian, to the extent that he had translated an allegorical work by the fifteenth-century poet Jāmi, Cowell encouraged him to take a similar interest in Khayyām. He transcribed the 158 quatrains in the manuscript and helped FitzGerald with its nuances. Then, in the autumn of 1856, he sailed for India with his wife to take up a chair in modern politics in Calcutta, turning down an offer of a substantial annual stipend from FitzGerald to remain in England until he could find a suitable teaching job at another university.

FitzGerald had become attracted to Khayyām from the start, for he had found a kindred spirit in the eleventh-century Persian. But at the height of the pain of his ill-advised marriage, he found translating the poems the distraction he needed. He would reflect on several stanzas for several hours, then go out for a walk to ponder their spirit and wonder how he might produce one or two English versions out of them. After his separation from his wife, he plunged into the task even more furiously and wrote often to Cowell for guidance. Cowell remained as attentive as ever, despite his wife and Lucy being best friends, and he sent FitzGerald a new manuscript, one that he had found at the Bengal Asiatic Society. That manuscript, however, was corrupted on a large scale with many dreadful insertions. It had 516 stanzas, many of them extremely poor or devoutly Islamic. FitzGerald also embarked on a correspondence with a French scholar, J.B. Nicolas, who was in possession of 464 purported Khayyám stanzas.

He wrote to Tennyson about his new obsession: 'I have really got hold of an old Epicurean so desperately impious in his recommendations to live only for *Today* that the good Mahometans have scarcely dared to multiply MSS of him.' In other words, he had seen immediately that Khayyám stood head and shoulders above the crowd, and had become a cult figure precisely because he had been a rebel. By this time, poor Cowell, a devoutly religious man who would remain loyal to FitzGerald for the rest of his life, was sorry he had ever introduced his friend to Persian.

At the end of 1857, FitzGerald sent thirty-five of the 'least wicked' of the quatrains he had translated to *Frazer's* magazine.[10] But they were not used and, after waiting a year, he put them together with another forty and printed 250 copies privately in 1859. After keeping forty copies for himself, he gave the rest to the publisher Bernard Quaritch of Castle Street, Leicester Square, to distribute, but Quaritch could sell very few at their cover price of one shilling. He remaindered them in a bargain box at a penny each, one-twelfth of the original price.

They were still there two years later, in 1861, when the scandalous poet Algernon 'Swine-Born' Swinburne was shown a copy of the little booklet by a friend and was immediately won over by it. The next day he raided the box and bought a few more to give to friends in his Pre-Raphaelite circle, including Dante Gabriel Rossetti who was similarly overcome. In a letter to its translator that would take eleven years to arrive, Rossetti wrote: 'I do not know in the least who you are, but I do with all my soul pray you find and translate some more of Omar Khayyám for us: I never did – till this day – read anything so glorious, to my mind, as this poem.'

The rest of the story is well-known, but it may be worth mentioning here that out of the forty copies that FitzGerald had held back for his friends, he only gave away three, and so secretive was he about his own part in the venture that Carlyle was taken aback a decade later when he was told that his old friend might be the translator. The man who told him so was Charles Eliot Norton of Harvard University in the United States. He wrote that he had heard that a certain 'Reverend Edward FitzGerald who lives in Norfolk and is fond of boating' was behind the book. 'Why', Carlyle replied. 'He's no more Reverend than I am! He's a very old friend of mine – I'm surprised, if the book be as good as you tell me it is, that my friend has never mentioned it to me.'[11]

It was in the United States and largely through Norton that the identity of the translator was divulged. Quaritch confirmed it in 1875 when advertising another translation by FitzGerald, his *Agamemnon* by Aeschylus. The disclosure angered FitzGerald, but it was too late. London's literary circle was still a small one and most of it quickly found out the identity of the reclusive gentleman of Suffolk. Carlyle was among those who took an immediate dislike to the book because of its subversive message. He described Khayyām most inaccurately as 'that Mahometan blackguard', though he pulled his punches when he wrote to FitzGerald about it later.

In the 1870s, FitzGerald spent many a summer month each year at sea on his magnificent and sleek 43ft schooner, *The Scandal*, which he had had built for him at Wivenhoe in Essex. He had it crewed by his favourite men, that 'superior race' of Suffolk seafaring men, and he used the vessel to visit destinations ranging from Scotland to Holland and France. On one occasion, as he lay on deck reading a classic, he was so absorbed in the book that he did not notice the swing of the boom and was swept overboard.

Despite an acute sense of loss occasioned by the deaths of friends such as Carlyle, his last years were his happiest – certainly the most serene – since he had been at Cambridge in his youth. Although he sometimes complained that some of his London friends, such as Tennyson, had become too grand for him, his reclusion in the woods of Suffolk was largely of his own choosing, and although he suffered from bronchitis most winters, he retained sufficient strength to go to London for several weeks each year to visit the theatres and the concert halls. Although he never courted public recognition, he took quiet satisfaction in the Rubāiyāt having become 'a little craze' in the United States, while the enhanced esteem in which he was held by men of letters, including Tennyson who invited him many times in vain to go to stay with him on the Isle of Wight, made him feel that his life had not been wasted.

In his last spring, in April 1883, he made his last visit to London on business and, although he left by the evening, went on to Chelsea to inspect a statue which had been erected to Carlyle. He reflected sadly on the state of Carlyle's house which had been a second home to him for years. It was empty and 'To Let'.

On his return to Suffolk, he wrote to his lifelong friend, the actress Fanny Kemble in London: 'Next week, I am expecting my grave Friend Charles Keene, of *Punch,* to come here for a week – bringing with him his bagpipes, and an ancient Viol, and a book of Strathspeys* and Madrigals; and our Archdeacon will come to meet him to talk over ancient Music and Books: and we shall all three drive out past the green hedges, and heaths with their furze in blossom.'[12]

He lived to the end for his friends, to whom he was always a most welcoming host and for whom he would recite drama and verse and play his little organ. His end, too, came in the manner he wished, suddenly. While visiting friends in Merton, Norfolk, in June – to lend his own large farmhouse, Little Grange, to two of his nieces – he died quietly around dawn in his bed. Thus he was spared 'a lot of women messing about' around him. He was seventy-four, about the same age, so he thought, as Omar when he had died.

FitzGerald had once read some of Mark Twain's writings and been moved by them. He had wondered why he had not discovered the American writer earlier. Later, Twain would be so moved by FitzGerald that he would write his own 'Rubáiyát'. By 1929, it was estimated that FitzGerald's Rubáiyát had been reprinted 310 times in English alone. That was probably the last time anyone counted.

Why was it so successful? The simple answer must be that the world had begun by that time to embark on the most rapid process of change in its history; an intellectual revolution that was the tail end of the Renaissance and the Industrial Revolution and which still continues, at an even greater pace, though not always necessarily for the better. The year of the first edition of the Rubáiyát was, after all, the year of

* Music for a slow Scottish dance that was fashionable at the time.

Darwin's epoch-making book, a book that, without any doubt, shook the world even more deeply than had the discoveries of Newton and Copernicus. Old Fitz spoke through the mouth of an obscure Persian called Omar Khayyām, but he was really the latest incarnation of a long list of free-spirited men going back to Democritus.

ENDS.
Ze Khayyām ān bozorg-andīshé Iran,
Ze FitzGerāldé pīré Engelestan,
Begoftam dāstāni rafteh-az-yād,
Barāy e zīrakān, khūbān o yāāran.

Of the lord Khayyām, sage of Iran,
Of wise FitzGerald of Engelestan,
A tale of tears, toil and triumph,
For kindred minds have I here spun!

Via della Frattina,
Trinita dei Monti, Rome.
18 December 2006.

The Rubāiyāt: A New Translation

My coming did not profit this Wheel,
Nor will my going its glory seal.
Neither any man did to me reveal
What ills the cries of little orphans heal.

As I studied Khayyām's writings and those of others about him, it became clear that his life could be divided into a number of distinct stages. They are: a privileged, though not aristocratic, upbringing in Nishāpur; early recognition as a mathematical prodigy; youthful hedonism fuelled by professional success and the companionship of princes and kings in Samarkand, Bukhara and Isfahan; growing confidence in proclaiming his religious doubts and his pride in his pre-Islamic, Iranian roots to the annoyance of the Muslim clergy; an emersion in the awesome scientific and philosophical heritage of ancient Greece; despairing of his life when a fatwa of apostasy is issued against him after the death of Malik Shah and being abandoned by the queen Terken who suddenly needs to appease the clergy; and, finally, fleeing to find peace among his family and clan in Nishāpur. He died there four decades later as a revered sage, a companion of sultans, once more, and a wealthy nobleman.

These stages may all be seen here reflected in the quatrains that I have chosen for translation as the most characteristic of his poems.

There are between 100 and 200 quatrains that scholars attribute to Khayyām with varying degrees of certainty, depending on their occurrence in the oldest historical records and on their philosophical content and linguistic style. No contemporary anthology, let alone an autographed collection, of his poems has survived. Under the later Saljuq

Turks, who were either weak or genuinely orthodox, being found in possession of any vaguely subversive religious writing was instant proof of blasphemy, and most of the clandestine anthologies of his poems that must have existed probably perished in the further waves of Turkic and Mongolian destruction that swept over Iran from the east in the three centuries after his death.

Having been written over five or six decades, some of the quatrains inevitably repeat the themes of previous ones. Nor are they all poetically perfect, with Khayyām sometimes being tempted to let a less-than-satisfactory quatrain pass because he was pleased with the sentiment it expressed. So I decided to pick, at most, no more than a quarter of those that are supposedly his. I needed to feel comfortable with them myself and I needed to leave as little room for disputation by scholars as possible. As a result, the fifty quatrains I chose to translate are typical of his moods and beliefs and style, and they include all those that occur in the oldest historical quotations.

They also serve their purpose here. They are the ones that have made the occasional and amateur poet the beloved daily companion of his countless admirers over the past nine centuries. They express his love of the living world, they puncture the pomposity of those who claim to have all the answers to all our questions, they advocate caring for other human beings for their own sakes, rather than for reward in an afterlife, and, I think, they are sufficient in number to give the English reader a full sense of Khayyām, the man of flesh who was subject, as are we, to the vagaries of personal circumstance and impersonal Time.

But why translate any of them at all when we have FitzGerald's glorious version of 1859, one of the most inspiring feats of translation in world history? The answer is that the original quatrains are free-standing stanzas, while FitzGerald's 'rendering' – to use his own preference – is a single long poem based largely on one collection only, the Bodleian manuscript of 1460 at Oxford University. Since FitzGerald's time – although mostly due to his success – scholarship has moved on.

As I examined the 158 quatrains in the Bodleian manuscript, I thought that only fifty-seven had any chance of belonging to Khayyām. Even some of those were structurally too weak for the demanding craftsman that Khayyām tried to be. But I accepted that those might have been corrupted by generations of copyists. Many differed slightly from those found elsewhere and they were not all improvements.

By contrast, my own chosen quatrains are selected mainly from the 200 that the Iranian prime minister Muhammad Ali Foroughi chose in 1942 as likely to be authentic. However, even that meticulous scholar allowed some stanzas to pass through his fingers that sat awkwardly with their neighbours. While the great majority were clearly the work of a philosophical and religious sceptic, others professed devout faith and therefore made it difficult to see why such a strong believer would have attracted the wrath of the clergy of his time.[1]

Yet one more reason compelling me to risk ridicule by attempting a new translation was that language changes over time and every generation needs its own rendering of receding texts. When sometimes I recite FitzGerald at book clubs in England, I hear someone saying that they had difficulty understanding him, even though, prior to my visit, they had bought his Rubāiyāt and spent time studying it.

Nor, for such aspirant readers, will a verbatim prose translation be sufficient, as becomes painfully clear when one examines the translation by the poet John Heath-Stubbs[2] and the late Professor Peter Avery of Cambridge University. The thoughts and sentiments in Khayyām are not by themselves new, but as old as our oldest forebears. They need the theatricality of metre, the humour of rhyme and the fun of playing with words to bring them to life once more. For example, Avery and Heath-Stubbs offer the following for one of the most-loved stanzas of the Rubā iyāt:

> The cycle which includes our coming and going
> Has no discernible beginning nor end;
> Nobody has got this matter straight –
> Where we come from and where we go to.[3]

Compare their offering with the original Persian, where Khayyām resorts to the tricks of poetry and the use of only majestic – though simple – words to grab us by the scruff of the neck and take us where he wants us:

> In dāyerh-ī kāmadan-o raftané māst
> Ānrā na bedāyat, na nahāyat peidāst.
> Kas mī nazanad dami darin ma'nī rāst:
> Kin āmadan az kojā-vo raftan be kojāst?

Is it not better at least to attempt an imitation, as I have:

> This Circle in which we ebb and we flow
> Neither beginning, nor an end does know.
> The Riddle stands as posed long ago:
> Where do we come from? Where do we go?

A prose translation would have turned one of the greatest wits in world literature into a 'club bore', a pub philosopher who drones on with the most mundane statements all evening and puts to flight anyone who might have been kind enough to lend him an ear.[4]

I have not succeeded always in following the exact wording of the quatrains. Clearly this was impossible if I wanted to maintain even a semblance of rhyme and rhythm. As a result, sometimes literal accuracy suffered. But I thought that literality was much less important than the message and the 'feel' of each quatrain. Khayyām would have approved. To abide by the strict rules that govern the writing of quatrains in Persian, where at least three of the four lines (1, 2 and 4) must rhyme, he sometimes uses a throwaway phrase only to provide a suitably rhyming word or fill a void. None of the phrases I have left out are central to the theme or thrust of the stanzas concerned. No 'punch line' has been changed.

In one or two cases, I have substituted the names of some pre-Islamic heroes for others because the originals were of the wrong length or emphasis. But Khayyām would not have minded. He cherished equally all reminders of classical Greece and Rome, as well as Iran, which, for him, died in the Muslim invasion of the seventh century. Invoking the names of any of those heroes would have pleased him.

Still, many weaknesses remain and it is necessary to emphasise that I was never trying to write literature in a language in which I was not raised. I rely, instead, on the good sense of my readers not to allow technicalities to come between them and Khayyām. Perhaps, in time, some of them will write in with their ideas, so that, together, we might improve the translation for possible future editions.

Lastly, by chance, I seem to have come upon an important discovery while engaged in the task of rendering Khayyām's poems into English. The Rubāiyāt in Persian are not presented in the order in which they were written. That has been lost for ever. In Iran, for centuries, they have been arranged alphabetically according to the last letters of the rhyming words of each stanza. This has been for easy reference. But I thought that I would arrange them in order of youthfulness or age, depending on their internal evidence. Some were clearly written by a raw, light-hearted and arrogant young man. Others spoke of the travails of middle life, while yet others spoke of the onset of old age or were fare-thee-wells and last testaments.

Arranging the Rubāiyāt in this order, it suddenly occurred to me that Khayyām had left us a short autobiography after all. In the middle of the two extremes of youth and decrepitude, neatly fell some of the known events of his halcyon days, such as his scientific attainments and the turmoil caused by his conviction for blasphemy.

Arranged in this manner, the Rubāiyāt assume the course of a typical river as it forms in the foothills of a mountain and begins its descent towards the plains below. It starts as a small stream, falling noisily and impatiently over boulders. As it gathers more water, it deepens and broadens, and exudes dignity and a quiet confidence in itself. Farther on, in the autumn of its life on the floor of a great valley, it meanders and darkens, acquiring a sombre mood. Finally, it achieves grandeur in its estuary when it appears not to be moving at all. It merges into the sea and loses its separate identity, its 'self'.

1

What a handsome face, what beautiful hair!
My height a cypress, my skin so fair.*
And yet, my Maker, what purpose did He
Assign to my life when He painted me?

١

هر چند که روی وُ بوی زیباست مرا ،
چون لاله رخ وُ چو سرو بالاست مرا ،
معلوم نشد که در طربخانه ی خاک ،
نقاش ازل بهر چه آراست مرا .

2

Lovers and drinkers from Heaven banned?
What nonsense they speak! You must understand:
If God were to bar His best from His court,
Heaven would be as: the palm of my hand!

٢

گویند که دوزخی بُوَد عاشق وُ مست ،
قولیست خراب ، دل در آن نتوان بست ،
گر میخواره وُ عاشق به دوزخ باشند ،
فردا بینی بهشت همچون کفِ دست !

3

Since Venus and Mars trod the sky at night,
Than the juice of grapes naught has proved so right.
I ask my vintner, ask him often: Why?
Better than he sells, what hopes he to buy?

٣

تا زهره وُ مه در آسمان گشت پدید ،
بهتر ز مَی ناب کسی هیـــــچ ندید .
من در عجبم ز میفروشان ، کایشان ،
به زانکه فروشند ، چه خواهند خرید ؟

* He uses the word lāleh-rokh, lily-cheeked.

4

In Heaven, they say, lovers *can* entwine,
We shall be given honey, milk and wine.
I say: 'Cash is best, let credit be thine'.
My love! Fill my glass, put your lips to mine!

گویند بهشت وُحورِ وُ کوثر باشد ،
جوی می وُ شیر وُ شکّر باشد .
پرکن قدح باده وُ در دستم نه ،
نقدی ز هزار نِسیه خُوشتر باشد .

5

They say that people, after their demise,
In the same state will they from dead rise.
With lover and wine I pass each moment:
Thus might I wake up on Day of Judgement.

گویند هر آنکسان که با پرهیزند ،
ز آنسان که بمیرند ، هرآنسان خیزند .
ما با مَی وُ معشوق ازآنیم مدام ،
باشد که به حشرمان چنان برخیزند !

6

Drunk again, Khayyām? Doctor will be mad!
A maid in your arms? Love her, make her glad.
All will end in doom. No! Do not be sad:
We are still here. That cannot be bad!

خیام اگر ز باده مستی ، خوش باش !
با ماهرخی اگر نشستی ، خوش باش !
چوُن عاقبت کار جهان نیستـی است ،
انگار که نیستی ، چُو هستی ، خوش باش !

7

To drink, to laugh, is my religion.
Freedom from religion is my religion!
I asked Heaven about hers. She said:
Why, your irreligion is my religion!

مَی خوردن وُ شاد بودن آئین منست ،
فارغ بودن ز کفرُودین ، دین منست !
گفتم به عروس دهر: "کابین تو چیست" ؟
گفتا : که : "دل خرّم تو کابین منست"!

8

When my Creator my elements planned,
They say He meant me for the Promised Land.
Lover, lute and wine by a field of corn:
Give me those three now. Birds are best in hand!

من هیچ ندانم که مرا آنکه سرشت ،
از اهل بهشت کرد یا دوزخ زشت .
جامی وُ بتی وُ بربطی بر لب کشت :
این هر سه مرا نقد وُ ترا نسیه بهشت !

9

Some bread, some cheese and a jug of wine,
With you beside me beneath a lush vine!
I know a great king who would, if he could,
Barter his crown for that which is mine.[5]

گر دست دهد ز مغز گندم نانی ،
وز می دوُمنی ، ز گوسفندی رانی ،
با لاله رخی به گوشه ی بستانی ،
عیشی بوُوَد آن نه حدّ هر سلطانی .

10

Each tiny atom, of earth, air and sea,
Once moved another to write poetry.
This speck of dust on your hair was once
As loved by someone as you are by me![6]

هر ذرّه که بر روی زمینی بوده است ،
خورشید رخی ، زهره جبینی بوده است .
گرد از رخ نازنین به آذرم فشان ،
کان هم رخ وُ زلف نازنینی بوده است .

11

This jug was, like me, a lover distraught,
His heart was by one cruel beauty caught.
This handle you see around its neck bent,
Round that beauty's neck many a night it went.

این کوزه چومن عاشق زاری بوده است .
در بند سر زلف نگاری بوده است .
این دسته که بر گردن او میبینی ،
دستی است که بر گردن یاری بوده است .

12

Girl of the light foot, rise up to the day:
Bring out the harp, a dance tune play.
It hates happiness, this Relentless Wheel,
This old parade of Dey† succeeding Dey.

هنگام صبوح ای صنم فرّخ پی :
برسـاز ترانه ، پیـش آور می ؛
کافکند به خاک سد هزاران جم وُ کی ،
این آمدن تیر مـــه وُ رفتـن دی .

13

The stars ruling far-flung skies,
Have come to belong to the haughty Wise.
My son, listen well to this, my finding:
The Wise themselves know they philosophise.

اجرام که ساکنان این ایوانند ،
اسبـاب تردد خرد منـــدانند .
هان تا سررشته خرد گم نکنی :
کانان که مدبّرند ، سرگردانند .

14

One bull in the sky: they called it Taurus.
One bull below Earth: aloft it bore us.‡
Open your eyes now: you will see with ease,
Between the two bulls: a herd of donkeys.

گاویست در آسمان ، قرین پروین ؛
یک گاو دگر نهفته در زیر زمین .
چشم خردت باز کن از راه یقین :
زیر وُ زبر دوگاو ، مشتی خر بین !

15

Alas the story of my youth is told,
Alas bold spring into autumn grew.
The songbird they called my carefree youth,
Unloved it arrived, in haste it flew.

افسوس که نامه ی جوانی طی شد ؛
آن تازه بهار زندگانـــــی دی شد .
آن مرغ طرب که نام او بود شباب ،
افسوس ندانم که کی آمد ، کی شد .

16

This Sea of Being has come out of naught;
No glimpse of its truth has anyone caught.
Many a clown has put forth his thought:
From the Other Side, news cannot be sought.

این بحر وجود آمده بیرون ز نهفت ،
کس نیست که این گوهر تحقیق بسفت .
هرکس سخنی از سر سودا گفته است ،
زان روی که هست ، کس نمیداند گفت .

---

† 'Dey' is the mid-winter month of the Zoroastrian calendar. Here it stands for the annual cycle.

‡ This refers to the ancient legend that our world was held up on the horns of a supernatural bull.

17

Truth remains hidden, doubt remains strong,
I cannot endure hoping I am wrong.
Oh, give me that glass, dull my reason make:
A fool is a fool, drunk or awake.

17

چون نیست حقیقت وُ یقین اندردست ،
نتوان بامید شک همه عمر نشسـت .
هان ! تا ننهیم جام مَی از کف دست :
در بیخبری ، مرد چه هشیار وُ چه مست

18

An awesome secret grows in my heart.
One day, it will pull humankind apart.
Grains of sand in shells in hiding become
Perfect pearls to which mighty kings succumb.§

18

هر راز که اندر دل دانا باشد ،
باید که نهفته تر ز عنقا باشد .
کاندر صدف از نهفتگی گردد دُرّ ،
آن قطره که راز دل دریا باشد .

19

Shouted at a whore a raucous mullah:
'Drunkard, faithless, a menace you are.'
She replied: 'My lord, I am all you say,
But are you truly all you say you are?'

19

شیخی به زن فاحشه گفتا "مستی !
هر لحظه به دام دگری بنشستی" .
گفتا : "شیخا! هر آنچه گویی هستم ،
آیا تو هر آنچه گویـی ، هستی ؟

20

Lost to the wine of the Magus? I am!
Pagan? Zarathustrian? Haereticus? I am!
Every nation holds its notion of me.
I am my own man, whatever I am.

20

گر من ز مَی مغانه مستم ، هستم !
ور کافر وُ گبر وُ بت پرستم ، هستم !
هر طایفه ای بمن گمانی دارد ،
من ز آن خودم ، هرآنچه هستم ، هستم .

21

Mighty Lord, when He the world did ordain,
Why did He often from ideal abstain?
Who can be at fault if the tower leans?
If it does not lean, why start again?

21

دارنده چو ترکیب طبایع آراست ،
باز از چه سبب فکندش اندر کم وُ کاست ؟
گر خوب نیا مد این بنا ، عیب کراست ؟
ور خوب آمد ، خرابی از بهر چراست ؟

22

If I had Mazda's** omnipotent hand,
I would destroy each and every land.
A whole new world would I then start
In which not a soul†† nursed a broken heart.

22

گر بر فلکم دست بُدی ، چون یزدان ،
برداشتمی من از این فلک را زمیان .
وز نوُ فلکی دگر چنان ساختمی ،
کازاده به کام خود رسیدی ، آسان .

§ It seems safe to assume that what he thought he had discovered would be regarded as blasphemous. If so, was it because his extensive study of the movements of the planets had convinced him that the earth was not the centre of the universe, but moved round the sun?

** One of the titles of God in Zoroastrianism. The others are Izad and Yazdān.

23

Countless tufts of grass line every stream.
Shimmering, slight, unworthy they seem.
Do not trample them, for they are, to me,
Ghosts of past lovers once more here to dream.

هر سبزه که بر کنار جویی رُسته است ،
گویی ز لب فرشته خویی رُسته است .
پا بر سر سبزه تا به خواری ننهی !
کان سبزه ز خاک لاله رویی رُسته است .

24

As none ever told what the future brought,
What purpose is there in being fraught?
Let us drink, instead, to this Moon again,
For oft shall she look here for us in vain.

چون عهده نمیشَوَد کسی فردا را ،
حالی خوش کن این دل شیدا را .
مَی نوش به ماهتاب ، ای ماه ، که ماه ،
بسیـــــــار بتابد وُ نیابد مارا !

25

Choose a bowl of wine over the land of Tūs,
The mace of Caesar, the ring of Kāvūs.
The roar of a drunk at dawn in the street,
Thrashes the Peace of the Holy Cheat.

یک جرعه ی مَی ز مُلک کاووس به است ؛
از تخت قباد وُ مُلکـت توس به است .
هر ناله که رندی به سحرگـــاه زند ،
از طاعت زاهدان سالـــوس به است !

26

Lord of the *fatwa*, what a rogue you are!
Drinker I may be, I prefer by far:
From the juice of grapes to secure a thrill
Than to cheat orphans of their father's will.8 7

ای صاحب فتوا ، ز تو پُرکار تریم ؛
با اینهمه مستی ، ز تو هشیار تریم .
تو خون کسان خوری وُ ما خون رَزان !
انصـاف بده : کــــدام خونخوار تریم !

27

It is best today few friends to seek.
It is best with folks from afar to speak.
The one for hard times to lean on I chose:
When I needed her, she‡‡ sang with my foes.

آن به که درین زمانه کم گیری دوست ؛
با اهل زمانه صحبت از دور نکوست .
آن کس که به زندگی ترا تکیه براوست ،
چشم خود ار باز کنی ، دشمنـت اوست .

28

Goodbye! For to live in this blighted land,
Other than grief, would leave naught in hand.
But only let those rejoice on my grave,
Who could their own necks from the hangman save.

رفتم که درین منزل بیداد بُدن ،
در دست نخواهد بجز از باد بُدن .
آن را باید به مرگ من شاد شدن ،
کز دست اجل تواند آزاد شدن .

†† He uses the word Āzādeh or freethinker, but if pushed, he would have probably extended it to the whole of mankind.

‡‡ The Persian language has only one word, 'ū', for third person singular. I have used 'she' here because I believe the person of whose 'betrayal' Khayyām complains in several places, was the queen Terken Khātūn. See 'Chapter 9: The Queen Turns'.

29

Whoever in life has a loaf of bread,
With a modest roof up above his head,
Master to no one, nor a chief to dread:
Tell him envy none, when he goes to bed.

٢٩

در دهر هرآنکه نیم نانی دارد ،
از بهر نشست ، آشیانی دارد ،
نه خادم کس بُوَد ، نه مخدوم کسی :
گو شاد بزی ، که خوش جهانی دارد !

30

A loaf of bread every other day?
A sip of water from a jug of clay?
Better than servant to a peer be,
Let alone subject to a lesser stay.

٣٠

یک نان به دو روز اگر باید مَرد ،
از کوزه شکسته ای دمی آبی سرد ،
مامور کم از خودی چرا باید بود ؟
یا خدمت چون خودی چرا باید کرد ؟

31

This world, this ancient caravanserai,
This old resting place of the low and high,
How for fair Shirīn does it still grieve,
How for brave Farhād does it still sigh!§§

٣١

این کهنه رباط را که عالم نام است ،
وآرامگه ابلق صبح وُ شام است ،
بزمیست که وامانده ی صد جمشید است ،
قصریست که بازیچه ی صد بهرام است .

32

Tyranny triumphs. Your heart is in pain.
Time is on the wing. Seek the wise and sane.
You are no more than a whiff of powder,
A spark, a breeze and a drop of rain.***

٣٢

ترکیب طبایع چو بکام تو دمی است ،
روُ شاد بزی ، اگر چه بر تو ستمی است .
با اهل خرد باش که اصل من وُ تو ،
گردی وُ شراری وُ نسیمی وُ دمی است .

33

To a potter's shop did I go last night,
To my eyes his art made a soothing sight.
Suddenly murmured a tall jug of clay:
'May to December, December to May!'

٣٣

در کارگه کوزه گری رفتم ، دوش .
دیدم دوهزار کوزه ، گویا وُ خموش .
ناگاه یکی کوزه برآورد خروش :
"کو کوزه گرُو کوزه خرُو کوزه فروش" ؟

§§ These are two of the most celebrated lovers in Firdowsi's *Book of the Kings*. Shirīn was the Armenian queen of the Sasanian emperor Khusraw Parvīz when Farhād, a young nobleman, fell in love with her. The emperor set the bold young man an impossible task, to carve a road through the mountain of Bistūn or Behistun, but when Farhad had nearly accomplished his work, messengers were sent to tell him that Shirīn had died. He killed himself by throwing his pickaxe in the sky and standing underneath it.
*** This is an allusion to the four 'elements' of earth, air, fire and water that in classical times were thought to make up the world.

34

A vulture I saw on the wall of Tūs,
In its talons held the head of Kāvūs.†††
Cried it to the skull: 'Tell me, oh, great king,
Where are your trumpets, where your thumping Kūs.'‡‡‡

مرغی دیدم نشسته بر باره ی توس ،
در پیش نهاده کله ی کیکاووس .
با کله همی گفت که افسوس ، افسوس !
کو بانک جرسها وُ کجا ناله ی کوس ؟

35

Mighty God excels in thousands of arts.
Yet He everyday breaks numberless hearts.
Young innocent breasts, fresh cheeks of rose,
He afflicts with pain and into mud throws.

آنکس که زمین وُ چرخ وُ افلاک نهاد ،
بس داغ که او بر دل غمناک نهاد .
بسیار لب چو لعل وُ زلفین چو مُشک ،
در طبل زمین وُ حقه ی خاک نهاد .

36

Today I will shed my robe of restraint:
Let trails of red wine my white beard taint.
No more piety: I am seventy.
If not dance now, when might it then be?

من دامن زهد وُ توبه طی خواهم کرد ،
با موی سپید ، قصد مَی خواهم کرد .
پیمانه ی عمر من به هفتاد رسید ،
این دم نکنم نشاط ، کی خواهم کرد ؟

37

Never of teachers did I go deprived;
And more theorems I myself contrived.
Seventy-two years, day and night, I thought:
Only to conclude that I knew naught!

هرگز دل من ز "علــم" محروم نشد ؛
کم ماند زاســرار که "مفهــوم" نشد .
هفتاد وُدوسال فکرکردم ، شب وُ روز ؛
معلومم شد که هیــــــچ معلوم نشد !

38

My coming did not profit this Wheel,
Nor will my going its glory seal.
Neither any man did to me reveal
What ills the cries of little orphans heal.

از آمدنــم نبــــود گــردون را سود ؛
وز رفتن من ، جاه وُ جلالشَ نفزود .
وز هیچ کسی نیز دو گوشم نشنــود :
کاین آمدن وُرفتن من بهر چه بــود .

39

A vase of China, exuding charm,
Even drunkards do not wish to harm.
Yet these lovely heads, these delicate hands,
Who could hate them so? No one understands.⁹

ترکیــب پیاله ای که درهم پیوست ،
بشکستن آن روا نمیدارد مســت .
چندیــن سرویای نازنین وُ برودست ،
از مهرکه پیوست وُبه کین که شکست ؟

††† Tūs was the nearest city to the east of Nishāpur and Kāvūs is a mythological king of ancient Iran in the *Book of the Kings*.
‡‡‡ A war drum.

40

On the Great Riddle no light has been shed.
That coded script has never been read.
On a stage we sit, you and I, a while.
Then the curtain falls and the World is dead.

اسرار جهان را نه تو دانـــی وُ نه من .
این خط مقرمط نه توخوانـی وُ نه من .
هست از پس پرده گفتگوی من وُ تو :
چون پرده برافتد ، نه تومانی وُ نه من .

41

What a perfect day, neither hot nor cold,
The yellow roses paint the garden gold,
And a nightingale sings in the Old Word:
'Oh, come ye, make haste, wine must ye khword.'§§§

روزیست خوش وُهوا نه گرمست وُ نه سرد .
ابر از رخ گلزار همی شوید گرد .
بلبل به زبان پـــهــــلــوی با گل زرد ،
فریــــاد کند که مَـــــــــی باید خوَرد !§§§

42

This garden, this park, these broad skies,
Hillocks, waterfalls, meadows, butterflies.
Do send for my friends, those tingling wits
Who lighten my heart, who brighten my eyes.

چندانکه نگـــاه میکنم هر سویی ،
در باغ روانست ز کوثر جـویی .
صحرا چو بهشت است ، زکوثر کم گوی !
بنـشیـــن به بهشــت ، با بهشتی رویی !

43

Agreeable friends, where did they all go?
At the feet of Time, all of them fell low.
For a while we feigned brave defiance.
None triumphs over this Vale of Sorrow.

یاران موافق همـــه از دست شدند :
در پای اجل یکان یکان پست شدند .
خوردیم زیک شراب در مجلس عمر :
دوری دوسـه پیشـــتر مسـت شـدند !

44

At the vintner's house an old man, alone,
Sat in a corner, forlorn on his own.
Murmured he, at last, why departed friends
Did not send word to make their fates known?

پیری دیدم به خانه ی خمّـــاری :
گفتم "نکنی ز رفتگان اخباری" !
گفتا "مَی خور که همچو ما بسیاری
رفتند وُ خبر باز نیـــامد ، باری" !

45

Those who conquered all science and letters,
And shone as beacons among their betters,
Did not find the thread of this Tangled Heap,
Only told a tale, then they fell asleep.

آنان که محیط فضل وُ آداب شدند ،
در جمع کمال شمع اصحاب شدند ،
ره زین شب تاریک نبردند بُرون :
گفتند فسانه ایّ وُ در خواب شدند !

§§§ I have translated the 'Pahlavi' or 'Middle Persian' of the Sasanian state into 'the Old Word' here and 'khwārden' is the root for drinking and eating in that language, as it is also in modern Persian and Kurdish.

46

Wise old man, rise up early in the day,
Watch over that youth as he kneads the clay.
Advise him to treat with respect, please,
The hand of Caesar, the eye of Parvīz.

46

ای پیر خردمند ، پگه تر بر خیز ،
وان کودک خاکبیز را بنگـر تیز .
پندش ده وُ گو : "نرم نرمک میبیز
مغز سر کیقباد وُ چشم پـرویـز" !

47

Sober, I cannot face the dawn, alas:
I cannot pull forth this tired carcass.
I live for that breath when the maid offers:
One more cup to me, but it has to pass.

47

من بی مَی ناب ، زیستن نتوانم .
بی باده کشـیـد بـار تن نتوانم .
من بنده ی آن دمم که سـاقی گوید :
"یک جام دگر بگیر" وُ من نتوانم .

48

This Circle in which we ebb and we flow,
Neither beginning, nor an end does know.
The Riddle stands as posed long ago:
Where do we come from? Where do we go?****

48

این دایره ای کامـدن وُ رفتن ماست :
آنرا نه بدایت ، نه نهـایت پیـداست .
کس میـنـزند درین عـالـم ، راسـت :
کاین آمدن ازکجا وُ رفتن به کجاست .

49

Loved Ones! My ashes, disperse wide and far,
My many failings, count at the bazaar.
Or else, from my clay fashion a brick,
To make a stopper for the vintner's jar.

49

چون مرده شوم ، خاک مرا گم سارید ،
احوال مرا عبرت مردم سازیـد .
خاک تن من به باده آ غشته کید ،
وز کالبدم ، خشـت سـر خم سازید !

50

And when you gather at the old tavern,
Each others' latest trivia to learn,
Choose the best of wines, drink to absent friends,
Leave a glass empty, when it is my turn.10

50

یاران ! بموافقت چو دیـدار کنیـد ،
باید که زدوست ، یاد بسیـار کنیـد !
چون باده ی خوشگوار بنوشید بهم ،
نوبت چو بما رسد ، نگونسار کنید !

**** In the Persian original, one feels that by 'we' Khayyām means more than we human beings, but the whole of the universe, as if oblivion ought to be the rule, a total utter oblivion in which even the rule of oblivion itself could exist. The apparent necessity of a 'First Cause Without A Cause' must have been as paradoxical to his logician's mind as it is to many of us today.

The FitzGerald Rubáiyát*

I

Awake! for Morning in the Bowl of Night
Has flung the Stone that puts the Stars to Flight:
    And Lo! the Hunter of the East has caught
The Sultán's Turret in a Noose of Light.

II

Dreaming when Dawn's Left Hand was in the Sky
I heard a Voice within the Tavern cry,
    'Awake, my Little ones, and fill the Cup
Before Life's Liquor in its Cup be dry.'

III

And, as the Cock crew, those who stood before
The Tavern shouted – 'Open then the Door!
    You know how little while we have to stay,
And, once departed, may return no more.'

IV

Now the New Year reviving old Desires,
The thoughtful Soul to Solitude retires
    Where the White Hand of Moses on the Bough
Puts out, and Jesus from the Ground suspires.

*   The First Edition of 1859, which remains the preferred edition of most readers. FitzGerald published three more revisions and another, the Fifth, was brought out posthumously.

V

Iram indeed is gone with all its Rose,
And Jamshīd's Sev'n-ring'd Cup where no one knows:
    But still the Vine her ancient Ruby yields,
And still a Garden by the Water blows.

VI

And David's Lips are lock't; but in divine
High piping Péhlevi, with 'Wine! Wine! Wine!
    Red Wine!' – the Nightingale cries to the Rose
That yellow Cheek of hers to incarnadine.

VII

Come, fill the Cup, and in the Fire of Spring
The Winter Garment of Repentance fling:
    The Bird of Time has but a little way
To fly – and Lo! the Bird is on the Wing.

VIII

And look – a thousand Blossoms with the Day
Woke – and a thousand scatter'd into Clay:
    And this first Summer Month that brings the Rose
Shall take Jamshīd and Kaikobád away.

IX

But come with old Khayyám, and leave the Lot
Of Kaikobád and Kaikhosrú forgot:
    Let Rustum lay about him as he will,
Or Hátim Tai cry Supper – heed them not.

X

With me along some Strip of Herbage strown
That just divides the desert from the sown,
    Where name of Slave and Sultán scarce is known,
And pity Sultán Máhmud on his Throne.

XI

Here with a Loaf of Bread beneath the Bough,
A Flask of Wine, a Book of Verse – and Thou
    Beside me singing in the Wilderness –
And Wilderness is Paradise enow.

XII

'How sweet is mortal Sovranty!' – think some:
Others – 'How blest the Paradise to come!'
    Ah, take the Cash in hand and waive the Rest;
Oh, the brave Music of a *distant* Drum!

XIII

Look to the Rose that blows about us – 'Lo,
Laughing,' she says, 'into the World I blow;
    At once the silken Tassel of my Purse
Tear, and its Treasure on the Garden throw.'

XIV

The Worldly Hope men set their Hearts upon
Turns Ashes – or it prospers; and anon,
    Like Snow upon the Desert's dusty Face
Lighting a little Hour or two – is gone.

XV

And those who husbanded the Golden Grain,
And those who flung it to the Winds like Rain,
    Alike to no such aureate Earth are turn'd
As, buried once, Men want dug up again.

XVI

Think, in this batter'd Caravanserai
Whose Doorways are alternate Night and Day,
    How Sultán after Sultán with his Pomp
Abode his Hour or two, and went his way.

XVII

They say the Lion and the Lizard keep
The Courts where Jamshíd gloried and drank deep:
    And Bahrám, that great Hunter – the Wild Ass
Stamps o'er his Head, and he lies fast asleep.

XIII

I sometimes think that never blows so red
The Rose as where some buried Caesar bled;
    That every Hyacinth the Garden wears
Dropt in its Lap from some once lovely Head.

XIX

And this delightful Herb whose tender Green
Fledges the River's Lip on which we lean –
    Ah, lean upon it lightly! for who knows
From what once lovely Lip it springs unseen!

XX

Ah! my Belovéd, fill the Cup that clears
To-Day of past Regrets and future Fears –
    To-morrow? – Why, To-morrow I may be
Myself with Yesterday's Sev'n Thousand Years.

XXI

Lo! some we loved, the loveliest and the best
That Time and Fate of all their Vintage prest,
    Have drunk their Cup a Round or two before,
And one by one crept silently to Rest.

XXII

And we, that now make merry in the Room
They left, and Summer dresses in new Bloom,
    Ourselves must we beneath the Couch of Earth
Descend, ourselves to make a Couch – for whom?

XXIII

Ah, make the most of what we yet may spend,
Before we too into the Dust Descend;
    Dust into Dust, and under Dust, to lie,
Sans Wine, sans Song, sans Singer and – sans End!

XXIV

Alike for those who for To-Day prepare,
And those that after a To-morrow stare,
    A Muezzin from the Tower of Darkness cries
'Fools! your Reward is neither Here nor There!'

XXV

Why, all the Saints and Sages who discuss'd
Of the Two Worlds so learnedly, are thrust
    Like foolish Prophets forth; their Words to Scorn
Are scatter'd, and their Mouths are stopt with Dust.

XXVI

Oh, come with old Khayyám, and leave the Wise
To talk; one thing is certain, that Life flies;
    One thing is certain, and the Rest is Lies;
The Flower that once has blown for ever dies.

XXVII

Myself when young did eagerly frequent
Doctor and Saint, and heard great Argument
    About it and about; but evermore
Came out by the same Door as in I went.

XXVIII

With them the Seed of Wisdom did I sow,
And with my own hand labour'd it to grow;
    And this was all the Harvest that I reap'd –
'I came like Water, and like Wind I go.'

XXIX

Into this Universe, and why not knowing,
Nor *whence*, like Water willy-nilly flowing;
    And out of it, as Wind along the Waste,
I know not *whither*, willy-nilly blowing.

XXX

What, without asking, hither hurried *whence?*
And, without asking, *whither* hurried hence!
    Another and another Cup to drown
The Memory of this Impertinence!

XXXI

Up from Earth's Centre through the Seventh Gate
I rose, and on the Throne of Saturn sate,
    And many Knots unravel'd by the Road;
But not the Knot of Human Death and Fate.

XXXII

There was a Door to which I found no Key:
There was a Veil past which I could not see;
    Some little Talk awhile of Me and Thee
There seemed – and then no more of Thee and Me.

XXXIII

Then to the rolling Heav'n itself I cried,
Asking, 'What Lamp had Destiny to guide
　　Her little Children stumbling in the Dark?'
And – 'A blind understanding!' Heav'n replied.

XXXIV

Then to this earthen Bowl did I adjourn
My Lip the secret Well of Life to learn:
　　And Lip to Lip it murmur'd – ' While you live,
Drink! – for once dead you never shall return.'

XXXV

I think the Vessel, that with fugitive
Articulation answer'd, once did live,
　　And merry-make; and the cold Lip I kiss'd
How many Kisses might it take – and give!

XXXVI

For in the Market-place, one Dusk of Day,
I watch'd the Potter thumping his wet Clay:
　　And with its all obliterated Tongue
It murmur'd – 'Gently, Brother, gently, pray!'

XXXVII

Ah, fill the Cup: – what boots it to repeat
How Time is slipping underneath our Feet:
　　Unborn To-morrow and dead Yesterday,
Why fret about them if To-day be sweet!

XXXVIII

One Moment in Annihilation's Waste,
One moment, of the Well of Life to taste –
　　The Stars are setting, and the Caravan
Starts for the dawn of Nothing – Oh, make haste!

XXXIX

How long, how long, in infinite Pursuit
Of This and That endeavour and dispute?
　　Better be merry with the fruitful Grape
Than sadden after none, or bitter, Fruit.

XL

You know, my Friends, how long since in my House
For a new Marriage I did make Carouse:
    Divorced old barren Reason from my Bed,
And took the Daughter of the Vine to Spouse.

XLI

For 'Is' and 'Is-not' though *with* Rule and Line,
And, 'Up-and-down' *without*, I could define,
    I yet in all I only cared to know,
Was never deep in anything but – Wine.

XLII

And lately, by the Tavern Door agape,
Came stealing through the Dusk an Angel Shape,
    Bearing a Vessel on his Shoulder; and
He bid me taste of it; and 'twas – the Grape!

XLIII

The Grape that can with Logic absolute
The Two-and-Seventy jarring Sects confute:
    The subtle Alchemists that in a Trice
Life's leaden Metal into Gold transmute.

XLIV

The mighty Mahmúd, the Victorious Lord,
That all the misbelieving and black Horde
    Of Fears and Sorrows that infest the Soul
Scatters and slays with his enchanted Sword.

XLV

But leave the Wise to wrangle, and with me
The Quarrel of the Universe let be:
    And, in some corner of the Hubbub coucht,
Make Game of that which makes as much of Thee.

XLVI

For in and out, above, about, below,
'Tis nothing but a Magic Shadow-show,
    Play'd in a Box whose Candle is the Sun,
Round which we Phantom Figures come and go.

XLVII

And if the Wine you drink, the Lip you press,
End in the Nothing all Things end in – Yes –
    Then fancy while Thou art, Thou art but what
Thou shalt be – Nothing – Thou shalt not be less.

XLVIII

While the Rose blows along the River Brink,
With old Khayyám the Ruby Vintage drink:
    And when the Angel with his darker Draught
Draws up to thee – take that, and do not shrink.

XLIX

'Tis all a Chequer-board of Nights and Days
Where Destiny with Men for Pieces plays;
    Hither and thither moves, and mates, and slays,
And one by one back in the Closet lays.

L

The Ball no Question makes of Ayes and Nos,
But Right or Left as strikes the Player goes;
    And He that toss'd Thee down into the Field,
He knows about it all – He knows – HE knows!

LI

The Moving Finger writes; and, having writ,
Moves on: nor all thy Piety nor Wit
    Shall lure it back to cancel half a Line,
Nor all thy Tears wash out a Word of it.

LII

And that inverted Bowl we call The Sky,
Whereunder crawling coop't we live and die,
    Lift not thy hands to *It* for help – for It
Rolls impotently on as Thou or I.

LIII

With Earth's first Clay They did the Last Man's knead,
And then of the Last Harvest sow'd the Seed:
    Yea, the first Morning of Creation wrote
What the Last Dawn of Reckoning shall read.

LIV

I tell Thee this – When, starting from the Goal,
Over the shoulders of the flaming Foal
    Of Heav'n, Parwin and Mushtari they flung,
In my predestin'd Plot of Dust and Soul.

LV

The Vine had struck a Fibre; which about
It clings my Being – let the Súfi flout;
    Of my Base Metal may be filed a Key,
That shall unlock the Door he howls without.

LVI

And this I know: whether the one True Light,
Kindle to Love, or Wrath consume me quite,
    One Glimpse of It within the Tavern caught
Better than in the Temple lost outright.

LVII

Oh Thou, who did'st with Pitfall and with Gin
Beset the Road I was to wander in;
    Thou wilt not with Predestination round
Enmesh me, and impute my Fall to Sin?

LVIII

Oh, Thou, who Man of baser Earth did'st make,
And who with Eden did'st devise the Snake;
    For all the Sin wherewith the Face of Man
Is blacken'd, Man's Forgiveness give – and take!

*   *   *   *   *   *   *

KÚZA NÁMA†

LIX

Listen again. One Evening at the Close
Of Ramazán, ere the better Moon arose,
    In that old Potter's Shop I stood alone
With the clay Population round in Rows.

†   'Book of the Jug'.

LX

And strange to tell, among that Earthen Lot
Some could articulate, while others not:
    And suddenly one more impatient cried –
'Who is the Potter, pray, and who the Pot?'

LXI

Then said another – 'Surely not in vain
My substance from the common Earth was ta'en,
    That He who subtly wrought me into Shape
Should stamp me back to common Earth again.'

LXII

Another said – 'Why, ne'er a peevish Boy
Would break the Bowl from which he drank in Joy;
    Shall He that made the Vessel in pure Love
And Fancy, in an after Rage destroy?'

LXIII

None answer'd this; but after Silence spake
A Vessel of a more ungainly Make:
    'They sneer at me for leaning all awry;
What! did the Hand then of the Potter shake?'

LXIV

Said one – 'Folks of a surly Tapster tell,
And daub his Visage with the Smoke of Hell;
    They talk of some strict Testing of us—Pish!
He's a Good Fellow, and 'twill all be well.'

LXV

Then said another with a long-drawn Sigh,
My Clay with long oblivion is gone dry:
    But, fill me with the old familiar Juice,
Methinks I might recover bye and bye.'

LXVI

So, while the Vessels one by one were speaking,
One spied the little Crescent all were seeking,
    And then they jogg'd each other, 'Brother! Brother!
Hark to the Porter's Shoulder-knot a-creaking!'

*   *   *   *   *   *   *

LXVII

Ah, with the Grape my fading Life provide,
And wash my Body whence the life has died,
    And in a Winding-sheet of Vine-leaf wrapt,
So bury me by some sweet Garden-side.

LXVIII

That ev'n my buried Ashes such a Snare
Of Perfume shall fling up into the Air,
    As not a True Believer passing by
But shall be overtaken unaware.

LXIX

Indeed, the Idols I have loved so long
Have done my Credit in Men's Eye much wrong!
    Have drown'd my Honour in a shallow Cup,
And sold my Reputation for a Song.

LXX

Indeed, indeed, Repentance oft before
I swore – but was I sober when I swore?
    And then and then came Spring, and Rose-in-hand
My thread-bare Penitence apieces tore.

LXXI

And much as Wine has play'd the Infidel,
And robb'd me of my Robe of Honour – well,
    I often wonder what the Vintners buy
One half so precious as the Goods they sell.

LXXII

Alas, that Spring should vanish with the Rose!
That Youth's sweet-scented Manuscript should close!
    The Nightingale that in the Branches sang,
Ah, whence, and whither flown again, who knows!

LXXIII

Ah, Love! could thou and I with Fate conspire
To grasp this sorry Scheme of Things entire,
    Would not we shatter it to bits—and then
Re-mould it nearer to the Heart's Desire?

LXXIV

Ah, Moon of my Delight who know'st no wane,
The Moon of Heav'n is rising once again:
    How oft hereafter rising shall she look
Through this same Garden after me – in vain!

LXXV

And when Thyself with shining Foot shall pass
Among the Guests Star-scatter'd on The Grass,
    And in Thy joyous Errand reach the Spot
Where I made one – turn down an empty Glass!

TAMÁM SHUD‡‡

‡   'Finished'!

APPENDIX III

Omar the Greek

Each tiny atom, of earth, air and sea,
Once moved another to write poetry.
This speck of dust on your hair was once
As loved by someone as you are by me!

'No man is an island' and Khayyām was, in his time, one of a long line of thinkers stretching into prehistory. In particular, as cited in the accusations of heresy levelled against him, he was a product of that amazing outburst of curiosity, observation, reasoning and disputation that had characterised Greece fifteen centuries earlier. He was therefore, in a sense, an alien living among Muslims, but a theist or deist, rather than an outright atheist.

As with many of us to this day, his inner self, a combination of instinct and upbringing, demanded that every phenomenon in existence have a prior cause. But that immediately confronted him, as it does us, with a logical paradox: If all things needed a cause, what was behind the first cause? That, in turn, gave rise to a seemingly absurd deduction, that the world could have neither a beginning, nor an end:

This Circle in which we ebb and we flow,
Neither beginning, nor an end does know.
The Riddle stands as posed long ago:
Where do we come from? Where do we go?

It was convenient, for lack of a better word, to call the seemingly insoluble mystery at the heart of the universe 'God', as do some modern scientists. But his reasoning robbed him of the greatest benefit of religion: an omnipotent and everlasting father on a throne in the sky who knew and cared for each and every one of us. The logician's 'God' was merely a force of nature: as far removed as possible from the jealous, tribal Eloah or Allah of the Judaic religions, a grander version of the grumpy, illogical grandfather most of us remember from our childhoods, or even the more diffuse Mazdā of Omar's own Zoroastrian forebears. To Omar, there was no longer any 'He' in the heavens and there was no special place for man in the firmament. The only consolation was that the great universe around us, which might or might not have burst into being out of nothingness, was frighteningly awesome, almost deserving of our worship:

> This Sea of Being has come out of naught,
> No glimpse of its truth has anyone caught.
> Many a clown has put forth his thought,
> From the Other Side news cannot be sought.

Khayyām advocated that society be run along ancient Athenian lines, rather than through the observance of 'revealed' laws. But the ancient Greeks were a diverse herd, a crowd of argumentative men. Which were to be favoured over others? Khayyām's quatrains and his other writings indicate firmly that he belonged to the Atomist school, as championed by the pre-Socratic philosophers Leucippus and Democritus. His notion of the 'good life', which requires avoiding luxuries, shunning political power and cultivating personal friendships, is clearly inspired by Epicurus. Ironically, Epicurus later gained a notorious reputation for hedonism and excess – in direct contrast to the principles he actually espoused. Some commentators have been tempted to compare Khayyām to Lucretius, the tempestuous Roman poet who idolised Epicurus and whose poem *De Rerum Natura* Khayyam is said to have translated (see p. 316). A glance back at these illustrious names might help us tentatively to conclude which influences shaped Khayyām's ideas.

'I came to Athens and no-one knew me', Democritus complained in about 448 BC, when he arrived in that city to be a student. He must have either had a strong sense of his personal gifts – prodigies often have them – or else have come from a family of noblemen in his native town of Abdera in the north-east. Today, he would be surprised at the clamour that his arrival would cause. As he approached the Greek capital, he would have been greeted by the scientists of the Democritus Nuclear Research Centre waiting to welcome him in ceremony.

Democritus of Abdera (460–370 BC) was the most prominent of the atomist philosophers, though he had himself come across that theory at the feet of Leucippus of Miletus as a schoolchild. Democritus was about ten years younger than Socrates but belonged to the older, more brilliant Miletine school of thought from Asia Minor. While Democritus believed that all gods and divinities had been invented by men unable to explain natural phenomena, Socrates firmly believed in their existence, saying that the traditional gods of the Greeks were immortal though flawed human beings, while a greater, central divine force had created the world. Furthermore, while Democritus apparently did not oppose the return of democracy to Athens, Socrates criticised it vehemently and eventually lost his life because of this. One more difference between the two men was that Democritus travelled widely in the world. He travelled to Persia, apparently via Babylon, and he also visited Egypt, making him a truly-rounded man. He is known to have written many books on mathematics, although they have been lost.

More to the point, Democritus taught that the world had been caused by the interaction of motion with atoms, the infinitesimally small units of matter that could not be subdivided further. He believed that atoms moved constantly in empty space and collided with one another to form larger bodies. They differed only in shape and size.

Of course, Democritus was as guilty of leaping into the dark without the slightest empirical evidence in constructing his system as was Aristotle, later, in attacking the theory. Nevertheless, it remains the stuff of wonder that he came so close, on so many points, to what scientists would discover to be the case two millennia later with unimaginably precise instruments and hugely advanced mathematics. Almost the only error he made was to say that atoms were indivisible. Had he managed to be a little more prescient, he would have been able to look at the sun and see that the destruction of atoms and their recombining together to form heavier atoms provided the very energy of his daily life. One more point that he guessed correctly was the principle of the conservation of energy in the universe, though he did not express it as such.

Democritus also constructed a completely materialistic system of ethics for his followers, though it would fall on his principal champion among the next generation of philosophers in Athens to make it influential. That man was Epicurus, the founder of Epicureanism.

Epicurus, too, was born and brought up outside Athens. He came to live in the city at the age of thirty-five, although he had spent two years there earlier. Born of Athenian parents on the island of Samos, he had inherited Athenian citizenship from his father, but he had to undertake military service in the city in order not to lose it.

He arrived as a fully-formed philosopher, in around 306 BC, when Alexander's empire had long since fallen apart and life had become hard for most people. He brought with him his own group of students. He bought or rented a house with a large garden and set up a school in rivalry with Plato's Academy and Aristotle's Lyceum, both of which were now in other hands. But unlike the other two establishments, 'The Garden', as it became known, charged no fees, and he allowed women, as well as some of his slaves, to enrol in its classes. Students and friends contributed what they could to enable the place to continue, but its needs were modest. Epicurus lived on barley bread, and fruit when this was available. He ate cheese with his bread only on feast days. His students were allowed no more than a pint of wine each day. During one famine, he saved them by counting their allotted beans himself.

He abhorred all types of excess and heightened passions, including sexual ones, and discouraged sexual relationships among his followers, though he was not always obeyed. He taught that fear was the greatest enemy of human happiness, such as fear of loss or fear of losing luxuries to which one might become attached. For him, the best state of mind was contentment – for example the contentment that followed a modest meal. Fear of death was especially pointless, 'for death means nothing to us'. After death, the atoms of the soul would disperse as irrevocably as the atoms of the body, and even the pain of dying meant little, for it was temporary. On the day he died, at the age of seventy-two from a blockage of the bladder, he wrote one of his most joyous letters, asking a friend to provide for the children of a student who had predeceased him.

So, was Epicurus merely a commentator on the science and ethics of Democritus? Largely, yes, but he expanded on his idol's ethics and inspired a large and faithful following of his own that would later make Epicureanism one of the two most influential 'religions' of the Roman aristocracy. The other, more successful school, was Stoicism, and it was the Stoics who spread rumours of debauchery and excess in The Garden to give their rivals the unfortunate reputation that they now have. In fact, Epicurus's greatest weakness seems to have been a dictatorial mind which turned his school into a cult. So stern was he with those who sought to expand on his ideas that Epicureanism became an obstacle to the development of philosophy for several hundred years afterwards.

Apart from his clear inclination towards Democritus's atomism, as in the quatrain at the head of this chapter, Khayyām shared a number of ethical beliefs at the core of the teachings of Democritus and Epicurus. His advocacy of the simple life and rejection of political involvement are two examples:

> Some bread, some cheese and a jug of wine,
> With you beside me beneath a lush vine!
> I know a great king who would, if he could,
> Barter his crown for that which is mine.

Khayyām's questioning of divine intervention, or even interest, in human affairs made him a most dangerous heretic, as did his refutation of the idea of life after death:

> When my Creator my elements planned,
> They say He meant me for the Promised Land.
> Lover, lute and wine by a field of corn:
> Give me those three now: birds are best in hand!

I have assumed in this book that Khayyām was fluent at least in the reading of ancient Greek texts. This is for two reasons. First of all, it is most unlikely that anyone at the time could have become a renowned authority 'on the science of Yunān', as he did, without being able to read the original sources. The Arabic translations that were available were notorious for either being wrong, incomplete, deliberately distorted to make them compatible with the Koran, or all three. Secondly, due to widespread diplomatic and commercial relations between Isfahan, on the one hand, and Armenia and Byzantium on the other, it would have been extremely easy for him to find able tutors to teach him Greek. He would almost certainly have had some of them among his personal friends, possibly including the Armenian princess who was married to chancellor Nizām. He enjoyed a close friendship with her stepson, Mo'ayyad, if not her own son Ziā, while she would have cultivated the company of the charismatic young poet, musician and astronomer as an antidote to her unhappy exile. Furthermore, some of his known acquaintances read several languages, including Syriac and Greek.

With an ability to read Greek, therefore, Khayyām would have been expected to have a private library of philosophical texts in Greek. Commentaries on Democritus and some of the books of Epicurus would have sat on his shelves, not to mention the other illustrious names of Greek philosophy. Does not, for example, the following quatrain include a direct quote from the most famous of those sages?

> Never of teachers did I go deprived;
> And more theorems I myself contrived.
> Seventy-two years, day and night, I thought:
> Only to conclude that I knew naught!

The mullahs who drew up the fatwa of death against him were right to say that he 'loved the Greeks' and that, by implication, he rejected their claims of representing divine power on earth. In his eyes, they were pompous primitives. Under the circumstances, and with the empire having fallen into civil war after the death of Malik Shah, Khayyām was unusually lucky to escape with his life to find safety among his family and clan in his home region.

Khayyām's Mathematics and Other Writings

Beside the Rubāiyāt in Persian, three poems in Arabic and a number of treatises on mathematics, philosophy, nature and mechanics are attributed to Khayyām, together with a monograph on the history of the Iranian calendar.

A translation of the three Arabic poems into English may be advisable first, for they are in the same spirit as the Rubāiyāt in their writer's refutation of religious dogma. They emerged some thirty years before the first stanza in Persian and, as they are ascribed to Khayyām by solid figures, their authenticity has never been challenged. For example, Shahrazuri, writing in Arabic as early as 1189, says: 'Omar Khayyāmi was of Nishāpur by upbringing and descent, and he followed Avicenna in the various branches of philosophy. He wrote fine poems, in Persian and Arabic.' Here are my[1] translations of the three poems in Arabic that Shahrazuri goes on to quote:

1

If all the Heavens, the farthest sky, came into my grasp, I would abstain from the forbidden, even in private, in my own home. Then, by day and night, I would pass my time in my God's worship.

Many are the men who have gone astray and then found their way, through that overflow that is my cloud [?]. My path enlightens this vale of darkness [?].

2

Were I contented with bare subsistence, gained through hard work with my own bare hands, I would not fear life's tribulations.

Be my witness, Time. I ride poetry to raise my heart high. I touch the Greater and the Lesser Bears. But then, God decides to reverse my luck.

Accept it, my heart, as you try to rest. Zenith is always followed by Nadir. When you're riding high, you can be certain the fall approaches.

How strange! Dreams come so close. Yet, stubbornly, they stay out of reach, a little too far.

Try hard as you may, the end is the same.

3

I searched far and wide for a brother, one who would stand, shoulder to shoulder, with me in hard times. But often, alas, I chose the wrong ones. I abandoned them, when they proved, at last, their unworthiness. I learned, at the end, to stop looking.

By God, it's better to expect little from your fellow man, even if you live for a thousand years.

The first two have only near-equivalents among the Rubāiyāt, but the last seems, in part, an exact translation of one of them, suggesting that Khayyām was so pleased with the brilliance of the Persian, or vice versa, that he translated it into the other language himself:

> It is best today few friends to seek.
> It is best with folks from afar to speak.
> The one for hard times to lean on I chose:
> When I needed her, she sang with my foes.

Shahrazuri gives us the three apparently in the order in which they were written, for they are not arranged according to their rhyming words. Another implication is that Khayyām wrote very few poems in Arabic, despite being a renowned master in the language. Otherwise, the poems would have been rearranged as in anthologies and collections by their rhyming words.

The first poem suggests it is the work of a young man. It is frivolous and arrogant, showing a readiness to hurt others' religious sentiments to score a point. By contrast, the other two are not rebellious, merely reflecting the sombre mood of Khayyām's middle years, when the clergy had issued their *fatwa* of heresy against him and when his long-time friend Terken Khātūn had abandoned him in the civil war of 1093.

* * *

A chronological list of Khayyām's other, lost or extant, writings may be attempted next, even though it sometimes becomes a matter of conjecture as to which works preceded which. This listing reflects, in part, my own personal judgement:

1. Between the later years of his schooling in Nishāpur and 1066, *Difficult Problems of Arithmetics (Mushkilāt al-Hisāb)*. Only the title page has survived, in Leiden, Holland. It provided proofs of Hindu achievements in deducing the roots of integer numbers, 'as many as you like', as he said about it elsewhere.

2. *Treatise on the Difficulties of the 'Book of Music'* (by Euclid), written or completed in Samarkand. Only one chapter entitled 'Classification of Types by Fourths' ('Al Qawl alal Ajnaās Allati bil Arba'a') has survived. It implies that a musical education had been part of his schooling in Nishāpur.

3. *Treatise on the Division of a Quarter of a Circle* in which he says he hopes to write his next book on algebra. Again written in Samarkand.

4. 1072 or early 1073, *Treatise on the Proofs of the Problems of Algebra and muqābala*. Dedicated to Abu Tāhir, the governor of Samarkand. In it, Khayyām makes his major contribution to the development of mathematics.

5. Between August 1074 and July 1077, *The Book of the (Persian) New Year (Norūz Nāmeh)*. Written in the immediate years before the inauguration of Khayyām's reformed solar calendar in 1079 (see below). Later additions and evidence of corruption at the hands of numerous copyists make it difficult to judge how much of it might have been written by Khayyām, but it did make sense for him to attempt it.

6. 1077, *Treatise on the Difficulties in the Introductions to the Book of Euclid (The Elements)*. He had probably started this work in Samarkand, but either completed it or improved it in December 1077 at a library in another city, probably Shiraz, where he often stayed with his friend Abu Nassr bin Abdol-Rahmān, the governor of Fārs province. Khayyām had moved to Isfahan by then, but travelled regularly to other cities to give lectures or to meet fellow researchers. Abu Nassr admired Khayyām as the greatest living authority on the teachings of Avicenna.

7. Between the spring of 1079 and the spring of 1080, *A Translation of Avicenna's Treatise on Monotheism*. Khayyām translated this into Persian 'at the request of friends' in Isfahan, implying that he is really not interested in such subjects (see below).

8. 1080 or 1081, *Treatise on Being and Obligation*. Written at the 'request' of his friend Abu Nassr, the imam-governor of Fārs province in Shiraz. Almost certainly a conspiracy between the two men to stifle accusations of heresy against Khayyām and, by implication, Malik Shah (see below).

9.   In the next several years, *Answers to Three Questions: The Necessity of Contradiction in the World, Determinism and Permanence*. Apparently again urged to write this by Abu Nassr, who was pleased with the effects of the previous paper. Thus these monographs cannot be regarded as reflecting Khayyām's real beliefs (see below).

10. Precise date unknown, *The Requested Book (Darkhāst Nāmeh)*. This was written in Persian, with two titles in Arabic given to it probably by later copyists: *Treatise on the Generalities of Being* and *Treatise on the Chain of Order (in the Universe)*. Written at the request of Mo'ayyad al-Mulk, his close friend and the senior son of Chancellor Nizām. It is an orthodox explanation of the universe according to Eastern Aristotelianism, written in the form of a short manual for a students. The end passage cannot be by Khayyām at all, but added by a Sufi mystic. It classifies all the searchers after truth and it places Sufis at the highest stage of attainment, for 'they do not seek knowledge through reason and thought, but through the cleansing of the inner self'. It also places Ismailis above Muslim clergy, even though the Ismailis were at the time a terrorist movement which was pursued by the armies of Khayyām's own friend Malik Shah.

11. Probably in the middle 1080s, *An Intelligent Man's Guide to the Problems of Knowledge in General (Al-Qiā al-aqli fi mowdu' al-ilm al-kulli)*.

12. Probably in the 1080s, *Treatise on Existence (Risālah fil-Wujūd)*.

13. Probably in the 1100s, after the flight to Khorāsān, *Two Treatises on the Level Balance*. By then, he no longer needed to write orthodox papers to cover up his real beliefs, though neither did he dare to voice those beliefs openly.

14. 1121, *On Determining the Proportions of Gold and Silver in an Object made of Them*. He began by weighing a chunk of pure gold in air and then in water, noting the ratio of the first figure over the second. He repeated the process with a chunk of pure silver. Repeating the process yet again with an object made from a mixture of gold and silver, he placed the resultant ratio on a scale, at one end of which was the ratio for pure gold and at the other the ratio for pure silver. The comparison gave him an accurate measure of how much of each of those two metals was present in the alloy. This article makes its appearance a decade before his death, in a book published by one of his former students, Abdol-Rahmān Khāzeni. The latter, a slave captured in Byzantium and brought up as a castrato by the khāzen or treasurer to the court of the sultan Sanjar in Merv, attributes the article to Khayyām, together with the papers on the level balance, above. It would seem that Khayyām had written them earlier for the treasury. The method regarding alloys is thought to have been known to the ancient Greeks but the level balance, a drawing of which has survived, is a most

elaborate instrument, with five pans and a weight that moves along a scaled arm.[2]

15. *A Treatise on the Workings of Nature*. Now lost, it is said to have been inspired by the long Latin poem of that name by the Epicurean Roman poet Lucretius. See p. 307.

16. *On Necessities for Places*. This was a guide for travellers that drew on Khayyām's own experience of visiting many distant parts of the Saljuq empire, from Bukhara to Baghdad. Again lost. No hint of a date has survived in connection with the latter two works.

*   *   *

It is important to put Khayyām's achievements in the field of mathematics in context, for although he is rightly regarded as one of the two greatest mathematicians that the world of Islam produced – the other being his fellow Persian and predecessor, Khārazmi – he suffered from Khārazmi's failure to take full advantage of the inventions of the Indians. Although he based his new system of arithmetic on the Indian invention of the zero and the principle of position, he did not adopt their use of symbols in algebra. Instead, he continued with the Greek depiction of formulae in words, making further advance in mathematics cumbersome.

A good way of demonstrating this lost opportunity is to give an algebraic formula and its solution as described by Khārazmi, followed by our modern depiction of it:

What must be the amount of a square, which, when twenty-one dirhams are added to it, becomes equal to the equivalent of ten roots of that square? Solution: halve the number of the roots, the moiety is five. Multiply this by itself, the product is twenty-five. Subtract from this the twenty-one which are connected with the square, the remainder is four. Extract its root, it is two. Subtract this from the moiety of the roots, which is five; the remainder is three. This is the root of the square which you required and the square is nine. Or you may add the root to the moiety of the roots, the sum is seven. This is the root of the square which you sought for, and the square itself is forty-nine.[3]

$$X^2 + 21 = 10X ;$$
$$X = 10/2 \mp \sqrt{[(10/2)^2 - 21]} = 5 \mp \sqrt{(25 - 21)} ,$$
$$+ 5 \mp \sqrt{4} = 5 \mp 2 = 3, 7 .$$

Frederick Rosen, who in 1831 translated the passage given here from Khā razmi's book on algebra, the first to contain that work, pointed out that in the text even numerals were always expressed in words. Indian figures, he said, were only 'used in some of the diagrams, and in a few marginal notes'. This is not meant to undervalue the work of such men as Khārazmi and Khayyām. Even though they were only commentators on, or at best expanders of, their predecessors in Greece and India, they showed originality in many instances, with Khārazmi's work clearly being more than the sum of the achievements of the Indians and the Greeks. This raises an interesting point: did he, hailing as he did from the heart of the former Persian and Parthian empires, have access also to works by ancient Iranian mathematicians that are now lost, or are all his innovations his own work?

As for Khayyām, his place in the history of mathematics is assured: 'Three centuries after the great Khārazmi had finished his labours', wrote the Scottish-American mathematician E.T. Bell in 1940, 'the Persian poet-mathematician Omar Khayyām reached a considerably higher mathematical level than any of his predecessors. This devil-may-care, somewhat cynical philosopher had imagination. Not content with collections of rules, Omar classified cubic equations and devised a method of geometrical solution for numerical cubics. . . .'[4] In the words of an earlier writer, Florian Cajori of Colorado College in 1894, he was 'the one who did most to elevate to a *method* the solution of algebraic equations by intersecting conics. . . . Omar al-Hayyami of Chorassan divided cubics into two classes, the trinomial and the quadrinomial, and each class into families and species'.[5] Indeed, Khayyām went further. He also produced solutions for three classes of cubic equations that had defeated many a genius before him.

Khayyām failed to discover negative roots and he did not always notice positive ones. An attempt to find arithmetical solutions to equations defeated him, though he hoped that 'someone else coming after us might succeed'. According to an extensive profile of him posted on the Internet site of the Department of Mathematics at the University of St Andrews, Scotland, those future mathematicians whom he anticipated proved to be del Ferro, Tartaglia and Ferrari in the sixteenth century.

Khayyām put his mathematics at the service of his astronomy and the reform of the solar calendar. Here, he achieved truly wondrous results. His calculation of the average length of the year to within five seconds of what an atomic clock would have produced remains awe-inspiring and his help in paving the way for differential calculus and non-Euclidian geometry turns him into one of those 'giants' on whose shoulders Newton said he had stood.

* * *

The *Norūz Nāmeh* or *The Book of the New Year* is a theatrical tale, written between the autumn of 1074 and the summer of 1077, of how mythological ancient Iranian kings devised a solar calendar and what names they gave to the months and days. None of the book's various titles are likely to be original and, as we have seen, its exaggerated glorification of old Zoroastrian customs has caused some modern commentators to doubt its authorship by Khayyām.

A sample is given here from the opening pages of the text that are reminiscent of Khayyām's preference for simple language in his Persian writings. At the time of writing, he would have been no older than twenty-nine, a young man given to passions and proud of his professional success and his companionship of an emperor. The text also bears signs of severe corruption by copyists.

> This is a book devoted to discovering the truth about [the festival of] Norūz among the kings of Persia, why that date was chosen, which king chose it and why they honoured it. It is a short book. . . .
>
> It is said that when Gayūmarth, the first of the kings of Persia, ascended the throne, he wanted to name the months and the days, so that the people might know how to find them. He looked into it. The morning when the sun entered the first minute of Aries, he summoned all the [Zoroastrian] mūbads of the realm and commanded them to make it the beginning of the calendar and divide the year into twelve months. They gathered together and named the months and made that day the start of the new era. . . .
>
> And so have declared the mūbads of Persia, who were the wisest in the world, that Izad Almighty has twelve angels. Four of those He has installed in the Heavens to protect them and [keep] all that is in them free from demons. Another four angels He has installed in the four corners of the world to stop demons descending from the Qāf mountain. The remaining four angels roam the skies and the earth to keep demons away from His creatures. . . .
>
> As the kings settled on the date, both to honour the sun and to make it easier for the people [to remember it], they designated the day a feast day

and they informed the rest of the peoples of the world of it to help them to keep a calendar. . . .

It is wise for rulers to keep the feasts and traditions of their predecessors, for their own good and for posterity. The sages have said that whoever celebrates Norūz will live in happiness till the start of the next year. Philosophers have proved the truth of it...

[The first month is called] Farvardin: It is a Pahlavi word, meaning the time of the year when seeds germinate. . . .

[The second month is] Ordibehesht. It derives from 'Ord Vehesht', meaning 'like paradise', for in this month, the world takes on the mantle of heaven in its luxuriance. . . .

The above extracts are based on a number of old manuscripts, including one at the British Library dated 1487, but such is the extent of accumulated corruption in the text at the hands of numerous copyists that it is difficult to see how much of the monograph might have been written by Khayyām. For example, the book seems to attribute the founding of the first Persian calendar to two kings, Gayūmarth and his grandson Jamshīd. That cannot be the work of a meticulous mathematician such as Khayyām. Its introduction and an epilogue that describes the customs of ancient Iranian kings at Norūz are believed to have been written some forty years after Khayyām's death by a man from the city of Herat, Abdol-Rāfe Harawi.

*　　*　　*

The philosophical papers we have of Khayyām's, though certainly written by him, can be dismissed as, at best, driven by expedience and, at worst, as acts of dissimulation designed to divert suspicions of heresy from him and, more importantly, his friend and emperor Malik Shah. Apart from the circumstantial evidence we have that they were a ploy, forged at the insistence of two of his other influential friends, they contradict all else that we know of him, including the letter and spirit of his poetry. We ought to remember that the widespread rumours of grave heresy levelled against Khayyām could seriously undermine Malik Shah's position in a deeply religious society awash with conspirators and Assassins. Though the office of the chief astronomer in the land was not insignificant in itself, an outlandish, hard-drinking, artist-type executive at the head of that office could have been ignored, for it did not endanger the sway of the established religion, Sunni Islam. But this particular astronomer was an intimate of the sultan, and the sultan sometimes shocked the clergy by expressing doubt on the nature of Allah and Islam (see p. 198). Omar's malign influence on the increasingly impatient and headstrong emperor had to be confronted, even though it was still really the chancellor who ran the empire.

Thus we can imagine spies keeping a careful watch on Malik Shah's closest friends, if only to provide evidence for the Grand Vizier to prove to Malik Shah that he knew he kept unsuitable company. We are told by Nizām himself that the sultan was coming under the influence of women, meaning in particular Terken Khātūn, and drinking companions. At the same time, Malik Shah was thinking of abolishing the caliphate in Baghdad – perhaps even at the behest of Khayyām – something to which Nizām was vehemently opposed, as it would have been followed swiftly by Nizām's own dismissal.

Here is a sample passage of Khayyām's philosophical piece *On Being and Obligation* that he wrote in 1080 or 1081 at the request of Abu Nassr Muhammad bin Abdol-Rahīm, the governor of Fārs province. It is about the necessity of the existence of God, argued along Aristotelian lines, and on man's duty to pray to his creator along Muslim lines. The governor was known as an admirer both of Khayyām and Avicenna, and was therefore himself under suspicion of heresy. It is also possible that he thought he was acting in the best interests of his emperor. It is immediately clear why the piece can be dismissed as a ploy.

> . . . If people ask why Allah Almighty has created opposites, the answer is clear: to refrain from the greater good to avoid the lesser evil would itself have been to commit an evil. The boundless wisdom of the Central Being has given all beings the ability to achieve their maximum potential. I issue no final judgement here and only quote some of the philosophers . . .
>
> On the subject of obligation, it must be said that its nature is implicated in its 'whyness', for the 'whyness' of things necessitates their existence. And so we say that God has created human beings so that they cannot survive and attain their potential unless they cooperate with one another . . . and specialise . . . and thus they need just laws . . . and those laws need to be issued by someone who is superior to others in intelligence and in cleansing the self, desiring nothing except the grace of God, so that what

is revealed to him, he enforces justly. Such a self then deserves being chosen to convey divine revelation to the people and he is in turn rewarded with the possibility of seeing God's glorious Heavens with his own eyes . . .[6]

How humiliating to have had to stage such a charade.

*   *   *

A question arises here: why did such an energetic genius and 'chatterbox' produce only a slender body of writing? The answer has to be that he did not have the freedom to write what he thought worth teaching, except in mathematics and a few innocuous subjects, such as scales.

Up to the inauguration of his reformed calendar in 1079, Omar was primarily engaged in mathematical research and astronomy. In both of those subjects he was outstanding, and in those subjects it is quality that matters, not quantity. As we have seen, in the opinion of historians of mathematics, without Omar such great innovators as Descartes, Newton and Leibniz would probably have been hindered from achieving their full potential. By paving the way for differential calculus and non-Euclidean geometry, Khayyām is truly one of the founders of the modern world, affecting the daily lives of all of us to this day.

But the polymaths of his time were expected to write on virtually every branch of learning, as we see in the case of Avicenna, a most prolific writer who lived a couple of generations earlier. But Avicenna lived under the relaxed rule of the Persian dynasties, the Samanid and the Buyid.

By contrast, with the coming of the Turks and their conversion to Islam, the orthodox Sunni clergy were given new power over the populace and Khayyām began to be intimidated by them from about 1080, when he was only thirty-two years old. Thus we see that at that age he has to deny his real beliefs, inspired by such rationalists as Democritus, Epicurus and Rāzi, in favour of orthodox Islam, not necessarily to protect his own life – for he was safe as long as his friend and fellow sceptic Malik Shah lived – but to avoid giving any pretext to the men of Nizām al-Mulk to undermine Malik Shah's standing in society.

We may be certain that Omar found such concealment of his views in public disheartening. This is evident in the quatrain that describes the mass of humanity as 'a herd of donkeys' or in the other quatrains that defy the *fatwa* issued against him and exude pessimism and rage.

Thus when Khayyām's mini-biographer and contemporary, Zeid Beyhaqi, tells us that Khayyām was 'miserly' when it came to writing and teaching, it is because he does not know Khayyām well. He is much younger, lives in another part of Khorāsān, and belongs to a family of Muslim clerics with whom Khayyām does not want to associate.

Later, Qifti, the devout Muslim and patriotic Arab, feels no embarrassment in disclosing the true extent of Khayyām's alienation from Islam. On the contrary, he feels it his duty to do so. He tells us that 'After the people looked into his religion and his life was threatened, he curbed his pen and reined in his tongue', going on to make exaggerated profession of religiosity.

The threat did not diminish completely even after the death of Malik Shah when Khayyām fled to the relative safety of his home city. There he kept his own counsel and travelled only to visit a few former colleagues and trusted friends. The Rubāiyāt were a different matter. They were his personal secrets and his only way of expressing his rage, his sorrow and his real philosophy, clothed in an art form that might, just might, survive the unforgiving age.

Principal Characters

Toghril: Senior chief and eventual sultan of Saljuq Turkish nomads who fled from central Asia into north-eastern Iran and defeated the Ghaznavid emperor Mass'ūd in 1040, eight years before Khayyām was born there. A little later he captured Isfahan in central Iran from its Persian monarchs of the Buyid dynasty and had himself crowned in Baghdad as the supreme temporal ruler of eastern Islam. He was succeeded by his nephew Alp-Arslan.

Nizām al-Mulk: Persian chancellor or Grand Vizier to the sultans Alp-Arslan and Malik Shah. Alp-Arslan divorced one of his senior wives, an Armenian princess, to give to him to marry and appointed him on his deathbed as guardian over Malik Shah. The latter addressed him as 'Father' for the rest of his life. Recruited Khayyām, twenty years his junior, as an astronomer and moved him from Bukhara to Isfahan. He promoted a severe interpretation of Sunni Islam.

Shams al-Mulk: King of the Qarakhanid kingdom of Samarkand and Bukhara in central Asia who made young Khayyām one of his closest companions in 1073 before Nizām al-Mulk made his kingdom a vassal of Malik Shah in Isfahan. He had previously betrothed his daughter Terken to Malik Shah.

Hasan Sabbāh: Founder of the Ismaili Muslim sect of the 'Assassins'. About the same age as Khayyām, he worked in Isfahan for a year or so at the same time as Khayyām and made a failed attempt to meet the Ismaili caliph in Cairo. In 1090, he seized one of Malik Shah's castles in the Alborz mountains and used it to terrorise the Saljuq state, eventually causing it to fall apart in a dynastic war.

Malik Shah: Saljuq sultan under whom the empire expanded to its greatest extent. Ascended the throne at seventeen and reigned – under Nizām al-Mulk's guidance – for twenty years. Made Khayyām one of his closest companions. In matters of religion, he was a sceptic.

Princess Terken or Terken Khātūn: Daughter to King Shams al-Mulk, was betrothed to Malik Shah while both were small children. Date of birth not known precisely, but still of childbearing age in 1092 when Malik Shah died at thirty-seven and she became a faction leader in the dynastic war that followed. Knew Khayyām since her girlhood in Bukhara.

Princess Zubeida: Malik Shah's other wife and first cousin. Seemingly a few years younger than Terken, she was similarly betrothed to Malik Shah while both were small children. After Malik Shah's death, the Nizāmiyah championed her son Berkyaruq as the rightful heir to the throne, in opposition to Terken's son Mahmūd.

Mo'ayyad al-Mulk: One of Grand Vizier Nizām's senior sons and a close friend of Khayyām, later became Grand Vizier to princess Zubeida. Sacked by Zubeida, he strangled her.

Michael Psellus: Byzantine diarist, fake monk, chancellor and man of peace under empress Eudocia, starved the army of funds while Anatolia was being overrun by the Saljuq Turks and countless Christians were slaughtered or taken into slavery.

Empress Eudocia: Byzantine ruler who eventually cast aside the advice of the 'peace camp' at her court and married the army commander Romanus Diogenes in a desperate attempt to stem the tide of the Turkish onslaught in Anatolia.

Romanus Diogenes: Byzantine nobleman from Anatolia who struggled to reduce the influence of effeminate men at court on Empress Eudocia and championed the cause of a stronger army to save Greek and Armenian Anatolia from Turkish marauders. Eudocia eventually made him her co-emperor.

Badr al-Jamāli: Armenian ruler of Egypt. Captured as a boy in Anatolia by the Turks and sold into slavery, he rose through the ranks to become the army chief of a regional governor. On being invited by the Ismaili caliph in Cairo to rescue him from his Turkish 'slave' guards, he made the caliph his puppet. He expelled Sabbāh when the latter arrived in Cairo to ask the caliph to help the oppressed Ismailis of Iran.

Emperor Alexius Comnenus: Byzantine ruler at the time of the First Crusade in 1096. Pressed in the west and east by Normans and Turks, made peace with the Roman church to recruit mercenaries in Europe, but did not quite foresee the consequences.

Pope Urban II: Roman pontiff who preached the raising of an army of knights to go to the rescue of eastern Christians. He underestimated the response.

Muhammad al-Ghazāli: Muslim fanatic and protégé of Nizām al-Mulk who became Khayyām's most active tormentor. Was instrumental in inspiring Muslims to turn their backs on the scientific rationalism of ancient Greece.

Family Tree of the Saljuq Emperors of Iran

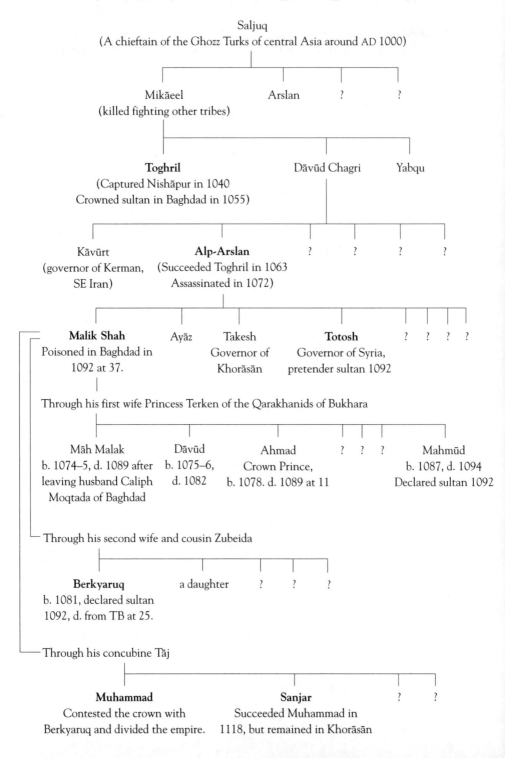

Saljuq
(A chieftain of the Ghozz Turks of central Asia around AD 1000)

Mikāeel   Arslan   ?   ?
(killed fighting other tribes)

Toghril   Dāvūd Chagri   Yabqu
(Captured Nishāpur in 1040
Crowned sultan in Baghdad in 1055)

Kāvūrt   **Alp-Arslan**   ?   ?   ?   ?
(governor of Kerman,   (Succeeded Toghril in 1063
SE Iran)   Assassinated in 1072)

Malik Shah   Ayāz   Takesh   **Totosh**   ? ? ? ?
Poisoned in Baghdad in   Governor of   Governor of Syria,
1092 at 37.   Khorāsān   pretender sultan 1092

Through his first wife Princess Terken of the Qarakhanids of Bukhara

Māh Malak   Dāvūd   Ahmad   ? ? ?   Mahmūd
b. 1074–5, d. 1089 after   b. 1075–6,   Crown Prince,   b. 1087, d. 1094
leaving husband Caliph   d. 1082   b. 1078. d. 1089 at 11   Declared sultan 1092
Moqtada of Baghdad

Through his second wife and cousin Zubeida

Berkyaruq   a daughter   ?   ?   ?
b. 1081, declared sultan
1092, d. from TB at 25.

Through his concubine Tāj

Muhammad   **Sanjar**   ?   ?
Contested the crown with   Succeeded Muhammad in
Berkyaruq and divided the empire.   1118, but remained in Khorāsān

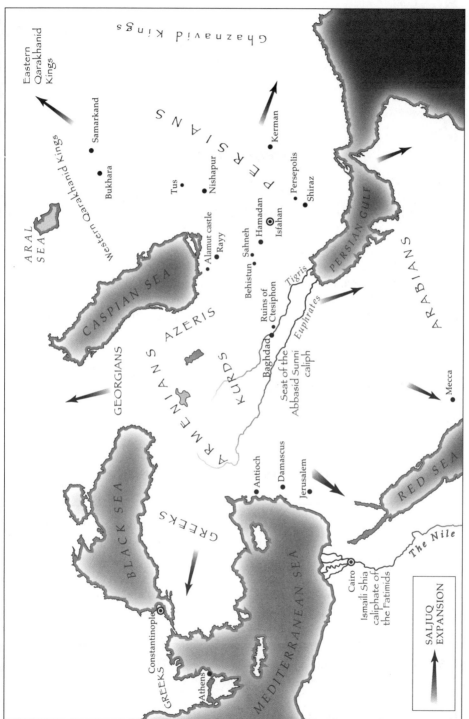

Map of the Saljuq Empire at the Time of Malik-Shah's Death.

Chronology

1018   10 April: The future Grand Vizier Nizām al-Mulk, is born to a tax collector near Nishāpur in Khorāsān.

1020   Firdowsi, the epic poet and champion of renewed pride in the old Persian empire, dies at the age of eighty-four on his estate east of Nishāpur.

1031   Saljuq Turkoman nomads invade Khorāsān from beyond the Oxus River.

1033   Large numbers of Christians make a pilgrimage to Jerusalem to mark the millennium of Christ's Passion.

1037   Avicenna, the great scientist/statesman and future role model for Khayyām dies.

1040   A devastating drought coincides with the final fall of Nishāpur to the Saljuqs.

c. 1046   In Rayy, central Iran, Hasan Sabbāh, the future founder of 'the Order of the Assassins' and leader of the Ismailis of the east is born to a Yemeni Arab immigrant.

1048   Thursday 18 May: Khayyām is born in Nishāpur to Ebrāhūm Khayyāmi, a physician. Abu Rayhān Bīrūni, the Khorāsānian geographer and sociologist dies.

1050   Polyphonic singing replaces Gregorian chant. Guido d'Arezzo (b. 995) dies. Time values are given to musical notes.

1052   Pisa takes Sardinia from the Arabs.

1054   4 July: When Khayyām is 6, the Crab Nebula appears for the first time and is so bright it remains visible for twenty-four days.

1055   Malik Shah, the future sultan, is born to Alp-Arslan, the ruler of Khorāsān and a nephew to Toghril.

1056–7 Famine causes thousands of deaths from Egypt to Transoxania.

1058   Ghazāli, Khayyām's future tormentor, is born in Tūs, near Nishāpur.

1063   Toghril dies and is, a little later, succeeded by his nephew Alp-Arslan.

1064   Alp-Arslan invades the Caucasus and forces Bagrat IV, the Armenian king of Georgia, to give him his daughter 'in marriage'. He later hands her to Nizām.

c. 1063 Sabbāh begins to question his Shia Twelver faith in favour of Ismaili version of Shia'ism.

1066   8 May: Halley's comet in the sky for seven nights. Gazed on simultaneously by 17-year-old Khayyām and an Otho Geraldino, the first known ancestor of the FitzGeralds of England and Ireland.

1066   Sabbāh burns his bridges and swears oath of allegiance to Egypt after hallucinatory illness.

1066   Khayyām's father and his Zoroastrian mathematics teacher Bahmanyār die.

1067   On the last day of the year, General Romanus Diogenes arrives in Constantinople to marry Empress Eudocia and become co-emperor in the hope of stemming the tide of invaders on all sides.

1068   Khayyam settles down in Samarkand.

1071   The Battle of Manzikert, north of Lake Van. Alp-Arslan captures Romanus and ensures continued Turkish migration into Anatolia.

1072   May or June: Ismaili leader visits Rayy and tells Sabbāh to prepare to be his future envoy in Cairo. Khayyām in Samarkand has published three books on mathematics and music and is asked to move to Bukhara to be nearer the king of the western Qarakhanids.

1072   24 November: Alp-Arslan dies from wounds inflicted by a noble prisoner whom he was going to crucify. His eldest son Malik Shah succeeds him.

1072–3 Aged 25–6, Khayyām first emerges in history as a drinking companion of King Shams al-Mulk in Bukhara, who takes advantage of the cancelled Saljuq offensive and captures Termez and Balkh. Nizām al-Mulk, acting as regent for Malik Shah, invades Transoxania and turns Shams al-Mulk into a Saljuq vassal. Malik Shah, and the king's daughter Princess Terken, who have been betrothed since early childhood, marry.

1074   Khayyām, who has been recruited to work on a new observatory in Isfahan, passes through his city of birth, Nishāpur, probably as a member of Princess Terken's bridal party. Malik Shah also probably in attendance, but not Nizām. Aged 26, Khayyām settles down in Isfahan for the next eighteen years as a close companion of Malik Shah, the royal family's chief doctor, and the most brilliant member of a team of eight astronomers given the task of reforming the ancient Persian solar calendar and building a new observatory for the capital.

1075   Khayyām and his team of astronomers temporarily halt the further recession calendar by reinstalling leap years.

1076–7 Hasam Sabbāh, the future founder of the cult of 'the Assassins', flees Rayy for Isfahān, incognito.

1077   Khayyām and his colleagues now in the home straights in the race to come up with the most accurate calendar ever. He travels widely in search of other mathematicians and instrument makers.
        Pope Gregory VII crosses the Alps to meet the German magnates to settle the fate of Henry IV.

1078   Sabbāh leaves Isfahan to arrive in Cairo on 30 August in great secrecy. He stays there about eighteen months. The building of the Tower of London starts.

Michael Psellus the former fake monk and man of peace dies in Constantinople in obscurity.

1079   14 March: Approaching his thirty-first birthday, Khayyām's reformed solar calendar is inaugurated by the shah.

1079–   Khayyām says he is still in Isfahan after the inauguration of his
80   calendar and translates 'at the request of a group of friends', seemingly including Malik Shah, who must remain anonymous, a treatise by Avicenna from Arabic into Persian. The language he uses is highly provocative to Nizām and the clergy. Ghazāli is making a name for himself in Nishāpur.

1080   News reaches Isfahan in July that Shams al-Mulk has died. Has Terken Khātūn gone to Bukhara for his last days? Has Khayyām gone with her?

1080–1 Khayyām shows first signs of coming under pressure for being a sceptic. He is in Shiraz.

1081   10 June: Expelled by Egypt, Sabbāh arrives back in Isfahān, in disguise.

1082   Late April: Caliph Moqtada's vizier arrives in Isfahan to ask for the hand of Malik Shah's daughter, but is told it is up to her mother Terken Khātūn.
        December: One of Nizām's senior sons dies. Rumoured poisoned by Malik Shah.

1084   Khayyām's friend Mo'ayyad is appointed by his father to be the new chief of staff of the chancery. Malik Shah and Nizām drive the Kurdish Marwanid kings out of Diyarbakir. Mosul also conquered.
        27 November: Prince Sanjar is born in Sinjar and is named after the town. Robert Giscard frees Pope Gregory who had been confined to Castel Sant'Angelo by Henry IV. Antioch is captured for Malik Shah.

1086   Nizām's south dome of the Friday mosque in Isfahan is finished. A year later, his rival Tāj al-Mulk builds the north dome. Malik Shah, Terken Khātūn and Khayyām presumably at both inaugurations.

1087   Thirteen years after becoming sultan, Malik Shah makes his first visit to Baghdad at the insistence of Terken for the wedding of their daughter Māh Malak to Caliph Moqtada on 22 May.

Malik Shah's name recited for the first time in prayer sermons in Mecca. Khayyām, as doctor, gives up hope for Prince Sanjar.

1088   12 March: Urban II becomes pope. Unable to enter Rome.

1089   30 May: Two emirs escort Terken's young daughter out of Baghdad. She dies in November in Isfahan from smallpox, leaving Terken to bring up her baby son, heir to the caliphate. Terken is, at most, only 34, the same age as her husband.
        Malik Shah and Nizām invade Transoxania at the behest of Khayyām's old mentor Abu Tāhir, the governor of Samarkand, to overthrow Terken's nephew Ahmad Khān, and go on to conquer East Turkistan.

1090   Recorded glimpse of Khayyām as royal companion. Malik Shah now more sedentary than his predecessors and spends more time at court.
        Wednesday 4 September: Sabbāh seizes the castle of Alamūt and stays inside it for the next 34 years, climbing to the roof only twice.

1091   Nizām sends fanatical young Ghazāli to Baghdad to be the main director of his Nizāmiyah college there. The chancellor has also been expanding his book on the art of government, the Siāsat Nāmeh. Warns against 'the influence of women' and against abolishing the caliphate.
        November: Malik Shah pays his second visit to Baghdad and stays till at least March, but his personal dislike for his son-in-law has so intensified that he does not grant the caliph a single audience.

1092   Spring and summer: Sabbāh refines his grand plot.
        14 October: Nizām is assassinated. 15 November: Malik Shah dies, almost certainly poisoned. Terken hides his body. Is Khayyām with her? Rumours spread quickly. Zubeida is in Isfahan.

1093   Terken in charge of Isfahan but apparently little else. Zubeida and Berkyaruq have been released by the Nizāmiyah and fled to the north.
        In April: Totosh takes Mosul.
        Ghazāli in Baghdad, a prominent Islamic jurist and Zubeida's man.

1094   January: Khayyām makes pretend pilgrimage to Mecca to ward off accusations of heresy.
        3 February: In Baghdad, prayers recited in the name of Berkyaruq. Nizām's son Izz al-Mulk is his Grand Vizier, 'but he drinks too much'.

His elder brother and Khayyām's former friend Mo'ayyad is Terken's vizier and their other brother Fakhr al-Mulk is Totosh's.

4 February: Caliph Moqtada dies immediately after blessing Berkyaruq's sultanate. Khayyām, in Baghdad, wonders how to pass through the war zones to reach safety in Nishāpur.

Ismaili Shia Caliph Mustansir dies in Cairo. Sabbāh breaks away from Cairo a couple of months later and the chasm within Ismailism is formalised.

El Cid takes Valencia from the Moors. St Marks Square, Venice, completed. Khayyām's old enemy Ghazāli leaves Baghdad for Nishāpur.

18 November: Urban II opens the Council of Clermont and calls for a Christian army to rescue the faithful in the east and reopen the pilgrimage routes to Jerusalem.

1099   Crusaders capture Jerusalem.

1100   Ibn Funduq, the future historian and mini-biographer of Khayyām, is born.

1105   Late November: 25-year-old Berkyaruq, supreme sultan at last, dies from TB. Khayyām is now wooed by princes once more.

c. 1110   The philosopher Zamakhshari recalls a dispute over Ma'arri's poetry with Khayyām.

1112/   Khayyām, in the city of Balkh with his secretary Nizami Arūzi, visits
13   the local emir for lunch and describes where he will be buried.

1114   He accompanies Sultan Sanjar on a hunt. Forecasts the weather.

1117–   Arūzi is in Nishāpur and 'eternally grateful to my lord Omar'.
18

1118   18 May: Khayyām is seventy. Writes quatrain about it.
Muhammad dies in Isfahan and younger brother Sanjar, 'sultan' of Khorāsān, becomes supreme sultan, but stays in Marv. Friend to Khayyām, despite exaggerated report of his grudge against him since childhood. Siege of Alamūt fails.

1123   Āmir, the caliph of Egypt, sends a second epistle to Syria against the followers of Sabbāh. He describes them as the Hashishiyah, which eventually becomes the European word 'Assassin'.

1124   Friday 23 May: Sabbāh dies in Alamūt. A whole string of castles and mini-states owe him loyalty.

1130   Caliph Āmir in Egypt is assassinated by Sabbāh's followers.

1131   Friday 4 December: In the evening Khayyām dies, aged 83. His last day described by his son-in-law.

1135   April or May: Arūzi visits Khayyām's grave 'to pay my respects' and, seemingly, to research his life.
         One of Khayyām's former students, a distinguished jurist, is burnt alive for heresy. A new federation of Turkish nomads begins to invade and devastate Khorāsān anew.

1203–4 The poet Shāhpūr Khayyāmi Nishāpuri dies in Tabriz, Azerbaijan, 72 or 73 years after the death of his apparent ancestor.

Notes

Chapter One

1   From a new translation of the Rubāiyāt by the author. See Appendix I.

2   Today we know it as Halley's comet. It is depicted in the Bayeux Tapestry, apparently made by the Normans in Kent in the 1070s to commemorate their victory.

3   According to my calculations based on the tables of *The Islamic and Christian Calendars* by G.P.S. Freeman-Grenville, Garnet Publishing, Reading, England, 1995.

4   In one of the two oldest surviving anthologies of verses attributed to Khayyām, the *Tarabkhāneh* (or Pleasure House) of Yār Ahmad bin Hussein al-Rashīdi al-Tabrīzi, finished in 1463, Khayyām's place of birth is given as the village of Dehak near the town of Fīrūz Gand near the city of Astar Ābād, today's Gorgān, at the bottom eastern corner of the Caspian sea. As the author is contradicted by others and makes other mistakes, his assertion is suspect. However, the wealth of his detail can not be dismissed easily. It may well mean that the family had originated in that region or had sent a younger son, Khayyām's father or grandfather, to Nishāpur for a higher education. If so, they would have probably been an old Iranian family of the 'dehghān' or landowning class, confined to rural districts by then, as were, for example, Firdowsi's or Nizām al-Mulk's.

5   The ancient name 'Iran' was not used to refer to a political entity in Khayyām's time. It described, rather, all the independent and semi-independent kingdoms and principalities that spoke any of the various Iranian languages, from New Persian or Fārsi on the shores of the Oxus River in central Asia to Kurdish in the Zagros mountains bordering Byzantine Anatolia in the far west. In short, it meant the heartland of the former Sassanian empire that had been overrun by Arabs in the south in the seventh century. It is often said that it refers ultimately to the Aryan or Indo-European tribes that arrived in the Iranian plateau from the north some 4–5,000 years ago.

6   This was also the year in which in a little known country called Scotia far in the western extremity of the world, a chieftain called Macbeth would kill his

suzerain Duncan to crown himself king. However, the reign of Macbeth would be a prosperous one, compared to Toghril's.

7 Daqiqi was a Zoroastrian who began an epic history of pre-Islamic Iranian kings in verse, but died young in 978. The great poet Firdowsi later incorporated into his own epic masterpiece, *The Book of the Kings* or *Shāhnāmeh*, the verses that Daqiqi had completed about the life of Zarathustra or Zoroaster, the ancient prophet.

8 He was a native of the city of Tūs to the east of Nishāpur but died in 1072 as a refugee in Azerbaijan in western Iran. His main works are the first dictionary of New Persian (today's Fārsi) and *The Epic of Garshāsp*, a Zoroastrian hero of Middle Persian tales.

9 Professor Peter Avery of Cambridge University in 1979 wrote of Manūchehri: 'Like Khayyām, he belonged to a society of cultured Persians living precariously under the menace of destructive marauders from the north and north-east'.

10 An often unspoken antagonism on the part of the Muslim clergy in Iran towards all things Iranian continues to this day, when Islam rules the country once more. Behzād Nabavi, a member of the 'Islamic parliament' and former minister in the government in Tehran, told a newspaper in February 2002 that he had recently been talking to a mullah about his own descent from a long line of influential Muslim clerics. The mullah had said: "That's wonderful. There's only one bad thing about you, then, and that's your Iranian first name". Indeed, after the Islamic republic was established in 1979, many registrars refused to accept the names of any children which took apparent pride in Iran's pre-Islamic past. In the same interview, Nabavi criticised the altering of the name of a girls' school in Tehran from Nargess to Narjess to make it sound Arabic. (Classical Arabic does not have the 'g' sound.) Numerous other place names with a history were replaced with Arabic ones and Persian was encumbered with thousands of new Arabic lone words.

11 There are a number of suggestions put forth to explain the origins of the name, the most popular among scholars being 'Ne Shāhpūr', with 'ne' in Middle Persian meaning 'of', in the sense of 'owned by'. This is plausible, since in modern Kurdish, which is closely related to Middle Persian, the word 'of' is 'heen'. Thus 'Of Shāhpūr' would be 'Heeni Shāhpūr' in its Kurdish equivalent, with the first syllable of 'heeni' being dropped later in popular usage. Indeed, the word may be related even to 'own' in English at the western end of Eurasia. But could it also have been 'No Shāhpūr'? 'No' in modern Persian means 'new', as does 'nū' in Kurdish.

12 'Abar' is believed by scholars to derive from the Parthian word 'aparkan' or 'foal', also young boy and upstart. If true, Abar Shahr would have meant New Town.

13 At least it is imaginative, far better than the usual 'fell from his horse while hunting wild boar'!

14 This is the Western name of the famous book of fairy tales. In the Middle East it is known as *The Thousand and One Nights* and hails from the original *Hazār Afsāneh* or *Thousand Tales*. The settings have in many cases been transferred to Baghdad of the caliphs, but the bulk of the stories have their roots clearly in Iran and India.

15 *The Crab Nebula* by Simon Mitton, Faber, London and Boston, 1979.

16 *Byzantium: The Imperial Centuries*, by Romilly Jenkins, Weidenfeld & Nicolson, London 1967.

17 The political, as opposed to the religious, break between Rome and Constantinople occurred 300 years earlier. In 754, Pepin, the Frankish impostor 'gave' the city of Ravenna, the capital of Byzantine Italy, to the bishop of Rome, Pope Stephen III, in return for being recognised as the new king of the Franks. By accepting the gift, the pope broke his legal ties to his hitherto sovereign, the emperor in Constantinople. The process culminated in the coronation of Pepin's son, Charlemagne, as the new Holy Roman Emperor in Rome by Pope Hadrian on Christmas Day, 800, when the interdependence between the papacy and the new Western empire became complete. The Frankish leader could not become emperor without being crowned by the pope, while no-one could become pope without the approval of the emperor. Yet all was done under a pretence of legality. Charlemagne's justification for his defiance was that the empire in Constantinople had been usurped. His lawyers argued that because the sovereign there, Irene, called herself emperor, not empress, she had disinherited herself by resorting to lies. More relevantly, however, Charlemagne had by then captured the whole of Italy from the Lombards, the pope's enemies, occupied Rome and confirmed his father's gift of Ravenna to the papacy.

18 *The Dreadful Day*, by Alfred Friendly, London 1981.

19 Ibn al-Athīr's *Annals of the Saljuq Turks*, trs. Professor D.S. Richards, Routledge, London 2002, p. 114.

20 Bahmanyār had, in turn, studied under the great Avicenna.

21 Ibn Funduq was an orthodox Muslim of Arab descent who wrote only in Arabic and does not seem to have admired Khayyām. His full name was Zahīr ad-Dīn Abul-Hasan ibn Zaid al-Beihaqi. He spent his adult life in Beihaq, today's Sabzvār in western Khorāsān.

22 In a commentary on Nizāmi Aruzi's *Four Discourses*, Dr Muhammad Moin of Tehran University speculated in 1952 that Khayyām might have spent part of his youth in Isfahan. This is erroneous and based on a preface in one of Khayyām's own books in which he uses the phrase: 'my teacher Avicenna and I'. He could not have meant it literally, for Avicenna died in Isfahan in May 1037, 11 years before Khayyām was born in Nishāpur. But Avicenna had been the teacher of his teacher Bahmanyār and, the word 'student' was sometimes used at the time to mean a 'follower' or someone who had studied the writings of an earlier

thinker. Khayyām's mini-biographer Ibn Fundoq, who met him, uses that word to describe the relationship between Khayyām and Avicenna while naming Avicenna's real students elsewhere.

23 This account is based on a chapter in Beihaqi's *History of Sultan Mass'ud* (Tārīkh Beihaqi), Tehran 1997. vol. 1, p. 163.

24 He died in 1014. His name was Abu Abdullah, but he is everywhere referred to simply as 'al-Hākim', *The Judge*. Being a clergyman, Hākim saw himself as a Muslim first and wrote in Arabic only.

25 In the *Book of the Kings*, Shírín is the beautiful Armenian lover of the Sassanian emperor Aparviz.

26 Today, one farsang or parasang generally indicates a distance of about 6km or 3.7 miles, but, according to the travel journal of Nasser Khosrow, the Ismaili leader who passed through Nishāpur in 1046, it stipulated a greater distance, approximately 8km or 5 miles, in those times.

27 *The Life of Avicenna* by Dr Sādiq Gowharin, Tehran, 1968, p. 543.

28 Abu Muslim, whose Iranian name was Behzādān, was a Khorāsānian general who overthrew the Umayyad caliphs in the middle of the eighth century and replaced them with the Abbāsids in Iraq.

29 *The History of Nishāpur* by Al-Hākim, Tehran 1995, p. 217.

30 Ibid.

31 Hākim, p. 212.

32 Khayyām's contemporary, Nasser Khosrow, also describes the Andalusians of southern Spain in his time as a blonde and blue-eyed people, showing that racial mixing between the Spanish and their North-African Muslim conquerors had similarly not proceeded very far despite several centuries of Moorish rule in Spain.

33 Tāzhīk was the Middle Persian word for Arab. In the early years of Islam in Iran, those Iranians who converted to the religion of the Arabs were looked upon as collaborators and were called 'Arabs' to depict them as traitors, but presumably because the new Muslims either did not mind being called Arabs or, else, did not dare to admit to their Arab masters that they minded, the name acquired general currency. The word has survived in the name of today's Persian-speaking republic of Tajikistan in Central Asia.

34 The Parthians are believed to have descended from the Parni tribe, who were themselves a branch of the Scythians and inhabited the eastern region of the Caspian sea around 300 BC. The Scythians were a vast group of Indo-European tribes who roamed and plundered a huge area from the Danube region in eastern Europe to the steppes around the Caspian and produced a number of states.

35 Philip Bond, the mathematician and former memory champion of Great Britain, describes Khayyām as one of his 'top ten intellects in all history'.

36 Beihaqi, Vol. 1, p. 278.

37 Few people in the West know quite how powerful, advanced and organised the Sasanian empire was. For over 400 years until it went down to the Arabs in the mid-seventh century, it was the equal of the eastern Roman Empire in armed might and sometimes captured whole Roman armies together with their emperors. The fatal rivalry eventually exhausted the two empires to such an extent that they became prey to the lightly-armed, unsophisticated fighters of the new Muslim sect of Arabia. In particular, had it not been due to the emperor Aparviz's intervention in the internal affairs of Constantinople to install his own favourite on the throne there – a futile war that lasted twenty-four years – Islam might not have survived and the world today might have been a very different place. In any case, the Sasanian emperors gave the various Iranian peoples, such as the Persians and the Kurds, the strong identities that have sustained them to the present.

38 The long epic in verse is largely based on earlier texts and poems in Middle Persian, or Pahlavi, the official language of the later Sasanian emperors. Firdowsi says it took him thirty years to finish it. He died in 1020 on his estate near the town of Tūs, to the east of Nishāpur.

39 One of the most cherished lines in the *Shah Nāmeh* is: 'I toiled greatly these past thirty years, with this Persian, revived Old Iran'. He may have exaggerated at the time. The success of his book proved that Persian had not been vanquished, that the language was not only spoken widely but there was a class of Iranian who read and wrote in it. Nevertheless, so tenacious would the effort of the Muslim clergy in later centuries be to replace it with Arabic that, without Firdowsi, Iran today might have been a member of the Arab League.

40 In my capacity as a commentator on the Middle East for *The Times*, I have written countless obituaries of once-powerful men.

41 Beihaqi, Tehran 1997, volume 3, p. 884.

42 *Armenia: The Survival of a Nation*, Christopher J. Walker, Croom Helm, London, 1980.

43 Quoted by Brian Harper in his *The Official Halley's Comet Book*, 1985.

44 Throughout this book, I have preferred to base my story of Sabbāh's life on the writings of the two Persian historians Ata-Malik Juvayni and Rashīd ad-Dīn. Immediately after the fall of the Ismaili castle of Alamut, the former was given access to Sabbāh's autobiography and quotes from it in detail before, he says, destroying the parts that enraged the Muslim in him. The latter seems to have had a fuller copy than we have inherited from Juvayni, for his quotations are more detailed.

45 This is an approximation. At the time, the old solar Zoroastrian calendar which was used for civic purposes was not being corrected precisely with leap years to keep it in step with the sun. The observance of anniversaries therefore slowly regressed against the seasons.

46 This is exactly my own story when, in 1959 in Kurdish western Iran, my father decided to send me to England for my higher education.

47 *Zār bar sar-e-Sabzeh*, Mass'ud Khayyām, Stockholm, 1996.

48 None of the sources refer to any siblings, but there are indications that he had at least one sister.

49 Rostam is the most celebrated of all the knights in the *Book of the Kings*. He saves Iran several times in the fifth and sixth centuries AD from being overrun by the Hephthalites or White Huns, a people who originated in north-west China and were related to the Huns who had earlier devastated many parts of Europe in the fourth and fifth centuries. Of the same basic stock as Mongols and Turks, the Hephthalites were eventually scattered or absorbed by the Turks in Central Asia. A marauding and parasitic people, they did not practice agriculture and nothing has survived of their language.

Chapter Two

1 Or Scheherazade, in its Western incarnation. The name is still common among the Iranians of today. In its Arabic adaptation, the original Persian title of the king, Shahryār, has similarly survived.

2 I shall for ever be indebted to Britain's Royal National Theatre for their staging of the play in 2001. It was not staged in Euripides's own time, but it won first prize in Athens after the playwright's death in 406 BC when it was produced by Euripides the Younger, the great man's son or nephew.

3 Who could this ancient Greek philosopher be? Quotes by him seem to have been in circulation in Khorāsān at the time.

4 The constellation of the Plough is called the Seven Sisters in Persian. It is said to be seven sisters following their mother's coffin in single file through a winding lane to a cemetery.

5 A corruption of the Middle Persian Margāb, Marv Water.

6 Chārsu literarily means 'four-sided' in Persian.

7 *The Lost Heart of Asia* by Colin Thubron, Penguin Books, London 1994.

8 Note that his aim is to go to 'China' in the east as quickly as possible and so may have taken a different route from that of Khayyām's caravan bound for Samarkand and Bukhara in the north.

9 Obviously the turban.

10 *The Travels of Marco Polo*, Andre Deutch, London 1959.

11 He admits that towards the end of the reign of the emperor Constantine IX, he had became so bored with trying to amuse the emperor that he pretended to be dying, so that the emperor would allow him to become a monk in the hope of being cured. Earlier during the same reign, he had feared being ousted from the emperor's inner circle because the emperor had frequently tired of his

enthusiasms. As soon as Constantine had died, he had given up the monastery for the excitement of the court once more.

12 From Michael Psellus's *Chronographia*, translated by E.R.A. Sewter and published in Penguin Classics in 1966 as *Fourteen Byzantine Rulers*. 'He was the greatest scholar and clearest thinker of his day', wrote Professor George Ostrogorsky of Psellus in the 1960s. 'His *Chronographia* is the outstanding memoir of the middle ages, unparalleled in its intellectual vigour, its lively descriptions, its discriminating psychological insight and its clear-cut and brilliant characterisation.'

13 More accurately, the word is a compound adjective meaning 'gold sprinkler'. It refers to the shining specks of gold dust in its bed in its head waters.

14 The Arabs had imposed their own script on Iran since the seventh century, but there are indications that, as with Firdowsi a generation earlier, Omar was proficient in the old, Middle Persian, script and could read commemorative plaques still surviving on old buildings.

15 *Paper Before Print*, by Jonathan M. Bloom, Yale University Press, New Haven and London, 2001.

16 According to the Muslim Persian historian Tabari (839–923), the libraries in Ctesiphon were burnt down on the orders of Omar, the second Muslim caliph, who said that all books other than the Koran were either superfluous or harmful. It is difficult to believe that the same caliph would have issued a different order regarding the libraries of Alexandria which were also captured in his brief reign. The Arab historian, Ibn Khaldun (1332–1406) tells the same story thus: 'Sa'ad Bin Waqqass (the Arab commander) asked the caliph what to do with the books among the booty of Ctesiphon. Omar wrote that they be thrown into the river, for if there were any guidance in them, Allah had sent us better ones (in the Koran), and if there were mischief in them, Allah had warned us of them. So the books were thrown into the river or burnt and the sciences of the Persians which were bound in books did not reach anyone afterwards.'

17 Bernard Lewis, the renowned scholar of Near Eastern history at Princeton University in the United States says that it was Iranians who probably invented the book as we know it. 'We are on stronger grounds in ascribing to Persians the book, that is the book in the form of the codex. The Greco-Roman world used scrolls, and so did much of the ancient Middle East. The codex, stitched and bound in the form which we now know as the book, seems to have originated in Iran. The cultural impact of such an innovation was obviously immense.' (*From Babel to Dragomans – Interpreting the Middle East*, Weidenfeld and Nicolson, London, 2004, p. 49). The earliest reference to a codex is found in a couplet by Martial in Rome in 83 or 84 CE: 'This bulky mass of multiple folds / All fifteen poems of Ovid holds.' (*Libraries in the Ancient World*, Lionel Casson, Yale University Press, London 2001, p. 124).

18 My translation from *Avicenna*, by Dr Sādiq Gowharīn, Tehran, 1968, p. 547.

19 Yāqūt, *Geography*, IV, 509.

20 *Historium Compendium* by George Cedrenus, Bonn, 1839, p. 668.

21 My translation, slightly shortened, from the original Arabic.

22 Scylitzes, a writer and soldier who deeply admired Romanus and despised Psellus and the Ducas family.

23 Ibn al-Athir relates that when Toghril was laying siege to Jazirat (today's Cizre in south-eastern Turkey) in the late summer of 1057, some of his men went to the nearby Syriac monastery of Akmul. Of the 400 monks there, 'they slaughtered 120. The remainder purchased their lives with six makkūks of gold and silver [about 80lb or 35kg]. And so ended 800 years of Christianity in that region'.

24 According to the historian Sam'ānī, he was Sadr Ismā'īl bin Abi Nassr as-Saffār, the chief imam of Samarkand, who had dared to urge the king to 'observe the ordinances of the faith and to desist from what was forbidden'.

25 Ibn al-Athīr (1160–1233) in *Al-Kāmil fil Ta'rīkh*, his history of the Saljuqs.

26 If, as we may expect, she had been forced to convert to Islam, she would have been given a Muslim name, but none of the sources refer to her even by that.

27 *History of the Georgian People*, W.E.D. Allen, London, 1932, p. 93.

Chapter Three

1 Khātūn is an old Iranian title current in pre-Islamic Soghdia (the region of Samarkand) denoting a lady of rank, such as a princess. It was later widely adopted by the incoming Turks. As for Terken, it was a Turkish equivalent that was also used as a personal name. Iranian historians later erroneously wrote it down as 'Turkān', thinking that it must somehow relate to the word 'Turk'.

2 C.E. Bosworth in the *Cambridge History of Iran*, Vol. 5, p88. Cambridge, 1968.

3 Ibn al-Athīr's *Annals of the Saljuq Turks*.

4 A few months later, Qavurt's semi-autonomous state of Kermān, which included the city of Shiraz, was given back to his sons and the family ruled there for 140 years until they were overthrown by another wave of Turks from central Asia.

5 'Kudatghu Bilig' or 'Knowledge that Brings Happiness' was completed in 1070 in the city of Kashghar by one Yūsef Khās Hājib, a Muslim Turk educated in Persian and Arabic. It is a long narrative poem in the Qarakhanid dialect depicting the ideal of a just monarchy on the Sasanian model. See the *Encyclopaedia of Islam*.

6 The royal parasol has a long history in the region and goes back at least to the emperors Darius and Xerxes of ancient Persia.

7   The twelfth-century Arab geographer Al-Idrīsi, who lived in Sicily at the court of the Norman king Roger II, wrote generally of the Turks: 'Their princes are warlike, provident, firm and just, . . . , but the nation is cruel, wild, coarse and ignorant.'

8   In my translation from the original twelfth-century text and tenth-century poems.

9   This is a euphemism for wine. It implies that some of the very first grapes of early summer had been fermented already.

10 A district of Bukhara. For a detailed description, see later in this chapter.

11 My translation.

12 Women from the city of Tarāz, believed to have been near today's Talas in northern Kyrgyzstan, must have been regarded as particularly beautiful. Formerly a stronghold of Zoroastrianism, Christianity and Buddhism, the Iranian language of the Soghdians of Samarkand was still spoken in Tarāz at the time.

13 Rūdakī here uses 'Izad', the Zoroastrian name of God, rather than the Muslim 'Allah'. Furthermore, his use of 'Our Izad' would have implied to at least some of his readers that he was contrasting the Iranians to the Arabs, that he believed the Iranians had had a kinder religion in Zoroastrianism before Islam had been imposed on them by war. This hidden message, if indeed it were so, would not have been lost on bright young Omar.

14 One theory is that before the Mongol invasion of the early thirteenth century, it had been buried under the sand dunes which were blown over parts of Bukhara by storms, so that the invaders never saw it.

15 'A fire temple in Islamic dress. . . . A precocious masterpiece in brick integrating compact monumentality with refined all-over geometric ornament. The pre-Islamic open-plan domed square is enlivened by engaged columns, gallery and corner domes.' *Islamic Art and Architecture* by Robert Hillenbrand, Thames & Hudson, London, 1999.

16 From Narshakhi's tenth-century *History of Bukhara*. My translation.

17 Omar's former mentor, the chief Islamic judge and governor of Samarkand, would seem to have been among these clerics, as we shall see later.

18 Ibn al-Athīr says 1064, but he is wrong. Malik Shah spent the whole of that year accompanying his father Alp-Arslan fighting in Georgia, Armenia and Kerman and campaigned in Transoxania the next year. Another, earlier historian, Sibt ibn al-Jawzi says the marriage contracts took place in 1065 when Alp-Arslan campaigned elsewhere in Transoxania.

Chapter Four

1   'Dey' is the mid-winter month of the Iranian calendar and here stands for the annual cycle.

2 Armenius Vambery's *History of Bukhara*, London 1873, p. 97.

3 He died in 935 at the age of eighty-one.

4 Aruzi says he heard it in the Islamic year 510 (May 1116 to May 1117). Khayyām would have probably dismissed it as an old wives' tale, particularly if he had met Abu Reza.

5 The seasons in Isfahan are extremely regular, with the coldest months of deep snow and biting frost being December and January. It is therefore unlikely that any caravan that had left Bukhara with the first cool breezes of September would have reached Isfahan before the frost had set in. Far more sensible would have been for the travellers to overwinter in one of the cities of Khorāsān or Rayy before setting off on the last leg of the journey. My guess is that Omar, possibly with Malik Shah and Queen Terken, arrived in Isfahan in March or April 1074.

6 The measure of weight kharvār may have started – I could not find any sources for it – as 'khar bār' or donkey load, but it has in recent centuries come to mean as 100 'mann' of Tabriz or roughly 100kg. Thus 1,300 kharvārs may have either meant 1,300 mule loads or roughly 13 metric tons.

7 *The Travel Journal*, p. 145, my translation.

8 Zarrīn means 'golden' in Persian and is given as the name of the river by Khayyām's contemporary historian Māfarrokhi. For some reason, Zarrīn has now become Zāyandeh or 'birth-giving'.

9 From *Al-Kāmil*, trs. D.S. Richards, RoutledgeCurzon, London 2002, p. 189.

10 One of the legendary kings of ancient Iran and a prominent hero in the Shah Nāmeh.

11 One of the Zoroastrian names of God.

12 My translation. See Appendix IV, Khayyām's Mathematics and Other Writings.

13 My translation. As in *The Life of Avicenna* by Dr Sādiq Gowharin, Tehran, 1968.

Chapter Five

1 This temporary adjustment has given rise to some of the original sources mistakenly dating the beginning of the reformed calendar to 1074, instead of 1079, as we shall see later.

2 The first month of the Muslim calendar which, in 1040, began on 11 September.

3 A spicy hot meat stew.

4 Mass'ūd was slain by his guards soon afterwards during his flight to his Indian domains. His dynasty survived in Ghazni (in today's central Afghanistan) for several more generations.

5 E.R.A. Sewter in the introduction to his translation of *Fourteen Byzantine Emperors: The Chronographia of Michael Psellus*, Penguin Books, 1966.

6 The English word 'clock' comes ultimately from the Latin word 'clocca' for bell. In early medieval monasteries prayer times were proclaimed to the monks by ringing handbells. Later, larger bells were installed in churches.

7 Pronounced 'Jūtī' in ancient Egyptian, he was the moon god who also represented the sun god Re. He was regarded as the inventor of writing and language, and the protector of scribes.

8 To what extent should we credit Islam with technical or scientific progress made in the 'golden age of Islam'? Most of the individual innovators and scientists were agnostics or belonged to other religions. Furthermore, freedom to express doubt in philosophical matters existed only rarely, when a local ruler happened to be a bad Muslim, rather than an observant one. In the same vein, would it be right to credit Christianity with the work of Galileo Galilei when that same Christianity did its utmost to throttle him? No one in the West does so, though innovations in the lands of Islam are often credited to Islam.

9 The late Senator S.H. Taghizadeh writing in the *Encyclopaedia of Islam*. He says it occurred on a Friday, but my calculation using Professor Freeman-Grenville's excellent *Islamic and Christian Calendars*, 1995, London, suggests firmly that 15 March 1079, fell on a Monday. Today, Norūz falls always on 21 March.

10 Ibn al-Athīr, the Arab historian of the late twelfth century, says of the year 1074–5 that Nizām al-Mulk and Malik Shah gathered together a group of leading astronomers, including Khayyām, who fixed 'Nayrūz' to the spring equinox. As he makes clear mistakes regarding dates elsewhere in the same passage, his claim must be taken cautiously. He is probably referring to the temporary halt that the astronomers made that year to the further regression of the solar calendar against the seasons. See earlier in this chapter. But it is possible that Norūz, too, had fallen out of unison with the vernal equinox and needed correcting.

11 Only in Arabic sources is Khayyām referred to as al-Khayyām or al-Khayyāmi. For the English reader, probably the best way of writing his name as pronounced in Persian would be Omar-e-Khayyām. It remains the common practice in the Iranian world to this day.

12 He would be thirty-one on his next birthday, 18 May, in just over two months' time.

13 David Ewing Duncan in *The Calendar*, London, 1998, Fourth Estate.

14 This was said to me by the famous British astronomer Sir Patrick Moore, in 2005. His eyes lit up when I told him I was writing his idol's biography.

Chapter Six

1 10 April.

2 It is appropriate, in my opinion, to describe the princess Terken as 'the queen', even though Malik Shah had another wife and a concubine beside her. This is because the other wife, the Saljuq noblewoman Zubeida, emerges only after Malik Shah's death as a rival to Terken. As long as Malik Shah lived, it was only Terken who was influential in matters of state, and it was only Terken whom he took on state visits to Baghdad. At times, in fact, it was Terken who dragged him along. This will emerge more clearly in the pages ahead. The title 'khātūn', which followed the names of all the princesses of the Qarakhanid and Saljuq royal families, is of ancient Iranian origin and apparently meant 'the wife of the chief'.

3 My translation from the original, finished in 1092.

4 27th of Ordibehesht, the second month of the Zoroastrian solar calendar.

5 Mo'ayyad would soon be dispatched to be governor of the town of Takrit, north of Baghdad. While studying Arabic and Islamic law at the Nizāmiyah school which his father had built in Baghdad, he nearly lost his life several times in clashes between the Shia and Sunni districts of the city.

6 'f' and 'h' are pronounced separately.

7 'Pākā! Shāhā! Dādārā . . .' You cannot possible distance yourself from Arabic any more visibly than this.

8 Juvayni uses the word 'Batinis', the Esoterics, those who believe in hidden meanings of scripture, the common description of the Ismailis at the time.

9 My translation.

10 Dey is the name of the tenth or midwinter month of the Iranian calendar. He uses it here to convey the passing of a whole year.

Chapter Seven

1 This was the second rebellion by Takesh and he was blinded for it. Earlier, he had been forgiven and his principality restored to him on a sworn promise of obedience. Malik Shah and Nizām usually gave a second chance to rebels unless they had committed acts of particular cruelty.

2 The sources give its date as the Islamic lunar year 479, which began on 18 April 1086, and ended on 7 April 1087. But Malik Shah and Nizām were campaigning in Syria by September 1086 and are found in Baghdad in the following March for the wedding of Terken Khātūn's daughter to the caliph in May. It seems that Malik Shah and Nizām went there straight from Syria.

3 Khayyām is universally referred to by the contemporary sources as the khājah, the lord, and this title normally implied closeness to the ruling house. Elsewhere, it is attached to high religious dignitaries who were revered by rulers.

Obviously this latter category does not apply to a young man known for his scandalous scepticism.

4 Two other sources say that the caliph paid an initial sum of 50,000 dinars for 'the right of suckling' – a Turkish custom – and an additional 100,000 dinars as the normal bride price. From *Al-Kāmil*, trs. D.S. Richards, RoutledgeCurzon, London 2002, p. 203.

5 In the Persian variety of the Arabic script, it can also be read as 'Māh-e-Malik', meaning 'the Moon of the King', invoking her father's first name. Whether this double meaning was instrumental in choosing the curious combination, we cannot say. Nor do we know exactly when she was born. If my research in Chapter II is well founded and Malik Shah's marriage to Terken Khātūn could not have been consummated before the summer of 1073, then at the earliest the couple might have had a child in the spring of 1074. If she were that first child, she would have been fourteen years old at her wedding. If she had been born later, she would have been even younger. In any case, given her mother's strong protectiveness towards her, she would have been at least twelve years old when she went to her bridal chamber. This is a real credit to Terken, for Islam's minimum age for females to marry is nine lunar years, or approximately eight years and nine months solar. For a comprehensive account of the dates of birth of Malik Shah's sons, see *The Cambridge History of Iran*, Vol. 5, 'The Saljuq and Mongol Period', p. 77.

6 Presumably, her condition that the Caliph Moqtada not sleep with any other women applied to after the wedding only, for he already had two infant sons by concubines.

7 Yet he would not be declared a saint until 1881.

8 *Ganj-i-Soxan*, by Dr Z. Safa, University of Tehran Press, 1960.

9 Khosrow tells a humorous, though tragic, story of his flight from Balkh. He had gone into a cobbler's shop to have his shoes mended when a clamour rose in a neighbouring street. The cobbler left to investigate and returned with blood over his clothes. Khosrow asked the cause of it. The man answered: 'Oh, it was nothing. We found one of the followers of Khosrow.' The Ismaili leader says he left the city immediately without collecting his belongings.

10 C.E. Bosworth, *The Encyclopaedia of Islam*.

11 We shall see later how important leaving a historical legacy was both to Malik Shah and Nizām al-Mulk.

12 Bosworth.

13 In the event, her nephew was treated gracefully and taken to Isfahan to live in comfort there. After the deaths of both Abu Tāhir and Malik Shah, he was restored to his throne.

14 Rawandi began to write his dynastic history of the Saljuqs, *Rāhat al-Sudūr*, in 1202.

15 Khāqāni.

Chapter Eight

1 The highlands to the south of the Caspian Sea which had never been conquered by Muslims. The region had largely converted to Shi'ism, the minority branch of Islam later, but it remained a stronghold of Iranian patriotic sentiment, with many families trying to link their descent to the Sasanians.

2 By which is meant a Twelver Shi'ite, of the type that runs Iran today. At that time, they were the 'quietist' branch of Shi'ism, the Ismailis being the rebellious branch and sympathetic to Cairo.

3 Not quite. In the local language of Daylam, it means 'eagle-taught', which, in turn, is said to allude to a legend in which someone saw eagles nesting on the high rock and thought to himself that it would make an easily-defended fortress.

4 'Deh-Khodā' or 'village god' in Persian is the equivalent of the title 'esquire', but it can also be a family name. It is significant that though Sabbāh was of recent Yemeni descent, he had chosen an Iranian name. This would have endeared him all the more to the locals.

5 'White Stone' in Turkish.

6 My translation. Juvayni's writing is often dense and the theological discussion was particularly obtuse. So I have summarised extensively.

7 Ibid.

8 The interesting aspect of this story must be that the vizier knows his sovereign Malik Shah and the other members of the royal family do not take offence at Turks being described as ignorant, even though, ethnically, they are all Turks. The same applied to Mahmūd, under whom Nizām himself was born. But elsewhere, Nizām uses the term Turks as those who serve in the Saljuq army and to whom the state is indebted.

9 I have translated these excerpts from a Tehran edition of the *Siāsat Nāmeh* published in 2537 of the short-lived Shāhanshāhi calendar of Shah Muhammad-Reza Pahlavi.

10 My own place of birth 848 years later.

11 Ibn Athīr.

12 'Cow Fish Water' in Kurdish.

13 *Al-Kāmil*, D. S. Richards, RoutledgeCurzon, London, 2002, p. 259.

14 Bundari, Ibn Athīr, etc.

Chapter Nine

1 I have exercised a little poetic license here. The Persian word 'ū', pronounced 'oo', has no gender and can mean either 'he' or 'she'. But because I believe that the treacherous former friend to whom he refers can only have been the princess Terken, I thought that taking the liberty was justified.

2 The sources say forty-seven, but they mean lunar years.

3 Ashtiani, the modern historian.

4 The original sources often find it difficult to admit that a woman might have been in charge. So Zubeida's activities are attributed to Berkyaruq.

5 He asked why two points on earth were chosen as the poles when they did not differ from all the other points on the globe. Ghazāli, a foul-mouthed and unstable character, believed that even studying medicine was a waste of time, let alone the pursuit of the sciences. He believed that studying the Koran only was worthwhile.

6 Khayyām would have read in the brief autobiography of his hero Avicenna that, earlier in the century, he had fled from Hamadan to Isfahan with his brother and a servant disguised as travelling dervishes.

7 Studying the tactics used by the British police from 1989 onwards to protect the novelist Salman Rushdie from Muslim activists may be instructive here. I spent an evening in one of the houses in London he had just vacated and was told that he never spent more than a few days in any one house. Soon he was transferred to the country where the movements of suspicious characters could be detected more easily.

8 See the top of this chapter, as well as 'Appendix I: A New Translation'.

Chapter Ten

1 My translation from the original Arabic with some help, over the more opaque phrases, from my Coptic Egyptian friend, Dr Fuad Megally, a writer and broadcaster with the World Service of the BBC. I asked Fuad whether the phrase 'His hair flew in the air' might not be metaphorical. He was certain it was a physical description.

2 Some religiously inclined commentators have said that Qifti contradicts himself when he calls Khayyām the 'imam' of Khorāsān and then goes on to say that his poems were 'snakes' on the body of the holy Shari'a law and full of treacherous hatred for it. I see the word 'imam' here as the repetition of Khayyām's later, honorific title, used in polite society to address all leading learned men, not a Muslim leader. See the appendix on Khayyām's other writings for a translation of the poems that Qifti quotes to prove Khayyām's heresy. For a discussion of the alleged contradiction, see Mehdi Aminrazavi's *The Wine of Wisdom: The Life, Poetry and Philosophy of Omar Khayyām*, Oneworld, Oxford, 2005.

3 Later, he told me that it had been a mistake and that, of course, he had not meant it.

4 This sounds like a direct quote from the writings of Khayyām himself, used sarcastically here to imply that old Iranians had been pagans.

5 My translation from the original Persian. The piece is called 'Thoughts'.

6 Or Tzachas. (Runciman and Angold).

7 *The Birth of Europe: Colliding Continents and the Destiny of Nations*, by Michael Andrews, BBC Books, London 1991.

8 Pronounced by today's Iranians as 'Tīsfūn' and by Arabs as 'Teysafūn'. It first emerges in history as a Greek military camp after Alexander's conquest of Persia in the third century BC. The succeeding Parthians who expanded it are thought to have pronounced it as 'Tispūn'.

9 Ibn al-Athīr. My translation.

Chapter Eleven

1 Ibn Funduq.

2 *A History of the Crusades*, Vol. 1, by Sir Steven Runciman, 1951. *The Crusades*, by Hans Eberhard Mayer, 2nd Edition, 1986.

3 From the account of Robert the Monk who was present at Clermont, but wrote his *Historia Hiersolimitana* much later. Here quoted from *Infidels* by Andrew Wheatcroft, Viking Penguin, 2003, p. 172.

4 The reader may not mind being reminded that as far back as 1030 in northern Italy, a monk, Guido de Arretzo, had given us our present, full system of musical notation. Without him, Bach, Mozart and Beethoven's achievements would not have been possible and the whole world would have been unimaginably the poorer for it.

5 *The First Crusade* by Runciman, p. 141.

6 Mayer, p. 47.

7 This account is based largely on *The Crusades through Arab eyes* by Amin Maalouf, Saqi Books, London, 1984.

8 See Chapter Two.

9 Its name is linked to mules (astars) in local folklore, but it is not inconceivable that in times forgotten, a Jewish woman there expanded a farmhouse into an ābādī, a hamlet. It certainly existed long before Islam.

10 Arūzi is not reliable on dates of historical events, only those he saw himself. In this story, he says that the rebellion of Sadaqa occurred in the reign of Malik Shah. It did not. It happened under Muhammad, in 1107.

Chapter Twelve

1 *Chahār Maqāleh (Four Discourses)*, Seventh Edition, Tehran, 1963, p. 100.

2 See the Prologue.

3 *Chahār Maqāleh*, p. 101, my translation.

4 'Sheikh al-imam Khayyāmi'.

5 A popular poem by Ma'arri says: 'People are of two types: Those with brains but no faith, and those with faith but no brains.' On the whole, however, he was a mild sceptic. In one of his collections, he visits Heaven and finds that heathen poets have been allowed in. See *Risalat ul Ghufran, A Divine Comedy*, trs. by G. Brackenbury, in 1943. Ma'arri died in 1057.

6 See the start of Chapter 10.

7 For reasons why neither of these two men write about Khayyām's poetry, see Epilogue : The Story of the Rubāiyāt.

8 *The Assassins*, by W.B. Bartlett, Sutton Publishing, 2001, p. 76.

9 Iranians mostly refer to him as Beihaqi, for he was born in today's Sabzvār, formerly known as Beihaq, in western Khorāsān.

10 This Arabic word can mean any relative through a wife, such as a brother-in-law. It can also mean son-in-law. Most sources interpret it as the latter.

11 'Imam' was often used as an honorific, such as 'maestro', rather than meaning a prayer leader, and 'Baghdadi' could easily be a title derived from having studied in Baghdad. It would seem most unlikely that Khayyām would allow his daughter to marry a Muslim cleric.

12 See the Prologue.

13 Bertrand Russell in a letter to Lady Ottoline Morrell, 27 August 1918.

Epilogue

1 The last quatrain of the first edition of the FitzGerald translation. See 'Appendix II'.

2 Dashti died in prison after the Islamic takeover of 1979.

3 This continues to be the unspoken attitude of millions of Iranians today. One of the best-loved poets of modern Iran, Mehdi Akhavān Sāles, wrote such a strong denunciation of Islam and praise of Zoroastrianism after the Islamic revolution of 1979 that it cannot be published anywhere in the world for fear of assassins. It is distributed clandestinely and, if anyone possesses it in Iran itself, they risk execution for blasphemy.

4 For Zamakhshari's account of the clash, see Chapter 12. Ghazāli calls Ma'arri 'a Zandīq [Zoroastrian, but here meaning an unbeliever] who harbours a bitter hatred of Islam and of all the prophets.' *Omar Khayyām*, Ali-Reza Zekāvati Gharagozlou, Tehran, 1998, p. 88.

5 See 'Appendix IV, Khayyām's Mathematics and Other Writings'.

6 *Mirsād al-Ibād (The Watchtower of the Faithful)*, Tehran, 1995, p. 693.

7 For some of these quotes, I am indebted to an excellent biography of FitzGerald by the late Robert Bernard Martin, which deserves a reprint. *With Friends Possessed* is both enlightening and moving. It was published in

1985 by Faber & Faber in London and Boston. Other quotes are from *The Life of Edward FitzGerald*, Alfred McKinley Terhune, Oxford University Press, 1947.

8 Carlyle estimated that FitzGerald had given Tennyson £300 a year 'for many years' at a time when a man could bring up a family on a third of the sum. Dick Davis in his introduction to the Penguin edition of the Rubáiyát. London, 1989, p. 17.

9 Martin, p. 139.

10 Terhune, p. 205.

11 Martin, p. 220.

12 Terhune, p. 344.

Appendix I

1 My other authorities for Khayyám's quatrains are the collections by Sádiqh Hedáyat (1934) and the modern scholars Rahím Rezá-Zádeh Malik and Ali-Rezá Zekávati Gharagozlou. My chosen quatrains also occur among the 200 chosen by the late Peter Avery of Cambridge University and his partner in translation, the poet John Heath-Stubbs. See 'Bibliography'.

2 When Heath-Stubbs died in late December 2006, all the serious British newspapers devoted long obituaries to his life. Yet only one made a passing mention of his Rubáiyát.

3 Strangely, even though they had the freedom of prose, Heath-Stubbs and Avery also often took liberties with their translation that were unnecessary. For example, in a dozen places, they make Khayyám address his companion as 'boy', when I have seen only one such reference, and the quatrain is of doubtful attribution. Both men were homosexual. Elsewhere, whenever Khayyám does address a companion, he invariably implies the female form. A further error in their translation is their inclusion of dozens of stanzas that clash with Khayyám's beliefs and therefore cannot be his. While one quatrain in their selection is defiantly sceptical of received doctrine, the next may be devoutly religious, the third the utterance of a superstitious astrologer. Their collection of 235 quatrains is also almost relentlessly negative, in opposition to Khayyám's joyous personality. See *The Ruba'iyat* (sic) *of Omar Khayyam*, Penguin Books, London, 1981, p. 39.

4 Khayyám does not actually say that he knows a great king who yearns for the unfettered life of one of his subjects. His original words are that the pleasures of a simple life 'are not always within the reach of every sultan'. But his audience would have known that he spoke from personal knowledge. As told in his story above, he was a close drinking companion to two great kings, three if we count the sultan Sanjar in the latter part of his life. In this quatrain, I have also changed 'a leg of lamb' into 'some cheese', believing that the latter conveys the

spirit of the original better to a western reader. He seems to have chosen 'a rān' or thigh of lamb merely because it rhymed with 'nān', or bread.

5   This quatrain is the fifth oldest to emerge in the medieval sources of Khayyām's poems. It bears clear signs of his having been familiar with the atomistic theory of Democritus. See Appendix III : Omar the Greek.

6   He must mean some of his fellow astronomers who had too much confidence in their learning.

7   His exact words are 'I drink the blood of grapes, you that of people', by which he means to say that, as Islamic judges, the clergy were the arbiters of wills and other contracts and often charged too much for their services.

8   This is the earliest Khayyām quatrain to emerge in history, though indirectly. Juvaini, the Persian governor and historian under the Mongols, wrote between 1253–60 that, after Genghis Khan had devastated the city of Marv in 1220, a group of survivors returned and began to gather the dead. On the thirteenth day, the number surpassed one million and three hundred thousands and one of them recited the above quatrain in lamentation. Obviously Juvayni possessed that record, but it has now been lost. See 'Appendix IV'.

9   He does not mention any kind of drinking vessel, but implies it. He says merely: 'negunsār konīd', 'turn downwards'. This could be interpreted as either, dramatically, 'pour a glass onto the earth underneath which I lie', or, more becoming of an old man, 'drink one more glass, for that is what I would have wanted you to do'. I wished to replicate FitzGerald's memorable phrase 'turn down an empty glass', but proved unequal to the task.

Appendix IV

1   I am grateful to my friend Fouad Megally of Egypt for his counsel over some of the more opaque passages in these poems. We were, nevertheless, defeated by the first and there was clear evidence of corruption at the hands of copyists in the others, too.

2   *Dictionary of Scientific Biography*, Vol. 7, New York, 1981, p. 347.

3   *A History of Mathematical Notations*, Florian Cajori, New York and London, 1928.

4   *The Development of Mathematics*, E.T. Bell, New York and London, 1940.

5   *A History of Mathematics*, Florian Cajori, New York and London, 1894.

6   My translation.

Selected Bibliography

Original sources

Arūzi Samarqandi, Ahmad bin Omar bin Ali Nizāmi: *Čahār Maqāleh (Four Discourses)*, ed. Muhammad Moin, Tehran, 1964.

Avicenna: *The Autobiography*, as quoted in full by Sādiq Gowharin in *Ibn-e Sīnā*, Tehran, 1968.

Beihaqi, Abul-Fazl Muhammad bin Hussein: *Tārīkh-e Beihaqi (Beihaqi's History)*, 3 vols., ed. Khalīl Khatīb Rahbar, Tehran 1997.

Firdowsi (d. 1020): *Shāh Nāmeh (Book of the Kings)*. The Amīr Bahādor Edition, Tehran, 1904.

Hākim al Naishābūri, Abu Abdullah (d. 1014): *Ta'rīkh al-Naishābūr (History of Nishāpur)*, ed. Muhammad-Reza Shafī'i Kadkani, Tehran, 1996.

Ibn al-Athīr, Izz ad-Dīn: *Al-Kāmil fil-Ta'rīkh (Complete History)*, translated and annotated as *Annals of the Saljuq Turks* by Prof. D.S. Richards, Routledge Curzon, London 2002.

Ibn Funduq, Ali bin abil-Qāsim Zeid al-Beihaqi: *Tatimma Suwwān al-Hikmah (Supplement to the History of the Philosophers)*, Punjab University, 1935.

Khayyām, Omar (d. 1131): *Dāneshnāmeh-ye Khayyāmi (The Complete Works of Omar Khayyām)*, ed. Rahīm Rezāzādeh Malek, Tehran, 1998.

Khosrow, Nasser (1050s): *Safar Nāmeh (Travel Journal)*, ed. Vahīd Dāmqānī, Tehran, 1960s.

Nizām al-Mulk, Grand Vizier Ali Tūsi: *Siāsat Nāmeh (Book of Politics)*, ed. Mortezā Modarressi, Tehran, 1955.

Sabbāh, Hasan: *The Autobiography* as censored by Atā Malik Juvayni (or Juwayni) in 1260 in his *Tārīkh-e Jahān Goshā (History of the World Conqueror)*, Vol. III, Luzac, London, 1937.

Monographs, biographies, reference books.

Avery, Peter, and Heath-Stubbs, John: *The Rua'iayat of Omar Khayyam*, Allen Lane, London, 1979.

Bernard Martin, Robert: *With Friends Possessed: A Life of Edward FitzGerald*, Faber and Faber, London, 1985.

Brill: *The Encyclopaedia of Islam*, Leiden, Netherlands, 2006.

Dashit, Ali: *Dami bā Khayyām (A Moment with Khayyām)*, Tehran, 1966.

Khayyam, Mass'ūd: *Zār bar sar-e Sabzeh (Weep for the Grass)*, Ārash Förlaq, Stockholm, 1996.

Rezāzādeh Malek, Rahīm: *Omar-e Khayyām*, Tehran, 1998.

Tabatabaie, Javad: *Khājeh Nizām al-Mulk*, Tehran, 1996.

Terhune, Alfred McKinley: *The Life of Edward FitzGerald*, Oxford, 1947.

Zekavati Ghargozlou, Ali Reza: *Omar-e Khayyām*, Tehran, 1998.

Travel journals

Polo, Marco (c. 1300): *The Travels*, ed. Manuel Komroff, Rochester, N.Y., 1933.

Thubron, Collin: *The Lost Heart of Asia*, Penguin Books, London, 1995.

Wellard, James: *Samarkand & Beyond*, London, 1977.

Poetry and prose

FitzGerald, Edward: *The Rubāiyāt of Omar Khayyām & The Salāmān and Absāl of Jāmī*, Bernard Quaritch, London, 1879.

Keshāvarz, Karīm: *Hezār Sāl Nasr-e Pārsi (A Thousand Years of Persian Prose)*, Tehran, 1975.

Safā, Dr Zabīhollah: *Ganj-e Sokhan (Treasury of Words: A History of Persian Poetry)*, Vol. I, Tehran, 1969.

History (the Muslim east)

Āshtiāni, Abbass Eghbāl: *Tārikh-e Iran, A History of Iran*, Eighth Edition, Tehran, 1997.

Barthold, W: *Turkestan Down to the Mongol Invasion*, London, 1928.

Bartlett, W.B.: *The Assassins*, Sutton Publishing, 2001.

Cambridge University: *Cambridge History of Iran* (Vol. V, The Saljuq and Mongol Period), 1968.

Casson, Hugh: *Libraries in the Ancient World*, Yale, New Haven and London, 2001.

Daftary, Farhad: *The Assassin Legends: Myths of the Isma'elis*, I.B. Tauris, London, 2001.

Girshman, R.: *Iran*, London, 1954.

Gerayeli, Freydoon: *Naishābūr: Shahr-e Firūzeh (City of Turquoise)*, Tehran, 1978.

Hedin, Sven: *The Silk Road*, London, 1938.

Lewis, Bernard: *The Assassins*, Al Saqi Books, London, 1985.

Maalouf, Amin, tr. Ron Rothschild: *The Crusades Through Arab Eyes*, Al Saqi Books, London, 1984.

Thomson, James Westfall: *The Medieval Library*, Chicago, 1939.

History (Byzantium, the medieval church and the Crusades)

Andrews, Michael L.A.: *The Birth of Europe: Colliding Continents and the Destiny of Nations*, BBC Books, London, 1991.

Angold, Michael: *The Byzantine Empire, 1025–1204*, Longman, London, 1997.

Bartlett, W.B.: *The Crusades: An Illustrated History*, Sutton Publishing, 1999.

Friendly, Alfred: *The Dreadful Day: The Battle of Manzikert, 1071*, London, 1981.

Garland, Lynda: *Byzantine Empresses*, Routledge, London and New York, 1999.

Jenkins, Romilly: *Byzantium: The Imperial Centuries*, Toronto, 1987.

Lynch, Joseph H.: *The Medieval Church*, Longman, London and New York, 1992.

Mayer, Hans Eberhard: *The Crusades*, Second Edition, Oxford, 1988.

Oxford University: *The Oxford History of Byzantium*, 2002.

Psellus, Michael (d. 1078): *The Chronographia*, tr. E.R.A. Sewter, Penguin Books, London, 1966.

Runciman, Steven: *A History of the Crusades* (Vol. I), Cambridge, 1951.

Russell, Bertrand: *A History of Western Philosophy*, Unwin, London, 1969.

Khayyām's mathematics and the calendar

Bell, E.T.: *Development of Mathematics*, McGraw-Hill, New York and London, 1945.

Cajori, Florian: *History of Mathematics*, Macmillan, New York and London, 1894.

Ewing Duncan, David: *The Calendar*, Fourth Estate, London, 1998.

Freeman-Grenville, G.S.P.: *The Islamic and Christian Calendars*, Garnet, UK, 1995.

Whitfield, Peter: *Landmarks in Western Science*, The British Library, London, 1999.

Index